# Swansong 1945

## A Collective Diary from
## Hitler's Last Birthday to VE Day

Walter Kempowski

*Translated from the German by*
Shaun Whiteside

**GRANTA**

Granta Publications, 12 Addison Avenue, London, W11 4QR

First published in Great Britain by Granta Books 2014
Paperback edition published by Granta Books 2015

Original German edition first published in 2005.

Walter Kempowski: *Das Echolot. Abgesang '45. Ein kollektives Tagebuch*

Copyright © 2005 Albrecht Knaus Verlag, Munich, a division of Verlagsgruppe
Random House GmbH, Munich, Germany
English translation copyright © Shaun Whiteside 2014
Foreword copyright © Alan Bance 2014

This book has been selected to receive financial assistance from English PEN's 'PEN
Translates!' programme, supported by Arts Council England. English PEN exists to
promote literature and our understanding of it, to uphold writers' freedoms around
the world, to campaign against the persecution and imprisonment of writers for
stating their views, and to promote the friendly cooperation of writers and
the free exchange of ideas. www.englishpen.org

A CIP catalogue record for this book is available from the British Library

9 8 7 6 5 4 3 2 1

ISBN 978 1 84708 641 9
eISBN 978 1 84708 642 6

Typeset by Avon DataSet Ltd, Bidford on Avon, Warwickshire
Printed and bound by CPI Group (UK) Ltd, Croydon, CR0 4YY

www.grantabooks.com

For Cherry Duyns

# Contents

# Foreword

Despite being one of Germany's best-known and most respected authors, Walter Kempowski (1929–2007) is not yet recognized in the English-speaking world. This book will begin to build a wider reputation for a writer who believed that history should not be left solely to historians. As Julian Barnes once wrote, 'History isn't what happened. History is just what historians tell us.' Over the second half of the twentieth century, Kempowski dedicated his life to researching and memorializing the common experience of the Second World War. While his own story is essentially German, his painstaking and devoted work has international breadth and relevance.

Kempowski was born into a comfortable family of shipowners and timber exporters in the picturesque Baltic port of Rostock, where a happy childhood was to end prematurely with the coming of war. He experienced Allied bombing in both Rostock and Hamburg: he later confessed that as a schoolboy he hoped for an Allied raid on Rostock (which duly came) to save him from handing in his Latin homework. The family, though patriotic, was anti-Nazi, but Walter was inevitably recruited to the Hitler Youth, where playing truant to listen to his brother's banned jazz records landed him in a punishment unit. In February 1945, aged sixteen, he was conscripted as a messenger into a Luftwaffe youth auxiliary, anti-aircraft unit. Two months later, in the last days of the war, his soldier-father, a veteran of the First World War, was killed by a Russian bomb in East Prussia.

After the war, Kempowski began an apprenticeship in a printing works, but a year later he took a job with the US Army of Occupation in a 'labor supervision' company in Wiesbaden. In 1948, keen to see his mother and his home city again, he returned with his brother Robert to his beloved Rostock, where both were arrested by the Soviet authorities and sentenced by military tribunal to twenty-five years in a labour camp for espionage: Kempowski had given the US authorities bills of lading proving that the Soviets were taking more goods from Germany (reparations) than the Allies had agreed. His mother, too, received a ten-year prison sentence, of which she served six, for complicity in the brothers' crime.

Kempowski served eight years in jail, mostly in the Soviet, and later GDR, prison Bautzen, notorious for its high death rate. On his release in 1956 as the result of an amnesty, he moved first to Hamburg and then, in 1957, to Göttingen, where he finished his schooling and trained as a teacher. Marriage in 1960 to another teacher, and two children born in 1961 and 1962, completed his family. He taught first in the village school of Breddorf in Lower Saxony, then moved in 1965 to another village, Nartum, near Bremen, where he later designed a beautiful house with a tower to hold his vast collection of writings and photographs. Today the collection is housed in the Academy of Arts in Berlin, although there is still a small personal archive in Rostock, holding manuscripts and some memorabilia, such as the boots he wore on his release from Bautzen, and a small library of his favourite authors, including Theodor Fontane and Thomas Mann, both, like him, associated with the Baltic coast.

Kempowski had embarked on his literary career with *Im Block* ('In the Cell Block'), published in 1969 to little acclaim. An expanded and republished version, called *Ein Kapitel für sich* ('A Separate Chapter'), was filmed for TV in 1979. The rest of his literary career and his fame as a writer were shaped by two massive series of publications. The first was his *Deutsche Chronik* ('German Chronicle'), consisting of six novels and three 'enquiry' volumes. The novels represent something like a history of the Kempowski family from the late nineteenth century. *Tadellöser und Wolff* (1971), the first to be published, dealt with the interwar period and earned him a national reputation, especially after it appeared on German TV. The best known of his 'enquiries' was *Haben Sie davon Gewusst? Deutsche Antworten* ('Did You Know about It? German Answers'), for which he questioned Germans about their knowledge of concentration and extermination camps.

The author's second great series was his *Echolot* ('Sonar' or 'Echo Soundings') project, made up of ten volumes, which concludes with

*Abgesang '45* ('Swansong 1945'). The title *Das Echolot* brings to mind sonar signals sent into the depths of the ocean and bouncing back to configure the seabed or contours of objects out of sight beneath the surface. Kempowski first conceived the idea of gathering ordinary people's accounts of their personal experiences of the Second World War in Bautzen prison, where the inmates endlessly shared their war histories. Later, in Göttingen, he salvaged from the pavement a dead soldier's diary, letters and photographs, trampled on by passers-by. From this beginning, he went on during the 1970s to collect autobiographies, letters and diaries, and to commit himself to the idea that these private, 'insignificant' but authentic testimonies must be preserved and made available to posterity. The simultaneity of these writings across the whole social spectrum sets up in itself a striking resonance.

He called it 'rescuing the voices of the dead'. His mission developed to include international participation in the war, so that, having initially concentrated on material supplied by his immediate circle, he broadened and intensified his search at the beginning of the 1980s, scouring second-hand bookshops and flea markets and putting advertisements in newspapers to solicit contributions, and thus to create an archive of 'unpublished biographies'. It grew into an ambitious plan, paralleled only by the great – and very differently resourced and organized – British Mass Observation project, which aimed to create a 'collective diary' of the years 1943 to 1949. Kempowski put much of his own money into funding his project.

From quite early on, the notion began to develop of composing published volumes from his collection. Originally, he wanted to present every day of the war through his collective diary, but he soon realized that this was an impossibly over-ambitious project and chose to select only certain dates for coverage. He also modified his plan to give voice only to unknown, ordinary people, deciding instead that the voices of important participants, from Hitler to Churchill, would help to display the war in all its aspects.

The *Echolot* project – and, in particular, *Swansong 1945* – is not a mere collection or compilation of documents: it is, rather, a composition. Kempowski's own word for his creative method was 'collage', a concept derived from early twentieth-century modernist visual art, describing the sticking together of disparate elements to make a whole picture. According to Simone Neteler, Kempowski's long-time assistant, *Echolot* has two underlying principles of composition, horizontal and vertical. The volumes are consistently chronological, covering specific, significant dates over three years; individual authors regularly turn up. The volumes also have a 'vertical' depth, where individual voices seem to be communicating with each other: 'it's like a long conversation which begins anew with each new date'. The work is a polyphonic dialogue employing both contrasts and parallels for compositional effects, although Kempowski intended to be sparing with contrasts, which he believed produced too 'crude' an effect. But they occur, nonetheless: for example, during the hopeless last stand in the east, Hitler bestows military medals to the very end, even as some soldiers prematurely exult in his demise.

The first four volumes of *Echolot,* which appeared in Germany in 1993, were instant best-sellers: the publishers, Knaus, went on to bring out all ten volumes, including *Abgesang '45*, along with the diary Kempowski compiled about the project's problems and progress, *Culpa* (2005). The first four volumes, their documents arranged chronologically in diary form, dealt with January and February 1943 and the Battle of Stalingrad. Of the ensuing six volumes, *Fuga Furiosa* (1999) comprised four volumes concerned with the flight of Germans from the east ahead of the advancing Red Army, and *Barbarossa '41* (2002) dealt with the German attack on Russia. The final volume, *Abgesang '45*, appeared in 2005.

The exhausting work of compiling *Echolot* did not prevent Kempowski from writing further novels, including *Heile Welt* ('Intact World', 1998), about his twenty years as a village schoolteacher. Two others, *Hundstage* ('Dog Days', 1988) and *Letzte Grüsse* ('Last Greetings', 2003), feature his alter ego, the fictional writer Alexander Sowtschick, and display the best of Kempowski's humour. His very fine last novel, *Alles Umsonst* ('All in Vain', 2007), sums up in its title Kempowski's recurring theme of futility, and his sense that Germany had irredeemably forfeited its former identity as a nation of 'poets and thinkers'.

*Swansong 1945* is given particular colour and coherence by the choice of four particular days, between Hitler's fifty-sixth birthday on 20 April and VE Day on 8 May 1945. The Kaiser's birthday had always been celebrated in pre-First World War Prussia/Germany as a public holiday, and with the Nazi rise to power in 1933, Hitler's birthday likewise became an occasion for triumphalism, parades and flag-waving. But by April 1945 Germany was on its knees: the Wehrmacht had been fleeing before the Russians since July 1943, and the lost battles of Stalingrad and Kursk loomed large in German minds. Dresden and Hamburg had been obliterated by fire-bombing (Dresden as recently as February 1945) and Berlin was a shattered monument to Nazi megalomania and swagger. There is no better example of the desperation of the German military than the description of Germany's Volkssturm (Home Guard) donning civilian clothes to cover their uniforms, while the pathologically vain Hermann Goering is ordering a made-to-measure high-ranking American officer's uniform.

The irony of celebrating the birthday of the man responsible for this disastrous war is not lost on the many military and civilian Germans whom Kempowski quotes. They guess that this is almost certainly Hitler's last birthday and the mood is funereal rather than celebratory. The few military actions undertaken in these last weeks are the swansong of Nazism, and of the great German *Kultur* the Nazis usurped and perverted. Kempowski quotes Hitler's last 'political testament' and the last 'Birthday Speech' broadcast of Propaganda Minister Josef Goebbels, astonishing in their sustained fantasy. Goebbels's relentless mendacity attempts to wring propaganda value even out of the catastrophe: '[Adolf Hitler] will go his own way to the end, and what awaits him there is not the downfall of his people but a new and happy start to a flowering of all things German.' Ordinary Germans at last respond cynically to Goebbels's duplicity and begin to see that they have been mocked and duped from the start.

As the official documents and the accounts of ordinary people gather pace, readers are invited gradually to reflect on historical reality and the question of German complicity. Kempowski took upon himself the momentous task of compiling *Echolot* partly to explore German guilt, as made explicit in the title of his diary, *Culpa*. He felt that German accounts of the Second World War never adequately represented the ordinary soldier's experience, nor the complexity of the Germans' response to Nazism and the war. Into his vast composition the author wove contributions from German exiles as well as from anti-Nazi Germans, and the thoughts of Americans, Russians, British, Italians, French and many other foreign nationals. He summoned the voices of soldiers and nurses, prisoners, journalists, writers and housewives; the famous and the obscure. *Echolot* is not history, it is the stuff history is made of.

Literary accounts of these war years are often at variance with conscientious academic research, even those by such luminaries as Nobel Laureate Heinrich Böll. *Echolot* augments the record with a comprehensive and true account of the impact of the war. For this reason I suggested that Granta should translate *Abgesang '45*. Perhaps most significantly, compiling and composing *Echolot* allowed Walter Kempowski to show that, alongside Nazi war crimes, the suffering of German victims should also be represented, a previously taboo idea, at least until Günter Grass's novella *Im Krebsgang* ('Crabwise') in 2002. And perhaps here at last, in Kempowski's *Echolot*, literature meets history.

Alan Bance
Southampton, June 2014

# Preface

When I started working on the 'Echolot' project twenty years ago, I was preoccupied by three paintings.

The first was Brueghel's *Tower of Babel*, that depiction of a conically rising tower, of the arching spirals placed on top of one another, screwing its way into the clouds and pushing up towards God. The tower that people built to be equal to the Almighty, but which they also built out of longing, perhaps in order to reach him prematurely and seek refuge in his lap. The Tower of Babel collapsed, we know, and the confusion that ensued continues to this day.

The second was *The Battle of Alexander at Issus* by Albrecht Altdorfer, that well-known painting showing thousands of warriors killing one another. Nameless people, meant for death, long since mouldered and forgotten, and yet these were men who had wives and children sitting at home, whose seed we bear within us as their descendants.

The third picture was *The Surrender of Breda* by the Spanish painter Velázquez. In this a victor faces his defeated foe. Not only does the victorious general have his arm upon the neck of the subjugated man, who is humbly handing him the key of the city, he is benignly bowing to him – indeed, he is helping his inferior to his feet. The picture was painted over 360 years ago, and even today its message has not been deciphered.

Now, during the days of remembrance, two generations after the end of the war, I find myself thinking of different images: the camera panning across the ruins of Warsaw, across the piles of corpses in Bergen-Belsen and over a prison wall scattered with bullet holes, mass graves being opened and the dead exhumed. The bell is ringing in Hiroshima.

In these days I also remember the quiet treks of the refugees, the frantically fleeing German soldiers – every man for himself! – and the foreign workers going cheerfully homewards, with their national cockades. And I can't help thinking about the weeping child soldier resting on the limber of his shattered gun.

My parents had a tobacco tin from the days of the Seven Years War. It stood on the radio next to the strawberry geranium and moonlight cactus, and had these words on it:

> *Everything changes,*
> *After war and bloodshed*
> *Let us enjoy heaven's favour*
> *And enjoy the delight of peace.*

No, we can't really talk about 'enjoyment'. Our film may have finished, but others are being cued up, and we will see them all. Again and again there will be pictures of war and bloodshed, with no end to the show in sight. The skyscrapers are already burning.

I can't help thinking about the Doré picture Bible that I used to flick through as a child while lying on the carpet, and its illustrations of the Flood. The waters recede, and piled on the cliffs are the bodies of the drowned. We're still waiting for the dove to bring us the olive branch. But in Doré's picture no rainbow stretches above the dead.

Walter Kempowski,
Nartum, February 2005

# Editorial Note

In most cases the texts I chose for *Swansong* were not abridged. I have not indicated omissions at the start or the end of a self-contained text, but I have identified deletions inside a text with […]. Peculiarities of style, spelling and punctuation have been kept as they were in order to preserve the authenticity of the documents. Obvious slips have been corrected. Additions or explanations that I thought necessary in some places are in square brackets. In the date line at the beginning of the individual days, the number of days that have passed since the start of the war is given on the left after the sign <, while on the right the number of days remaining until the end of the war is shown before the sign >.

With regard to the headings, where authors did not want to be named either initials or pseudonyms have been used. When copyright holders could not be identified we have used our editorial judgement as to the information that appears. Where possible, birth and death dates have been given. Places appear in round brackets if the texts cannot be matched to a particular day; those places that were not under the control of the unified armed forces of Germany are in italics.

It is in the nature of things that the veracity of certain facts and events could not be checked. This, together with the subjective character of the sources, helps to explain obvious contradictions.

W.K.

# Note on the English Translation

This is a faithful translation of the German edition published in 2005, with some small changes. Where entries were written in English in the first instance, we have gone back to the originals apart from two instances (see Joseph Lewis, p. 212, and Ethel Inglis, p. 231) where it proved impossible to locate them in the Mass Observation archives; here we have translated the German. We have not been able to include extracts from *My Three Years With Eisenhower* by Harry C. Butcher (pp. 409–415 and, pp.442–448 of the German edition), which would otherwise have been on p. 399 preceding the Norman Kirby entry and on p. 430 preceding the text by Leonid Voytenko. We have also not been able to include the extract from *Inside the Third Reich: Memoirs* by Albert Speer (pp. 18–20 of the German edition), which would otherwise have been on page 10 preceding the entry by Wilhelm Bodenstedt. Where the German edition preserves peculiarities in the German entries, we preserve peculiarities in the English. In his editorial note, Walter Kempowski explains the use of round brackets and italics in the headings; we have corrected a few inconsistencies in the German edition, following this system. In addition, without removing any of the existing information, we have added the nationalities of authors, the majority of them German, in the index, counting as German those who were born in territories which were German before the Second World War but may not have been German after, German citizens who left Germany and took other citizenships by 1945, and ethnic Germans who were raised in countries other than Germany. We have also updated biographical details when possible and would be glad to add more, or correct any errors, if notified.

# Abbreviations

| | |
|---|---|
| BDM | Bund Deutscher Mädel: League of German Girls |
| HJ | Hitlerjugend: Hitler Youth |
| KLV | Kinderlandvershickung: the Children's Evacuation Programme |
| KPD | Kommunistische Partei Deutschlands: the German Communist Party |
| MAN | Maschinenfabrik Augsburg-Nürnberg, parent company of the MAN Group of car manufacturers |
| NKFD | National Komitee Freies Deutschland: National Committee for a Free Germany, a German anti-Nazi organization that operated in the Soviet Union during WWII |
| NKVD | Narodnyy Komissariat Vnutrennikh Del: People's Commissariat for Internal Affairs, the Soviet secret police |
| NSDAP | Nationalsozialistische Deutsche Arbeiterpartei: the National Socialist German Workers Party, the Nazi Party |
| OKL | Oberkommando der Luftwaffe: Luftwaffe Supreme Command |
| OKW | Oberkommando der Wehrmacht: High Command of the German Armed Forces |
| RAD | Reichsarbeitsdienst: Reich Labour Service |
| RM | Reichsmarschall: Reich Marshal |
| ROA | Russkaya Osvoboditel'naya Armiya: Russian Liberation Army |
| SBZ | Sowjetische Besatzungszone: Soviet Occupation Zone |
| SED | Sozialistische Einheitspartei Deutschlands: Socialist Unity Party of German |
| SHAEF | Supreme Headquarters Allied Expeditionary Forces |

| SPD | Sozialdemokratische Partei Deutschlands: Social Democratic Party of Germany |
| SS | Schutzstaffel: the Nazi Party's 'Protection Squadron', responsible for a huge number of war crimes |
| U-boat | *Unterseeboot*: submarine |
| VE | Victory in Europe |
| WAAF | Women's Auxiliary Air Force |

**Additional terms**

| Obersturmbannführer | 'Senior assault unit leader': a rank in the SS and other paramilitary organizations equivalent to lieutenant colonel in the army |
| Stalag | Stammlager für kriegsgefangene Mannschaften und Unteroffiziere: prisoner-of-war camp for enlisted men and non-commissioned officers (NCOs) |
| Standardartenfüher | 'Standard leader': a rank in the SS and other paramilitary organizations equivalent to colonel in the army |
| Sturmbannführer | 'Assault unit leader': a rank in the SS and other paramilitary organizations equivalent to major in the army |
| Sturmführer | 'Assault leader': a rank in the SS equivalent to a junior or senior lieutenant in the army; obsolete by 1945 |
| Volkssturm | a German paramilitary organization in the last years of the war, set up by the Nazi Party as part of a German Home Guard |
| Waffen-SS | the armed branch of the SS |

*Spring Faith*

The winds again are mild and light,
they whisper and wander day and night,
through field and forest wending.
O fresh perfume, o youthful sound,
now, wretched heart, be thou unbound!
for now must all the world be mending.

The earth grows lovelier day by day,
what yet may be, no one can say:
the blossoming seems unending.
The farthest, deepest valley flowers;
now, heart, forget the painful hours,
for now must all the world be mending.

Ludwig Uhland, translated by J. W. Thomas

When our enemies heard thereof…
they were much cast down in their
own eyes: for they perceived that this
work was wrought of our God.
DAILY READING: NEHEMIAH 6:16

Diesen hof ausfegen
Deezen hoaf ous faygen
Sweep this yard
*STARS AND STRIPES*,
DAILY GERMAN LESSON

**Flight Captain Hans Baur, 1897–1993**       **(Berlin)**
Hitler's last birthday was a grim and sad affair. Grand Admirals Raeder
and Dönitz, Himmler and Goebbels came to congratulate him.

**Martin Bormann, 1900–1945**       **Berlin**
*Hitler's birthday*
    Sadly not exactly a 'birthday mood'.
    Advance unit ordered to set off for Salzburg.

**Dr Theodor Morell, 1886–1948**       **Reich Chancellery, Berlin**
Injected him with Strophantose, Betabion forte i.v. plus Harmin
s.c. – or rather I asked Dr Stumpfegger to do it as my hand was too
unsteady.

*

**Benito Mussolini, 1883–1945**                    **Palazzo Monforte, Milan**
*Interview*

I felt and feel the greatest respect for Hitler. One must distinguish between Hitler and some of his highest-ranking men.

**Adolf Hitler, 1889–1945**                                        **(Berlin)**
*To Benito Mussolini*

My thanks to you, Duce, for your words of congratulation on my birthday. The battle that we are waging for our very existence has reached its climax. With unlimited deployment of ammunition, Bolshevism and the troops of Jewry are doing all in their power to unite their destructive forces in Germany and to throw our continent into chaos. In the spirit of dogged contempt for death, the German nation and all those who are similarly minded will halt this attack, however hard the struggle may be, and with our unique form of heroic courage, we will change the destiny of Europe for centuries to come.

I send you my warmest regards,

Adolf Hitler

**Joseph Goebbels, 1897–1945**                                    **(Berlin)**
*Radio address*

After this war Germany will *blossom* within a few years as never before. Her ravaged countryside and provinces will be built with new, more beautiful cities and villages in which happy people live. All of Europe will be involved in this revival. We will be friends once more with all people of goodwill. Together with them we will heal the grave wounds that disfigure the noble face of our continent. In rich fields of grain the daily bread will grow to assuage the hunger of the millions now starving and suffering. There will be work in abundance, and from it, as from the deepest spring of human happiness, blessings and strength for all will flow. Chaos will be tamed! This continent will be ruled not by the Underworld, but by order, peace and affluence.

That was always our goal! It still is, even today. If the enemy powers were to enforce their will, humanity would drown in a sea of blood and tears. Wars would alternate with wars, revolutions with revolutions, and in their terrible wake the *last remains* of a world that was beautiful and lovable and will be so again would be doomed to perish.

**Winston Churchill, 1874–1965**                    (*London*)
The indispensable political direction was lacking at the moment when it was most needed. The United States stood on the scene of victory, master of world fortunes, but without a true and coherent design.

**Bernard Law Montgomery, 1887–1976**        (north-west Germany)
I had always put Berlin as a priority objective; it was a political centre and if we could beat the Russians to it things would be much easier for us in the post-war years. [...] Berlin was lost to us when we failed to make a sound operational plan in August 1944, after the victory in Normandy.

**Georgy Zhukov, Soviet general, 1896–1974**          *outside Berlin*
On 20 April [...] the heavy artillery of the 79th Rifle Corps of the 3rd Shock Army opened fire on Berlin. The storming of the German capital began.

*

**Alfred Kantorowicz, 1899–1979**                  (*New York*)
Franklin Delano Roosevelt died – like Abraham Lincoln – knowing that he had won a victory. A fine death: to die at the end of success, even before the opposing forces who will defile the victory and make its fruits rotten have come into play – Roosevelt was spared Wilson's fate. He will not have to endure others spoiling his peace.

It is a strange encounter: Roosevelt in the western hemisphere the crucial adversary of the crazed rabble-rouser from Braunau; he came to the peak of state power at the same time as the latter did. The vanquished Hitler will not survive the victor for long. The raging hater probably detested Roosevelt more than any other individual in the world. Jews, Communists, intellectuals, against whom he yelled himself hoarse, were collectives, abstracts to a certain degree, the hallucinations of a lunatic, objects of his manic rages, but when he uttered the name Roosevelt, his voice broke into a screech of loathing. It was the aristocrat in Roosevelt, his intelligent, radiant, magical side, that made the ragged petit-bourgeois' dank inferiority seethe.

I don't want to turn him into a 'superman', not even in the hour of grief. Rather, I must consider injustices that have appeared in my own notebooks for years. I have written down bitter words about him; they came from disappointed trust, disappointed hope. And I can now take some of them back.

The statesman, the visionary, the intellectual leader; Roosevelt has all too often made concessions to the politician who must deal with everyday intrigues. He said nothing when – after Pearl Harbor and the declaration of war by Nazi Germany – he would have had the chance to settle his scores with the friends and defenders of Nazism and Fascism in his country. He let the war degenerate into a police action against gangsters, after whose defeat his troops acted as the gendarmes of restoration. The districts of the poor were bombed to pieces, but his special envoys brought compliments to the palaces of kings, marshals and industrial leaders. He exchanged handshakes with French Fascists in Casablanca – within sight of the concentration camps in which the surviving anti-Fascists were still being abused. That he was indistinguishable from the trite milquetoasts of daily politics makes me insanely furious.

*

### Anaïs Nin, 1903–77 (*New York*)
Frances gives me a small velvet hat with a trailing feather, the latest fashion. Pablo repainted the feather a more vivid pink. I wear this dashing hat when we go to the theatre or ballet.

### Thea Sternheim, 1883–1971 (*Paris*)
What glory in the gardens! Lilac, laburnum, hawthorn and pink hawthorn in bloom. Above the walls hang the heliotrope clusters of the clematis. What enchantment lies in the white blossoms. On the hill, a view of the city spread out below. How many cities have been turned into piles of rubble by now? The angels have protected Paris.

**Hans Henny Jahnn, 1894–1959**          **(Bornholm)**
*To his aunt Helene Steinius*

For the last two days we have had spring weather, and work in the fields is progressing at full speed. This week I hope to finish sowing the barley; after that will come oats and grapes. In the meantime another three colts are due to arrive here, and hopefully some calves too.

\*

**Eberhard Fechner, 1926–92**          *Schloss Waldeck*
On 20 April 1945 I was a corporal, lying wounded in the Baroque library in Schloss Waldeck. We had been taken prisoner by the Americans and were lodged there.

The door opens, and three German commanding officers come in, salute and hold a birthday party for the Führer. With Nazi 'Heils'! And there were six of us lying there, and I thought I'd gone mad. Americans allowing German officers to hold a birthday party for Hitler. And I lay in bed, with bullets in my leg and didn't object, but raised my arm and thought I was mad.

**Captain Fritz Farnbacher, 1914–2012**          **Bohnsack, near Danzig**
10 o'clock officers' meeting of the whole regiment to celebrate the Führer's birthday. First a short memorial address for Herbert K., then *Pathétique*, played by the doctor, then various speakers, a choir, Haydn's *Emperor Quartet*, a tribute to the Führer, and finally sandwiches and alcohol, with the appropriate effect; but in the end the regimental commander orders another 20 minutes of good music, which must end with 2 Bach chorales.

**Günter Cords, b. 1928**          **Antiesenhofen, Austria**
Führer's birthday. We arrived at the party in the village square, shielded against sightings from the air by fat-bellied lime trees. Enticed by our marching, a dozen and a half children stood around while their parents watched cravenly through the curtains. Just before the conclusion of the address the children disappeared as well. In their place Jabos

appeared in the sky and brought the festivities to an end before the brass band could play the national anthem.

### Volkssturmmann Fritz Steffen, 1893–1979                          Stettin

On 20.4.45, 7.00 p.m., we have to go to the 'Party for the Führer's Birthday' in the mess at the Landeshaus. A Kreisleiter talks about the final victory! The free bottle of red wine and small portion of ham and sausage with bread weren't enough to persuade us of it.

### Dieter Borkowski, 1928–2000                          Kreuzberg, Berlin

Most party members were sitting or lying in the gutter, drunk. The Ortsgruppenleiter had distributed pilfered alcohol. He, himself quite a young man, then stood white as a sheet in front of the Führer's old fighters who could hardly get up and some of whom had vomit on their uniforms. 'Comrades, the hour of truth has struck! You will be deployed at the Reich Chancellery and save our beloved Führer.' [...] At last we set off to march via Blücherstrasse to Hallesches Tor and then to Wilhelmstrasse.

*

### Theo Findahl, Norwegian journalist, 1891–1976   (Dahlem, Berlin)

When I get to the Hotel Adlon at around half-past twelve, the shells of the Russian artillery are striking the entrance to the Linden with great rumbling and crashing. In the dining room the few guests are overcome by the willingness of the waiters to pour out copious amounts of wine, when hitherto the rule has long been: one glass per head. Well, yes, better have the last guests pay for it than give it all to the Russians.

[...]

Goebbels's shouting has subsided somewhat in Berlin. He no longer has the same hold on the people as before, and the prevailing belief among the foreign journalists here is that there will not be a serious battle for the German capital. The barricades, built of cobblestones and reinforced with all kinds of rubbish, rusted cars and bathtubs, do not look imposing, and we can't imagine them being a major obstacle for Stalin's big tanks. In two or three days it will all be over, we say.

We have heard from the most diverse sources that the Volkssturm will not fight, and the Communists will of course welcome the Russians as liberators. Only a few are shaking their clever heads and saying the madness of the Red Army will prompt German despair, so that the heat of battle will itself unleash a massive fire. The battle for Berlin could even be a terrible one, they say, don't be foolish, flee while there's still time. Remember that the Red Army has the best artillery in the world. The Russians have about a thousand cannon per kilometre, one cannon per metre – a barrage. It feels as if the world is coming to an end.

In the Press Club on Leipziger Platz the disintegration is complete. The offices are a chaos of paper, shards of glass, chairs and tables, all scattered about, under a trickle of chalk dust. No receptionist. No censorship. Everything in flux. It looks as if all press activity from Berlin has ceased. The waitresses huddle together on the stairs when the cannon roar. There's no food to be had. Even the bar is shut. Most of the reporters have fled. Even now one must talk of Berlin as a city under siege; the Russians have, as far as we know, the most important means of access under their control. As if by miracle, telephone calls from Stockholm and Copenhagen are coming through, and lucky individuals are able to send sensational telegrams home – no one bothers about censorship, everything's in a state of breakdown. Listen, listen, they say at the end, listen to the *thundering cannon* in Berlin! We hear, we hear, say excited voices from Stockholm and Copenhagen.

\*

**Captain Arthur Mrongovius, 1905–92**                                       **Tabor**
On 20 April, Führer's birthday of all days, we had reached Tabor, the holy city of the Czechs. In a crowded waiting room we heard Goebbels's speech on the occasion of Hitler's birthday. It was ghostly to hear the familiar voice in these bleak surroundings – it no longer radiated any kind of confidence. When the speaker swore loyalty to 'our Hitler' it sounded like a swansong. The downcast silence of the gathered crowd of refugees and scattered soldiers was the echo of this address.

**Marie 'Missie' Vassiltchikov, 1917–78**              **Gmunden, Austria**

Adolf's birthday. A ridiculous speech by Goebbels: 'The Führer is in us and we in him!' How far does he want to take that? He added that there will be no difficulty in rebuilding everything that has been destroyed. Meanwhile the Allies are advancing on all sides, and the air raid warnings go on all day. The colonel's wife seems not to believe any of these announcements, however. She is convinced that Germany has a secret miracle weapon that will be deployed at the last minute; the poor woman can't imagine how they could say such things otherwise. She insists that we have breakfast with her. It's very kind of her, because it's our only meal of the day.dsadada 'asda'

**Rittmeister Gerhardt Boldt, 1918–81**                               **Zossen**

The rumour is spreading of a liberating army. Flyers are being dropped over Berlin: 'The Wenck army is coming, and will bring you freedom and victory'. But that 12th Army, named after its leader, Tank Commander Wenck, is not in fact an army at all. Of its nine divisions six exist only on paper, so only three divisions, one corps, could be fully deployed. These three divisions are very badly equipped and armed. Almost 90 per cent of their number are 17- and 18-year-old trainees who know nothing of war. There are groups in which not even half the soldiers are supplied with weapons. That's the 'liberating army'. When Hitler gave them to Wenck on 5 or 6 April, he said solemnly: 'Wenck, I place the fate of Germany in your hands!'

*

**Ernst Jünger, 1895–1998**                               **Kirchhorst**

Read Job. No philosophy grasps more; pain is the deepest gold-digger.

**Thomas Mann, 1875–1955**          *Pacific Palisades, Los Angeles*

Got down to the novel again and wrote a little more of XXVI. Walked nearby with K. [...] Transcription of my German speech, practised.

**Heimito von Doderer, 1896–1966**           **Aalborg, Denmark**
*Park Hotel, breakfast* […]

Yesterday before bed and today getting up I had to forgo a smoke because I had no matches: the consequence of this was that my breakfast cigarette made me slightly dizzy.

It seems to me, walking in one's uniform, that one senses the general situation here in ephemeral trivia: the bad manners, by Viennese standards, of the Danish waiters (like those in north Germany) in their attitude towards Danish guests, and so on. Getting a bit of jam on the breakfast table requires awkward prompting, and at first one is told that there's none there, until eventually it turns up twice… That's how we're going through the world today: responsible for the collective. The bridge between inside and out, the bridge of reality, is broken.

Today three pages of prose, Melzer's farewell.

**Wilhelm Hausenstein, 1882–1957**                      **Tutzing**
Last night I read *The Giant Toy* by Emil Strauss to the end in long chunks. I am usually a slow, pedantically precise reader, a rather awkward one, but in the case of this book I was gripped with impatience; the detail (the casual conversations, for example) seems to me to be at odds with the whole; the excursive and discursive passages wearied me and made it impossible for me to concentrate. So I did something that I *never* do and skipped whole pages, and in the end I parted painlessly from the book, even though I found its descriptive aspects very compelling. At the same time I couldn't fail to recognize the skill and the good phrases that occur in parts.

*

**Officer Udo von Alvensleben, 1897–1962**                      **Norway**
Hitler's birthday. A party in Saetermoen with string quartet, medals, pudding and special awards. At the same time the Russians are encircling Berlin. All the while German troops are standing pointlessly at the North Cape, in the Apennine Mountains and on Crete. In the cauldron of the Reich people are running aimlessly here and there while a hail of bombs rains down on villages and crossroads.

**Christian Graf von Krockow, 1927–2002**          Cavalry School,
                                                  Næstved, Island of Seeland

As if in mockery: big review for Führer's birthday. It will probably
be the last time. Medals are awarded. Our Cavalry Captain, highly
decorated, is dissatisfied with the Cross of Merit in War that is pinned
to his uniform: 'Am I a civilian or something?' Above all, pithy
speeches are delivered, with oaths of loyalty devoted to THE FÜHRER.

**Jacob Kronika, Danish journalist, 1897–1982**          Berlin

Hitler's birthday!

This time it's the Führer's last birthday, the Berliners are saying.

In years past they called out 'Heil!' Now they hate the man who
calls himself their leader. They hate him, they fear him, they suffer
misery and death because of him. But they have neither the strength
nor the courage to free themselves from his demonic power. They wait
desperate and passive for the final act of the war.

Last night unknown hands put up a big, rough-and-ready banner
on a ruin on Lützowplatz. The lettering appears across the wall of the
first floor and reads, 'For this we thank the Führer!'

The phrase is well known. It was invented by Dr Goebbels. The
words have been used countless times. But they were not intended as
an epitaph for Germany's ruins!

*

**Wilhelm Bodenstedt, postal official, 1894–1961**          Breslau

The night was very troubled again. The artillery fire didn't ease up
until the morning. During the day the pressure became more intense.
Received a letter from my little Wifey today, dated 10.3, which means
that the letter had been on the road for over 40 days. It is the 11th letter
since 10 February. Unfortunately this one was *without* hairs, unlike
all the previous letters. The injury to my hand is healing very slowly,
it still needs to be bandaged. I had thought a little plaster would be
enough, but I still need to wear a bandage. It's 10 p.m. now. We have
already had a visit from the airmen: the lads dropped explosive bombs.
Now goodnight, my little Wifey.

**Volkssturmmann Emil Heinze**                          **Breslau**
On 20 April, Führer's birthday, a propaganda officer delivered a
speech in which he said consoling words about, among other things,
the devastation of Breslau: 'I have spoken to an engineer. A street
like Albrechtstrasse can be rebuilt in four weeks.' This prompts loud
laughter from the assembled company. Complaints are voiced that
many people are wearing civilian suits under their uniforms.

**Hugo Hartung, dramaturg, 1902–72**                    **Breslau**
In the big seminar room a funeral celebration is held for the Führer's
birthday. With rather hollow pathos, the colonel delivers a speech
proclaiming his confidence in victory. Most of the other officers look
very sceptical. Again medals are awarded and promotions handed out.
The best thing about this day is that we are given a delicious lunch
and a bottle of wine. On the city fronts of Breslau things are also still
relatively calm.

**Albrecht Schulze-van Loon, paratrooper**             **(Breslau)**
Our marksmen used every trick at their disposal. They had crept
through the rubble into a street on which the Russians were driving a
truck to bring reinforcements forward. Poldi was sitting on the left, his
comrade on the right of the street, which was blocked by a high gravel
embankment. When the Russian truck stopped, Poldi's comrade fired
from the right. The Russians reacted sensibly and at lightning speed:
they leapt from the truck on the left and thus into our Poldi's line of
fire. Our two groups of marksmen had eliminated about two units of
Russian soldiers in the course of the fighting.

**Senta Tittmann, b. 1919**                    *Obernigk, near Breslau*
On 18 April 2,000 German prisoners came through. They were lying
in the Palace Park. Hildburg and I went to peel potatoes with some
other women after dinner. It looked like a stage, all shadowy, with
backdrops.

In front of us lies a huge mountain of potatoes. On the left are three
field kitchens, served by a German.

In the background of the white farmyard is the dark front of the hungry prisoners. Behind us the ruins of the castle stands black and accusatory, illuminated by the flickering light of the Russian campfire. A starlit sky arches over us. As if on command, the show begins over Breslau. Searchlights, tracer bullets, firestorm. Somewhere Russians were singing – sound travels long distances at night.

The doors of the oven are opened so that we have a little light to work by. A Russian major issues orders in an unpleasant voice. We took the opportunity to talk to the prisoners when we walked past them at the field kitchens. 'Chins up, be brave and stay true to us.'

Oh, those men know very well what dangers they face. A Berliner soon showed up. The sounds of home in my ears. Oh, what pain we feel in our hearts when we think of our own men.

*

**Erna Seiler, 1906–90**                                    **Czechoslovakia**

In the meantime we hadn't even noticed how close the Russians had come and how busy the Czechs were. But how could we hope to get out of there now? No trains ran, the bombs were falling.

Now our aunt Lena came up with a plan that only she could have carried off. There were still German soldiers, a whole barracks full, in Tschaslau. Aunt Lena went there every day and said to the captain, 'We have 11 children, do you want to have them on your conscience? Come out to us!' And one day it actually came to pass that Aunt Lena was given the message: 'Tomorrow there is a convoy from Tschaslau to Passau. We will drive via Winterberg and drop you off there. A truck will be provided for you.' Aunt Lena had to say goodbye to lots of things, but she took an old wardrobe (which was valuable) and the children's beds. We didn't have much to pack. The truck was empty, but everything was piled up behind, an old sewing machine last of all. The rest of the room was for the 11 children, 2 of them in the pram, and for us 2 mothers. A Czech woman, an elderly woman, lived downstairs. She pressed a big piece of bread into my hand and said, 'For your children. The Germans are withdrawing, but the Russians are coming. I don't think it's going to get any better for us.' Then an adventurous journey began, mostly at night. By day the cars stood at the edge of the forest and were guarded by the soldiers. 'Partisans,' they said. At night we drove through Prague; whistles, shouts, shots.

**Hildegard Holzwarth, seminarian, b. 1928**                    **Prague**
Yesterday we went to the circus. It was terrific. I just looked at everything and was as delighted as a little child. I particularly liked a magician, he did such exciting things. I'm glad that I was able to be so childishly happy again. But now the sad seriousness of life stands before me with great clarity. I've been in Prague for exactly a year this week. I'm grateful for the lovely year that I've been able to enjoy in the 'golden city'. It was so full of variety, so full of merriment and sadness. I will never forget those days, you beautiful city!

Here all the preparations against the enemy are being made. There is terrible tension between Germans and Czechs. There have been some minor disturbances. Why should German women and girls risk themselves for this? My duty calls me to my parents. We are no longer needed. Prague, adieu!

Today it is the Führer's birthday. What a day of celebrations that used to be. This year the day is a day of mourning. Führer!

**Lieutenant Hans Kranich, 1919–80**        **Altvatergebirge, near**
                                                                **Jägerndorf**
Now I could almost believe that I was still with my battalion on the Führer's birthday, because I heard the Führer's short speech on the radio, expressing his gratification that Roosevelt, his worst enemy, had died unexpectedly, while on 20 July he himself had been saved by providence.

Things started to change in April while I was an adjutant with the battalion. It was spring and a wild cherry tree blossomed on the mountainside, a weary blue haze hung on the horizon.

Orders came fast and furious: they came almost daily from the Army Group, but most of them were only for officers. They made for amusing reading, Field Marshal Schörner in particular demonstrated his literary gifts. I liked his letters because they finally addressed reality again and the clichés of the soldiers fighting bravely night and day were suddenly forgotten. They were like this: 'I am standing on a tower looking out over the section of a division. What spreads across the parade ground is the expression of lax apathy, not to say cowardice. The grenade launchers have been placed as far back as possible. The artillery hasn't looked for the place for the most effective deployment, but the position from which it can get away as quickly as possible. Three (!) military policemen bring back one measly Russian prisoner rather than dealing with the rabble slouching around on the daily march.' The aura of the wild man hung around him as it did around no other. Luckily the division knew in advance that Schörner wanted to view the procession of sick and wounded men, and promptly received the highest praise from the head of the Army Group: 'The squadron of the 78th St. D. was exemplary.'

*

### Göring's adjutant                                          Carinhall, Berlin

Today I am setting off for the first time from Carinhall with RM [Reichsmarschall Hermann Göring]. Leaving the rooms in which he has lived for years, and which have witnessed his rise, will be terribly hard for him. I had never seen tears in his eyes before – when he took leave of his employees, he could contain them no longer.

The atmosphere in Berlin is oppressive, as it has been for the last few weeks. AH comes very late and accepts only very brief birthday wishes, then the strategy meeting. It is worth making some remarks about this event and the people taking part in it. It ended at around 10 p.m. RM has an order (or permission) to drive south, and goes without lengthy goodbyes. Between two air raid warnings we try to leave, but have to turn round, and in the second break we only make it as far as the Zoo bunker. There RM goes quickly through the rooms of the field hospital and then sits down in the antechamber of the general air raid shelter. The attitude of the inhabitants is amazing: I would understand if they booed 'Meier'*, but on the contrary, the news runs through the bunker like wildfire: our Hermann is here! And then everyone rushes over enthusiastically to hear a word from him or shake his hand. We can't get away from the bunker until after midnight.

---

* Göring had famously said, 'If even a single enemy plane flies over our territory, you can call me Meier,' the latter phrase meaning more or less 'then I'm a Dutchman'. As the enemy planes approached, Göring was popularly known as 'Meier'.

**General Karl Koller, 1898–1951**                    **OKL, Wildpark-Werder**
Göring had, incidentally, come from Carinhall to the Führerbunker fully prepared to travel, and had already made the necessary arrangements for his convoy. His cars were all fully laden.

Then, at the strategy meeting in the Führerbunker, after my departure he asked the question about relocating once more, and demanded of Hitler that at least one person from the OKL, either he or the head of the General Staff, should go to the south, because the situation there required a common, senior leadership from the Luftwaffe. Hitler replied, 'Then you go. Koller is staying here.'

Christian told me this second-hand from the bunker after my arrival in Wildpark-Werder. He tells me Göring is leaving for Berchtesgaden immediately after the conference. He informed me that I was to stay and deputize for him.

**Dr Hans Graf von Lehndorff, 1910–87**                    *Königsberg*
My equipment currently consists of the following: a short-sleeved tropical shirt, a pair of underpants, a pair of corduroy trousers half a metre too big for me, which I found in the street, also my own long trousers, laced at the bottom, a jacket inherited from a relative, the military coat, the felt boots and a hat that I also found. In a sack over my shoulder I am carrying my old shoes and the camouflage jacket I found. The weather is slightly better. The sun shines from time to time. The streets are still unusually busy, and the air full of aeroplanes bound for Pillau. In front of the carts I find a team of East Prussian horses, which are already thoroughly apathetic, and have got used to this dreadful way of walking: sharp trot in three-four time. It's a torture to hear them dashing along the cobbles, neck dragged back, head at an angle, mouth torn bloody. [...]

Crouching side by side on the floor, we are guarded by a thick-set, fair-haired Russian, who can speak a little German. At noon in the antechamber he cooks us thick porridge in a bucket on a tiled stove. He clearly enjoys the hunger in our eyes.

In the afternoon we are questioned individually. It goes remarkably quickly for me. From my remaining papers the grim-faced major probably sees that I am a doctor. Otherwise he doesn't get much out of me. He clearly doesn't understand that I've just joined this unit. Again I am amazed by the possibility of a system amidst this confusion. Why do they even make distinctions? Most people won't come out of this sorting machine alive anyway. The major thinks I'm exaggerating the rest of my information. Plainly I'm not very interesting at the moment. He doesn't believe that I wasn't a party member. The interpreter asks, 'Why party bad for you?' I can't explain that very quickly, I reply. Urged several times to give an explanation anyway, I make the sign of the cross. The interpreter taps his temple and nods to the interrogating major. He gives me back my papers and lets me go.

The other men are questioned for much longer. The boy is asked among other things how many Russian prisoners he killed during Hitler Youth exercises. An old man who used to be a policeman is never seen again.

### Frau Bruno                                                     *Königsberg*

On 20.4 all people who were not politically suspect were driven to Königsberg on foot. During the journey back the women were repeatedly abused, it was a Via Dolorosa. In Königsberg corpses were lying in the streets; Germans, Russians, horses, whole blocks were burned out, so that in the city and also on the farms nothing but the walls were left standing. I dragged myself wearily to my flat and found nothing there. It was all destroyed. Only the staircase was still intact, and the radiators hung on the walls. There was nothing but rubble and ashes! I was so dulled inside that the sight of it barely shocked me. In the camp I'd made friends with an old chemist and his wife, and, with Herr Wiehler, the four of us now moved into Herr Wiehler's flat. Of his 5 rooms, 2 rooms and the kitchen were usable, and we formed a makeshift community, which is something quite uncommon.

### Willi Holtzer                              *Fischhausen, near Königsberg*

We spent the first night in a little room in the farmhouse. We were guarded by a Russian at the door. It must have been midnight when the Russian woke me with the butt of his rifle and beckoned to me to follow him. I had to leave my rucksack behind.

He then led me into a dark corner of the farm. There, under a low ceiling, there was a long, narrow box with a lid, in the shape of a coffin. Was it a trap? After the Russian had fiddled around with something on a shelf, he came out of the dark with a tin of red paint and a brush. With hand gestures he ordered me to paint the coffin red.

The sentry headed back towards our quarters. What lay ahead of me now? Should I try to escape?

The surprise was all the greater when the sentry came back after a short time and led me into the kitchen. There the Russian field kitchen had left behind a generously laid table. With friendly nods I was encouraged to eat. Was this to be my last meal?

As I ate I was able to observe that the next comrade was being led to the barn to paint. And now I also learned the reason why the sentry had taken us to the barn without our luggage. It meant that he was able to go through our bags undisturbed. Heavy luggage would probably only have weighed us down, and there might have been a watch or two hidden in there. I was no longer worried about my watch. I was grateful for the good food, and the bits and pieces I'd 'found' in the kitchen.

### Klara Gawlick, b. 1907                          *Königsberg*
Every day the Russians came to take what remained of our things. They even pulled an old gentleman's jacket from his shoulders. It was late on the evening of 19 April when a Russian sentry brought us home from our hard day's work. Another Russian coming towards us on a bicycle ordered us all to come to the commandant's office. There we were interrogated until well into the night, and then locked in the cellar after being roughly tweaked on the nose and called 'Nazi swine'. Then we were told we were going to be transported to Russia. My worries for my three little children, who had stayed behind in the cottage, were indescribable. In the morning we were left alone for a few minutes, before being locked in the cellar again. Luckily a senior-ranking Russian came and asked us what we were doing. When we told him and pleaded, he let the women with small children go home. I know nothing about the fate of the others.

*

**Erich Zimmermann, musician, 1900–1987**    (*Heubude*)

Omi Paula looked through all the food in our cellar, the food that had been crushed and trampled in the mud. It was our salvation that all kinds of things were uncovered. The potatoes were there, and from my food chest came two jars of lard.

We lived in a pile of junk and devastation, and I insisted that Omi Paula left it like that – as a good housewife, of course, she wanted to clean up straight away – because among all the junk there were lots of things that were valuable to us, which Omi Paula could have taken from our flat. The devastated appearance of our room was our best protection. Then, if the Russian and Polish soldiers came to our house, they usually just said with a grin, 'All kaput!' and didn't bother looking any further.

Worst of all were the nights. We could never settle down until 1 in the morning, because every night the Russians went through the flats in search of women. Omi Paula and I had agreed with everyone in the house that she would present herself as my wife, and I had drummed into the two boys that they were only to call me 'grandfather' from now on.

It was clear to me that I owed my survival so far largely to Omi Paula's help. But since we had come back to her house, it turned out that I could pay her back for her help with my presence and the state I was in. A healthy, strong man would immediately have been dragged away by the Russians. I hadn't shaved for weeks, and my long beard and my starved condition gave me such an appearance that I often heard the soldiers using the expression 'old invalid'.

As we waited for the Russians at night, Omi Paula and I lay fully dressed in bed, she with an old scarf around her head, which she never took off by day either, to hide her face. Then, when we heard the Russians coming, she pressed herself against the wall as invisibly as possible, while I quickly crept out of bed and sat on my travelling wheelchair. If the Russians came, I got in their way as an invalid. They muttered something and set off again. Among all the residents of the house it had been agreed that if a woman started screaming somewhere in the house, all the other women should join in with the screaming, because that was the best way of driving the Russians away.

One night three Russians came into our room. There was something special about them. They were fully armed, with guns over their shoulders.

I gave them the usual welcome. One of them was a small, evil-looking Kalmuck type, the second a big, dark Russian, the third actually looked quite human and was even friendly. I found these fellows particularly unsettling, because there was something strangely calm and sly about them. They wanted me to give them salt, which was in very short supply at the time. I said we hadn't any, and was very frightened as I did so, because there was a big stone pot full of salt in the room which was extremely valuable to us.

Then they wanted me to go with them into the kitchen, and I was glad at least to get them out of there again. They demanded cooking pots from me, and when I pretended not to understand them they took two as if it was perfectly natural. Then they left, and of course I thought I'd seen our irreplaceable cooking pots for the last time, even though one of them tried to make me understand that he would bring them back in a few hours.

These fellows stayed in the house for three days and nights. They had lodged themselves in the cellar, where they did their cooking and fried rabbits in our pots, which you could smell all over the house. Once the ringleader went fishing with explosives in the Martwa Wisła, and brought us a bowl full of little fish. After three days they disappeared and even brought me the pots back first. They had behaved with great restraint and care and hadn't done anything to anyone. A few days later Omi Paula happened to see them again in the street outside the house, being led away unarmed by Russian soldiers. So they must have been runaways or deserters.

*

**Brigitte Kramer**                                    **Pillau–Copenhagen**
A ship was waiting there, but it was very small with room for only a few people. My mother was shocked, she said we could never cross the Baltic in such a thing. I didn't worry about it. The sailors would know whether or not it could be done. I wanted to get away at once. To go anywhere a person could live properly again.

And then another terrible thing happened. The Volkssturm wouldn't let my father on to the ship. My mother and we children were already on deck when we noticed that they were stopping him from boarding. More people were fighting their way on, so that we couldn't get off again either. We shouted and cried; it wasn't possible that we should be parted now, after we'd survived so much.

My father saw us on board. He was pale and unable to speak. Because of his injury his voice failed completely when he became distressed.

Then one of the lower-ranking officers noticed our desperation. He ordered the Volkssturm man to let my father on board. He refused. Then, when no one was looking, the officer showed my father how to climb through the railing. He did so and was back with us once more. No one fetched him down again, because it had all been done very quickly.

We left the harbour straight away, and right after that the siren went off in Pillau. From the ship we saw the city being bombed. Everything was ablaze! Then we were pursued by a Russian aeroplane, but our anti-aircraft guns forced it to turn back.

We were quite exhausted with excitement and tried to sleep wherever we could. Mother and I on the bare iron panels, some on their suitcases, my sister on a coil of rope, and my father sat and slept on the corner of a chest. And above us was the cold night sky.

In the middle of the night we reached the Hela peninsula, where we were to be transferred to a bigger ship. Three ships were burning in the harbour, and the remains of others loomed blackly out of the water. It was a bleak sight. We stayed on deck. There, in complete darkness, lay the *Lapland*, a freighter that was to carry us across. Ferries and little boats were heading towards it from all directions. Towards morning, with the sun already rising, it was our turn. Along a very narrow gangway, with a rope on the right as our only support, we had to get from the small ship to the big one, across the open sea that lay darkly below us. The luggage was heaved across in nets at the same time. One of those nets opened above the water and all its contents, suitcases, bundles, chests and prams, fell into the sea.

Then we were on board. The upper decks were mostly occupied by the wounded. We heard them groaning when we were sent down to the bottom, to the bilge. Straw had been laid on the floor.

The *Lapland* was part of a convoy along with three bigger ships and several escort vessels. Next morning people said that the island of Bornholm was in view, towards midday the island of Rügen, and in the evening we were said to have arrived in Copenhagen. I could hardly believe it, but it was really true.

Coming from the stuffy, dark bilge of the ship, our minds filled with everything we had experienced, and with the image of our devastated, chaotic, burnt-out home before our eyes, we saw Copenhagen in front of us. A radiantly blue sky, the bright green patina of domes and roofs, the fresh spring green of the trees and people on the quayside dressed in bright summer colours, waving at us.

### The German Red Cross Tracing Service, 1989
Subcommittee for the Tracing of Children UK – 01227 – female
  Surname: unknown
  First name: unknown
  Assumed date of birth: 20.4.1945
  Found: delivered to the Royal Institute of the Blind on Refsnæs near Kalundborg, Denmark on 20.4.1945. Is rumoured to be the child of German refugees.
  Clothing: unknown
  Description: eyes grey, hair dark blonde

### Navy Lance Corporal Klaus Lohmann, 1910–2002    Travemünde
Evening. Chopped wood with three comrades in vicarage! Otherwise a day with a lot of work in the study and the usual alarm. In the evening a few English fighter planes roared low above us, the anti-aircraft guns fired like mad but no hits.

*

### Eva Braun, 1912–45                                                (Berlin)
*To a girlfriend*
  Dear Hertalein!
  Many thanks for your last two letters, and please accept my belatedly written birthday wishes. The bad telephone connection

made it impossible for me to call. I hope you see your Erwin again soon and well. I'm sure I'm very close to your thoughts and feelings when I say that. I hope your birthday letter from him arrives soon. It can't have gone missing!

I'm very glad that you decided to keep Gretl company at the Berghof. Since the attack on Traunstein yesterday I'm no longer so firmly convinced that you're safe in Garmisch. Thank God mother is coming to you tomorrow. That means I don't need to worry any more.

Here we can already hear the artillery fire from the eastern front, and naturally have air raids every day. From east and west, just as you like! Unfortunately I'm under orders to be on hand because of possible flooding, even though my whole life is being played out entirely in the bunker. You can imagine how little sleep we get. But I'm very happy to be close to *you* now. Admittedly not a day passes without my being told to take myself to safety at the Berghof, but so far I've always been the winner. Besides, from today there's not a chance of getting through in the car. If all else fails, though, I'm sure there will be a way for us *all* to see you again.

An amazingly awful thing happened to Brandt, i.e. it was something that he did. I can't tell you more about that here.

The secretaries and I fire pistols every day and have already become such crack shots that no man dares compete with us.

Yesterday I had what was probably my last conversation with Gretl. Since today I haven't been able to get through. But I'm firmly convinced that everything will turn out all right, and *he* is much more hopeful than usual.

What's Anneliese doing? She certainly won't have been able to escape, because of the factory. I offered her and her aunt, on his behalf, the Berghof as a place of shelter. If they turn up they'll be very welcome. And where is Ilse now? Please write again, if possible. Perhaps it could go by airmail! Captain Bauer has a lot of air traffic with Bavaria. Frau Bormann will also know how best to get a letter through.

Where is Käthl? Georg, Bepo, and how is Gretl? Please write soon and often! Sorry if the style of this letter isn't as good as usual but in a hurry as always.

With warmest wishes for you all, I am still your Eva

PS The photo is intended for Gretl. One of those little things is to be her property.

Please tell Frau Mittlstrasser as a serious order to give the girls from Austria leave to travel home. But please only for a limited time. I'm thinking 14 days or so. Please send them my warmest regards as well.

\*

**Sigmund Graff, 1898–1979**   *Bad Kreuznach prisoner-of-war camp*
Just before midnight I arrived in Kreuznach on a transport of several thousand prisoners, all officers. We were sent inside the wire, where in the faint moonlight we saw comrades sleeping in open holes in the ground. They had covered themselves with cardboard and newspaper as protection against the cold. We were shivering too, and wanted to make ourselves little fires. But because someone who had gone to inquire about building a fire was immediately shot at by the sentry standing by the brightly lit fence, we had no option but to walk around till morning. When it was light we established that we were in the highest part of an enormous enclosure, which rose at an angle out of the valley. A few days later the whole terrible surface was covered with a whimpering grey carpet of humanity.

**Gerhard von Rad, 1901–71**   *Bad Kreuznach prisoner-of-war camp*
Overall the weather was very good; it rained relatively little. Then admittedly when it did rain the misery was great. It was a curious sight, when at the start of the downpour the whole camp, which otherwise presented an image of mostly recumbent men, leapt to its feet and everyone covered his head with a piece of cardboard or a blanket. Within a few minutes the muddy yellow ground was an unfathomable slurry that turned each footstep into an enormous effort. And yet, when the damp started to penetrate your skin, you had on all accounts to keep moving. When the rain abated, you scraped the mud a little to the side and lay back down so that you could rest a little till the next shower came. When the sky was clear, the nights were extremely cold, and you could only ever lie on the ground for a short time. Some of the prisoners had a strange way of getting warm quickly again. On

one of my nightly rounds, from far away in the moonlight I saw a big cluster of men tightly crammed together. But that heap – there were always several hundred – was in constant motion; it wobbled back and forth like a jellyfish, so that the ones on the outside often couldn't follow the movements and fell over. Of course it wasn't an enthusiastic game, there was lots of cursing and squabbling, the noise could be heard a long way off. But it was still a coming-together of people in an effort to keep warm. A group like that grew quickly. Because everyone was trying to get from the edge into the middle, the pressure built up, which meant that one's body was kneaded and one was soon warm. No one gave much thought to the vermin to which one was thus exposed. As the pressure was naturally never very even, the huge mass of people was constantly moving back and forth. Once someone lost a shoe in the rough ground and was thus of course put in a highly uncomfortable position. He circled the heap again and again, and begged them to part for just a second so that he could get his shoe. But no one listened to him.

There was a pretty cottage not far from our house. Early in the morning the attic room windows opened and, as soon as the sun was shining, the beds were laid out. But we were up even earlier. Did the people realize the yearning with which the eyes of tens of thousands settled on those beds and those little rooms?

**Franz Bittkowski, b. 1915**     *Bad Kreuznach prisoner-of-war camp*
Rained almost all night. Cold and fever even worse. Even less to eat! Sun every now and again. April weather, delousing.

Received a mess kit.

*

**Waltraut Fach, b. 1925**                    (Gross Soltikow, Pomerania)
Six of us are living in a tiny room on Koball's farm. We sleep on straw, have nothing to eat. Mother begs the farmers for eggs and bacon. The pickings are sparse. On the ground we find food and washing powder and help ourselves without asking the farmer for permission. So mother is able to wash our louse-ridden clothes – did I say we've

discovered clothes lice? So now we have an occupation to fill up our days: cracking lice and nits!

**Jutta, schoolgirl**                          **Tantow, near Stettin**
On the morning of 20 April such heavy fire began that we were all scared. It didn't let up! The decision to get away was made, because our lives were now at stake. My father ran to the coachman to tell him to hitch up the horses. First we loaded up, as we were ordered to, the company documents, then the coachman packed things for himself and his family on to the cart, so it was nearly full when it got to us. We had another two-wheeled barrow in the stable, so we went and got it, loaded it up with our most necessary things and coupled it to the horse-cart. I insisted on my doll with the real hair coming with us. Admittedly I was already fifteen, I know, but I said she belonged to me. My little sister couldn't be parted from her angora cats, she cried so much that the animals were put on the cart.

**Walburg Lehfeldt**                          **Lönnewitz**
At about 6 o'clock we stopped for a rest near Nexdorf. By that time we had trekked for 9 hours without stopping. We stopped in the forest and covered the carts thoroughly with bushes as air raid camouflage.

The American planes circled above us all day, bombing the nearby munitions factory at Schlieben! Karin in particular was very scared of the bombs from the planes. In spite of our own fears we had to keep reassuring the children and horses and comforting each other. We couldn't take to the road so we cooked in the forest with four bricks on which we put the cooking pot containing meat from a wether slaughtered in the Clementinenhof at the last minute with preserved salted beans and potatoes. We ate the hot stew from flat tin plates with tin spoons, which we had brought for this purpose from the oak dresser in the hall. As the tin became very hot, this turned out to be impractical.

It was warm spring weather! Jobst was put in his pram, which we took down off the cart. We tried, in so far as this was possible with the air attacks going on, to sleep on the fur blankets after our sleepless night. The two bigger children slept on hay in a deer manger that we found in the forest. Suddenly some Russians came galloping towards us with battle cries and circled us. We thought we were in the hands of the Russian army, but they were only scattered Vlasov troops firing up their own courage. They asked us the way and then galloped westwards on their fast little horses.

## Klaus Reinhardt, agricultural apprentice                    *Prositten*

Then came 20 April 1945. I arrived on the farm with a load of hay and saw a lorry. Standing beside the lorry were two Russian soldiers with machine guns at the ready. On the lorry there were already a few German boys who were also working on the kolkhoz. When the Russians saw me, I had to get down from the hay-cart straight away and climb up and join the others. After a while two Russians arrived who'd been searching the whole farm for Germans but who had found only old people and children that they didn't want to take with them. Then after a while an officer arrived from the house who had probably been negotiating with our guards. The Russians then sat down in the lorry, the officer as the driver in the driver's cabin, and the three other Russians, to guard us, on the bed. So we set off. As we did so an old woman threw another bag of food on to the lorry which, it later turned out, would save us from severe hunger, because for three days we had nothing to eat from the Russians.

Our journey took us to a kolkhoz in Prowangen. There were already 30 to 40 Germans here, gathered together from just about everywhere. Among these people I discovered three of my schoolmates: Lieselotte Bolk, Ulrich Columbus and Heinz Schulz. Of course I was glad that I'd found some acquaintances. After a while we had to marshal ourselves and we were driven off once again by the Russians. Lots of other Germans joined us on the way. We reached Prositten like that on the first evening. We had to go into a big house in which straw beds had already been spread out; presumably a group of Germans had been brought here by the Russians and driven on. We lay down on the straw bed and spent the night like that. At night we heard screams from women and girls being raped by the Russian guards.

**Walter Mehlberg, d. 1968**                          *Prokopyevsk*

On the night of 20.4 we arrived in Prokopyevsk, after 25 days of train travel. The city is in southern Siberia in the foothills of the Sayan Mountains, about 100 miles from the Chinese border. We had put about 6,000 miles behind us, and passed through four weather zones. When we arrived in Prokopyevsk, there were still high snowdrifts behind hedges and houses. After the long train journey our limbs were stiff, so walking was hard. We had only been able to leave the truck briefly in Moscow and at a stop in the Urals, to move a little and get some fresh air.

At the final stop we noticed that the train had got significantly shorter. About half of the transported men had been taken to another camp. After a good half-hour's march we reached our camp. Before we were scattered around the three barracks, a thorough body search took place. My pocket knife, which my father gave me in Köselitz, and the bag with my belongings in it were both taken from me. The same thing happened to my comrades. With everything we had left wedged under our arms we went to the barracks assigned to us, which was to be our shelter for a night. Piles of snow heaped up on either side of the entrance led us to conclude that the camp had been unoccupied for quite a long time. We tried to find a bunk, but they were all occupied, so we had to bivouac on the floorboards. As it had only just started thawing, and the ground freezes two metres deep, they gave off cold like an iceberg.

*

**Ernst Jünger, 1895–1998**                          **Kirchhorst**

In the meantime I read the memoirs of the Danish Countess Ulfeldt, which she left under the title *A Memory of Lament*. Long and difficult imprisonments such as hers in the Blue Tower suggest an astrological influence, a form of external compulsion. It can occur indirectly, through unlucky stars, or else it can be a matter of character. These questions are of little consequence, because prison opens its doors to both the innocent and the guilty; and both virtues and vices can lead to prison.

The uncontrolled urges of life above all lead to fetters. On the one hand that is obvious with regard to criminality. But it also applies, as with Casanova, Sade, Schubart, Trenck, to the erotic world. To the wanderlust connected with that world, fetters are the pendant to which, I think, Weininger first referred. Don Juan has to switch stages like a fugitive; Kant hardly ever left Königsberg. Balanced natures are the ones least threatened; for them imprisonment is also more bearable.

Maxims: that which our internal bonds cannot do is imposed on us from without. Hence our titanic nature is under particular threat; Prometheus is the greatest prisoner of all. That is one of the reasons why prisons are now on the rise. They are part of the equipment of the technical collective, just as monasteries belonged to the Gothic world. Hence too madness as the straitjacket of the titanic mind.

Outside, the procession of liberated Russians and Poles continues, and the looting at the same time. Yesterday we had three Frenchmen with us, pleasant people, because we help anyone who approaches us where possible, whether with food or with lodging. That is not only a human commandment, but at the same time the best security against being looted.

In this position the pre-eminence of primal labour is preserved again – the farmer can go on working, and so can the author, but no one who is dependent on bureaucracy, electricity or other distributors.

The important thing for the author is no longer to grasp the situation but, at the same time, to tame it, to bring it into a mirror, in which terrifying images also appear.

*

**Nina Mursina, forced labourer, b. 1925**                    **Namslau**
For over two years I have worked for the 'Greater Germany'. I would rather not remember that slavery. I wept every night and dreamed of the home I no longer had. On my chest on the left I had a birthmark. When I was still a child, my mother told me it would always bring me luck. But it only ever brought me bad luck. I remembered the words from a song: 'Why did I come into this world?'

We were only allowed to work, nothing else. We were not fed like human beings – our provisions were poor and low in calories. We worked with potatoes but were not allowed to fry any on the fire for ourselves. If the guards smelled the smoke they set fierce dogs on us. Everything was forbidden. In 1944 I was 19 years old. At that age you're already dreaming about love. The German women employed with us came to work with make-up on, they had done their hair in front of the mirror. And we, as *Untermenschen*, wore dreadful rags and wooden clogs that clattered when we walked.

**Anna Popovskaya, forced labourer, b. 1926   Görzig, near Köthen**
In the spring of 1945 I caught a cold and developed angina. Our farmer even called the doctor for me, something we couldn't have dreamed about before. The doctor examined me and prescribed medicine. I was off work for a week. But everything around me was very troubled. The bombs were falling constantly on the nearby towns.

Our colleague from Russia, a beautiful blonde called Ludmila, had an unwanted child by a Polish forced labourer. The farmer wanted to take her back to the labour exchange, which would have meant her being sent to Ravensbrück. We also have real Gypsies from Romania working with us. Ludmila abandoned her child with them. When we found out we were shocked.

Our farmer was very strict about love. He wouldn't acknowledge secret love. But if the young people were serious about it, he immediately made a separate bed available for the loving couple. On Sunday we were allowed to go to the village dance. With us was a beautiful girl, Lida. A German boy fell in love with her. When our farmer found out he thrashed her mercilessly with a whip. He was very angry with both of them, particularly with the 'Russian swine' who wanted to dishonour the German race. But the boy was so in love that he persuaded his mother to buy Lida from the farmer.

**Polina Moiseeva, forced labourer, b. 1925                 Hamburg**
I spent almost three years in Hamburg as a forced labourer. The first 13 months working in a jam factory in the camp, where I and my friend from the Ukraine sometimes furtively put berries in our mouths. Our

foreman was an old man and very good-natured. When things were stolen he always threatened us with being sent to the concentration camp. But in fact he turned a blind eye and silently waved a threatening finger.

Then we were deployed for a few weeks sweeping the streets, until we were taken to work in a fish factory in Altona, Hamburg, where we had to breathe in the horrible stench of fish for years. Our camp leader, Frau Böhme, a beautiful woman, was very strict but fair. One day she called me in to give me a job to do. But I couldn't understand what she was trying to explain to me. So I stood in front of her and blinked. Frau Böhme was beside herself and raised her arm to hit me. At that moment tears came to my eyes, and Frau Böhme lowered her hand. She started to say comforting words and brought me a tin of fish. Then she ordered a Pole to explain the task to me. She even apologized to me. We got very little to eat, we were always hungry. So we stole herrings from the work place, hiding them in our stockings or even weaving them into the braids on our heads. Strangely, we were warned in advance every time a raid was due, and on those days we didn't take anything. I'm sure Frau Böhme was behind those warnings. Once she gave me stockings of her own: 'Take them, yours smell so horribly of fish!' I blushed, but Frau Böhme said nothing and walked away.

### Joseph Goebbels, 1897–1945 (Berlin)
*Radio address*

He [Adolf Hitler] is the core of the resistance against the fall of the world. He is Germany's bravest heart and our people's most glowing will. I may allow myself a judgement about this, and it must be said today: if the nation is still breathing, if the chance of victory still lies ahead, if there is still a way out of this deadly serious danger – we have him to thank for it. He is steadfastness personified. I never saw him become uncertain or despondent, weak or weary. He will go his own way to the end, and what awaits him there is not the downfall of his people but a new and happy start to a flowering of all things German.

Hear it, people of Germany! Today in every country of the earth millions of people are watching this man, still doubting and wondering whether he knows a way out of the great disaster that has struck the world. He will show those nations, but we have our eyes on him, filled with hope and with deep, unshakeable conviction. Defiant and combative, we stand behind him: soldier and civilian, man and woman and child – a people, resolved to the bitter end, for it is a matter of life and honour. He is to keep his eyes on his enemies; for that reason promise him that he need not look behind him. We will not waver or yield, we will not leave him in the lurch at any time, be it the most breathtaking and the most dangerous. We stand by him as he stands by us – in Teutonic loyalty to his followers, as we have sworn and as we want to keep our vow. We do not call out to him, because he already knows, he must know: Führer, give us an order – we will follow! We feel him inside us and around us. God give him strength and health and protect him from all dangers. We want to do the rest.

Our misfortune has made us mature but has not stripped us of character. Germany is still the land of loyalty. In danger, they are to celebrate their finest victory. Never will history be able to say of this time that a people abandoned its Führer, or that a Führer abandoned his people. But that is victory. That for which we so often asked the Führer in our happiness tonight has now in suffering and peril for us all become a much deeper and more fervent plea to him: let him *remain* what he *is* and *always was* for us – *our Hitler*!

**Dr Julius Voss, chemist, 1898–1968**　　　　**Biebrich, Wiesbaden**
This order that has come in from the supreme leadership to defend every city – the explanation given is that every city is an important traffic hub – is based on an enemy report to the effect that 4,000 German aeroplanes have been destroyed in 14 days!

And what does Dr Goebbels have to say about that? He said in his article last Friday that we are now fighting for honour and no one will respect us if we surrender. Clausewitz so often quoted in the past, holds a different view. For him a failure to surrender has nothing to do with honour, and everything to do with narrow-mindedness.

Yesterday he spoke on the eve of Adolf Hitler's birthday. It was the most insane speech he has ever delivered. It bore a desperate resemblance to the behaviour of a man with tuberculosis who believes that everything will be for the best. Or was that a total lunatic speaking? Because otherwise how can one say in this situation that, if we do not capitulate, we will still remain on top, our ideas will conquer the world, that in a few years our cities will re-emerge more beautiful than ever, the fields will bear ripe fruit and work and affluence will be there for the taking. And the person who dares to say this once demanded to be taken seriously as a representative of the German intelligentsia! The answer comes on the radio from the opposing side. Today, as a birthday present for the 'Führer', Churchill will bring revelations about the German concentration camps, particularly about Buchenwald, and what comes out of that promises to be terrible. And where affluence is concerned, one can learn more from Eisenhower's challenge to the German seamen, in which he announced that German ships are now being used by the Allies to bring supplies to Germany. That won't stop the Nazis from sinking them. They don't care how many people in Germany die.

Otherwise, the foreign press are talking unanimously about the Führer's 'last' birthday, and they could be right.

### Hans-Jochen Vögel, b. 1926            near Pisa

On the evening of 19 April 1945, along with a handful of comrades in a half-ruined farmhouse, I listened to Joseph Goebbels's speech on Hitler's 56th birthday. Even though we knew that the Allies and also the Soviet troops had advanced far into Germany, and most of our home towns had already been occupied, and even though the definitive collapse had already begun in our section of the front, this diabolical seducer managed to cast his spell on us once again. Might the miracle weapons he talked about not bring about a last-minute turnaround? And might not the death of the American President Franklin D. Roosevelt, which he compared with the death of the Russian Tsarina Elisabeth during the Seven Years War, lead to the collapse of the alliance between the western powers and the Soviet Union; just as the death of Tsarina Elisabeth had led to Russia leaving its alliance against Frederick the Great? That was what we wondered. But the effect of this last attempt at mass suggestion fled within a few minutes. Bombs going off nearby and the sight of soldiers flooding back, either singly or in groups, quickly brought us back down to earth.

**Field Marshal Wilhelm Keitel, 1882–1946**                    **Berlin**
The last large-scale raid by the English and American air fleets on
the centre (government district) of Berlin took place at about noon
on 20 April. With my wife, Herr and Frau Dönitz and the adjutants
we observed this massive, terrible spectacle from the little hill in the
garden of the official flat of the Grand Admiral, who had returned to
Berlin the previous night from his command post 'Coral' (district of
Eberswalde).

The Reich Chancellery, already seriously damaged, had not been hit
again in this bombing raid. There was no resistance; German fighter
planes didn't join the battle to fend off the attack, anti-aircraft guns
were ineffective given the enemy's altitude. The air raid, lasting almost
two hours, was carried out as if during peace-time manoeuvres, in
precise formations, the bombs being dropped exactly as commanded.

From 4 o'clock in the afternoon we were ordered to the Reich
Chancellery (Führerbunker) for the strategy presentation. Jodl and I
entered the bunker, and saw the Führer with Goebbels and Himmler
going up to the day rooms of the Reich Chancellery; I didn't comply
with an adjutant's demand that I join them, because I had previously
had no opportunity to greet the Führer. I was told that a number of
Hitler Youth members had assumed position upstairs in the Reich
Chancellery, to be awarded medals for bravery for their excellent
attitude in enemy air raids in the air protection and anti-aircraft service,
including several Iron Crosses.

After the Führer returned to the bunker, Göring, Dönitz, Keitel and
Jodl were in turn ordered to his little living room, beside the bedroom,
to present their birthday greetings one at a time. The Führer greeted
all other participants in the strategy meeting with a handshake as they
entered the room, without paying any further attention to his birthday.

When I found myself facing the Führer, I wasn't capable of
giving him birthday wishes. I said something along the lines of: how
providence had so mercifully spared him on 20.7 in the assassination
attempt and that today, on his birthday, in these most serious of days so
far, when the existence of the Reich he had created was most seriously
under threat, he still held the leadership in his hand, and that gave us
confidence that he could make the decisions that could no longer be

postponed. I was of the opinion that he would act before the Reich capital became a combat zone.

I wanted to go on talking, but he wouldn't let me, and interrupted me with the words: 'Keitel, I know what I want, I will strike before, in or behind Berlin.' He was clearly aware of my attempt to resist this idea, which sounded like a slogan to me. With the words: 'Thank you, call Jodl in for me, we'll speak later,' I was dismissed.

So on the way back to Dahlem on 20 April, I told Jodl of my decision to send everything dispensable on by plane to Berchtesgaden, after my special train had already set off in that direction on 18 April. Piloted by my adjutant Schimonsky, my plane – doubtless launched as a daytime flight by Senior Flight Engineer Funk – flew, with full crew including General Winter, Dr Lehmann, Frau Jodl and my wife, to Prague, from where the passengers travelled on to Berchtesgaden in an official car that was waiting for them. My plane was at my disposal again in the evening, at Tempelhof airport, Berlin. All of this was done to relieve and prepare for the imminent transfer of the Führer's Headquarters to Berchtesgaden, which was held to be a complete certainty at the time.

*

**August Thurn, private soldier, 1925–2003**                    **east of Berlin**
Army high command is moving to Bavaria. This means that the guard regiment will no longer be required. In the evening the cellar master opens the wine cellar to everybody. We enjoy ample quantities of the good wine, and fill our flasks with the best tipple. Even before darkness falls, we are driving our lorries to the eastern front. Slightly intoxicated, we meet whole columns of refugees. We soon sober up at the sight of these people's misery.

After midnight we're at our destination, somewhere to the east of Berlin. With me are men from the guardsmen's regimental band, almost all of them sergeant majors. They've stuck assault rifles in their hands and sent them to the front. They have no experience whatsoever of the front. The man who sent his musicians here could probably have commanded a smart guard parade in Berlin. But that's about it. He has served his people up to the Russians on a plate. In the open, without cover, they just had to wait for the Russians to attack.

**Petty Officer Bruno J. Paap, b. 1916**          **Wittenberge, Elbe**
The battalion staff had the idea of promoting me to sergeant on Hitler's birthday, effective from 1.4.45. I wasn't proud of that as I would have been before, it was an embarrassment. But in order to comply with military duty, with the staff, I had to report to the commander of our fortress. So off to the staff, to make my report to the sitting commander: 'Captain, reporting, Petty Officer P. promoted to sergeant from 1.4.45.'

From the answer, the smile and the glitter in his eyes, as well as the full and empty bottles of alcohol standing around, I deduced that the officers had been drinking for some time, perhaps they were still celebrating Hitler's birthday? It was his 56th. This evening we listened to the last speech by Joseph Goebbels about Hitler's birthday on our radio.

To maintain discipline and order within the fortress of Wittenberge after 20 April, as before, strict checks of the public air raid shelters and bunkers as well as the accommodation were undertaken. Trusted old soldiers, NCOs and petty officers, the 'watchdogs' with their breastplates, had this difficult duty. One night two young men, about 18 years old, were checked and had no proper papers. These poor fellows, they were brought before the assembled court martial the following day and were found guilty of desertion, condemned to death and, the next morning, in the Singer sewing machine works very early in the morning, put on a high wall in front of the rifles and shot. I saw them shortly afterwards, dead, lying in their blood.

**First Lieutenant Fritz Radloff, 1916–89          Blumeshof, near Berlin**
Every day in the Wehrmacht report we hear that the eastern front is fighting hard. Anti-tank barriers are going up in Berlin. People are just dashing from one discussion to another, from one war game to another: we need arms, arms, arms! What am I supposed to do with French rifles? What am I supposed to do with the Luftwaffe auxiliary personnel? What are the girls still doing here? And no one dares to make a decision. The Volkssturm is edging towards the fortification, and who's still there? Only us! So we'll be thrown back on our own

devices. 'Chaps, we're alone!' On the eve of the Führer's birthday we listen to the propaganda minister's speech. We listen to the Führer's declaration. 'Berlin stays German!' So, it has to be, that's what we feel. Everyone is adjusting to the inevitable, the dance is beginning.

**Dieter Wellershoff, b. 1925**                                    **Chorin**
Meanwhile the news is seeping through that the Red Army had crossed the river Oder to the north and south of us, and is heading for Berlin in a pincer movement. So we've been bypassed, and probably our retreat has been cut off long ago. As messenger I was commandeered to the Regimental Commander's dugout. He was a pleasant, calm, worried-looking man, a teacher in civilian life, who asked after me and talked to me very paternally for a long time. It was 20 April. The sound of fighting on the Oder abated for several hours and then started up again. On the radio, Goebbels delivered a lunatic speech from an almost enclosed Berlin for Hitler's birthday. The Führer was in Berlin, he said, personally leading the defence of the Reich capital, on whose walls the Russian juggernaut would be smashed to pieces. 'Berlin remains German, Vienna is becoming German again,' screamed the master of fairy tales, now to general disbelief.

The Ukrainians had suddenly vanished. Instead a confused trek of German villagers came through the forest from the Oder valley, barely able to move from exhaustion. Still nothing happened. Probably the connection with the senior army staffs was broken and here in the forest we were living in a dead corner of the battle.

*

*Neue Zürcher Zeitung*
When the American infantry moved into Leipzig, they were greeted by the population with cheers and enthusiasm. In places the troops were heaped with flowers. But the enthusiasm of the population has less to do with the fact of liberation from the Nazi yoke than with the fact that it was the Americans and not the Russians who took Leipzig. According to a staff officer from General Hodges's headquarters, the scenes recalled the days of the liberation of Normandy and Brittany.

**Mary Wigman, 1886–1973**                                    *Leipzig*
Shattered, body and soul.

An excruciating day.

The bombed-out women in the basement were boozing with Frenchmen and US soldiers. The shouting, and the singing, the revolting duet of the voices of men and women who had lost all self-control. I was so ashamed for those females, who don't deserve to be seen as 'German women'. Oh, I sympathize with the starving sex which – whether friend or foe – is torn in its misery and isolation. But there is still something like the last shred of dignity, even in the deepest humiliation. I have never encountered lechery so naked, so shameless as I have in the United States.

What would these American boys say if they saw their own women and girls throwing themselves so freely at foreign soldiers, the conquerors of their own soil?

At 10 two American soldiers appeared. House search. For weapons. They took two cameras.

There's looting in the city. That's the Germans' doing! We have entered the third phase of the war.

The first: conquest and victory

the second: defeat and retreat

the third: occupation and start of collapse.

The fourth?

The Via Dolorosa is long –

**Elisabeth Kraushaar-Baldauf, b. 1915**                       *Leipzig*
Today played out like an overwrought film. The victors found the warehouse of a Leipzig distillery. The result is a piss-up on a grand scale. I would allow them to enjoy their flush of victory if it didn't make them so dangerous.

This afternoon one of the victors distressed me. Little Prietz, very worked up, called me into the estate office. He said there was a Yank in there throwing the furniture around, he'd already taken the little cash register, and he was also fiddling around with the pistol.

When the American saw me, he said in English, 'Oh, what a nice girl – come on, I am the victor and I have a pistol!' In response to my remark, also in English, that he was a good boy, but drunk, he stumbled, then put his arm around my waist and said, 'Come on, let's go.' I'd come up with a plan for such situations. I always took the victors, on the pretext that I had something to do there, down to the cellar, where the dead German soldier lay. I tried to do the same thing this time. That had always led to a salutary sobriety. We were crossing the courtyard when this victor was suddenly overcome. He shouted at me that I was his now and he had a pistol. In desperation I showed him my wedding ring, which made him furious. My husband was a Nazi swine, he said, and he'd soon show me. I reacted purely instinctively, with a diversionary manoeuvre. I asked him how his president was (Roosevelt, I had heard on Radio Luxembourg, had died on 12 April). It was like a blow from a club! He sat on the ground in the middle of the courtyard and sobbed: 'My president is dead!' The weeping warrior has ceased to be dangerous. The dead president had saved me.

In the evening the two Americans from the first night came back. They had asked for me, but then just stood around, and I didn't know what they wanted. After a while one of them started describing his home to me. He came from a farm, and that was why he liked the atmosphere here on the estate. He was simply homesick. Because the two of them were sober and very respectable, it occurred to me to invite them to shelter here for the night. The rumour was actually going around in the village that the victors wanted to celebrate their 'victory' with women tonight – how, one could easily imagine. I asked them both if they'd heard about that too, and whether they didn't know of an officer who would stay on the estate and protect us. They smiled, reached into their trouser pockets and showed me their insignias on the palms of their hands. When I looked at the unfamiliar badges, they said they were officers, and I had no need to worry.

Today I was called to the stables, where I was told that an American officer was shooting the pigs dead with a machine gun. When I entered the pigsty, the man was standing with his back to the door in the middle of the dead pigs. Rather startled by this sight, I challenged him in English. He turned round, looked me up and down and then said in fluent German, 'Go, before I forget myself. In Poland you killed more than pigs!' That was enough for me to get out of there in a flash.

Later the pigs were taken away on a lorry. The man who had requisitioned them was a Pole in American uniform.

**Margaret Bourke-White, photographer, 1904–71**            *Leipzig*
On Friday morning, April 20, *Life*'s Bill Walton hunted me out, his hair standing up from excitement in little fire-coloured whorls.

'Hurry to the Rathaus before they clean it out,' he said. 'The place is like Madam Tussaud's waxworks!'

We rushed in the jeep over the Zeppelin Bridge and [...] drew up before the Leipzig City Hall. Here the siege had been intense, and the deeper carvings of artillery were added to the outlines of the fine old Rathaus.

Bill and I raced up three flights of stone steps, climbed over a tumbled bust of Frederick the Great and a scattering of other fallen Prussians, and burst through a pair of padded, sound-proof doors.

Inside was a Baroque office, hung with sentimental landscapes and furnished in the heavy style which represented the nineteenth-century German's idea of luxury. Reclining on the ponderous leather furniture was a family group, so intimate, so lifelike, that it was hard to realize that these people were no longer living. Seated at the desk, head bowed on his hands as though he were resting, was Dr Kurt Lisso. On the sofa was his daughter, and in the overstuffed armchair sat his wife. The documents for the whole family were laid out neatly on the desk, beside the bottle of Pyrimal by which they had evidently chosen to die. Dr Lisso had been Stadtkammerer, Leipzig City Treasurer, with one of those low Party numbers which indicated that he was among the early faithful.

In a nearby room, seated in an equally lifelike circle, was Mayor Alfred Freiberg, Ober-burgermeister, with his wife and pretty daughter, Magdalena. Adjoining rooms held similarly peaceful and silent characters, of whom the most striking was the Commander of the Volkssturm in his fine uniform, with a portrait of Hitler beside him [...].

On the afternoon of the same day that Bill Walton and I had canvassed the City Hall, we had driven to the outskirts of Leipzig to hunt up an aircraft small-parts factory which had been an 8th Air Force bombing target. [...]

As we searched for the factory along a narrow country road bisecting ploughed fields, we began to smell a peculiar odor, quite different from anything in our experience. We followed the smell until we saw, across a small meadow, a ten-foot barbed-wire fence which, curiously, seemed to surround nothing at all. Parking the jeep, we ran through a small gate into the enclosure, and found ourselves standing at the edge of an acre of bones.

There was no one there; that is, there was no living person. But flying grotesquely over the patch of skulls and charred ribs, from a tall slender flag-pole, was a white surrender flag. There was eloquent testimony that the men who had been there so recently had not willingly surrendered to death. Plunged into the four-foot wide barrier of close-meshed barbed wire were blackened human figures whose desperate attitudes showed their passionate attempts to break to freedom. Caught in the spiked coils, they had perished, flaming torches, as they tried to escape.

Nothing was left standing among the ashes, except the incongruous flag-pole at the far edge. Dotting the ghastly mottled carpet which covered the area were dozens of identical little graniteware basins and among them a scattering of spoons.

*

**General Karl Koller, 1898–1951**         **OKL, Wildpark-Werder**
At 2.20 in the morning Göring passes the sentries, his car pulls into the big courtyard, the horn blares. Immediately Brauchitsch confirms his arrival by telephone. (I later learn from Senior Staff Physician Dr Ondarza, who accompanied Göring on the drive from the Führerbunker through Berlin, that they spent a considerable amount of time in various public Berlin air raid shelters. Göring wasn't given an unfriendly welcome by the population, the doctor told me, that Göring himself had been very companionable and made jokes, particularly about his notorious remark that 'if [even a single enemy plane flies over our territory,] you can call me Meier. Messengers were

even sent from neighbouring shelters to ask him to pay them a visit. He actually went, too, and was thoroughly popular among the Berliners.)

I tell Brauchitsch that I need to speak to Göring outside my official building, which he will drive past when he leaves. I have something important for him. I urge him to hurry, because otherwise it won't be possible to get across the Elbe before daybreak.

At three o'clock by my watch Göring drives past my house at high speed at the head of his motorcade, and through the gate past the sentries. He leaves without a word.

\*

### Colonel Richard Wolf                                    *Nuremberg*
In terms of combat the night of 19 April was relatively quiet. It must have been about 0.30 when Mayor Liebel left me. He was very depressed. [...] Soon after Liebel had gone, I heard a sharp report. Seized by a grim premonition, I dashed to the room in the bunker that was occupied by the Gauleiter and his staff. Liebel lay dead on his bed-frame with a bullet in his head. The gun had fallen from his hand... In the early hours of the morning reports reached us of the continuing advance of the Americans. The SS unit in the north had abandoned its positions. A wireless message from Hitler came in, awarding the combat commander the Knight's Cross with Oak Leaves and expressing thanks for his steadfastness.

The situation had become untenable. Further resistance was pointless. It must have been at about 10.30 in the morning that I radioed orders to all units to suspend fighting, and released them from duty. I myself had resolved that we would not surrender Nuremberg.

Nuremberg, historically such an important German city, could be conquered in combat, but even in this, the darkest moment in its history, it could not be surrendered.

All the next day the scattered sounds of battle could still be heard, as tanks clattered their way into the city. I tried to flee north with my information officer. We waded through the Pegnitz River during the night hours. We must have been spotted by the bridge guards. We were pelted by bursts of machine-gun fire, hand grenades went off. My information officer went missing during this attack. I spent more than two hours scouring the terrain for him. When I sought shelter from the coming dawn in a basement, I was surprised and taken prisoner by an American sentry.

### A schoolboy                                        *Nuremberg*

My father used to say that his greatest experience was at the age of 50 on 20 April 1945, when, as a Volkssturm member – armed with a French rifle from 1865, ten cartridges that only fitted an Italian rifle from 1870, and an anti-tank grenade with no detonator and witnessed only by two living oxen chained up in the city moat, which were to serve as food during the siege – he hoisted the white flag and handed the castle over to the liberators.

### Paula Nemeskei, 1904–89                            *Nuremberg*

20 April 1945, the Führer's birthday, will be the day when the 'city of rallies' will be definitively conquered! We can see from the attic that shots are still being fired in the north of the city. The towers of St Sebaldus's church have lost their spires – must everything in a city already so effectively destroyed be broken? But the Nazis remain true to themselves: they will sacrifice everything, because they see their own end approaching.

We carry the beds upstairs – sleeping quite undressed in freshly made beds, is that even possible?

It's been so long since we've been able to do that. The day is lively and colourful again, things are being organized all over the place. Americans come to the flat, looking for arms, looking for various other things, and are surprised when we tell them about our living conditions. They are amazed by our demolished flats, they shake their heads, 'what a life!' We listen to the firing from the attic again, and notice that the last resistance seems to have ceased towards evening. As night falls we sit by candlelight in the flat and celebrate.

### Hanns Lilje, 1899–1977                             *Nuremberg*

Last night, while I was dragging my bed below the barred window where it was better protected against splinters from shells, the smell of frying and the sound of tipsy men wafted up from the cellar, where the prison warders were busy organizing a farewell party, while up in their cells hundreds of men caught between hunger and terror were feverishly hoping for their imminent liberation. I myself slept, and see that one day I shall have to write a theological dissertation about sleep as a way of praising God.

I was quite calm the following morning and could barely detect a change in artillery fire, when after a moment's noise in the corridor the cell door was yanked open and one of our partners in suffering tumbled in with tears of joy: 'The Americans are here!'

They were real tears in his eyes, and it was with genuine outrage that he notes: You aren't even pleased.

It's true, I'm not pleased. At least not in that superficial, almost rather naïve sense in which my cheering, excitedly gesticulating colleagues are. It's immediately clear to me that for most people a very arduous journey back into life will begin. There will be tedious formalities, the search for families, the question of where my home will be henceforth. It will be some while until we can finally move around outside as free human beings.

There is suddenly a rising bitterness that it has to be foreigners who are giving us back the precious gift of freedom that our own compatriots stole from us; and there is also – a quite different feeling – somewhere within me, a very quiet amazement (or must I call it regret?) that the time of our ordeal is now suddenly and irrevocably here – did it bring us all that it was meant to, are we cleansed, purified, are we stronger?

*

**Reich Governor Franz Ritter von Epp, 1868–1946        Bavaria**
When the military situation further deteriorated during the first few months of 1945, and Bavaria and Munich also seemed to be under threat from the Allies, of course I discussed the situation with my colleagues, particularly with Major Carraciola, and the then deputy Commanding General of the VIIth Army Corps, General Kriebel. Kriebel explained to me that he would need at least two divisions to defend Munich. I knew that he did not have those divisions within his corps, that on

the contrary those few substitute formations which still had combat capability had been withdrawn over the past few weeks and sent to the front in Württemberg. Only sparse information reached us from the front itself, giving no picture of the number and strength of the units still fighting, and certainly not of their command conditions. Kriebel had told me he would withdraw with his remaining forces to a mountain fortress on the northern edge of the Alps near Garmisch. As I had to stay near him for the reasons already mentioned, I also had quarters prepared for my duty station. Kriebel, with whom I had had a very successful collaboration, was released from duty on 20.4.1945. I later learned from his successor, Griener, that there had been differences of opinion with Gauleiter Giesler about issues concerning the conduct of the war, which was why Giesler had suddenly insisted that SS General Fegelein in General Headquarters dismiss Kriebel forthwith.

### Heinrich, Prince of Hesse, 1927–2000          *Kronberg/Taunus*
The health of my grandmother [a sister of Kaiser Wilhelm II] deteriorated. Now she has developed pneumonia in both lungs.

On 19 April at four in the afternoon there was a knock at the cottage door. A sergeant and several soldiers informed us that we were to get out of the house by six o'clock.

We had to clear out all our possessions; we were allowed to take only clothes, bedlinen and provisions, nothing else. He explained to us curtly that they were not in a position to make concessions, they were only carrying out orders.

At every door, in the cottage as well as in the castle, soldiers are checking all the suitcases. If they find something that isn't on their list, they take it out and throw it back into the house. When it's the turn of my small suitcase, the soldier confiscates my private papers and my briefcase. He also grabs my diary, but I beg to be allowed to take it back to my room. Permission is granted; as soon as I am in the room I tear all the written pages out of the book and hide them in my father's old coat, which luckily escapes examination.

**Walter Dirks, 1901–91**                                    *Frankfurt am Main*
On 21 April I was appointed personnel officer at the labour office
in Hesse. So the acting director of the office and I were busy on the
rebuilding project, with our shirt sleeves rolled up, so to speak, two
and a half weeks before the day of capitulation. We had to fill the
country's labour offices, left headless by the fleeing Nazis, with reliable
democrats: Social Democrats, people of the centre, trade unionists.

*

**Heinz Linge, valet, 1913–80**                                        **Berlin**
Before, the Führer's birthday was usually 'introduced' as follows:
Hitler's personal staff appeared at midnight on 19 April and
congratulated him, although not until I had already done the same;
for first I had to tell Hitler that the staff were there to congratulate
him. This time everything was quite different. Hitler had previously
told me that he would not receive anyone offering congratulations,
and I was to inform the gentlemen who were coming to see him of
this. There was nothing that anyone could congratulate him about.
Nonetheless, at about midnight, the following were introduced to the
antechamber as usual: Adjutant in Chief General Wilhelm Burgdorf,
SS Gruppenführer Hermann Fegelein, Hitler's personal adjutant Julius
Schaub, Navy Adjutant Albrecht, the Head of the Adjutancy of the
Reich Chancellery, Adjutant Otto Günsche, Ambassador Walter
Hewel, deputizing for the Reich Foreign Minister in the Führer's
headquarters, and Werner Lorenz as deputy for the Reich Chief Press
Officer. After I had told Hitler of this, he gave me a weary, downcast
look. I had to tell the waiting men that the Führer had no time to
receive them now. That was how things remained for the time being.
But then Fegelein, who was married to Eva Braun's sister Gretl and
was on familiar terms with Eva, used his family connections. He went
to his sister-in-law Eva and tried to enlist her to persuade Hitler to
receive the well-wishers, who would not move from his side until they
had congratulated him. Eva managed it. Reluctantly Hitler got to his
feet and walked, bent over, dragging himself into the antechamber,
where everyone was able only to say 'Congratulations' – before they

saw Hitler's bent back from behind. Hans Baur, Hitler's chief pilot, his second pilot Betz, Rattenhuber, the deputy head of the Führer's Security Service, and Franz Schaedle, the head of the SS bodyguard unit in the Reich Chancellery, who also wanted to congratulate him, missed their moment. When they appeared at the start of the nightly review to congratulate the 'boss', he was on his way from his study to the conference room. In passing he shook hands with each of them.

After the strategy meeting, which took only a short time, Eva Braun joined him in the study, where they drank tea together and wanted to be alone. The birthday was appropriate to the situation.

As soon as Hitler and Eva Braun had gone to bed, at about 9 o'clock in the morning, General Burgdorf appeared and asked me, practically wringing his hands, 'to wake the Führer, for God's sake', so that he, Burgdorf, could pass on a very important report from the front. I did so. Hitler, who got up immediately but didn't get dressed, and didn't even leave his bedroom but just went to the door, asked through it, 'What's up, Burgdorf?' After the general, who was standing next to me, had replied through the door that the Russians had broken through between Guben and Forst, and counter-attacks had already been launched and the commander of our own units had been shot for 'failing' to defend his section of the front, Hitler gave me an order: 'Linge, I have not yet slept. Wake me an hour later than usual at 14.00.'

I woke Hitler at 14.00 in accordance with that order. Then he had breakfast and had me drip cocaine drops into his right eye. There was no conversation. He wanted to have Wolf brought to him, the puppy of his Alsatian Blondi. Then he played with the little dog, his favourite puppy, until lunch, which he took with Eva and the secretaries. He had locked himself away completely, and apart from Eva and me he didn't want to see any other human being. At around 15.00 delegates from the Hitler Youth under Artur Axmann's leadership, officers of the Herresgruppe Mitte, the Commander of the Führer's Headquarters, the Head of the Führer's Guard unit, a colleague of Bormann's and some SS men were at the exit of the Reich Chancellery to greet him as well. Hitler, who was wearing a field-grey uniform coat, turned up his collar and, accompanied by Navy Adjutant Karl-Jesko von Puttkamer and by me, went to see the well-wishers, who, at our appearance, silently assumed the attention position and gave Hitler the Nazi salute. In the park, at the gate to the Wintergarten, stood Himmler, Bormann, Burgdorf, Fegelein, Hewel, Lorenz, Hitler's doctors Theo Morell and Ludwig Stumpfegger, Schaub, Albert Bormann, Albrecht, Willi Johannmeier, Nicolaus von Below and Günsche. Heinrich Himmler walked up to Hitler and congratulated him. Hitler shook his hand but I saw that his handshake expressed utter indifference. After Hitler, tired, bent, grey in the face and feeble, had sluggishly paced along the 'front' and accepted the congratulations of the well-wishers, men arranged themselves in a semicircle around him to hear what he had to say to them. What they heard from his lips could not, however, given the current oppressive situation, free them of the conviction that total defeat was imminent, even if Hitler tried to create the opposite impression.

As the daily meeting was scheduled for 16.00, Himmler, Bormann, Burgdorf, Fegelein and the adjutants joined the Führer when he returned to the bunker, which he would never leave again. Then came Göring, Ribbentrop, Dönitz, Keitel and Jodl, each of whom I announced individually and took to Hitler to congratulate him. None of them spoke about the disastrous end. Each of them assured Hitler only of their loyalty to death. After this procession, which had by no means improved Hitler's mood, Hitler thanked everyone in the antechamber for their good wishes and vows, and asked General Chief of Staff Hans Krebs how the situation on the Oder had developed.

*

**Donald J. Willis, American soldier, b. 1919**              *near Dessau*
Some good news for all the troops. Our mail has finally caught up to us. This is always a sure sign our sector is becoming safer. Received several letters, including one from Mom. Was very glad to hear from home.

Everyone is saying that the war is nearly over. I don't know. It is almost too much for me to believe. Anyway, this is the main topic of conversation here. No one wants to take any unnecessary risks now.

**Edwin Chapman, British soldier**            *north-west Germany*
*To his parents*

Dear M & D

Thanks very much for more newspapers.

There is not much to report here. The weather is now magnificent.
There are still no baths (I have had none for fifteen days now). I don't
think the regiment can do anything about it: there just are not any
in the district & continental houses are not usually equipped with
baths.

We are getting plenty of eggs from the people here. I was given ten
yesterday.

The regiment is again playing the local team at football tomorrow.

It is not worth it, sending chocolate here. We get plenty, thank you.

Please don't forget that I would be delighted to receive some
envelopes large enough to put postcards in.

Yours ever, Edwin

**Norman Kirby, British sergeant, b. 1913**      *north-west Germany*

During our investigation of the fire and its unlikely threat to the main
body of the camp, we again encountered the all-too-frequent problem
of German deserters and would-be prisoners of war. Instead of going
quietly home as so many had been ordered to do by hard-pressed
front-line units, they persisted in giving themselves up. Could this
have been inspired by the thought of Allied rations and the associated
lightening of a burden on their starving families? To us who had to
cope with these increasing numbers in addition to our official duties
it began to seem as though barbed wire had a strange attraction for
German soldiers, disoriented by their unaccustomed freedom from
military discipline and the loss of the feeling of security which years of
barrack servitude and camp life had given them.

Two soldiers of the Wehrmacht dressed in civilian clothes doggedly
waited for three hours to report to us with the same determination
with which Londoners were queuing to see *Gone With the Wind*.
During the night a young member of the Luftwaffe in uniform came
to tell us that he had been on leave to see his child who had died. The
Allies had swept past his village during that time and now he was ready

to give himself up. He had an open wound in his leg and was wearing a soft slipper on one foot. We told him to spend that night at home and we would call for him in the morning.

**Maurice F. Jupp, British captain**                    (*north-west Germany*)
Your farm would have, if in Germany, to hold about 14 people. Food is not more [*sic*]. Their husbandry is admirable. The main routes are an incredible sight. Our transport moves in an endless stream in one direction. In the other, against the tide, some German prisoners, under guard, German soldiers with white flags wanting to give themselves up, German civilians, refugees, groups of liberated POWs of all Europe, it seems an unbelievable amount to the inmates – is ¼ Army ration. My friend took a roll of silk from a German factory for some of the women who have helped organise things. They were awfully overcome with joy, and collapsed. I heard him addressing a Jewish rabbi (who asked me for a parachute, to provide clothes for the women), to wait a fortnight before giving them such luxuries, otherwise the effect might be dangerous.

I am convinced that the average German is not aware of what goes on in these camps.

Kind regards

Yours, Maurice

\*

**Walther Teich, author, 1894–1962**                          **Hamburg**
The cliché could only really flourish as the art of book printing continued to progress. But what is a cliché? On the spot, I would define it thus: in a cliché form and content are not congruent. Content is smaller than the form that envelops it. The form wants to simulate a significant content. So a cliché is a piece of dishonesty. There are people who are dishonest by nature. They must express themselves with clichés. That can develop into an actual art. The poet will never make clichés, he leaves that to the artist . There are great talents who can write wonderful clichés. The times rush to welcome them. One might claim that in the last century art and literature have lived on

clichés, indeed, that the daily life of 'cultured' people is unimaginable without the cliché. The seeds are sown in school, its flowers blossom at the universities. The German language seems to conceal particular dangers within itself, where the temptation to the cliché is concerned. That is due to the fact that we have too much freedom in the use of concepts. This happiness easily turns to unhappiness. People become as pianists often are. They sit at the grand piano. It gives them the possibility of expressing an incredible amount. But they are technically impoverished. Then they start playing phrases, musical clichés, they try to achieve a virtuoso tonal richness with inadequate means. And so, dishonesty, blurring, a gap between content and form.

As long as readers do not notice that simplicity says more than extravagance and truth more than fraud, there is little hope for improvement. But as the human eye, people's vision, says more and says it more penetratingly than the word, the rubble of our cities may tell us where the clichés, the half-truth, can lead a people.

The journey from half-truth to whole lie is a short one. We have taken it very far, diabolically far.

\*

### Alexei Kalinin, Soviet captain, b. 1911     *in the east*
*To his son Vladimir*

Hello, Vovochka!

Vovochka, I have just received your letter, in the midst of the battle, and as I write the answer I am sitting in a trench that we have dug in the soil.

We are beating the Germans, my son, and we are moving five or some-times eight kilometres forwards every day. We are trying to destroy all the Fritzes as quickly as possible, so that the war is over, so that you can live better.

You write that you have holidays, while our holidays are over, and we are now showing the Fritzes, which is to say, we are beating them so that they lose their desire for warfare.

My son, I have already sent you three parcels, I have also included paper.

After our burst of gunfire the infantry pushed forwards, now we are advancing too.

So goodbye for now, Vovochka!

Warmest kisses

Your Papa

**Boris Markus, Red Army soldier**                           *Austria*
*Letter to unknown recipient*

So we have already reached the fourth state. It is like neither the first nor the second nor any other. In Hungary the language was difficult, but then I did not try to learn it, I found everything there unpleasant: the landscape, the architecture, the people (and after my encounters with the Serbs and the Bulgarians that is hardly surprising). Here in Austria one can understand the language (possibly better than in Germany itself, because it seems to me that the Austrians in comparison to the pure-blooded 'Aryans' speak a German that is close to our 'school German').

At any rate, speaking and understanding among the Austrians is easier than it is among the imprisoned Fritzes. So, in terms of language, it is easier. But the people are even stranger than the Magyars. Either they are petrified by Hitler's propaganda, or that's just their manner, at any rate neither their appearance nor their expressions arouse any sympathy.

I was able to convince myself that they are not Germans, but Austrians (that is, the first to feel the effects of German violence), but still I cannot help but feel a certain unease when I deal with them. And if that is how it strikes me, I can imagine what our ordinary soldier must think.

Still, we have taught our people how to behave to a certain degree (which one cannot, however, claim of some infantry units, particularly not of the advancing reconnaissance troops, who do what they like, and exceed all bounds, thinkable and unthinkable). Much must still be done to teach them that they should not fight with the ordinary people and not with objects, but only with Hitler's people. In real life that is hard to achieve, so we are often moving on extremely unpleasant trails that the advance troops have left behind.

But that is all between ourselves. At the moment these questions concern me more than anything else, because one will encounter them so frequently; one must often, in broken German (that is, in a 'mixture of German and the Russian of Nizhni Novgorod', so to speak), make it clear to the inhabitants that what we intend to do is something thoroughly noble, that it is not a matter of grabbing things and stealing etc. In the end these are lessons in political culture, which end with us talking about the Soviet Union, our laws, our conquests and achievements in all areas of science, culture and technology.

And so far there has been no village and no little town in which the people have not come from their houses as we left and said goodbye to us. And in this we see that they have received a good impression of our unit. And hence also of the Red Army.

Best wishes, Boris

### Vladimir Alexandrov, Red Army soldier       *East Prussia*
*To his parents near Novgorod*

Greetings, my dear ones. I send you my greetings and wish you all the best and above all health. I can tell you that I got the card you wrote me on 6.4.45, and I also got the letter you wrote me on 8.4.45. For both, thank you. I was delighted to hear in these letters that you got the presents from me. And above all that everything arrived unharmed, as they say, and nothing went missing. I have been very worried, and I will tell you why. You, Father, should receive four pairs trousers and also four shirts, so now I will know for certain: when summer comes, my father will have something to wear. And with the material I also send he can have a shirt made to measure. Of course I don't know whether or not you have received the packet with five metres of silk and seven metres of blue material in it, and also three pairs of trousers and two shirts. Well, and I have also sent something to Mother, of course, dresses, four, silk of course. I do not care what she does with them.

And there is also a dress in another package. All in all I sent her five. And also material from which she can sew something. So I will have the certainty that you have something to wear. You should also get a parcel from one 'Pavel Alexeiev'. Well, Father probably knows from whom. He must understand. He sent you two lots of material, red fleecy material and some canvas from which a nice shirt could be made. Enough of that. Dear parents, I have a request for you. In a parcel I sent a coat and trousers, and I ask you to keep that and what is still in it for me.

Another few words about me. As you see, I am healthy and cheerful. There are no particular changes. We are advancing and destroying the German bandits on their territory, and we are taking revenge for your suffering and tears. Greetings to Aunt Dasha and everyone I know. Best wishes and kisses,

Your son Volodya

*

**Benito Mussolini, 1883–1945**                    **Palazzo Monforte, Milan**
*Interview*

Let these stormy years pass. A young man will rise. A single-minded man. A leader who fully embodies the ideas of Fascism. Collaboration and not class struggle; charter of work and socialism; property sacred, as long as it does not encourage poverty; care and protection of workers, particularly the old and invalids; care and protection of mother and child; fraternal support for the needy; morality in every field. Struggle against ignorance and submissiveness towards the powerful. In so far as there is still time, strengthening of self-rule, our single hope until this utopian day when there will be division of the raw materials that God has given to the world, among all nations; glorification of the pride in being Italian; education in depth and not only at the surface, as has unfortunately happened because of events and not because of ideological inadequacy.

A single-minded young man will come, who will find our postulate of 1919 and the programme of Verona of 1943, who will put them into action in a fresh, bold and worthy way. The people's eyes will then be open, and the triumph of these ideas will be prepared. It was in too many people's interest for these ideas not to be understood and valued, and many believed that they infringed the moral and material interest of the people. We have lived through 18 centuries of invasions and misery, of falling birth rates, servitude, internal struggles and ignorance. Above all, however, centuries of poverty and malnourishment. Twenty years of Fascism and seventy years of independence have not been enough to give the soul of every Italian the strength to overcome the crisis and understand the truth. The great and numerous exceptions were not enough.

The Italian people have not overcome this crisis, which began in 1939. They will rise again, but the convalescence will be long and sad, and full of woe if there are setbacks. I am like the great clinician who has not succeeded in providing the correct treatment, and who has now lost the trust of the important patient's family. Many doctors are pushing for a successor. Many of them are already well known as failures; others are nothing more than bold or avaricious. The new doctor is yet to come. And when he comes, he will use my medicines. He need only use them better. An accuser of Admiral Persano replied, when asked what the admiral was guilty of, 'Of losing'. The same is true of me.

*

**Weert Sweers, b. 1917**                    *Cherbourg prisoner-of-war camp*
Today is the Führer's birthday. This day was once a big party for the whole nation, and now in captivity that is not the case. There is terrible agitation; lots of people claim, as ever, that they knew what was on the cards. But one thing is certain, according to the state of things today it is irresponsible for the war to be taken further. The war is lost, there is nothing to be done about that.

The Russians and the Americans are outside Berlin, and have launched the final attack.

The weather was still quite fine, and I spent the whole day on puzzles and other diversions. I can't sit dozing around the place all day, as most people do. We must deal with this life.

**Rita Ullrich, b. 1922**                          *St Sulpice internment camp*
We have a 'new man' here, who represents an exception among the inspectors. […] He never speaks to us. Today our three-year-old Christa

crossed his path, with her blonde curls, the darling of the whole camp, including the French, sweet and funny and trusting. I don't know how nature has managed to preserve the dimples on her plump little arms and calves! It must be the treats that all the lady supervisors keep aside for her; and by being spoilt and given piggybacks she became as a little sparrow becomes in winter: a bit cheeky, and that's why everyone likes to have her around for a while for their amusement. So today it was the little Stalin's turn to demonstrate his love of children. When she was digging there in the gravel he smiled down at her and said a fond word as he reached his hand out to her. And that was when the curious thing happened: Christa, who at such times would normally run to anyone's knee and ask to be picked up, she stayed rooted to the spot – she kept her eye on him, no smile revealed her cute little mouse-teeth – then she thoughtfully put her muddy hands on her back and suddenly she turned around and scurried away.

Little Stalin pursed his lips and strode furiously back to the children's barracks, saw the bouquets from yesterday's walk – swept one from the table, vase and all – a second, a third, hissed, '*Pas de fleurs aujourd'hui*' and stomped off to the next barracks! We saw Madame Duliac walking to the third barracks, with the words '*Pas de fleurs aujourd'hui*' on her lips, a phrase that spread from block to block.

No flowers today! What was that supposed to mean? Then someone remembered: it's the Führer's birthday.

**Rudolf Bradatsch**          *Hayes prisoner-of-war camp, England*
The colonel assigned to carry out the survey appeared in the camp, we had already arrived. When he entered the camp he saw a swastika flapping between the two big tents. He immediately called the alarm and the guards arrived, some with machine guns, some with their bayonets at the ready. Now we were asked if the perpetrator would identify himself. After a while, when no one had identified himself, the guards became a wild pack of shouting, raging soldiers. Until then we had always got on well with the guards. The prisoners of war were now divided into groups, and then the circus began. Some of us had to stand to attention, another group had to sing, and still other prisoners were chased at a running pace through the camp, while the guards

fiddled with their guns and shouted like a horde of Indians carrying out an attack. In the second act of the circus we had to break up the camp; the double wooden underfloors of the tents were, just like the tents themselves, stacked in a pile outside the camp.

Next it was the turn of the duckboards, which had proved very useful as paths between the tents; they too were removed and stacked up outside the camp. Around the individual tents the prisoners of war had, over time, arranged little flowerbeds and lawns to make the camp look a little more human. There was no evidence left of this because the little flowerbeds had quickly disappeared and been trampled away. Of course the big tents had to be torn down too, and the benches and tables stacked on the growing pile. The prisoners were spurred on with a great deal of shouting, and if individual prisoners didn't run fast enough (in the guards' opinion), rifle butts and bayonets were used. Some prisoners of war suffered bruising and stabbing injuries and had to be treated in the sick bay [...] What repelled me a great deal was that the German and English officers watched all this activity in the upper part of the camp, but no one stopped the show.

\*

**Ludwig Munzinger, 1921–2012**          (*prisoner-of-war camp, France*)
Fresh, harmless little humiliations eventually turn you into one of those unit prisoners who comes when they whistle and goes to sleep when it's dark. Then you no longer raise an eyebrow at the young Frenchmen slouching around on the sentry towers, acting as if they'd saved Europe from the Nazi barbarism. But perhaps they're only behaving so wildly because they weren't the ones who managed it, others did.

Then on Sunday you're not bothered by those Frenchmen who drift past the camp cheering with all their kit and caboodle, and express their 'feelings of sympathy' in unmistakable lewd gestures. Neither are you shocked in the slightest that the camp commandant is getting fatter and fatter and you're getting thinner and thinner, and you are only sometimes surprised at how little one actually needs to live. How shamelessly we used to eat!

But we don't become entirely stupid. Intellectual activity is allowed. People are enthusiastically learning English here, shorthand there. Whole notebooks made from the toilet paper that is supplied in ample quantities are filled with cooking instructions for the most delicious dishes.

And other talents develop in such an environment, meaning you become an expert on supplies. Even from far away they can tell in which pot the soup is thicker or thinner. Everything is counted: when the column laden from the provisions store comes back to the camp in the morning: 45 sacks red, 3 sacks white beans, 4 boxes biscuits, 4 cases raisins, 6 tins milk powder etc. A short time later you are surprised with a precise prediction of the 'menu'.

You can learn to admire the human sense of cleanliness. For 3,000 people there is one tap available and a few wash basins under the open sky.

**Mariela Kuhn, b. 1909**   *(Oxford Military Hospital – Head Injuries)*
Sulger, now alone with himself, is very lonely and bored. He has been here since 12 March. Talked to him for a long time, mostly about the (terrible) discoveries in the concentration camps of Buchenwald and Nordhausen – today there were pictures in the newspapers. They can't believe these things, even when they see them in pictures. Sulger says, 'Yes, but have you seen the terrible pictures of the Polish crimes before the war? Those atrocities were what really unleashed the war!'

Röhl on ward M1 was awake and in quite a good mood – I talked to him for a long time about the same subject, because it's the first time it's been possible to show them actual pictures of these crimes. He says, 'I can't believe it,' but he accepts that it's true and believes they didn't know anything about these things. He won't come down on either side. I also showed him pictures of the 'Blitz' over England in 1940–41, because German propaganda only ever spoke of the 'terror attacks' on Germany. All of them (the prisoners of war) want to know how heavily London was really bombed etc.

Ward M3: Heinz Kasburg leaves tomorrow, a bit too soon, as he is still a long way from being well. But he wants to go to the Watford prisoner-of-war hospital because he feels lonely here, and he hopes to meet friends there. So we had one last long conversation. He was so shocked by the newspaper reports and photographs that I really felt sorry for him; he kept saying, 'That can't be true, Germans don't do things like that,' and buried his face in the pillow.

Then he told me about the Polish crimes. He said, 'For years I was in the Hitler Youth, and we never saw or heard of anything of the kind, and I believed so firmly in National Socialism and that it was something good, and I tried to compare it with socialism and plutocracy and democracy and repeatedly came to the conviction that National Socialism is the best form of government for the German people.'

We talked about Hitler: 'I always believed in the Führer, I would have torn myself to pieces for him.' And he kept repeating, 'I can't tell you what this means for me all of a sudden. Only 14 days ago I was in the army and never doubted the truth of German radio or what we were told, and all of a sudden it's all supposed to be false and untrue and bad!'

I felt sorry for the boy. He told me his father was a headmaster, and initially against Hitler, he was loyal to the Kaiser. Later he volunteered for the army, even though he was already 45. Anti-Semitism entered the family when his grandmother, in Cottbus after the death of her husband, asked a Jewish businessman to take over her big shop. He seems to have ruined the shop, fled with the money and left the family anti-Semitic from that point on. A very typical story.

Kasburg repeatedly said how concerned he was about Germany's future. What would become of Germany under Russian rule? What would his own fate be? He thought it would be better to shoot himself than to live in shame and slavery, etc. I tried to say all that one can say on the subject, I felt terribly sorry for him, he's taking everything so seriously and is really concerned. During his active service he was in the Hermann Göring Division.

**Erich Kuby, b. 1910**                    *Landerneau prisoner-of-war camp*
Three Americans came to the tent, one of whom asked me about a bookshop and took notes. Perhaps he wants to write about it. One looked with interest at the woodcuts. He asked for a set. I said at the

moment we only had the sample prints so far, and could he wait until new finished ones were available. He respected the request, without saying a word against it.

If only they weren't so terribly naïve, our conquerors.

*

**General Siegfried Westphal, 1902–82**                                    **in the west**
In mid-April the US Army attacked Nuremberg. Some units turned towards Passau. On 20 April French troops are invading Stuttgart, Sigmaringen and Freiburg im Breisgau. On the same day – Hitler's last birthday – Field Marshal Kesselring came to the Reich Chancellery again.

I had asked him as a matter of urgency to win Hitler's agreement to a ceasefire, as further resistance was pointless and a crime against the nation. After a very difficult car journey – flying had long been out of the question – Kesselring returned, largely by back roads as the north–south route was already too tight for that. He spoke of the 'court of congratulations'. I was dying to hear what decision had been reached. But they didn't get that far. Hitler had been very 'distant'. Of course he had avoided factual discussions with his customary skill.

*

**Hans Erich Dalgas, 1896–1987**                                          **Bremen**
'Kaiser's birthday'. The situation is becoming increasingly hopeless. I can no longer think of a reasonable way out. Armed attacks often in the city. I'm having another little bunker built in the garden.

**Luise Solmitz, 1889–1973**                                              **Hamburg**
Prayer on the radio: 'Dear Lord, stand by the Führer; may thy work be his work, let his work be thine!'

Just one flag, 81 Gustave Falke Strasse on the left. People were talking about it. Dr Henneberg said unfortunately there would be a big battle in Hamburg, German troops are assembling near Lauenberg! No milk, as the road to Elmshorn is down. The whole day there were dull rumbles from the Harburg front. We collected provisions, took R. along. Precious blossoms on the magnolia, almond and fruit trees, so beautiful, so innocent. Who can delight in them!

X. fears imprisonment in Hamburg... He has plain clothes, but he's not allowed to wear them.

Late in the evening explosions woke R. He screamed. I fetched him. He went to sleep on my shoulder, so touching. It's supposed there are 60,000 children in Hamburg.

Frau W. quite excited, she was just outside with low-flying planes above her, she saw the flash of the guns.

Now, in the night, there's frightening gunfire, no sirens; the enemy is probably in Harburg already. It's weird, horrible. I am so worried about R.

Goebbels speech yesterday, repeated today. Yes, now we're really facing the bitter end, one way or the other.

## Mathilde Wolff-Mönckeberg, 1879–1958                    Hamburg

Now we're facing the final catastrophe! The Americans have advanced as far as Harburg, and the boom of cannon rolls over our city. [...] Hamburg is a fortress. Strange barricades are going up in the streets, erected from house rubble, which you have to climb over using steps made of rough stone slabs, the kind children make for fun. Will they be of any use? Hamburgers laugh and shrug, they don't believe in it. Every evening in his deep bass voice Baldrian announces the reassuring litany that our governors mean well for us, citing as proof very welcome extra rations: 100 grams coffee, 50 grams tea, 2 pounds sugar, ½ pound margarine. We have also received portions for the 75th week, flour and fat and sugar, which has all made its way down to the cellar as emergency rations. [...]

At the Dammtor shells and blockbuster bombs crashed down, the Alsterterrasse no longer exists, just piles of rubble, smoking, smouldering. On Klopfstockstrasse not a single window, the university a ruin with empty window frames, opposite whole houses gone, the English Seminary also windowless and with doors torn out, even the tabletop of Father W.'s table was pulled off by the blast And that's also how things look in Johnsallee, on the Mittelweg and in Badestrasse.

Whole big blocks of flats have been destroyed, blown around like a house of cards, except not so quietly. There must have been huge fires, an infernal spectacle. Poor Annie Stammann, sister of Aunt Lili Siemssen, was buried under her collapsing house and only found after three days. 90-year-old Adele Mönckeberg died as a result of that terrible night. [...]

Perhaps children and grandchildren will be interested to read this later on. It's terrible for us, and the pressure of the last 6 years weighs down terribly upon one. This evening the rumour is going around that Hamburg is being declared an open city. If only that were so!

**Ulli S., b. 1928**                                                    **near Hamburg**
Today Adolf Hitler is 'celebrating' his 56th birthday, and precisely because it is his 56th birthday, he should treat it as a proper holiday. But he doesn't feel like celebrating, which one can in the end understand.

This year things haven't got very far with the birthday surprises that are normally so spectacular. The only surprises for him today are unwelcome ones: Nuremberg, the city of his rallies, is in American hands, and the Russians have broken through outside Berlin and conquered Freienwalde, Wriezen, Seelow, Lebus, Beeskow, Forst and Weisswasser, and are now 30 km outside Berlin and Dresden.

So Goebbels's birthday speech sounded very whiny. There's a ban on bunting, as our comrades in the front zones are largely colour-blind and could easily confuse red and white.

The last German warship, *Lützow*, was hit by two armour-piercing bombs off Swinemünde on 16 April. The 10,000 tonne ship sank to the bottom near the beach. The damage is so severe that it must be regarded as lost.

American reporters bring stories from the occupied concentration camps of Buchenwald, Nordhausen, Belsen and Ohrdruf, so appalling that one might think one's brain had packed in. The whole world is frozen with horror. One wants to say, 'That is not true! That is a lie!' Such a thing cannot happen in the land of Goethe! Not in 'the most primitive country on earth could it be possible!'

**Dr Erwin Garvens, 1883–1969**                                    **Hamburg**

So it was Hitler's 56th birthday, which he hoped, they say, to experience because according to his horoscope this day promised to be particularly significant for him.

According to the evening news, the British are at the Lower Elbe – only one kilometre from Harburg! – and firing on the troops escaping northwards. The people in the street barely paid attention to the shooting, lots of them probably didn't even understand what was happening. By day, however, there was a permanent siren in the background that didn't bother anyone – not even me; at four o'clock I went to see a rather sweet and cleverly made film, *The Wedding Hotel* in the Kammer-Lichtspiele. There were no alarms in the evening or at night, so our precautionary measure of going to bed with our clothes on – I really don't like it! – was superfluous. Might the bombings be over for us as well? It would be a blessing!

*

**Benito Mussolini, 1883–1945**                    **Palazzo Monforte, Milan**
*Interview*

I have proof here that I have tried with all my power to prevent war. This allows me to be absolutely calm and carefree about the judgement of posterity and the conclusions of history. I don't know whether Churchill is as calm and carefree as I am.

Take note: we have startled the world of the big businessmen and the big speculators. They didn't want us to be given the chance of living…

If the outcome of the war had been to the Axis's favour, I would have suggested to Hitler the socialization of the world, meaning borders only of historical kinds; abolition of all customs posts; free trade between countries, regulated by a global convention; unified currency and hence the whole world's gold common property, the same with raw materials, which are to be distributed according to the needs of the different countries. Real and radical destruction of all weapons. Colonies: the developed ones to become independent states, the others distributed among the countries most suitable according to population numbers or for other reasons, to colonize and civilize.

Freedom of opinion, freedom of the press? Yes, provided that they are regulated and reined in by precise boundaries that are clearly established. Without that we would have anarchy and debauchery. And note this: it is most important that morality will be victorious. All religions are at complete liberty to spread: we were the first to give the Catholic Church back its lustre, dignity, freedom and authority. We are witnessing an extraordinary spectacle: this same Church prefers its weak enemies to its strong friends. Facing an enemy which it fundamentally isn't afraid of, and which provides the Church with arguments for the revival of faith, is doubtless an advantage.

*

**Werner Hütter, Wehrmacht radio operator, b. 1917      near Berlin**
We had gone mad. We've been completely exhausted. Our driver in particular was demoralized – always travelling in crowded streets, back and forth, this direction and that, even driving around in circles, constantly going through other units and columns, which put him under a lot of stress.

Towards morning there was a general meeting and a chance to take a breather. A lieutenant went off in our car to get petrol. Cigarettes were handed out. Weary and shattered, we then waited hour after hour for further developments. New units were equipped with anti-tank grenades and marched 'forward'. We were also given brief explanations in the use of the weapons. The division general came in the opposite direction with a number of cars.

Around midday our journey continued. The company was supposed to meet in a forest about 1 km east of Radebruck. The troops were prepared for deployment and given a few drums of cable. And there were front-fighting packs: additional supplies for the crews of armoured fighting vehicles etc. We washed in a puddle. The sun came through a little.

In the afternoon we received the order to drive to Hohenfliess-Eggersdorf and establish a connection between the division switchboard and the Artillery commander. Of course it was supposed to be done quickly, so we had to start straight away – even though it wasn't clear which way the communication would go. After we had, with a great deal of effort (including crossing the road) rolled out two lengths of cable, the oh-so-welcome order reached us that we were to roll them back up again! In the meantime the new division command post had been set up and we were given new instructions. What did it matter that we had worked in vain for two hours?

There was terrible traffic on the main road. A great number of heavy vehicles and armoured cars were coming through, all heading for Altlandsberg.

So we started all over again and laid a line through the long estate from the south end to the north all the way to the main road, where a unit was supposed to meet us.

It had grown dark by now – but flares kept coming down and transformed everything into bright daylight again. And one could almost talk about a hail of bombs, it was getting increasingly dangerous.

At last we had laid our cable – but no sign of the other unit. A light rain began to fall. We now had to go in search of them. We couldn't contact our lieutenant. He was urgently needed now, but we couldn't get through to him. Corporal N. was getting impatient because it was supposed to be a quick job getting that line through.

So on with the carbines – and off on foot, we couldn't get any further by car, the street was jammed in both directions! It was full of orders and shouting like nothing else!

After we had marched a few kilometres it became quieter – and that calm struck us as suspicious. We had seen no sign of the other construction unit. Different orders must have come in the meantime, and not reached us.

Unfortunately we didn't have a telephone connection either – what could we do? We met groups of private soldiers of all kinds – that struck us as very strange. Some comrades asked us where we were coming from and where we were headed? To Altlandsberg! They couldn't believe their ears – the Russians were there already. We knew nothing!

We talked to a lot of comrades – the cheer, the hope are gone. Some squaddies express themselves in the harshest terms. One company even marched through the town singing – as if the war was already over. Which way to Berlin? We saw drunken officers, not to speak of the lower ranks. People looked at us in amazement – what were we still doing here? No one could stem this flow of returning soldiers.

So that was 20 April and the night that followed. Who gave a thought to the Führer's birthday? The sky was grey almost all day – no more 'Hitler weather'.

**Helmut Vaupel, reserve recruitment officer, b. 1928 Kladow, Berlin**
On 20 April, the last 'Führer's birthday', we went to the troop drill ground in Spandau and practised sniping at life-sized cardboard comrades. In between, we lay in cover under fir trees, while streams of Allied bombers flew off towards the centre to drop their final 'birthday greetings'. When we reached Kladow again in the evening, we met the first remnants of our regiment, which had escaped the collapse of the front. They told us terrible things: about the carpet bombing of the Stalin organs [rocket launchers], terrible losses, many, many dead comrades who had been sent into their first battle only ten days before, and how Colonel Braun, a hard taskmaster in training, had wept at the sight of so many young victims. Over the next two or three days further survivors of the inferno came in; they were to assemble in barracks again, they were told. There were about 80 in the end, 80 out of 800! Now we go on waiting in paralysing uncertainty.

**Léon Degrelle, Waffen-SS officer, 1906–94**                      **Berlin**
On the evening 19 April 1945 General Steiner briefed me on the full extent of the disaster. The Red tanks were already almost at the Ringbahn, Berlin's well-known bypass.

Many of our comrades were in Berlin on official duty. With unusual cold-bloodedness they published our daily French-language newspaper, *L'Avenir*, the day before the encirclement. I jumped into my Volkswagen to inform my colleagues of the impending danger. It was an hour and a half's drive from my command post to Berlin. I drove past the wretched streams of refugees pouring in all directions, and at nine in the evening I reached the old Prussian capital.

The Hotel Adlon was still in operation, in spite of the bombs and grenades that were already landing in the street. In the brightly lit dining hall, waiters in tuxedos and maîtres d' in tailcoats went on solemnly and unflappably serving purple pieces of kohlrabi on the silver trays meant for better days. Everything was still orderly and smart, without an agitated word or a sign of haste.

Tomorrow or the next day the building would probably be in flames. Or else the Russians would be forcing their way into the gilded hall. But those dire prospects didn't alter the running of the establishment in the slightest.

It was very beautiful. The attitude of the Germans, their self-control and their sense of discipline down to the finest details and until the last moment, will remain a greatly moving memory for everyone who experienced the end of the Third Reich.

There was not the slightest sign of panic in collapsing Berlin.

And yet, who could doubt the outcome of the battle? Defences in the suburbs were ludicrous. There were very few infantry. The number of tanks was insignificant.

The last bulwark had been set up by Küstrin, after it had been taken the road was free.

In the night I drove through the city under artillery fire. I even got as far as Potsdam. No trace of looting. No sign of revolt. The old men of the Volkssturm and the boys of the Hitler Youth waited for the enemy with anti-tank grenades, and were as serious as Teutonic Knights.

*

**Elvira Stürhmann-Boljahn**                                              **Berlin**
I was a local music examiner in the BDM, and I organized the Hitler Youth celebrations for the Führer on 20 April 1945. We began with the Berlin flag march led by the Radio Orchestra conductor Willi Träder.

> Let us raise our flags
> Into the fresh morning wind...

The lyrics were by the worker poet Fritz Sottke. The celebration took place in the domed hall of the Olympic Stadium. Groups of Hitler Youth and the girls of the various different districts took part.

Next to me sat the composer of the songs 'Sacred Fatherland' and

'Nothing Can Be Taken from Us', Professor Heinrich Spitta. He has also composed the song 'Earth Creates the New', whose lyrics he penned himself.

> Inspired by faith we boys all march
> Our faces towards the sun

And

> We declare our faith to Hitler
> Till the grave.

The whole thing was a pure Hitler Youth event, there was a fanfare procession and the district band played. A speech was given by the district leader.

On 20 April all public transport was still running, and we were surprised that there was no air raid siren. Are they paying attention? we wondered.

## Artur Axmann, 1913–96                                              Berlin

On 19 April 1945, the eve of Adolf Hitler's 56th birthday, the ten-year-old boys and girls were, in line with tradition, accepted into the German Youth In past years the acceptance ceremony was held in the Grosse Remter in Marienburg in the east of the Reich, but it had been in enemy hands for a long time. So this year's ceremony was held in the domed hall of the Reich Sports Field in Berlin. We had taken all the necessary precautions in the event of an air raid. It was to be our last Reich event. Every last seat was full in the amphitheatre-style space of the domed hall. The scene was no longer dominated by uniforms. The boys wore white shirts and the girls white blouses. With their bright voices they sang the songs of the youth movement. The chamber orchestra of the Hitler Youth played. In here there was peace, while the rumble of the nearby front could be heard outside. It was very hard for me to find the right words that day. Where was one to draw one's hope? But in spite of everything hope is still being planted on the grave.

Also sitting among us were the 16- and 17-year-old fighters of our close-combat tank brigade who had already been wounded and distinguished for bravery. I had spent time with them two days before, when the Soviets had, amidst massive artillery fire, arrived from the area of Frankfurt/Oder and the Seelow Heights [...].

On the afternoon of 20 April I went to the garden of the Reich Chancellery with our delegation. A unit of the Courland Army and the 'Frundberg' SS Division had arrived there. Our delegation took up position between them. Hitler appeared from the Bunker with Dr Goebbels, Heinrich Himmler, Albert Speer and Martin Bormann. Hermann Göring was not there, but had been with Hitler earlier. I reported to the Führer. Then he walked along the front of the delegation with me. He walked with a slightly bent posture, and held his trembling hands clasped at his back. He delivered a brief address. He compared our people with a seriously ill patient for whom science still had a medication that would save him at the last minute. But it was crucial that the patient retained his will to live. The battle for Berlin had to be won. He ended his words with the exclamation: 'Heil to you!' There was no reply, only shocked silence. The enemy was already only a few kilometres away. What was astonishing was the strength of will and the resolution that this man still emanated. Everyone was under his spell, myself included. [...]

When the Führer's closest colleagues congratulated him, I was standing near Himmler and heard his words: 'My Führer, many congratulations on your birthday, also in the name of the SS, and all the best.' To my mind that sounded cool and uninvolved. [...] Had relations between the two men soured in the meantime? I wondered.

**Lothar Loewe, b. 1929**                          **Tempelhof, Berlin**
On 20 April, Hitler's birthday, we received special rations: two bars of chocolate (only now available to pilots) and a bottle of red wine. Ghostly orgies played out in the airport cellars. Soldiers and officers disported themselves with the women auxiliaries. Their need for protection and their desperate hope that they might escape from Berlin with the help of an officer or a sergeant made all their inhibitions evaporate. The last night in Tempelhof before the first grenades of

the Russian long-distance artillery hit the streets of Berlin, we were dancing on a volcano.

\*

**Friedrich Pechtold, b. 1929**                        **Bayerischer Wald**

It's 20 April, the Führer's birthday. The company is sitting on a slope with wonderfully blossoming apple trees. Lieutenant Weber delivers a speech and says the important thing now is that the Führer's work must not be destroyed, and we should not help in that process. In the afternoon he makes us stop behind a barn and delivers another address: 'Anyone who does not want to join in should now step forward and say so, but we will pursue him and his line until the end of the world!' And then we swear an oath to the Führer. I'm slightly disappointed: it isn't at all solemn, we don't even have a flag, we're still in our motley uniforms, and apart from a few training models we have no weapons.

But we have concerns of our own, and we take them to Petty Officer Stolze: if things get serious now, we need pay books, not our draft cards. After all, the draft card shows that one is not currently with an official unit. We know that the Americans are very precise on this: anyone who has no pay book but a rifle does not have combatant status according to the Geneva Convention, and anyone who doesn't have that doesn't need to be taken prisoner but can be shot straight away. In Kohlscheid, where I dug trenches, they caught seven Luftwaffe auxiliaries and shot them. A hero's death – if it has to be – yes! But not like this!

But Petty Officer Stolze hasn't a clue; we're not getting any pay books, and that's how it's going to stay.

When we get back to quarters in the evening, someone runs up to us shouting, 'Tank siren!' The head of the battalion comes and says it's just a false alarm. The French prisoners of war working on our farm put on their best suits.

Then a tractor drives up to the farm with two trailers that are unloaded immediately: camouflage suits, tent carpets, boots, armour-piercing grenades, sub-machine guns, machine guns and rifles. When we creep into the straw to sleep at 10.00 p.m., everyone has a camouflage suit; we have to take the SS eagles off them first. The suits are thickly lined and loosely cut; I can keep on all my stuff underneath. The fabric and the caps both have a fine camouflage pattern. A unit of 15 men also get an MG42, four to five armour-piercing grenades, eleven Russian sub-machine guns converted to German ammunition, a rapid-fire rifle with telescopic sights and a 98k carbine. A leaflet has been inserted into the tube end of the armour-piercing grenades, precisely describing how the German combatant – whether man or woman, child or old person – can very easily fire at enemy tanks. You just have to be careful because when you fire a massive jet of flame comes out the back.

> 'Tank assault or tank attack
> Keep well clear, both front and back!'

**Friederike Grensemann, b. 1924**                    **Wilmersdorf, Berlin**

On 20 April, the Führer's birthday, I went to the office, where I was given leave. When I was at home, Father arrived. He just wanted to fetch a leather coat, he said. He was wearing a uniform with an armband reading VOLKSSTURM, he had been called up at last.

It was time to say farewell – we didn't say much to each other. When he was finished, he gave me his pistol. 'It's over, my child, promise me you'll shoot yourself when the Russians come, otherwise I won't have another moment of peace.' He also instructed me to keep the barrel in my mouth. Then another hug, a kiss! All in silence. He went. Outside, Dr Ott was waiting in the car. He got in – they set off, around the corner into Mannheimer Strasse. He raised his right arm, it wasn't a Hitler salute, but it wasn't a wave either.

I went back into the house. What was I supposed to do? I remember sitting at the other end of our couch by the still-warm stove. What am I going to do? It is all over? I collected a few pictures and put them on my piano. Pictures of all my loved ones. Then I played 'Ave Maria' by Bach–Gounod. I had played it so often in the good days, my desert island piece.

Only five years later skeleton parts were found in the zoo south of Sommerstrasse during an excavation, and scraps of a post office savings book card. You see, I had the savings book at the time, and he had kept the card. The main post office savings office was in Vienna, and that was where they identified the owners. It must have been our father, because he had been assigned for deployment nearby, to protect Goebbels's private villa!! He was then interred in a mass grave in Plötzensee, Berlin.

## Eva Richter-Fritzsche, artist, 1908–86                    Berlin

When I came home I learned from Frau Simke that there would be coffee and butter on the new food cards. The grocer's was just around the corner, so we set off to fetch our ration.

The Russians had already advanced as far as Köpenick, and were firing grenades at the Adlershof. There was a fierce battle for house fronts and even whole houses. We had to walk home to the thunder of the guns. Frau Simke had just come into the hall, I myself was already holding the handle of the apartment door, when the accident happened. A grenade exploded right next to us, and the detonator hit me. I fell to the floor with a scream the like of which I'd never uttered before. The accident happened and, as I was to discover later, so did my farewell to the healthy life I had lived hitherto; impossible for me to grasp, after surviving our flight and the low-flying aeroplane attacks on our escape route across the Vistula lagoon.

The detonator had shredded my calf. The doctors did everything they could to save the leg. One day later the doctor told me it would have to be amputated. At that moment I couldn't pray to God, I doubted his existence. I agreed to the operation silently hoping that I wouldn't wake up after it. But three hours later the nurse brought me back to life.

I woke up with only one sound leg. My left calf was missing, and the knee had had to be removed as well. Today the outcome of the operation would have been different.

*

## Dr Felix Kersten, 1898–1960                    Gut Hartzwalde

On 19 April at 2.00 p.m. I flew with Norbert Masur [representative of the World Jewish Congress, who helped in the rescue of concentration camp victims at the end of the war] from Stockholm and was driven here in an official SS car. Masur and I were the only passengers on the scheduled flight between Stockholm and Berlin, which was otherwise packed full of parcels from the Swedish Red Cross to the Red Cross in Berlin. The flight lasted four hours, we saw neither Allied nor German planes in the sky. When the plane arrived at the Tempelhof airfield, we were greeted by a five-man police guard, standing to attention with a Nazi salute. Masur doffed his hat and said a polite 'Hello'. At the airport I was given a letter of welcome from the Reichsführer SS for Masur, signed by SS Brigade Leader Schellenberg.

Schellenberg joined us in Hartzwalde at 2.00 in the morning. We thoroughly discussed the wishes of the Swedish government, and agreed that as many Jews as possible should be released to Masur as an expression of goodwill.

Schellenberg was disappointed that Himmler was not prepared to make new concessions because of the intense pressure being exerted on him by the party leadership in the person of Bormann. During a discussion lasting several hours we considered how best to approach Himmler. Schellenberg agreed with me that help was urgently required.

**Walter Schellenberg, 1910–52**                    **Gut Hartzwalde**
By now the news had come in that Kersten and Norbert Masur had arrived at Tempelhof airport and had driven to Kersten's farm in Hartzwalde. As Count Bernadotte [Swedish diplomat who negotiated the release of 31,000 prisoners from German concentration camps during the Second World War] was expected in Berlin at the same time, there was a danger that the two meetings might clash, particularly since the tense military situation made Himmler difficult to contact. So Himmler asked me to go to Kersten during the night and enter into preparatory negotiations with Herr Masur. At the same time I was to agree a date for a meeting between him and Masur. I had dinner in Hohenlychen. Contrary to his usual custom, Himmler suddenly ordered a bottle of sparkling wine to raise a glass to Hitler's birthday at exactly twelve o'clock.

**Dr Felix Kersten, 1898–1960**               **Gut Hartzwalde**
At 9 o'clock in the morning I introduced Schellenberg to Masur, and
Masur had the opportunity to present his wishes. Schellenberg gave a
firm pledge to support Masur's demands to Himmler.

**Walter Schellenberg, 1910–52**               **Gut Hartzwalde**
In the morning I was woken by the roar of the planes, and while I
was getting dressed, a bomb fell nearby. Over breakfast I talked to
Herr Masur. He pressed for a meeting with Himmler as he had to leave
imminently. I knew Himmler would repeatedly try to postpone the
appointment, and I would have to use all my powers to make sure it
happened soon.

*

**Marthel Kaiser, b. 1925**               *Neheim, Westphalia*
This is a memorable day for us, 20 April, Hitler's birthday. Many
Germans, almost all of them in fact, will curse this day, and how glad
we once were of it. And how much has changed in the meantime.
All the things this man has done. Good things, certainly, it cannot be
denied that there were some things that were good and idealistic, but
the good does not outweigh all the terrible things that in the end befell
our German people because of this man. Today we stand in the world
more humble than ever before, and it is all the worse and all the more
painful in that we lately stood higher than ever before. How gullibly
trusting we were, how patiently our people bore all that misery because
they thought one day there would be a change for the better. But it was
not to be, just suffering and the endless rows of dead – all in vain –
pointless. It is such a bitter truth that it is almost beyond comprehension.
The destruction and annihilation of our glorious, proud and beloved
fatherland, that is all that has been completely achieved. Crimes have
been committed, crimes no one could have guessed at, and for which
we must all rightly atone. And the fact that they could happen here in
Germany weighs on us all, and if a German officer says at the sight of
the concentration camps that he too has now lost all his honour, then
he has spoken the truth. What must the enemies think of us! They

are now our masters, and we must be grateful if they treat us with mercy, and all that we owe to the man whose birthday it is today!! Perhaps no man has ever been more loved and revered, but perhaps also more hated by the same people after everything was revealed as lies and deceit. If a man such as Goebbels can present the people with such slapdash praise as he did in his annual birthday speech, one can only imagine that either we are all insane or, more probably, that he is. It sounds like mockery to our ears when he says that the Führer lives only for the people and has only their wellbeing at heart, and that we are approaching the end of the war that will bring the final victory. If it were not so pitiful, one would have to laugh at this man raving about an imminent final victory, without saying how he is going to go about driving out the enemy, who has already occupied more than half the Reich, and to the people themselves his words were once like a gospel. If I think about Frau Pfeiffer, for example, and so many other dear people and about myself, I feel truly miserable. What are they going to bring us now? What will the final settlement be like? What will become of us, and of our youth, which has been so squandered? I do not fear for my family, because we are – I believe – strong enough to survive anywhere and always to remain on top, but our fatherland will be torn apart until we no longer recognize it. How sad I am, and how impotent.

*

**Benito Mussolini, 1883–1945**　　　**Palazzo Monforte, Milan**
*Interview*

'Is there still hope? Are there secret weapons?'

'There are. It would be ludicrous and unforgivable to bluff. If the attempt on Hitler's life had not been made last summer, there would have been enough time to activate those weapons. Even in Germany that act of betrayal caused the collapse not of a party, but of the Fatherland.'

'But we were always loyal to you and always will be…'

'So many oaths! So many words of loyalty, of devotion! Only today do I recognize that the only person who is truly loyal is the one who is a true Fascist! You are the ones who are always loyal, in good times or in bad. It was easy to celebrate me in 1938! I have a whole list of people who no longer knew what to do to please me! And at the first sign of a storm they withdrew, cautiously at first, to observe how things developed, and then they changed to the side of the enemy. How deplorable! But how comforting to see at last who the pure, the true, the honest people are. One can betray the idea, one can betray me, but not the Fatherland.'

*

### Odd Nansen, 1901–73                                    Lübeck

I'm sitting on the omnibus and writing. On the bus – to freedom. Our journey takes us through Germany, northwards, across the north German lowlands. We are not far from Lübeck, but our destination is further north, we hope Sweden. The news arrived last night, after we had gone to bed. We were to be woken at four o'clock and ready to travel at 6! We could only take as many clothes as we could carry, and very little food.

I didn't sleep much last night. I walked around outside for hours, I couldn't calm myself down enough to go to bed. Outside there was a great deal of agitated activity. The air raid sirens sounded without interruption. Bombs exploded, cannon thundered, and machine guns rattled in every direction. One had the impression that one was standing right in the middle of it all – although that was not the case, because no bombs fell, no splinters and grenades. Even that had become unreal. But there was unease in the camp. Some prisoners somewhere had stolen parcels. They were caught and beaten. Their screams and roars rang out strangely in the moonlit night, among the thunder of the bombs and the protracted distortion of the air raid sirens. Hundreds of prisoners were busy carrying their mattresses out into the parade ground and pouring the straw on to a great pile. Why? Was it to be burned along with the millions of lice and bacilli? I don't know. The pile was still there when we left this morning. Like everything else under this regime, everything was done amidst a lot of shouting and yelling, furious commands and cursing. But this gave last night a familiar, 'homely' melody. We are now stopping in Lübeck. We have driven through the city centre and seen all that has been destroyed. It was sad to see the Rathausplatz with the beautiful old city hall, the Marienkirche and the cathedral, all in ruins. The most beautiful part of Lübeck lies in rubble, and yet Lübeck is probably one of the cities that got off lightly.

## *Cap Arcona* documentation                    Neustadt, Holstein

At about 5 o'clock the transport of the 4,255 Danish and Norwegian concentration camp prisoners left their section of the Neuengamme concentration camp on the 'white buses' of the Swedish and Danish Red Cross.

The Red Cross provision parcels meant for the Scandinavians which were no longer required were left for the use of the remaining concentration camp inmates.

This brought to an end Count Bernadotte's operation to save the Scandinavian prisoners. Other Neuengamme concentration camp inmates were brought in cattle trucks each holding 50 people, to Lübeck and from there to the *Thielbek*. Because of the aerial bombardment, the railway lines were often disrupted, so that the prisoners had to sit on board the trains for a very long time on the side-lines. Some of them were taken on death marches from these intermediate stops.

In the morning 2,300 Neuengamme inmates boarded the *Cap Arcona* cargo ship. 280 guards also settled here. Only some prisoners received starvation rations from parcels dealt out by the aid organizations. The SS kept most of the donations for themselves.

The *Athen* was also laden with prisoners, and tried to pass these compulsory passengers on to the *Cap Arcona*. But for the time being the *Athen* went on lying in her berth in Lübeck harbour. Conditions in the crammed holds of the ships were unbearable. There were several hundred fatalities in the harbour area, and the death toll was increasing.

The 20 Jewish children abused for pseudo-medical research and 28 of their carers, along with Soviet prisoners of war, were hanged in the evening in the boiler room of the school on the Bullenhuser Damm.

**Youth group leader**                    **Waren, Mecklenburg**

Once the battle for the Oder had begun we were constantly unloading train and boat transports in which the injured arrived with makeshift bandages. There was one event that I will never forget. On about 20.4.1945 we had to go back on to the platform. The only ones left were us boys in our uniforms and the railwaymen. All civilians had to leave the station. Then an enormous freight train arrived. All the wagons had their windows covered with barbed wire. Each wagon was packed full of women in concentration camp clothes. They were crying out for water. Women in SS uniform patrolled outside with pistols and whips. No one was allowed near the train.

The engine was changed. Then the train travelled on towards Güstrow. Excrement dripped from the bottom of the wagons.

*

**August Richard Protz**       **Camp 2, Emsland, Aschendorf Moor**

On 20 April the rest, including myself, landed in Camp 2 again, a real funeral cortège. The man in charge was 2nd Captain von Köpenick, a trainee chimney sweep called Herold who had promoted himself to officer. This apprentice ordered all veterans who were supposed to have looted from the marsh-dwellers on the death march to be summoned from the barracks. Each one was given a spade and off they went to the nearby forest's edge. Here trenches were dug by the prisoners, the length of each group and 2 m deep. Once the depth had been reached, they were ordered to drop the spades and mad Herold fired his 2 cm anti-tank gun, which was mounted on a truck, at those poor human bodies until they all toppled into the trench. Then the next group had to fill up the trenches with the bodies still moving. 80–90 young people were murdered that way. May God have mercy on their souls.

For those of us unable to leave the barracks because of the approaching enemy and the danger of bombardment, and who had not eaten for days, the approaching Englishmen, or the Poles in the service of the English, had a big surprise in store. At about midday the English Artillery launched a murderous attack on the wretched barracks, and it is worth noting that it was well known through information from reconnaissance planes and probably throughout the whole world that such barracks in Emsland held only prisoners who were enemies of the state.

Once barracks 2 and 3 and the latrines were ablaze and the screams of the unfortunates within rang out across the barrack city, Tommy set his Mosquitoes and fighter bombers on these miserable people. They came in swarms and fired 2 cm exploding bullets at the barracks, until everything was on fire and everyone inside had perished [...]

Using all my remaining strength I crept outside through the burning back door of our barracks, no. 13, and dropped into a hole in the ground left by my colleagues. That was the saving of me, because now the aeroplanes launched a bombardment unlike anything else. With an infernal wail the Mosquitoes swooped down spewing 'Minengranaten' [thin-shelled grenades] and bombs on the remains of those barracks still standing, and even the peat stacks outside the camp were, as 'battle objects', the goal of their death and destruction. Truly, a glorious deed of battle – I couldn't help thinking of the Warsaw Ghetto in 1941.

The English pilots saw the figures of the wretched wounded creeping around, but they went on calmly murdering, and completed the work of Herold, a Bohemian deserter and corporal.

Camp 2 Aschendorf Moor, which held so much suffering and cruelty, was no more. Like a beacon, the flames stretched to the sky and obliterated the earthly remains of Hitler's henchmen, who had themselves destroyed Germany's sons and daughters. We, a handful of degenerates with phlegmon and oedema, were chased on to the moors. Here we dug holes for ourselves in the peat stacks and I lay down on the blanket that I had brought with me from the camp. It began to rain, and I lay in the seeping moor water. I can't remember how long I lay there, because my brain and my body were absolutely exhausted by the events and struggle. One day I was carried from the peat stack by English soldiers and brought to Papenburg. The Catholic nuns in the orphanage of Ems in Papenburg gave me my first food after days of hunger. I owe my life entirely to those noble-minded, generous people. From the city of Papenburg itself I and my friend Helmut Baumgarten from Pattensen in Hanover received absolutely nothing.

\*

**Samuel Charles Grace, British prisoner of war**              *Nanndorf*
Fri. Rest. Enjoyed a good smoke in bed, had bread & cheese & pineapple jam for b/f. & then at 11 we had the cat's pyjamas, a good old pot of Blighty tea with milk & sugar, together with sweet American biscuits, cheese & jam. An English padre visited us this morning, & after listening to our tale of woe, told us that parcels were coming from IIIA & that we would get preferential treatment. Spuds up this afternoon, we mashed them with milk, liver paté & salt, then sweet coffee. Bread & jam, only a little but very tasty. Still no signs of rations. Rumours that this is a support area. About 7 p.m. 100 Yanks came over and bombed a nearby dump, 1 kilo away. We brewed up on a homemade cooker & had a couple of slices in the open air. Last minute orders, standing by to move. The Russians are now much more our allies.

**Michael Gow, British lieutenant**       *Bergen-Belsen concentration camp*
Yesterday I went with our doctor to Belsen Concentration Camp, which you have no doubt read of in the papers. [...] We passed through the village of Belsen and followed the signs to the camp, driving through the gates into a most imposing collection of barrack buildings, far better of their kind than anything in England. This surprised us very much at the time, because we hardly expected to find such a pleasant looking place. We were told later that these barracks were merely camouflage, and that if foreign observers came to look at the Concentration Camp they were shown this place instead. [...]There was just this small road I have put on the map leading into it. The British had set up a hospital in 'B' [barracks] and we saw this first. As we stood outside the 'Decontamination shed' we saw ambulances coming and going, and couldn't make out why it was that all the stretchers were empty except for blankets, until we discovered that it was quite impossible to distinguish between a stretcher with only blankets on and one with a body, so emaciated had the prisoners become. We then went inside the shed, and on either side were the women prisoners being washed

and powdered with disinfectant. They were all so thin that it was practically impossible to tell that they were women, let alone what age they were. They were very nearly all suffering from typhus, enteritis or dysentery, and the death rate is still 500 a day. The men had not yet been dealt with, because the medical staff were so hard worked that they simply hadn't had the time. It was appalling to think that these women had once been normal and healthy, and that once they had come from good homes. Some had been in Belsen for three years. The washing was done by imported German nurses, who were quite appalled by what they saw.

[…]Outside most of the huts were dead bodies which had not yet been buried; the SS guards, who were captured when the British took the place, are given the job of corpse lifting and burying. Some objected, apparently, that it was against the 'rules' to make them do this work, but I gather that our troops gave them a very rough time indeed.

[…]

German captured statistics for last month record 15,000 deaths at Belsen 'C'. The precautions against escape were as you might expect – watchtowers etc., though how the Germans imagined that these people could escape with thighs the size of my wrist I don't know. It was the most appalling sight I have ever seen or indeed ever will see.

On leaving we were asked to send some chocolate from the battalion for the children (who had either been born in the place or put inside with their parents). The response from the men was wonderful, and it took two jeeps to get it there. I shall remember this visit, chiefly because it brought home so much more clearly what we have been – and are still – fighting against, and it made me sure that the lives of many friends lost have been worthwhile.

**Maurice F. Jupp, British captain**                *north-west Germany*

It took 2 days for the inmates to appreciate that, in future, there would be enough to eat and drink. At first, they fought for every available drop of water or bit of food. The usual request is for cigarettes: the better types ask for nothing, or for things like magazines. There are some SS 'ATS' [Auxiliary Territorial Services] here – hefty women who have been put on to digging graves and burying dead female inmates. There are a few SS guards there too. They take the dead bodies in lorries to a burying ground, followed by Brit Army guards. As they pass through the camp, those who are strong enough to throw stones at the SS do so. The day before yesterday, one SS man lost his nerve under the stones and bolted. He was riddled with bullets. Yesterday, the same thing happened with three of them. The interesting thing, my friend said, was that none of the inmates tried to get away from the firing: death, bullets, etc., had no terror for them.

*

**Erich Kessler, b. 1912               Theresienstadt concentration camp**
Today I was at the eye clinic, as I have a small hardening that will have to be removed by surgery. As the instruments need to be prepared, I have to come back tomorrow at 9 o'clock. There is little work at the moment, so that we are only occupied for half the day. In the afternoon I sit down in the park by the main square. Today the first transport of Jews arrived back in Theresienstadt from the various camps in Germany. Around 1,700 people came in about 30 cattle trucks. There's another transport of 27 trucks in Bauschwitz. The transport has been under way since 9 March, for 6 weeks. These people are in a terrible state; half starving, dressed in rags, the women's heads shaved. 70 corpses so far have been lifted from the trucks, people who have died over the last few days. Most of them can hardly stand. It's possible that Hans is among them, as apparently there are people from Schwarzheide. In a few days I will learn more from the inquiry. It's dreadful to see the ignoble ways in which people treat each other. That people can reconcile their consciences to doing such things. Harry came in the evening and said that he had helped to lift the corpses out of the trucks and carry them to the various ambulances. He too was quite depressed and shaken. When the poor devils were brought to the sick bays and saw the beds with the white sheets, they started crying. They were undressed and washed. They had an inch-thick layer of dirt on their backs. Then they were given a specially prepared soup so as not to overburden their stomachs.

**Alisah Shek, b. 1927**          **Theresienstadt concentration camp**
At 6.30 a transport of 25 trucks, 1,800 people, arrived. The news
flew around the ghetto: people from the camps. When they drove
past 'Crete' [a part of Theresienstadt], they called out 'Auschwitz',
'Birkenau', 'Hanover', 'Buchenwald', they called out all these horrible
names from the train. Then the heart of the town stopped, and now they
are there. Stinking, pestilential people, half alive, half dead or corpses.
They pressed themselves against the window, terrible faces, bones and
eyes. 80 women from Theresienstadt and otherwise almost all men.
How awful they look. Here was what we had been trembling over
for months. Over our lives and our deaths, over unrelieved suffering
a millionfold, and now it is here. It is here. The remains of the masses,
the remains of people. They threw out cigarettes, they pointed into
their mouths, they fell to the floor – drink, eat. They were unloaded
into the turnstile – unloaded. Lots of them turned up, names – mother,
daughter, lover of this one and that. Everyone is horrified. They are
driven in flat-top trucks to the quickly erected ramshackle cabins,
mothers don't recognize their children, there is no light behind their
eyes. People throw them bread, they pounce on it and lash out around
them. The trucks – I will never forget it. The gloom, the wooden
boxes and wood pulp, dirt, clothes, all filthy – and yet so empty.
An unbearable stench of old dung, and on the slippery floor, hidden
behind boxes, in the dark the bright white foot of a corpse, someone
who was still alive a year ago. And in all that misery I understood how
good it is to be dead. Carried out on stretchers... In the night 6 trucks
from Hungary.

**H. G. Adler, 1910–88**          **(Theresienstadt concentration camp)**
17,539 prisoners in Theresienstadt (c. 7,000 Protectorate, 5,500
Germany, 1,250 Austria, 1,250 Holland, 1,400 Slovakia, 1,000 Hungary)
36.6% of the prisoners non-Jewish.

Transports from concentration camps are coming in – by 10 May
c. 13,500–15,000 prisoners.

Himmler is negotiating with the Swedish Jew Masur and others
over Theresienstadt.

*

**Nicolaus von Below, adjutant, 1907–83**　　　　**Führerbunker, Berlin**
All prominent personalities still in Berlin turned up for the strategy
meeting on 20 April, Hitler's 56th birthday. I saw Göring, Dönitz,
Keitel, Ribbentrop, Speer, Jodl, Himmler, Kaltenbrunner, Krebs,
Burgdorf and others. Before the situation briefing Hitler received
their birthday wishes, but was then immediately informed of the
latest events. After that Hitler had individual conversations. Göring
explained to Hitler that he had important things to do in southern
Germany. He would only be able to get through today. He bade
Hitler farewell. I had a sense that Hitler was inwardly paying Göring
no attention now. It wasn't a nice moment. The Grand Admiral also
bade farewell to Hitler. Hitler gave him the brief instruction to take
over the leadership in north Germany, and to prepare himself for an
honourable battle. Hitler's words conveyed the great trust that he
placed in Dönitz. Hitler took his leave of the others present, such as
Himmler, Kaltenbrunner and Ribbentrop, without a great deal of fuss.
That day I had the sense that Hitler had not yet decided whether to
leave Berlin or to stay.

There was a great deal of unease in the bunkers of the Reich
Chancellery, a sign that a general decampment was on the agenda.
Puttkamer drove with two petty officers from our adjutancy to the
Obersalzberg, to destroy all the documents there. I asked him to
throw my diaries on the fire with everything else, which he promised
to do, and kept his promise. The same happened to Schmundt's notes.
Fräulein Wolf and other members of the personal adjutancy also
prepared to travel.

Late in the evening we assembled in Hitler's small living-room for a
drink. Those present were Eva Braun, Frau Christian née Daaranowski,
Frau Junge née Humbs, Hitler's special cook Fräulein Manziarly,
Schaub, Lorenz and myself. At that little gathering we didn't mention
the war. Gerda Christian was, as always, the best at turning Hitler's
mind to other thoughts.

*

**Edgar Kupfer-Koberwitz, 1906–91**     **Dachau concentration camp**
Today is Hitler's birthday.

Brünn is supposed to have fallen – in Berlin there are still street battles.

Himmler is said to be in Munich, ready to defend the city to the last. The Munich offensive is now expected. There are a lot of soldiers here in Dachau now, and people are saying there are tanks and cannon. I myself saw a lot of soldiers who have come here to the sick bay, all in different uniforms. An Austrian colonel says, 'It's all shit!'

In the afternoon some low-flying planes fired again. In the night three sirens, three bombings – the bombs were dropped individually, so they must have known their targets precisely. It was at a distance of about five kilometres. The barrack trembled each time one landed. What are we going to have to endure here? They say the population of Dachau is to leave the city at midnight tomorrow, and go 13 kilometres further south. Again I've heard the toll of the dead in recent times: December 1944 = 1,800, – January 1945 = 2,800, – February 1945 = 3,000, – March 1945 – 4,000. Those are the figures for Dachau camp, without outside units, so I was told. That's 11,600 fatalities in this short time, people who couldn't defend themselves against death from hunger and typhus. All this happened without bombing. Almost 12,000 dead. Shouldn't we face death from bombs and grenades just as calmly? Who wants to escape? We have to stay calmly where we are. If it hits us, it hits us. The many prisoners of war and the other comrades in other camps are in danger. None the less it's a strange feeling for us being between two belligerent sides, without any protection. Because behind us the Nazi enemy is holding Munich, and our liberators, the Americans, are on their way from Augsburg.

**K. A. Gross, 1892–1952**     **Dachau concentration camp**
There's certainly something beautiful, perhaps even poetic about carnivals and the bustle of fairgrounds – once a year. But getting up in a terrible hubbub and going to bed in a bustle, and not knowing where to put your bowl at mealtimes, that's where cosiness ends, and there isn't a trace of poetry left either. Man is not made for such a herd lifestyle, if we have any idea of the creator's intentions; certainly not.

Dear Hax, what did they do with the perfect barracks of all those years ago! Do you remember the old days, when you played the landlord, so to speak, of a Tyrolean peasant drinking house, seeing the pals as your guests, entertaining them with a round of tabletop bowling. Martin, from Nuremberg, as the pub pharaoh, played the feminine counterpoint who, with his *'Guat Nacht jetz und Ruah is!'* – 'So now goodnight, and peace!' – took some of the edge off before bedtime. And such exclusiveness! Yes, you set some store by order and selectiveness, many a student fraternity could learn from your example. Only Reich Germans were allowed into your club, and only Kapos were allowed into the first room, and perhaps a pretty boy or too. Yes, what they made of your block: an international dive, in which even greens and blacks [criminals and antisocial elements] were welcome and – fie! – Gypsies. And yet what is true must remain true and these Gypsies are still morally upright gentlemen in comparison with some of the Reich Germans who are now doing all the talking, and whom you Germans document by saying that they lay hands on compatriots like the boy Hiob, whom one of them thumped yesterday, sending him flying in a high arc into the corner by the stove.

We're having a bit of a time in the pub tonight: Gypsy music. Black Oscar is playing the zither in a way that's to die for. Who can tell that he only came back at the start of the week from the disaster unit, a kind of explosives brigade, after it blew up the unit rather than the ruins. He came back laden with booty, with a Gypsy bag full of bread crusts, jam and smoked ham. Those IDs are all that you need here to get access to the highest circles of society.

**Edmond Michelet 1899–1970**   (Dachau concentration camp)
Another picture comes to mind, one of the most impressive of the past few weeks. One evening Citron and I were out in the avenue that runs past the rabbit unit at the end of the camp. Over the past year I've often walked along there with my students, the Polish pastors.

The sky, bluish-grey until then, finally matched the scene.

The sound of tanks and artillery fire was getting closer and closer from the west; a purple strip screened what we could see of the horizon. A Wagnerian scene, an image of Apocalypse. We were now moving in a communication trench formed by a double row of piled-up corpses. In their watchtowers the SS men were seeing out the last hours of a sentry duty that had been going on for ten years. They let their bird-of-prey eyes and the muzzles of their machine guns circle above the unsettled ant-hills, ready to leap into action at the tiniest sign of any shared activity.

Then a curious singing reaches our ears: a mixture of a soldier song and a hymn. The sounds come closer. We can make out the words. Citron recognizes a Hitler Youth marching song. In this black and red twilight the impression is poignant. The last SS recruits are coming back from exercises.

'Let's admit it,' says Citron, 'there's something magnificent about this catastrophe.'

*

**E. Chereau, French prisoner**                              **on the road**
The evacuation is becoming a serious matter, we leave the camp at 10.30, and are given no provisions for the journey. We were able to gulp down a litre of soup before we had to set off. Our guards, both brutal and averse to any kind of humanity, are still showing no laxity in their watch over us. Again we are experiencing the vagaries of the past week. We pass through Freystein. So we've covered about 30 km, and at nightfall we are crammed together in a field to rest for a few hours. We are delighted to discover that only a very few of our comrades are missing. The stay in Flossenbürg allowed each of us to recover a little.

**Ray T. Matheny, American prisoner of war, b. 1925**        **Austria**
In the middle of the day of April 20th, while marching through a small valley, dotted with a few farms and ringed by well-kept fir trees, we came to a hostel next to the road. We Kriegies [POWs] were getting water at a tank, along with a group of Hitler Youth dressed in their smart-looking uniforms. Each of them wore a dagger, set in an elaborate black sheath. The boys were cocky, making deriding remarks about how we were dressed and how 'smart' they were in their uniforms.

Almost without warning an American P-51 came bearing down the valley aligning itself to fire on the sizeable group of uniformed men below. Reaction was slow among the prisoners since we had never encountered a fighter airplane zeroing in on us for a strafing run. The reaction of the Hitler Youth, however, was very different for they had likely been taught to respect those ground-strafing fighters. They went wild seeking cover in every direction, but there really was very little available to protect any of us. Fortunately, the P-51 saw our disorderly group and held his fire, passing 50 feet or so above looking us over and creating a magnificent roar with his Rolls Royce Merlin engine. Then, he pulled up steeply and around to the west and made another low-level run at about 90 degrees to us. At this point the Hitler Youth ran to us taking refuge among our quasi-American uniforms. One of the Kriegies, anticipating the possibility of being strafed, had previously acquired or made an American flag and displayed it boldly to the pilot by having men hold it up over their heads. We, all being airmen, knew that when the P-51 wheeled around 90 degrees to us it was a friendly act, but the Hitler Youth did not recognize it as such. They ran to use our uniforms and American flag as protection. After the P-51 left the scene amid waves and cheers from our rag-tag group, we unmercifully derided the Hitler Youth for their cowardly actions.

### H. M. Baker, Canadian lieutenant colonel                   *Friesoythe*

I visited some prisoner-of-war camps today which our troops had liberated within the last few days. One of these camps contained over 1,000 Polish women who had been captured after the fall of Warsaw a few months ago after their abortive uprising. The Huns had rounded up hundreds and hundreds of women from all walks of life and had herded them into this camp. They had not actually maltreated them, but they had herded hundreds into accommodations which normally were only suitable for scores. They had also done their best to break down their morale in a dozen other ways without actually resorting to physical violence. Such, for instance, as only providing one water tap for all purposes for a hundred women.

There were some real lovelies in the crowd, and Tommy O'Hara and I feasted our eyes on the collection of attractive breasts so temptingly displayed by open-necked shirts and sweaters. There wasn't a brassiere in the lot and everything was swinging freely in the breeze. They all appeared to be reasonably well-fed, and some of the gals were even sporting sheer silk stockings. This latter incongruity is easily explained, however, as soldiers from the Polish Armoured Division were swarming all over the place. Several of them had even found wives, daughters and sweet-hearts amongst the prisoners.

Tom and I also visited a camp containing Italians who had been captured by the Germans. Here we found a completely different picture. The Huns had not been pleased at all when the Italians had pulled out of the war and then come back in again on our side. The result was that they treated any Italian prisoners they captured very poorly. Most of the men in this camp were walking scare-crows. They told us that the German attitude had been 'Work or die', and 'To hell with you if you are sick'.

We were met at the gate by a tall gaunt individual in a tattered Italian uniform when we drove up to the place. We could not make much sense out of what he was trying to say, and as he seemed to be a bit of an ass, we brushed him aside and headed into the camp until we found the Camp HQ. The Commandant was not there but the officer on duty sent a runner for him. Imagine our surprise and embarrassment when who should turn up a few minutes later but our old friend the scare-crow from the main gate. Apparently he was a ruddy general in the Italian Army!

**Benito Mussolini, 1883–1945**                    Palazzo Monforte, Milan
*Interview*

The famous annihilating bombs are being manufactured. I received precise information only a few days ago. Perhaps Hitler doesn't want to strike before he has absolute certainty that it will be decisive. There seem to be three bombs of incredible power. The manufacture of each one is terribly complicated and tedious. The betrayal of Romania has also had an influence on that, to the extent that the petrol shortage was one of the main reasons for the loss of supremacy in the air. Twenty or thirty thousand static or destroyed aeroplanes. Lack of fuel. The most terrible tragedy of all.

\*

**8th Session of the Camp Committee      Buchenwald concentration camp**

*Statement by the new commandant*

Eiden informs me that the new commandant (Capt. Ball) has reviewed the camp and is basically in agreement with the work of the committee. He asks the international committee to stay in control of everything, and to give the comrades in the camp anything that they need. He is also of the view that the sad chapter of SS rule in Buchenwald is to be visibly brought to an end, and asks that anything suggesting former atrocities be removed. Above all it should begin with the crematorium. (Removal of ashes and urns and their burial at the Bismarck Tower.) The commandant indicates that the dead of the nations should be laid out in a room somewhere (suggestion: Hall 8, Gustl. Works).

Eiden suggested to the commandant that the comrades still dying be interred in a cemetery in Weimar. The commandant agrees with this proposal. At 12 o'clock a transport of dead comrades is to set off for Weimar, where they will be interred in the ground in a kind of honorary cemetery. [...]

From this afternoon a film is being shown. (Suggestion of the committee members.[)] Cinema visit by nation, they themselves have to ensure order during the cinema visit. Issuing of tickets. Russians, Czechs and Poles go to the first viewing.

**1 May: Pieck:**

On 1 May at 8.00 reveille and march of the band through the camp.

9.00 or 11.00 (according to circumstances, whether visitors are allowed to enter the camp or our comrades are allowed to leave), a centr. assembly in the parade ground.

Programme: 3 speakers (as yet to be determined, suggestion: Slv., Russ., Roman.)

Music – in conclusion a pantomime and possible march-past by our comrades.

In the afternoon, national get-together or meeting in the halls that may be at our disposal in the camp.

\*

The <u>decoration</u> of the halls will be done by Comrade Hurta, of Block 53. An Austr. Comrade will be entrusted with the task of <u>assigning the rooms</u>.

From 19.00 an internal <u>carnival</u> will be held, at which the individual nations will be assigned certain seats. The event will also be organised by the Cz.-Sl. Comrade Hurta.

The individual committees must of course make people available for work required for the organisation of the event.

Cz.-Sl. Comrade Sitte was entrusted with the organisation of the music and cabaret events.

The committee wishes to decide which pictures should be prepared for the large-scale rally on 1 May. The event commission proposes: Stalin, Roosevelt, Churchill and Thälmann.

The Cz.-Sl. Comrade <u>Neumann</u> would like to add the pictures of Tito and Benesch to the existing suggestion.

The <u>camp committee</u> agrees the following stipulation: production of paintings of Stalin, Roosevelt, Churchill and if technically possible of the additionally named paintings.

<u>Bartel</u> proposes that the development of code words be the responsibility of the committee.

<u>The Russ. Committee member</u> suggests that a brief developmental history of the time from 1 May 1944 until 1 May 1945 be worked out for the 1 May.

The march-past on 1 May should be carried out by nation and with banners.

Because of the number of flags the nat. Committees should contact the representatives of the Commission.

*

**Christa Schroeder, Hitler's secretary, 1908–84 Berlin–Obersalzberg**
When Hitler turned 56 on 20 April 1945, Berlin was encircled. The first Russian tanks were at the gates of the city. The thunder of infantry fire could be heard as far as the Reich Chancellery. The presentation of well-wishers from the personal staff and the military in the morning occurred in a very muted atmosphere in comparison to earlier years.

All the more audible were the group of Allied well-wishers, flying air attacks at Berlin almost without interruption from the early hours of the morning until about 2.00 at night. We didn't leave the bunker. According to the schedule, Johanna Wolf and I were to keep the boss company over lunch. During the meal there was a very gloomy atmosphere. In the evening, in the middle of an attack, it may have been just before 22.00, Johanna and I were summoned to the boss. Tired, pale and haggard, Hitler received us in his little study in the bunker. He said, '…the situation has changed a lot over the last few days.' On 16 April he had answered my question as to whether we would stay in Berlin almost indignantly: 'Of course we will stay in Berlin. You need not be afraid on that score!' I replied that I was not afraid, as I had made peace with life anyway. But I couldn't imagine, I said, how that would go on, when the Americans on the one side and the Russians on the other were getting closer every day. 'Calm yourself,' Hitler replied irritably. 'Berlin will stay German, we just need to gain some time!' During his last address to the Gauleiters on 24 February 1945, Hitler conveyed his unshakeable conviction: 'We must gain time!' Now he said to us, 'The situation has changed so much over the past few days that I find myself forced to dissolve my staff. As you are the older ones, you make a start. In an hour a car will be driving towards Munich. You can take two suitcases, and Reich Leader Bormann will tell you what to do next.'

As I had no family members, I asked him to be allowed to stay in Berlin, suggesting that my younger colleague whose mother lived in Munich be sent instead. But he would hear nothing of it. 'No, I want to found a resistance movement later, and for that I need both of you. You are the most valuable ones for me. If it comes to the crunch, the young will always survive, Frau Christian will manage in any case, and if one of the young ones really does snuff it, then that's just fate!'

He didn't take his leave from us as he always did, by kissing our hands, but with a handshake. He was probably saying that he would tolerate no contradiction, and that the conversation was over for him. He certainly noticed our muted mood, because he then said, perhaps trying to console us: 'We will see each other again soon, I will follow you in a few days!'

This order to leave Berlin on 20 April 1945 did not correspond to my ideas at the time, as I had already decided to use the brass cyanide capsule that von Skorzeny had given me in exchange for a bottle of whisky. [...] Suddenly and unexpectedly ordered journeys had always been torture to me. But this order of Hitler's greatly exceeded my earlier feelings of displeasure, and put me in a state of confusion. As if in a daze, I left Hitler to pack my things along with my colleague Frau Wolf. [...]

The antechamber to the bunker on Vossstrasse was crammed full of people who had escaped the continuing air raids. The room placed at the disposal of us secretaries had originally been designed as a 'transmitting station' for radio broadcasts. I had always felt very uncomfortable there, as the ceiling and the walls were covered with soundproofing slabs, which swallowed every sound even as one was speaking. A dead room of oppressive silence like the grave.

But packing struck me as pointless. Suddenly the telephone rang. The boss was on the line. Hitler said weakly, 'Children, the hole has already been closed [we were to have driven through the Protectorate]. You won't get through in the car, and now you'll have to fly tomorrow morning.'

After midnight Hitler rang again: 'Children,' he said, 'you will have to get yourselves ready, hurry up, the plane will launch immediately after the all clear.' His voice sounded dull and he broke off mid-conversation. I asked him a question, but even though the receiver hadn't been put back down he didn't reply. These were, incidentally, the only phone conversations I had in my 12 years with Hitler. [...]

A short time later, it may have been around half past 2 in the morning, we made our way back through the crowded corridors of the public bunker on Vossstrasse to the Reich Chancellery, which was humming and seething like a swarm of bees. Everyone stared at us and our two suitcases with great curiosity. I had quite pitiful feelings and was filled with shame as I walked past the terrified people. [...]

When at last we were sitting in one of the cars, we realized that the driver didn't know his way around Berlin at all. And he had not been given any instructions about whether he should drive us to Tempelhof or Staaken. At any rate, whether by mistake or good luck, he brought us to Tempelhof. It was a macabre journey through Berlin at night. Past burning houses, smouldering piles of rubble, ruins and clouds of smoke, and Volkssturm men who were busy erecting barricades. We could hear the thunder of the Russian artillery a very short distance away.

Once we reached Tempelhof airport, nothing was known about a Ju 52 of which Colonel von Below, Hitler's Luftwaffe adjutant, had spoken. The commander of the airport advised us to try to find a seat on the transport just announced from north Germany, which was supposed to be flying to Salzburg. We managed to do that after some negotiations.

Without our suitcases, just with a travelling bag and a rucksack packed at the last minute on the orders of SS Obergruppenführer Schaub, containing mostly round metal tins of Dallmann's Chocolate, the plane took off.

After take-off, which was made difficult by a shower of sleet, we arrived at Salzburg airport following an eventful flight over burning towns and villages at daybreak. The fear had been terrible, when noises that could only have been gunfire forced their way dully to our cotton-wool-stuffed ears, and the plane seemed to plummet. We sat in silence on the floor of the transport plane between soldiers we didn't know, on green-painted ammunition chests. I can't remember a single word being spoken. It was as if we were paralysed when we landed. The silence was suddenly oppressive.

A few hours later when we travelled by bus to the Obersalzberg, I was amazed even to have survived the flight alive.

*

**Ivan Litvin, b. 1924**                                   **near Artern, Thuringia**
I worked for three years to the day for the farmer Robert Bachmann in a little village. His other son was also called Robert, he was three or even four years younger than me. Just before the end of the war he was called up to the Wehrmacht. Soon I heard his mother saying her Robert was fighting somewhere in the west and if it came to it he would, thank God, be taken prisoner by the Americans. There

were three of us Ostarbeiter from the Ukraine on the farm. There had previously been two Frenchmen as well, but they were so demanding, they kept coming with new demands and letting everyone around them sense their bad mood. So Herr Bachmann had passed them on to a gardener in Sondershausen.

My compatriot Kolya Malashchuk was from Kiev and came from a highly intelligent family, he could even play the piano. He was a bit younger than me. Before the war he had been an athlete, so his body was very muscular. Working in a foreign land far from his beloved Kiev seemed unbearable to him. Every day he spoke in a choked voice about the Dniepr and Khreshchatyk [the main street in Kiev], he thought about it with longing, and was worth very little as a worker.

It was already mid-February 1945, I can't remember the exact date. We were to muck the field with Nikolai and clear it of stones. On the edge of the village our farmer had a neglected shaft into which we were to throw the stones that we had collected on the field. We were equipped with a wheelbarrow and a pickaxe in case the stones were too big. When we came to the shaft in the afternoon, Kolya took me by surprise and asked me to break his left forearm with the pickaxe. He had heard somewhere that forced labourers with such injuries were deported back home. And he couldn't bear it any more, he said, he wanted to go to Kiev, he had a premonition that he would soon lose his life, and he didn't want to die without casting one last glance at his beloved city and his house, where his piano stood covered in dust in a high-ceilinged room.

'Don't be such an idiot, man,' I said to him, 'the war will soon be over, yesterday I heard the farmer telling his wife that Russians were already at the Oder. First of all your Kiev is totally destroyed, Khreshchatyk is doubtless in ruins, and your piano will have been carried off to the dump long ago. And how do you imagine crossing the front in the east? Will the Germans book a plane for you, or what?'

But Nikolai refused to yield. If I didn't do him the favour, he would tell Herr Bachmann about all my crimes. He would inform him how many eggs I had secretly swallowed in the hen house when I was supposedly feeding the hens. He would show him the place where I had then hidden the eggshells. He certainly wouldn't pat me on the head for a piece of pilfering like that.

That was all I needed. The farmer trusted me. I ate with him and his wife at the same table in their dining room. They had recently taken me along when they visited the landlady's mother, and on that occasion I was allowed to put on a nearly new jacket belonging to her son. I didn't have to sleep in the barracks as Nikolai did, I slept in a room beside Herr Bachmann's bedroom, in a downy bed under a downy cover. And I was to lose that over a few stupid eggs? No, I wouldn't let that happen.

So we tipped the wheelbarrow over so that Nikolai could rest his arm on it, then we wrapped his arm in my vest so that the pick wouldn't leave traces on his skin, and I hit with all my strength. Kolya gave a brief shout, turned pale and lost consciousness. His arm quickly swelled up and turned dark blue. Then I dragged Nikolai to the shaft and threw another big stone on to his arm. Herr Bachmann had Nikolai driven to the hospital in Sondershausen. There his arm was put in plaster, and a few weeks later he was watering flowers at the flower-breeder's, along with the Frenchmen moved from the farm. I visited him there. He bore me no ill will, he was just concerned that he wouldn't be able to play the piano any more.

**A German soldier**                                        **(Rappenhof)**
Radiant spring day, the first cherry blossom. I'm sitting in my little study, reading Hans Carossa's *Secrets of the Mature Life*. Outside my window a Ukrainian soldier is digging our garden, and I have an uncomfortable feeling watching this man toiling for me as I sit here in idleness.

What are the causes of our fatal defeat? Was it only the disunity between political and military leadership that led to the crisis, and will there be another Versailles? Is it the triumph of Bolshevism, of evil over good? Or might we not be at a significant biological turning point in human development? Did ancient Rome in the century of its downfall not have an Aetius? Why should the biologically strong and fresh Slavic man not be intended as the inheritor of Europe? Did the Germanic peoples not seem like uncivilized barbarians to the Romans?

The fact that even now, before the end of the war, almighty England is completely under the heel of Moscow proves where the actual power is coming from. Our struggle is the last heroic rebellion against a remorseless destiny. England thought it might hold it in check through its alliance with the Russians. How soon it will be shaken awake from its error! Only America will be able to save its interests abroad from the war, but like England it will have to renounce all influence in Europe.

In East Asia there will be a new power struggle, in which America will play no part. The Germanic people are all advancing towards a biological 'Volkstod' [national death]. The growing Japanese people will collide with the equally growing Slavic one. Will the last representative of the white race then survive?

Bolshevism, now at the centre of the clash, is perhaps the means that the Russians are using in their power struggle. It is thinkable that in a higher stage of development it will collapse from within all by itself.

### Grete Dölker-Rehder, 1892–1946        Neumühle, Allgäu

Otto was just saying that someone – I don't know who – knows what Stalin, Roosevelt and Churchill decided about our fates at their last conference in Yalta in the Crimea: the Bolsheviks were to get all the land east of the Oder, the French the land to the left of the Rhine and Baden, and the British and the Americans would administer the rest between them. And of course they would take Austria and the Czech lands away from us. So in this fragmented entity there would be hardly anything left of the old Germany! And how we dreamed and raved about the Greater Germany with its 90 million, the thousand-year Third Reich! That was a brief joy… And yet the defeat is now so complete that we should be thankful to be alive at all. If the Americans were not as deeply inside Germany as the Russians, we would probably be entirely swallowed up by Bolshevism. One also has the impression that as fiercely as we fought in the east, so easy we will make it for the enemy in the west. […] Even our hasty retreat from France was probably not an attempt to flee the Americans, but a desire to let one enemy in to help us against an even bigger one. There is no remedy now for the unbearable bombings and destructions of German cities. Oh, if only a core of Germany is left, let us be grateful! If only our children and grandchildren are still allowed to live and work, then the German people will not die out completely, then its soul and its spirit will also resurrect from this gigantic death.

*

**Benito Mussolini, 1883–1945**                     **Palazzo Monforte, Milan**
*Interview*
   I've already told you. The Third World War will break out. Capitalist democracies against Bolshevist capitalism. Only our victory would have brought the world peace with justice. I was accused of tyranny, which I imposed on the Italians. How they will mourn it. And it will have to return, if the Italians want to be a nation again and not a bunch of slaves. And the Italians will want it. They yearn for it. The furious people will chase away the false leaders, the base little men who have submitted to foreign interests. They will carry flowers to the graves of the martyrs, the graves of those who have fallen for an idea, who will be the light and the hope of the world. Then they will say without flattery or falsehood: Mussolini was right.

**John Colville, 1915–87**                                       *London*
Before dinner the P.M. recorded, in my presence, a message which, with those of Stalin and President Truman [...], will be broadcast when the armies of Soviet Russia and the Western Allies link up. He [Churchill] then dined alone with Lady Lytton whom, he told me, he once nearly married.

**Wehrmacht report**
On the Lüneburg Heath, British troops continued their attacks on a wide front northwards.

*

*Spring*

When the earth's light shows itself once more,
The green vale gleams with spring rain and gaily
The white of blossoms down the bright stream,
After a cheerful day has bowed to humankind.

Visibility gains through bright contrasts,
The spring sky lingers with its peace,
That mankind views the year's charms undisturbed,
And heeds to life's perfection.

Your obedient servant
Scardanelli
15 March 1842

                                        Friedrich Hölderlin

<2,064 Days        Wednesday, 25 April 1945        13 Days>

> They shall be my people, and I will be
> their God: for they shall return unto
> me with their whole heart.
> DAILY READING: JEREMIAH 24:7

> Bringen sie uns speise
> Bringen zee oons spy za
> Bring us food
> *STARS AND STRIPES*,
> DAILY GERMAN LESSON

**First Naval Lieutenant Otto Westphalen, b. 1920   U968, Kolafjord**
Submerged, we travelled through the fjord and reached the open sea.
Our area of deployment was to be the Russian coast near Murmansk.
We travelled underwater along the Russian coast at periscope depth. As
darkness advanced we risked getting closer. But even though we were
submerged the coastguard must have spotted us, because suddenly
there was a lot of agitation on land. Lights went on, cars drove along
the coast road. Suddenly spotlights were scouring the water's surface.
But the commander had already downed the periscope, which meant
that we could no longer be seen by the Russians.

*

**Agnes Seib, teacher, 1901–83                    Brockhöfe, Kreis Uelzen**
In the afternoon almost everyone worked in the garden, in the glorious
weather. I helped plant beans and sow sweet peas, and then did some
ironing with Grandma Westermann's iron.

## Hans Carossa, 1878–1956                    Rittsteig, near Passau

On the afternoon of 25 April I left the garden, where the tulips were already bearing fat buds, and walked between green fields in an easterly direction, always with the city of Passau in front of my eyes. Children were standing around an older boy, holding one of last year's bird's nests in the palm of his hand. It looked as if it was woven through with silver, and this jewel consisted of those soft, thin threads of tin which were often scattered by enemy pilots to make German anti-aircraft gunners lose their bearings. The bird, with its eye for shiny things, probably some sort of finch, had woven the so-called 'chaff' into its wickerwork.

## Hildegard von Marchtaler, 1897–1995                    Hamburg

Went to the city in the morning, got hold of a veal shank from the butcher. Walked back via Rabenstrasse and Harvestehuder Weg. Gazing on the eternally beautiful silhouette of the city centre in the middle of the tender green of spring, infinitely nostalgic, one completely forgets that there is nothing else all around but doom, death and destruction. The pale pastel tones of the sunny April morning, the overwhelming magnificence of buds and blossoms, can't abide all that misery. We are still curiously calm here, even though the enemy are approaching our city in large numbers.

## Navy Lance Corporal Klaus Lohmann, 1910–2002     Travemünde

After a number of cold, wet days, it is now sunny and warmer again. The blossom in all the gardens is so beautiful! In the morning there's an air raid and I have the opportunity to enjoy the glory of the vicarage garden. In the evening I go alone, and stroll through the little forest – bleeding, the sun is going down – and there behind it is home!

Heard news later in the vicarage. The situation is getting stranger and stranger. If only the Russians weren't getting close. But God will also know what is right for us and our people. At any rate, we must *all* atone for the terrible crime that has occurred.

The Führer and his people are supposed to be in Berlin, encircled Berlin. Might that mean that the end is near?? Again and again the question also arises of whether and when the inevitable clash between

Russians and Anglo-Americans will come. Terrible prospects are opening up – there is in fact only *one* genuine reason for joy: the hope of God's coming kingdom.

**Cesare Pavese, 1908–50**                                    *Calabria*
Going one's way and coming across marvellous things, that is the great impulse – particularly yours.

*

**Major Joachim Schultz-Naumann, 1913–91     OKW, Neu Roofen**
The first meeting between the Soviets and the Americans took place at Torgau on the Elbe. Troops of the 58th Guard Division belonging to the Association of the 1st Ukrainian Army Group under Marshal Konev are assembling here with the 69th US Division under the orders of the 12th American Army Group of General Bradley.

**Winston Churchill, 1874–1965**                            *London*
PERSONAL AND SECRET MESSAGE
FROM MR CHURCHILL TO MARSHAL STALIN
   Thank you for both yours of April 23rd which I duly received.
   And thank you also for the greetings which you send from your brave armies to those of the western democracies who now join hands with you. I can assure you that we reciprocate these greetings.

**Strategy meeting**                          **Führerbunker, Berlin**
Hitler: The British and Americans are behaving calmly at the Elbe. They have probably agreed a kind of demarcation line. Things in Berlin look worse than they are. The area of Berlin must be exploited as far as possible. The 12th (Wenck) and the 9th Army (Busse) which form solid fronts in the west and east, must be drawn to Berlin. The divisions based in Berlin must be filled up from the population as soon as possible. Special units must be formed to round everyone up.

*

## General Walther von Seydlitz-Kurzbach, 1888–1976          *Lunowo*
*To Erich Weinert*

Dear President, Dear Herr Weinert

[...] I don't know if you know that there are lots of gentlemen here who have never seen Moscow. So we have a great wish – and perhaps you can fulfil this wish in the appropriate manner – for the prisoner-of-war camp administration to make two buses available for a journey through Moscow the day before 1 May, i.e. Monday, 30 April, so that we can view the city in its full May Day regalia. You would fulfil the most fervent yearnings of a great many men in the building.

## Lieutenant Alfred Schlenker, 1922–85          north of the Po

We poached three rabbits, which we are slowly – with mounting hunger each time – cooking in a canteen. With Po river water and dandelion leaves! It couldn't taste better to us if we were in the finest hotel!

So busy are we that we are even forgetting our necessary sleep. In order not to be surprised, we have transferred our camp to the dense riverside undergrowth, where gnats and mosquitoes won't leave us in peace.

## Albert L. Kotzebue, US lieutenant, d. 1987          *on the Elbe*

At nine o'clock, I took five jeeps east, leaving two jeeps behind to maintain radio contact with the Regiment.

Leaving Kühren that cold April morning, I had no orders to go further east. Instead, I was broadly interpreting my original instruction 'to contact the Russians'. Because there appeared to be no resistance between the Mulde and the Elbe, and since rumors had it that the Russians were so close, I thought that my patrol might as well go ahead and try to make contact. Besides, I had a special personal interest in the Russian people. One of my ancestors, the playwright August von Kotzebue, had been a court favorite of Russian Empress Catherine the Great. [...]

We passed through Lampertswalde, then across a series of country roads, and arrived in the tiny village of Leckwitz. Driving up the main street, I saw a lone horseman a few hundred yards away. He disappeared into a courtyard.

He looked strangely out of place. Was this it?

The jeeps spun around to the entrance of the courtyard. There – amid a ragged crowd of displaced persons – sat a Russian soldier on a horse. The time was 11:30 a.m.

This was the first reported contact between the armies of the United States and the Soviet Union.

The soldier was a cavalryman. He was quiet, reserved, unenthusiastic.

*

**Rachele Mussolini, 1892–1979**          **Villa Mantero, near Como**
We spent the day of 25 April alone. I was forced to buy a cooking stove, because absolutely everything was missing. It was said that there was no petrol for the rest of our journey, so I phoned police headquarters in Milan to speak to my husband. [...]

In the evening the news spread that Mussolini had arrived in Como. He immediately sent me about twenty loyal soldiers for our protection.

On the second night, when we wanted to go to sleep, some of the soldiers insisted on sleeping on the floor just outside our door to protect us, and we were touched by so much affection. At the urging of the children I lay down, but felt that I couldn't close an eye.

My torment was terrible.

**Vittorio Mussolini, 1916–97**          **Milan**
I saw my father alone for the last time on the afternoon of 25 April 1945 in his office, which had been in Milan police headquarters for a few days.

Over the past few months he had been in excellent health. The constant treatment by Dr Zacchariae, a nice old German doctor sent by Hitler in person, showed a degree of success that other doctors in better times never had. Both physically and intellectually my father was once again the strong-minded man of 1939.

**Luigi Meneghello, 1922–2007**          *Padua*
Extremely irritable, I went and joined the others under the arcades. There were three or four of us; we ran back and forth among the pillars,

zigzagged around each other and fired off a few shots for appearance's sake. When the Germans decided to come out of their cover, I thought: 'Here we go: time for the hand grenades. It's pointless anyway, but those chaps in there have deserved it.' But the Germans, a small group of gentlemen dressed in bluish green, had strangely enough raised their hands and left them up. Holy Mother of God! I'd never seen them like that before, I was quite startled. I saw a gang of armed civilians emerging from the right; I ran forward and was just in time to shout, 'Hey, quick, take charge of them,' before they disarmed them in any case.

**Klaus Mann, 1906–49**                                          *Rome*
Very busy: article *The great job in Germany* ('they don't understand'). (Got 'jabs' at Company HQ.)

*

**E. Taube**                                                            *Danzig*
Via the interpreters, Herr and Frau W[aldmann] from Riga, whom we had met at morning and evening prayers in the confirmation room, I learned a bit of Russian, and consequently got to know a few officers from the commandant's office. They were very good people, just like the commandant. The former was very humane when the requisitions were taking place. Our wing was spared along with some of the others, and I got a protection notice for my violin.

**Elsa Güttner**                                                      *Danzig*
After about 4 weeks we were able to return to our flats. What we saw was unholy chaos and great destruction. We couldn't get the kitchen door open at all. There lay the books, torn from their bindings, paper and ripped fragments all over the place. The dining room was exactly the same. All the glass in the pieces of furniture was shattered, great holes burned in the tabletops, the lamps pulled down, the hangings and curtains torn to pieces. The most horrible stench reached us from the bathroom. The air raid water had been left in the bathtub, and the Russians had used it, there's no other way of putting it, as a dung heap.

All the leftover food, old bread and even worse, had been thrown into it. There were clothes and bedlinen in there too.

But in spite of everything we were glad to be home again, and we started to tidy up as much as our strength allowed. I was lucky and found a few potatoes and pieces of coal in my cellar, which I shared with my neighbours.

### Elsa Kreisel, b. 1888                                                                                                 *Danzig*
A reaction to starvation and all the anxieties I had survived began. Both my feet and legs swelled up to high above the knee: it was water in the joints, there was nervous inflammation too, I couldn't take a step without violent pain. In the end my comrades from upstairs fetched help. The Polish doctor treated me kindly and with success.

Our hostess, who was over 70 years old, went exhaustedly to bed as soon as she got back. She had been suffering from open wounds on her legs, and had remained in safety in the Oliwa Church with her daughter. She thought – safety in God's protection. But in there she was raped by a young Russian, that was the last straw, now she stays in bed, resigned to this terrible world.

### Else Gloeden, 1913–95                                              *Gross Jenznick, Pomerania*
Our Pole didn't give me any work to do, so I'm to sow vegetables in the garden for a while. Alice has cooked something and we want to eat. Then two horse-riders come to the farm, I jump out of the window and hide, now here, now there, and soon I don't know what's what, I climb through the window into our kitchen. Then the Russian, probably the one who's always been pursuing me, comes up to the open window outside and tells me: he wants hay for horses. I point to our Pole, saying that he's the owner, but he insists: 'You show.' As soon as we've reached the stable, he grins at me and throws me with all his might into the dung in the stable, pulls my underwear off. It isn't going quickly enough for him, he uses his rifle-butt too. He's done it! I'm dizzy, a jolt inside, a rush of blood, I'm lying in a pool of blood. He jumps up, hits me with his rifle a number of times: 'German swine', and steps aside. He wipes the blood off himself and goes outside cursing.

*

**Flight Captain Hans Baur, 1897–1993**                    **(Berlin)**
Things looked bleak in the Reich Chancellery. Scraps of curtain blew
back and forth from the dark gaps in the window. All life had fled
from the huge rooms. Wilhelmsplatz and Vossstrasse had become a
theatre of war. The complex, about five hundred metres long, had an
underground level. […] It was possible to drive into the underground
parts in motor vehicles. In former times the trucks had gone down
there to bring coke. Now they were bringing the wounded – if they
were driving at all. Over the past few days about 600 wounded had
arrived, and between 900 and 1,000 civilians, women and children,
seeking refuge here after a crazy chase through Berlin.

Hitler lived in a bunker of his own. Here there were only a few
rooms for him, his servants, the doctor and his core staff.

**Traudl Junge, Hitler's secretary, 1920–2002**                    **Berlin**
After 23 April 1945 (the Russians had already reached the Reich capital)
he spoke only of the end and of downfall. He had terrible notions of
what the victors would do with Germany. According to his account
there wasn't a glimmer of hope for our people.

**General Helmuth Weidling, 1891–1955**                    **Berlin**
At 10.00 p.m. I arrived in the Reich Chancellery with the report on the
situation. The Führer was sitting back behind his table with the map.
The relatively small room was full of people. […]

In long, repetitive sentences, he [Hitler] set out the reasons that
forced him to remain in Berlin and either to win here or to go under. All
of his words expressed, in one way or another, only a single thought:
with the fall of Berlin, Germany's defeat will be beyond question. […]

I, a simple soldier, stood here in the place from which the fate of
the German people was once guided, and from which it was defined.
I began to understand some things. It became increasingly clear to me
why we had now to experience the end of Germany.

No one in the room dared to express his own opinion. Everything
that came from the Führer's mouth was received with complete

agreement. This was a group of courtiers without parallel. Or were they worried that they might be uprooted from this still-secure and privileged life if they voiced their own opinion?

Should I, a stranger, announce here in this circle, 'My Führer, this is madness! A big city like Berlin can't be defended with our forces and with the tiny amount of ammunition we have at our disposal. Bear in mind, my Führer, the boundless suffering that the population of Berlin will have to endure throughout these battles!'

I was so worked up that it took all my strength not to shout out these words.

**Strategy meeting**                                    **Führerbunker, Berlin**
Hitler: In Berlin General Weidling has central leadership, Colonel Kaether is his deputy. Some division staff are yet to come in. The units of military personnel are being sorted and bulked out so that we have divisions. Anyone still to come in will be incorporated into these divisions, so that proper order can be established.

*

**Anna Eleanor Roosevelt, 1884–1962**     *Hyde Park, near New York*
We came back to Hyde Park yesterday morning, just one week from the time we all gathered here for the committal service in our hedge-surrounded garden. My sons and I went to look at the grave. If two soldiers had not been on guard, and the beautiful orchids flown up from the South had not covered the spot where the sod had been put back so carefully, we would hardly have known that the lawn was not as it had always been.

Before very long, the simple stone which my husband described very carefully for us will be in place. But in the meantime the children and the dogs will be quite unconscious that here a short time ago a solemn military funeral was held, and they will think of it as a place where flowers grow and where the hedge protects them from the wind and makes the sun shine down more warmly. And that is as my husband would have it. He liked children and dogs and sunshine and flowers, and they are all around him now.

[...]

It was a wonderful day, but very windy and much colder than when we were here two weeks ago. We have had open fires in our living rooms all the afternoon and evening. But the house as a whole is very cold, and I don't dare turn up our heat because we have a very limited amount of oil.

[...]

Today our heavier tasks begin, as trucks arrive from Washington and things are unpacked and made available for the further business of settling an estate. I foresee that we have many long days of work in the big house before it is presentable for government visitors, and many long evenings ahead of us just opening and reading this incoming mail. Someday, however, we will actually find ourselves sitting down to read a book without that guilty feeling which weighs upon one when the job you should be doing is ignored.

*

### Ernst Jünger, 1895–1998 (Kirchhorst)

About perception. We enjoy aspects together and side by side of things which logically appear in sequence, as a chain. That struck me in the garden today, when I was looking at a deep, velvet-brown auricula with a yellow calyx. The peaceful enjoyment that it prompted was based on the fact that its colours radiate the gentle warmth of tamed and muted fire. Yellow was the hearth, brown its twilight. A scarlet rim around the yellow middle would probably have yielded a more vivid but more uneasy cheerfulness.

### Kurt Weill, 1900–1950 *Hotel Bel-Air, Los Angeles*
*To Lotte Lenya in New York*

And what does all of this mean when you bear in mind that the Russians are in Berlin, and if you look at the photograph that I enclose. This is what we've been waiting for, twelve years now. Isn't it fantastic how unprepared these Nazis were for defeat? Until the last moment they refused to believe that they could really be defeated – why else would they commit suicide in their thousands? I don't think a nation has ever been defeated more catastrophically. 'Twilight of the Gods' was always a romantic idea for these sick minds, and now that it's a reality they're too small to bear it. What stupidity! What cowardice! What a 'master race'! If we think of the courage, the pride, the confidence, that the English, the Dutch, the Russians and above all the Jews have shown in the hour of their defeat, it fills one with profound revulsion to observe this total breakdown of all human dignity. But stronger than this feeling of revulsion is the feeling of 'confidence in mankind' – at one of the great moments in history to see how capable the human spirit is of shaking off an illness, finding its way back to decency and overcoming the greatest threat to civilization and progress.

Now, as I write here, the sun has come out and a small blue bird is taking a bath in the stream outside my window – and life is beautiful.

**Thomas Mann, 1875–1955**          *Pacific Palisades, Los Angeles*
Written on XXVI. Haircut in Westwood. [...] Opening of the San Francisco conference today. Radio address by Truman from Washington. Mood pictures on the radio. Among the German suicides is the military commentator Lieutenant General Dittmar. Heavy bombing of Hitler's estate near Berchtesgaden, which was destroyed. If he was there, he may be dead. The Hamburg channel goes on to reassure its audience that the wretched man is at the battle front in Berlin, like the other members of the government (?). In that case they are trapped, because the city is entirely encircled and the airfields have probably been taken too. The Americans are firing on Regensburg, approaching Augsburg. German troops are surrendering to the Americans in great numbers for fear of the Russians. Pétain is on his way through Switzerland to France, to be put on trial.

*

**Thea Sternheim, 1883–1971**                              *Paris*
The sensation of the day: in Switzerland, Philippe Pétain declares himself prepared to appear before a French court.

The news produces a huge amount of excitement in circles hostile to Pétain. [...]

This reaction makes me think about the strange concept of justice that held the masses in a rage. I have certainly never felt any sympathy for Philippe Pétain – anyone who wears a uniform is suspect to me a priori – but that a Marshal of France who is accused of treason and God knows what should not even be allowed to defend himself, lest those who have got hold of the rudder be disturbed in their machinations, still strikes me as being only another step along the road to illegality.

The battle in Berlin rages on, and some of it, in hand-to-hand combat, is apparently being fought on the U-Bahn.

### Chobaut, archivist                                     *Avignon*

The French have crossed the Rhine north of Basle and taken Lörrach. Vissault de Coëtlogon, Breton separatist and member of the Waffen-SS, was executed in the fortress of Montrouge. The appeal against the death sentence in the case of Lucien Rotée, the former director of the intelligence service, was rejected. Carles, former prefect of the Northern Region, has poisoned himself. He was to appear before the court. Bollaert free.

### Léon Degrelle, Waffen-SS officer, 1906–94          **Prenzlau**

Prenzlau was an old city, the glory of its grand brick churches was set off by enchanting, narrow pointed arches.

As we were coming through the city on 25 April, the battle to the death was beginning. For several days the Soviet air force had been dropping bombs. Collapsed houses made travelling difficult. Exhausted civilians were fleeing in large groups.

Three thousand officers of the Belgian army had just left Prenzlau barracks, where they had been interned since the capitulation of 28 May 1940. They sweated and wheezed on the country road. Generals with red faces and skewed caps wiped their faces by the city moat or, like fat, breathless nannies, pushed in front of them prams on which they had packed all their luggage. Great athletic feats were not to be expected of them. The Russians would have them soon.

Our positions were a few kilometres north-west of Prenzlau.

I set up my headquarters in the castle at Holzendorf, which was aswarm with groaning refugees. Most of them had been evacuated eastwards from the Rhineland. Now the Russians assailed them from behind and drove them westwards, in the direction from which they had come.

The excitement was too much for them. Many of the women looked anxiously around. One of them drew three little children to her skirt. She was expecting a fourth child, and moved through this chaos with her enormous, rather pointed belly. In the evening she lost her mind. She lay flat on her back, wept, sobbed and refused all help.

Henceforth Flemish and Walloon volunteers were agreed on what the outcome would be.

**Naval Ensign Peter Meyer-Ranke, b. 1925**                    **Prenzlau**
On the morning of 25 April we were in Prenzlau, a morgue-like city that was occupied by the Russians two days later. We drove to the station straight away. The big military hospital had already been cleared and there was a military hospital train there, six cattle trucks and eight old third-class passenger carriages. The train should have set off the previous evening, but no engine had come.

Now we were loaded on last; Sanis, a doctor and a young Red Cross nurse doled out hot coffee, bread and red jam. I ended up in a compartment with five Flemish, who cursed 'Gott verdammich' [sic] at least once a sentence.

But we managed: I lay and slept like one of the young SS men in the luggage rack, two slept on the wooden benches and two on the floor. We had blankets thrown to us, then the train set off. The engine had finally arrived, it must have been around six in the morning.

**Erich Kuby, b. 1910**                    *Landerneau prisoner-of-war camp*
Two soldiers in German uniform came into the library and said in French: Do you speak French, sir?

Me: Yes, how can I help you?

Do you have any French reading matter?

A little, sadly nothing special. Are you French? Where from?

(One): From Brest.

(The other): From Rennes.

We were in the French legion against Russia, says one.

**Elias Canetti, 1905–94**                                          **(London)**
The defeat of nationalism lies not in internationalism, as many have
believed until now, because we speak languages. It lies in plurination-
alism.

*

**Grete Dölker-Rehder, 1892–1946**                    **Neumühle, Allgäu**
A lot of things are freely on sale in Wangen, they say. People have been
standing outside the shops since 2 in the morning.

The feeling of panic here has eased a lot. The big distribution of
cheese is over, and so is the selling off of stock. We have become calmer,
and are going about our daily work.

**Dieter Wellershoff, b. 1925**                      **Gollin, Schorfheide**
In the morning the regiment gathers in Gollin. Pigs that were left
behind in the sheds are slaughtered. A young girl sits in a house with
her sick mother. She refused to leave her. We move on. [...]

The regiment falls apart again, mingles with the scattered forces
from other troops. A soldier with a blood-red bandage walks beside
me for a while. Two of his fingers have been shot off. He tries to keep
up, but falls further and further behind. [...] I'm still carting a carbine
around with me. Many people have already thrown their weapons
away. Refugees are getting stuck in the sandy forest tracks with their
high-stacked horse-drawn carts, women and children, some old men.
'Soldiers, help us!' they beg. But it's pointless, and we move on. You
become a swine if what's at stake is your own life.

All of a sudden two riderless, saddled horses gallop across our path.
Are they Cossack horses?

**Martin Bergau, b. 1928**                          **March of Brandenburg**
We reached a more elevated crossroads and drove right into the arms
of the 'watchdogs'. Some SS men, standing beside a military utility
vehicle, demanded our papers. Terrified, the RAD warrant officer
produced the movement order, but that wasn't exactly what they
wanted. His whining and reference to the young age of his charges

didn't help. The 'watchdogs' had already apprehended about one hundred and twenty soldiers of all armed services branches, and wanted to set up a rear position. We joined them. One SS-Sturmführer said curtly, 'You're under my command now, and don't forget, I've got a long-range pistol.'

A lance corporal said in a broad Viennese dialect that sounded rather stupid, 'Lads, where are the German retreat roads?'

## Hugo Hartung, dramaturg, 1902–72                           Breslau

They bring a deserter to our command post. He is a Breslau mechanic, father of several children, trying to get away from defence duties, which became pointless a long time ago, and save himself for his family. The man has a good face and a decent attitude. But when the colonel asks him the reason for his action, he doesn't reply. He knows his fate is sealed. The hearing takes a nasty turn when we are joined by a young lieutenant who insults the young man in the most obnoxious terms and tells him bullets would be wasted on him. He should be stuffed in a latrine, covered with quicklime. In the evening the lieutenant comes back to the command post to check whether the deserter has been summarily executed.

*

## Albert L. Kotzebue, US lieutenant, d. 1987            *on the Elbe*

We drove at full speed to the road just north of Strehla which goes to the Elbe. Travelling down this road for several hundred yards, we spotted the river, then strained our eyes looking across it. I could see the remnants of a pontoon bridge and the wreckage of a column of vehicles on a road paralleling the east bank. [...]

I looked through my field glasses, and saw men in brown shirts. I knew they were Russians, because someone had once told me that Russians wore their medals into battle. Yes, these were Russians. The time was 12:05 p.m.

Turning to Pfc. [Private First Class] Ed Ruff, I told him to fire two green flares – the recognition signal which the American and Russian armies had previously agreed upon. The Americans were to fire green flares, the Russians red. Ruff's flares soared over the Elbe from the launcher attached to the end of his carbine. The Russians did not respond with red flares. Instead, all of them began walking from the road down to the river bank. I told ruff to fire another green flare, which he did.

**Petty Officer Schmied**                                        **near Torgau**
The two comrades wanted to go to the 'Yanks', who were supposed to be only a few kilometres away near Düben.

'No,' I said, 'don't, it would be desertion. It can only last another few days anyway. When we've been doing our duty for years, we don't want to betray our own people at the last moment. We'll report to the military commandant here and make sure that we find my battalion.'

Now we gave Dimmitzsch a wide berth and looked after our physical wellbeing. There were milk, eggs, bacon and bread wherever there were still farmers.

'We're happy to give it to you, because otherwise Ivan eats it all.'

We ate ourselves fat and round, and we also equipped ourselves with bread-bags, flasks and belts, and slowly we became soldiers again.

At about midday we found a box of tinned pork in the forest. A hole in the ground seemed to be the best place to have lunch, and each of us scarfed down two tins. For pudding we munched on some gingerbread, and then an opened cigar box was passed around.

**An unknown man, b. 1924**                                        **near Berlin**
I went into a forest, and there was a torn-off arm there, on a tree, with a sleeve still on it and an armband. On the armband it said 'Frundsberg'. There was no sign of a corpse. Perhaps the arm belonged to a wounded man that they took away.

*

**Erich Kessler, b. 1912**                        **(Theresienstadt concentration camp)**
Today we learned that Herr Dunant had come unexpectedly to the camp at the same time that the misery transports arrived. He said to camp commandant Rahm who was accompanying him, 'That's

terrible!' Rahm just said drily. 'You see, this is how people come to us.' As if he wanted to add, 'And I turn them back into human beings.' […]

The promise made by the Jewish Camp Elder that the new arrivals would not mean a reduction in rations quickly proved to be incorrect, since today the bread ration was universally fixed at 70 grams for 4 days. Among us workers, this means a 50% reduction. The quality of the food also leaves much to be desired. Last night's soup was very empty and thin. Small wonder, if the supplies from the package are quickly disappearing. In the afternoon I met an acquaintance who told me that half an hour previously a man had handed a woman a parcel over the wooden fence that divides the ghetto from the rest of the world, and gave her the message that the Allies have entered Berlin from three sides. Hitler himself has taken over the defence of the city.

**Alisah Shek, b. 1927**　　　　**Theresienstadt concentration camp**
Early, 250 women from Dresden. Afternoon, men from Dresden, Poland and Hungary, 'quite good'. Early to barrack building commandant's office. 40 are supposed to go. Where, they have known for four days now... Saw first punches thrown. Afternoon called off, the Germans take all the food away. And the details are flying back and forth, everyone knows, nobody knows. Only horror, horror, horror, I can't think any more, the same narcosis as in October. I only know now that I will wake up little by little. Every day a new pain comes, a new wound hurts. I pray it will soon be over, so that we do not wake up again.

**Strategy meeting**　　　　**Führerbunker, Berlin**
Hitler: South-west Germany is fragile. Even my influence from Berchtesgaden could not have prevented it. The defeatist mood was already there. The three men responsible are no longer alive. They have contaminated the whole western front from the start, a society debauched by affluence.

*

**Olga Gindina, 1902–66**                                        *Moscow*
*To her husband*

Dear Lasinka!

Many thanks for thinking of us and sending people. They've done the following: repaired the roof, fastened the rotten beam to the ceiling, plastered everything and painted both rooms. They painted all three windows, and the room door from inside. Apart from all that work, Ilyevsky took the stove half apart and cleaned it, changed the bricks, blocked all the holes with glue, and now everything's working terrifically well again. The second, Pyotr, made me two jugs from tins, and they've fixed the sofa. I was so grateful that I went on an outing with them at their request: first I showed them the centre, Red Square and so on, and then I showed them the most interesting stations (of the metro). I think they liked it.

For a few days our radio didn't work, and we heard the news of the march on Berlin at Vera Ivanovna's. But Ilyevsky sorted that out too, and the radio has been working since yesterday. There are only problems with the power. We have power for just 3–4 hours a day, then they turn it off again.

**Paul S., businessman**                            **Lienewitz, west Berlin**
*Letter diary*

Sensational news again today. There's no point relaying it all, as it's contradictory. That's enough now. All the people from every part of town are streaming into our forest and hiding like mortally wounded deer. We made our minds up too and are building a hut where you find yourself among the reeds after coming out of the kitchen around the back.

The hut is finished. Moving in with beds and all kinds of Gypsy comforts. Disguised with reeds. Roof of boards, watertight tent floors as walls. All under the thunder of the guns, anti-tank cannons, tanks, armour-piercing grenades, infantry fire, machine guns etc.

Goodnight, your Papi

**Gisela Grössel, b. 1933**                    **Ramhof, near Donauwörth**
We go into the forest, where the men have built a wooden bunker. The
grenades are whistling, and I'm scared. We aren't allowed to go home
until the evening. We sink into deep sleep.

**An unknown man**                              **Kaulsdorf, east Berlin**
We're sleeping in the rectory cellar. Luise on a chair. Me on a wire
children's bed frame. First we drink our last bottle of wine with Uncle
P. and Miss L. Soon afterwards the church warden and I carry the
corpse of a man who has just died into the church porch.

**Jacob Kronika, Danish journalist, 1897–1982**                 **Berlin**
St Francis's Day! Conference of a developing League of Nations? […]

We are in the immediate vicinity of the Zoo flak towers […], in the
middle of the Tiergarten fortress. The bunker is built on the edge of
the actual Tiergarten. It isn't far to the Landwehrkanal. Only a few
minutes to the Danish embassy. The Spanish embassy, the office of
Reich Minister Speer and the Swiss embassy are the bunker's closest
neighbours. The palaces of the Spanish and Swiss representations have
suffered heavy bombing.

We have to give shelter to a sixty-three-year-old fireman for a while;
he has been seriously wounded by bomb shrapnel. One of his arteries
has been hit. […]

We've agreed with the legation staff that some big Danish flags are
to be spread out on the roof of the embassy building, as the Russians
are flying their daytime raids at a very low altitude. This measure is to
be taken as soon as possible.

We have enough to eat and drink. That's a good thing in wartime
too! The Danish secretary of the prisoner-of-war aid organization,
Christian Christiansen, who is living with the Swedes, keeps us
supplied with English and American cigarettes.

Towards evening we have to seek shelter in the bunker for a few
hours. Bombs and grenades are raining down. We close all four steel
doors; each entrance has two. Even behind the thick walls you can hear
the noise from outside very clearly. When shrapnel hits the bunker it
sounds like metal striking a hollow steel body. In spite of everything

we feel completely safe. The bunker can survive all kinds of things, we know that. When we can open the door again at last, it turns out that a German munitions store has been hit. The ammunitions stored in the Tiergarten have been exploding for over an hour. It's a terrible racket.

Everything all around is on fire: in Schöneberg, Wilmersdorf, Charlottenburg and Moabit.

The Zoo flak seems less frequent. Will ammunition have to be stored?

*

### Dr Meerfeld                                                    Gönningen
On Wednesday, 25 April, the Frenchman Gaston left us having worked as a butcher with Herr Anstätt for five years, a very decent man who plainly found it very difficult to be parted from his family. He was taken back to France on a collective transport.

### Ursula von Kardorff, 1911–88          Günzburg, Danue
We were sitting in Bürklin under a blossoming apple tree in the sun, a radiant blue sky above us. Around us artillery explosions, grenade launchers – the last scenes of a terrible drama. So we talked about completely different things. He put a flower in my hair. Then the shooting became more violent, a squadron of fighter bombers circled above 'Jettingen Fortress', artillery crashes over in Wetzel's Forest.

### Marie 'Missie' Vassiltchikov, 1917–78          Gmunden, Austria
A sunny day at last. We tried to tan ourselves on the terrace a little. In the afternoon we took a long cycle trip around the lake. When we were sitting by the shore, we suddenly felt as if the mountains all around were rumbling and shaking. There must have been an air raid somewhere, but we couldn't work out where. It seemed so close, and yet we saw no aircraft. On the way home we heard that the attack had been on Berchtesgaden this time, about fifty kilometres away. It had only sounded so close because of the echo. Sita Wrede told us the details later over the phone. She called Berchtesgaden the 'rock'.

**Christa Schroeder, Hitler's secretary, 1908–84**              **Berghof, Obersalzberg**

Wednesday, 25 April, was a spring day with a radiant blue sky. There was still a bit of snow on the ground, but it wasn't cold any more. I'd booked myself in at Bernhardt the hairdresser in Platterhof for 10 o'clock on the morning. [...] At about 10 o'clock the pre-alarm sirens suddenly went off again. Immediately after that the sirens announced an acute threat from the air, and already American bombers were flying in over the high Göll. At that moment a bomb fell very close by. I only had time to grab my handbag, put on a coat and dash to Johanna Wolf's room (she had recently come back from a visit to her mother in Wessobrunn). I called out, 'Come quickly, bombs are falling!' Without waiting I ran down the stairs of the old building in Berghof, or rather I was driven forward by the blast rather than actually running to the entrance to the bunker, and had only a few metres of courtyard left to cross, the 60 steps up to the bunker. [...]

The bombs fell without interruption, some directly on to the bunker. The explosion echoed terribly around the cliffs, it was uncanny. With every fresh bang I hunched my shoulders. The technical equipment of the bunker facilities, praised as so safe, failed. The light and the air supply packed in. Water forced its way into the bunker and came down the steps. We were worried that Frau Fegelein, who was very pregnant, might give birth prematurely. The chaos and fear were indescribable.

At about half past two in the afternoon we were finally able to leave the bunker. We slowly climbed the long steps into the daylight. What we encountered was a picture of the most terrible devastation. The Berghof was seriously damaged. The walls were still standing (only one side was shattered), the iron roof hung down in scraps. There were no doors or windows left. In the house the floor was covered with a thick layer of debris, and most of the furniture was in pieces. All the adjacent buildings were destroyed, the paths were piled with rubble and the trees had been felled. There was nothing green to be seen, it was a landscape of craters.

**Strategy meeting**                                    **Führerbunker, Berlin**

Hitler: I can only achieve one success here. If I achieve a success, even
if it is only a moral success, it is at least the chance of saving face and
gaining time. I know one thing: there is absolutely no point sitting in
the south, because I have no influence there, and no army. I would only
be there with my staff. I could only hold a South German–Austrian
mountain range if Italy could also be claimed as a theatre of war. But
even there complete defeatism prevails among the leadership, which is
consumed from the top down.

Goebbels: We can achieve a moral global success in Berlin. This
success can only be achieved at this one point on which the eyes of
the whole world are focused. The fact that the Soviets are moving into
Brandenburg will be received with no less regret than their having
overrun Berlin. But if they are beaten back before Berlin, that would
be a reason for a big success in the eyes of the world.

*

**Alexander Gordiev, Soviet officer**                          *on the Elbe*

I went with my deputies Yakov Koslov, Tossoltan Bitarov and Vladimir
Lyssov to the ferry landing stage, where the Americans were. These
were a patrol of the 273rd Infantry Regiment of the 69th Infantry
Division under Lieutenant Albert Kotzebue. It wasn't long before
many of our soldiers and officers had joined us.

We were all very excited. The American soldiers respectfully studied
our guard badges, orders and medals, asked about their meaning and
wanted to know what the red and yellow braids on our field tunics
were. When they found out that they were wound badges, they were
very impressed by the heroism of our soldiers.

On lengths of tarpaulin spread out on the meadow, Russian vodka
and a simple lunch were served. Then the American soldiers and
ours exchanged toasts – that there should never be another war, to
friendship sealed in battle against a common enemy, to peace. The
American soldier Joseph Polowsky, deputy to the patrol commander,
was particularly cordial and enthusiastic. He thanked the Soviet
soldiers for the battle that they had waged against Fascism. He spoke

German, and his words were translated by our interpreter.

Polowsky asked me to give him my photograph as a souvenir. Unfortunately I didn't have one. Chief Lieutenant Yakov Koslov helped me out of my embarrassment with a photograph of our regimental commanders. I wrote a dedication on it and handed it to the affable American.

**Joseph Polowsky, US soldier**                *near Strehla, on the Elbe*
Would you believe it? There was a tremendous burst of lilacs as we approached the Elbe River. This exaltation of being alive, after all those days trapped in a trench war. There were even jokes that we were approaching the river Jordan, crossing into Canaan. [...] We also knew that the United Nations was being born in San Francisco on the very same day, the 25th of April. Can you imagine? The very day we linked up with the Russians at the Elbe River. [...]

The Elbe is a swift-running river, about a hundred and seventy-five yards wide. [...] Fifty yards on each side of the river was literally covered with bodies – of women, old men, children. I still remember seeing a little girl clutching a doll in one hand – it was right there. She couldn't have been more than five or six years old. And her mother's hand in the other. They were all piled up like cordwood at the bank.

[...]

At this historic moment of the meeting of nations, all of the soldiers present – ordinary soldiers, Americans and Russians – solemnly swore that they would do everything in their power to prevent such things from ever happening in the world again. We pledged that the nations of the world would and must live at peace. This was our Oath of the Elbe.

It was a very informal, but solemn moment. There were tears in the eyes of most of us. Perhaps a sense of foreboding that things might not be as perfect in the future as we anticipated. We embraced. We swore never to forget. [...]

I was so captivated by the event that it took possession of me for the rest of my life. It has coloured my life.

**Photo-journalist Allan Jackson (d. 1995)**                    *Torgau*

Because all the bridges were blown, Ann and I crossed the Elbe in a beat-up rowboat that was once apparently a racing shell of some sort. We found a full-blown party in progress on the Russian side of the river. Vodka was flowing, and there was lots of food set up on the tables in an old building. We met a number of American soldiers and low-ranking officers, but no top brass and – most important to us – no other correspondents. There were lots of Russian soldiers wearing different types of uniforms and carrying a variety of weapons. All of them were very friendly, but the language barrier made conversation difficult. Most talk was carried on in broken German.

I decided that the best way to represent the link-up would be to have a number of American and Russian soldiers stretch their hands towards each other on one of the broken bridges. With the help of a French-speaking Russian soldier who was some sort of official press representative, I rounded up a few Russian and American soldiers to go out on the bridge. I explained what I wanted, and coached them on the action I planned for my photograph ('Don't look at the camera!'). I made several shots of the action, trying for angles of faces that did not look directly into the lens.

Two days later – on April 28 – my photos hit the front page of the major London newspapers. It was, the *News Chronicle* reported, 'a picture the world will never forget.' That same day, it was on the front page of the *New York Times* and many other American newspapers. Through the years, my picture of the American and Russian soldiers shaking hands at Torgau has been called the second best-known photograph of World War II. Only Joe Rosenthal's flag-raising photo on Iwo Jima is better known.

**Michael Wieck, b. 1928**                    *Rothenstein camp*

The state we're in is like torture, and absolutely unbearable. But look, something's happening. When another unit turns up at the cellar, they drag us out and put us with the others. The cellar is long and labyrinthine. The sentry stops by one of the cellar doors and at least eighty of us are brought into an empty basement room, in which we have just enough space standing upright for the cellar door, which opens inwards, to be closed again. Then here we are in a cellar that has only two windows, and these are shatter protected. That means: the windows just below the ceiling of the cellar are walled up and have only two air slits, which isn't nearly enough to air a room crammed with so many people. We stand helplessly around for a while, then some people start sitting down on the floor, which in turn means that other people have no room. Gradually a tussle breaks out, shouting and cursing. Everybody is fighting, pushing and shoving for a patch of floor. But that's not going to be possible unless we all lie on top of each other. We would hit each other too, if exhaustion and paralysing resignation hadn't taken the upper hand. We feel like cattle ready for the slaughter, crammed into trucks, destined for death. Our pigsty might have been dirty, but it's a steerage cabin in comparison. Anyone who falls asleep now soon gets a rude awakening. Arms, legs, heads and even torsos lie on top of you, and it's not easy to shake these burdens off again. Anyone who goes to sleep ends up on the bottom layer, and anyone who's awake struggles to the top. The lack of oxygen becomes increasingly unbearable. Someone has some matches, and as this cellar is also completely dark, he lights one. Apart from the sulphurous head, the matches don't burn, the lack of oxygen is already so bad. And then there's the metal canister, that yellow jam bucket, that serves as a toilet. You can't get to it, and if you do, it's being hogged by some long-term shitter, as they're known. There isn't enough capacity and it runs over on the first day. A man coughs beside me, repeatedly trying to cough away from me. He's pretty well finished, but he's touchingly concerned about me, and puts up with me lying on top of him most of the time. 'Man, just stay away from me!' he says now and again, in broad East Prussian.

Only once a day, sometimes twice, are we able to leave the cellar. Then we're led under guard to some scrubby ground near the barbed-wire fence. There we're supposed to 'do it' in shallow dips, which takes some learning. You have to get quite close to the edge of the dip without falling in. The unfamiliar oxygen makes us dizzy, and we have no paper, nothing to hold on to, no coat hook.

On the way back we see a heap of piled-up corpses. They are lying by the barracks wall. The next day they've gone, and the day after there's an even bigger heap. You die, and the Russians don't mind. On the contrary.

One morning there's water to drink. It's unboiled water from the upper pond, which they distribute from a tub. The water is so cloudy that you can hardly see the bottom of the tub. I refuse to drink the water, but soak my stripped-off vest and put it on my face. It acts as a refreshing air filter. I also notice that the air is a bit better quite close to the floor. A fresh draught comes in under the door. Soup kitchen in the afternoon. I take soup for my two neighbours who have no vessels. The nice coughing man that I'm mostly lying against refuses my offer to share the soup with him. He confides in me that he's got tuberculosis and is very worried about me. I pour soup into his cupped hand, he can sip it like that. Every few moments a Russian comes to the cellar door and yells various names that he can't read or pronounce properly. Hans Gohngheim for Hans Hohnheim, and so on. Every now and again the name called out belongs to one of us. In the hope of being released from this hell, he happily follows him. After a few hours he comes back, beaten bloody, no longer in a state to speak; a jaw seems to have been broken, an eye is swollen. The next one whose name is called out goes along with a heavy heart, never to appear again. Another one comes back unharmed. Just as the powerful people want. It's particularly terrible at night. People are constantly being taken for questioning. Because a lot of people are sleeping, they shout and shine dazzling spotlights into the cellar. They want to be sure that no one's sleeping and won't hear them. And because that doesn't help either, everyone always has to get up from the floor when names are being read out. We also hear the summons at the other cellar doors. An additional torture if it's repeated ten to twenty times. Of course my name can't be read out because I'm not on any kind of list. So I imagine that I'll be in this hellhole for ever.

*

**William J. Fox, US war reporter**                                   *on the Elbe*
The dawn was still young, the air cold as six jeeps from E and H Companies rendezvoused with the other two jeeps. The first was the

radio jeep from Regiment headquarters, the second from V Corps. [...]

The patrol followed a circuitous, sweeping route up and down side roads and main roads through Gornewitz, Denwitz, and Fremdiswalde to Roda. Approaching each town, we slowed down and cautiously reconnoitred before driving in. Small, peasant communities, these towns were for the most part still asleep when our jeeps passed through. Other American patrols had already scouted some of these villages; desultory white flags hung from most of the houses. Here and there, an inquisitive youngster stuck his head out of an upstairs window. Small groups of impassive villagers watched the Americans move silently through the streets. There was no resistance. It was an unreal silence. On that early April morning, war seemed far away in these gray houses and on the lonely, winding roads.

The weather remained cold, the mist persisted. The patrol advanced slowly, carefully, alert to everything around it. After leaving Roda, Maj. Craig decided to go into Wermsdorf. From the distance, we could see a huge red cross glistening from the roof of what appeared to be a big hospital in the town.

We reached Wermsdorf at 9:15 a.m. Driving into the main portion of town, some elements of the patrol went directly to the hospital, while others searched out the area. A number of French, Belgian, Russian and Polish slave laborers who had been turned into farm workers showed up. Eager to help us, they pointed out German soldiers in hiding. [...]

At around 11:00 a.m., the patrol pulled out of Wermsdorf and headed up through the central wood which joins the Forsten Wermsdorf and Hubertusberg. Our column went into the forest and stopped at its northern fringe. There we took an entire German sanitary company without trouble. But this caused further delay. By this time, many of us were feeling increasingly eager to meet the Russian forces as soon as possible. [...]

At three o'clock the jeeps moved out of Calbitz. All along the route were streams of freed slave laborers and Allied POWs. Some were drunk, others looting. All waved at us and saluted and cheered. They were the flotsam of Europe at that moment – and they were free. Caught in the cataclysm were a number of German civilians who had panicked in the face of defeat. They were on the road in carts, wagons, sulkies, and in anything else which could carry them. They were fleeing – the very old and the very young, the sick and the crippled. They had been caught in the whirlpool of their own nation's collapse, and had now started to join the other wanderers of Europe.

Sometime around four o'clock, the patrol headed for Terpitz. Not far from the Elbe River we stopped on a hilltop to survey the area. We thought we might be able to see the Russian bridgehead from here.

Everyone was suddenly filled with excitement. Through field glasses, we could see several columns of troops moving north over the gentle hill beyond Liebschütz. We questioned a couple of German soldier strays. The troops were German, not Russian, retreating to the north.

We moved east into Clazschwitz. By then, the roads were very dusty. The air had grown warm, though there was still a chill wind. Moving through the village, the patrol was overtaken by several speeding jeeps. The column halted. The men in the jeeps were from Lt. Kotzebue's patrol. They conveyed the startling news that Kotzebue had made first contact with the Russians in the morning, that he was now on the east bank of the Elbe – not far away.

Craig immediately gave the signal to take off. The jeeps leaped forward, speeding out of town, heading for Leckwitz and the Elbe. After all the jeeps had cleared the last house and the lead vehicle was about 150 miles east of the city limits, the column ground to a halt in a typhoon of dust. Everyone looked to his right with an open-mouthed stare. There, on the tree-lined parallel road leading from Zausswitz, was a column of horsemen moving west. One word came from every amazed mouth: 'Russians!'

The horsemen apparently saw the jeeps at the same time, for they wheeled to their right and started galloping toward the Americans. Among the cavalrymen were several soldiers on bicycles and motor-cycles. All of us piled out of our jeeps. Time stood still as the first Russian approached.

'I thought the first guy would never get there,' one GI later told me. 'My eyes were glued to his bike. He seemed to get bigger and bigger as he came slower and slower toward us. He reached a point a few yards away, tumbled off his bike, saluted, grinned, and stuck out his hand. Then they all arrived.'

This was the contact. The time was 4:45 p.m. The sun was waning. The day was clear. Everyone grinned. No one could think of anything to say. The Americans said, '*Amerikanski*', the Russians said, '*Russki*'. That was it. It was an historic moment, and everyone knew it. But no one was able to say anything memorable. [...]

When the civilities were finished, the Russians offered to take us to an Allied POW camp which had been liberated several days earlier. [...] When the jeeps rolled into the entrance of the camp, it was almost dark, but not too dark to conceal the fact that we were Americans. The reaction was like a tidal wave. The first amazed onlookers exclaimed, 'My God! Yanks!' As the jeeps made their way along the streets of the camp, the welcome rose – then roared like thunder. Americans, Britons, French, Yugoslavs, Allied officers and enlisted men of all nations cheered us, screaming and crying their joy. [...] They were eager just to say hello and shake hands and simply touch these men from the States.

**Ernst-Günther Henken, private soldier, b. 1921**    **Rheinsberg**
Last night bumped into the company, of which only about 50 are left. The front is getting closer again. The Führer is in Berlin, which is apparently encircled.

In Rheinsberg I saw SS 'Heini' Himmler.

**Dr Felix Kersten, 1898–1960**    *Stockholm*
Yesterday and today discussions with His Excellency Günther. I reported that we had renewed negotiations with Himmler with a view to avoiding a Scandinavian war and bringing about the capitulation of the German associations in Norway. At Günther's request I confirmed that in writing.

I also informed him of Himmler's wish to suspend hostilities towards the west, but to continue them against the Soviets. Günther said it would have been impossible for Bernadotte to drive to headquarters, the communication must have come through the Swedish Foreign Ministry.

Later I learned that because of the orders I issued the situation had eased in all significant respects, a war in Scandinavia had been avoided and later discussions and technical developments could be carried out successfully by other offices and individuals.

### John Colville, 1915–87                                      *London*
Returned to find a telegram from Stockholm reporting Himmler's wish to surrender to the Western Allies and Hitler is moribund with cerebral haemorrhage. This may be a last-minute attempt to separate us from the Russians but the P.M. immediately summoned a meeting of the Cabinet and the C.O.S. and sent the whole story on to Stalin. At any rate it shows that, as the P.M. said to me, 'they are done'.

### Winston Churchill, 1874–1965                                *London*
There can be no question as far as His Majesty's Government is concerned of anything less than unconditional surrender simultaneously to the three major Powers. We consider Himmler should be told that German forces, either as individuals or in units, should everywhere surrender themselves to the Allied troops or representatives on the spot. Until this happens the attack of the Allies upon them and on all sides and in all theatres where resistance continues will be prosecuted with the utmost vigour.

Nothing in the above telegram should affect the release of our orations on the link-up.

### Joseph Stalin, 1879–1953                                    *Moscow*
PERSONAL AND SECRET MESSAGE
TO PRIME MINISTER MR WINSTON CHURCHILL

Many thanks for your message of 25 April concerning Himmler's intention to capitulate on the western front.

I consider your proposal to confront Himmler with the demand for unconditional capitulation on all fronts, including the Soviet, to be the only right one. As I know you well, I have never doubted that you would act in precisely that way. Please act in the spirit of your proposal, and where the Red Army is concerned, it will continue to advance on Berlin in the interest of our common cause.

**Strategy meeting**                                    **Führerbunker, Berlin**

Hitler: If this is really true, I have received a message that the discussions between Eden and Molotov have apparently yielded no compromise. The Russians are demanding the entire territory. That would mean total defeat for England. England began this war because I demanded: a corridor to East Prussia and Danzig with a vote under Allied control. And now they are to allow a power which already practically controls the whole of Europe and extends all the way to East Asia to advance still further?

*

**Renata Laqueur, b. 1919**                   *transport from Bergen-Belsen,*
                                              *Niederlausitz concentration camp*

At half-past five the next morning I was up again and wanted to get organized. We had nothing left. On my way back to the car, having forgotten something, I heard excited discussions and loud, joyful cries. A woman came towards me, gesticulating violently, and told me breathlessly about the arrival of the Russians. The people in charge of the German transport had been taken prisoner, and nothing more was known.

I couldn't believe it, too often J.P.A. ['Jewish Press Agency', the slang term used by inmates for rumours circulating within the camp] had fooled us with 'safe' reports. I needed to see for myself. I ran along the tracks until I reached the street, where a soldier stood about a hundred metres away. I hesitantly ran on, recognized a grey-green uniform, a long coat, a rifle – nothing special. Then he must have heard my footsteps. He turned to me, I saw his face, his cap and the red stern. It was true! [...]

In the village, Tröbitz, an incredible chaos prevailed. Now there was no doubt, Russian soldiers everywhere, Russian vehicles, and a column of heavy tanks roared down the main street. The Russians had reached the village at 2 o'clock in the morning, and the mayor had been sensible enough to hand it over without a fight. But the Germans remained fearfully in their hiding places. Suddenly I felt intense pangs of hunger again, and at that moment I understood what it meant for us to be 'free'. [...] I went into a house and found the inhabitants sitting in the kitchen, huddled together, a mother with four children and a grandmother. And aunts and nieces who had been evacuated here from the Ruhr. It was pleasantly warm in the crowded room, a pot of coffee steamed on the little table. I inhaled that aroma that I had missed for so long. I asked for a cup, asked for bread. I was given black coffee, and thick slices of bread with bacon on it. No one said anything. But they didn't want to get the bacon out quite so readily, because when I sat down and waited for the bread, the woman began to wail: 'We ourselves have nothing. The Soviets took everything during the night.' I knew she was lying. Because the army didn't need her bread, so I said in a resolute, firm voice, 'Give me bread with a lot of butter, and be quick about it.' It took just under a minute. I ate, quite calmly, until I was full, but said nothing more. My eyes fell through the kitchen window on to the village square. I saw a fountain and in the background the church tower. The mother stroked her child's hair and wailed, 'You see, now they're coming, now they will set fire to the church and we will all go up in flames. Children, hurry to the cellar. They're coming!'

For me that was the first example of how omnipresent the Goebbels propaganda still was – even after liberation. 'The Russians set all the churches on fire and murder woman and children.' The Germans in Tröbitz firmly believed it.

*

**Natalya Krishanovskaya, b. 1909**                    *Soviet Union*
*To her husband*

Dear Vitusik!

Today is a very special day: we heard on the radio that our troops have advanced on Berlin from the east and the south. This joyful news unleashed such excitement among us that I can't describe it! Pride, enthusiasm, the anticipation of seeing our loved ones again – those were the feelings that gripped us all... Berlin – that is, the lair of the Fascist monster – is on the brink of total destruction!

My dear Vitusik, I am sure that this postcard will reach you only after the end of the war, after the complete capitulation of the Fascist monster of Germany, and that this will happen in the next few days, is my firm conviction! See you very soon, my dearest one!!! We kiss you very, very warmly, Your Natalka, the Mamas and the children.

I await your letters. N.

**Boris Gindin, Red Army soldier, 1926–45**                         *Czechoslovakia*
*To his mother, Olga Gindina*

Dear Mama!

I am in a dense spruce forest. It has become rather cold, though we are just a little further north now. I have just had some hot tea: that warmed me up a bit. It has been sleeting since morning. I am looking at more or less the same scene as the one in the song, you know, that waltz, 'In the forest near the front'. The latest papers have been brought. They include some extraordinarily interesting stories. The troops of Marshals Zhukov and Konev have made it all the way to Berlin. They are fighting fiercely. And so are our Allies. I don't understand why the German is still baring his teeth. No matter, soon we will deal him the coup de grâce.

Goodbye. Greetings to all, all, all.

**Boris Bayanov, Red Army soldier**                         *outside Berlin*
*To his wife*

My dear Asko!

I drove through the hinterland of Berlin, everywhere you see the consequences of fierce battles, trenches, anti-tank ditches, burnt-out tanks, weapons left behind by the Germans. The region is beautiful, there are pine forests, lots of lakes and near them villages with weekend cottages. Nature is always nature. But in spite of the joy of victory one remains tangibly aware that one is on foreign soil, and one thinks with longing of our region around Moscow, which is so very dear to us.

I send you, my love, greetings from the hinterland of Berlin.

Greetings to our little daughters.

I kiss you

Boris

**Georgy Zhukov, Soviet general, 1896–1974**          *outside Berlin*
On 25 April the battles in the inner city become increasingly intense.
The enemy, supported by strong defences, put up a stubborn resistance.

Our troops had severe losses, but they went on enthusiastically
pushing forward towards the centre of Berlin, where Fascist supreme
command was still based. We could tell that this was the case from
listening to Hitler's speeches on the radio, hysterically ordering his
armies to relieve Berlin, unaware that those armies had already been
defeated by the 1st Byelorussian and the 1st Ukrainian Front.

**Alexander Vishnevsky, Soviet field surgeon**          *Ussuriysk*
In the morning I went to the Medical Administration, where Pesis
told me that lots of medicine had arrived, including about 5 tonnes of
glucose and 200 kilograms of novocaine. According to his calculations,
we should expect two hundred thousand casualties. It was reported
on the radio that the troops of Marshals Zhukov and Konev were
waging street battles in Berlin. Yes, I could be more useful there than
here.

*

**Martin Bormann, 1900–1945**          **Berlin**
Göring thrown out of the party!
First major attack on the Obersalzberg.
*Berlin encircled!*

**SS-Sturmbannführer**
**Erich Kempka, 1910–75**          **Führerbunker, Berlin**
A telegram from Göring arrived from the Obersalzberg. With great
fury we heard what it said, which was more or less the following: 'Since
you, my Führer, determined that I would be your successor should
you no longer be capable of continuing government business because
of death or other circumstances, I consider that the time has now come
to take up my office as successor. If I have received no answer from
you by 26 April 1945, 24.00 hours, I shall assume that you agree with
my demands, sig. Göring.'

In the small circle in which this telegram was known, its effect was greater than the impact of a bomb. [...]

Explaining that he was working on behalf of Adolf Hitler, Bormann gave the following wireless message to Göring: 'Your intention to take over the running of state is high treason. Traitors are punished by death. Bearing in mind the merits that you have acquired over your work for party and state over the years, the Führer wants to refrain from resorting to the death penalty, but demands that you resign immediately, on the grounds that because of your illness you are no longer in a position to undertake the deals transferred to you, signed Bormann.'

### Rittmeister Gerhardt Boldt, 1918–81          Führerbunker, Berlin

This message struck Hitler like a blow from a club. At first he wept like a child, then he raged like a man possessed. In his eyes it was an outrageous defection. He also saw the telegram as an ultimatum. [...]

Hitler's rage spread to the whole of the bunker. Goebbels too was seething with fury, and voiced his feeling in a torrent of words, whose swollen phrases of honour, fidelity, death, blood, honour, you, my Führer, to you, my Führer, and honour once again, was poor at hiding the envy that Göring was about to take his head out of the noose.

### Flight Captain Hans Baur, 1897–1993                    (Berlin)

Tempelhof was lost on 22 April, so all we had left was Gatow airfield. On 25 April, the planes departed for Munich and Salzburg for the last time. They took off at 2 o'clock in the morning to arrive before the light of the new day. Only Major Gundelfinger was unable to set off because some passengers were still missing. When he was in the air at last, he worked out that he would have to fly for about fifty minutes in sunlight. During the night or in the morning hours we had landing reports from all the planes except Gundelfinger's.

Hitler: 'I entrusted important files and papers to him, which are to grant posterity testimony of my actions.' Hitler was unable to calm himself for a long time, the loss seemed to cut him to the quick.

**Frau Henschel**                                          **Gatow airfield**
Just before we boarded our plane – the first three aeroplanes had already
taken off – there was an incident. Workers who were transporting our
luggage by torchlight started yelling about the 'Reich Chancellery
bosses', then they started abusing us and looted the suitcases. It was an
hour before order could be re-established and we were able to take off.

\*

**Lieutenant Erich Weitzsch, b. 1920**                         **Courland**
We are facing the 8th Battle of Courland and are ready to fight – and
so, doubtless, is the enemy. Supplies have continued to cross the Baltic
unimpeded. Everything's available here: provisions, ammunition, fuel,
weapons. The units are even working well together again. We're sure
that we'll fight down the enemy again in the 8th Battle of Courland. At
the same time, however, I have the vague feeling that whatever happens
it could be the last Battle of Courland. The whole arc of the front has
been shortened again.

Will it all not be over soon? Perhaps the enemy's waiting for further
advances on the other fronts. They've been hesitantly following the
shortening of the front line.

There is still talk of a ceasefire with the western powers. But it seems
to me all desperate situations provoke wishful thinking.

**Lieutenant Harro Ketels, b. 1915**                          **Courland**
They've published a lecture by Professor Baumgarten on 'The True
Future of Europe' as a special edition for commanders. B. holds the
chair in philosophy at Königsberg University, and delivered this lecture
recently when the Russians were already outside the city. It contains
an essential contribution to the understanding of our time. He forced
me to rethink a few things. National Socialism and Bolshevism have
much in common.

**Dr Arnold Schön, corvette captain**                         **Pillau**
When the front line was getting closer and closer and it was plain that
Pillau was going to fall the rest of the navy staff moved to Neutief. I

was ordered to leave the citadel on 24 April at 23.00 hours, and march with the rest of our company, 80 men, to the Hinterhafen, where a ship was to pick us up from the navy equipment office. We waited for hour after hour, but no one called, and no ship arrived. At last it was 3.00. The artillery fire on the railway area behind us gradually increased. The Russians had forced their way into the zone of the Hinterhafen from Camstigall; the houses on the Russendamm were ablaze, a sea of flames that lit up the whole district. It turned 4.00, and no ship came to pick us up. From the Russendamm and across the Hinterhafen we were already being fired at by machine guns. The artillery fire on the railway facilities and the Holzwiese continued to intensify. Then I decided to push through to the Vorhafen with my company, in the hope that there was another ship there. Individually, or in small groups, creeping on after every hit, we managed to get across the Holzwiese and the Hindenburg Bridge, past Consul Janzen's blazing house, across the rubble of the buildings on Königsbergerstrasse (Sparkasse, Strahlendorff), and on the market (Wendes's house), down Lizen-strasse, on which every building, from the 'Deutsches Haus' to the 'Kurfürstlicher Hof', had been hit by bombs, and then down Lotsen-strasse across the ruins of the 'Goldener Anker' – only the façade up to the first floor was still standing – to the corner of the Vorhafen.

There, by the skin of our teeth, we were able to board the last naval ferry barge, and thus the last vehicle to leave Pillau. A few minutes later, at 4.30 on the morning of 25 April, we set off.

**Georg Sukov, sailor**                        *Haussa*, **Swinemünde**
We had set off with over 3,000 refugees, injured and prisoners on the last large ship out of Pillau. [...] We moored in the Kaiserfahrt near the navy depot [of Swinemünde], just before the pontoon bridge that had been built by the pioneers. The refugees went on land and were transported on to Wolgast.

The holds, which were in a terrible state, were cleaned. You can't imagine what those spaces looked like, where people have had to live without any kind of hygienic facilities for several days. Then people started to load on military equipment and petrol in barrels. The cargo was meant for the army in Courland.

**Bruno Just, Volkssturm man**                              **Copenhagen**

We arrived in Copenhagen in the morning, and were led to the citadel.
We had hoped we could at least rest for a day and get something to
eat. No such luck. We have just 2 hours to take a look at the town.
We changed a few kroner, and off we went into the city. It's great
strolling around here. There's no sign of the war. All the shops are
open, and you can buy anything. What a difference between here
and what we've left behind in East Prussia. Everything there was
destruction and annihilation, for months we moved only among
ruined houses abandoned by their inhabitants, and here you can get
anything you want. The people are well dressed and clean, although
all the women seem to have been at the paint-box, because their faces
are all made-up. First of all I bought myself some fine chocolate.
Unfortunately it only looked good, really it was ersatz. The sausage
was highly coloured and unpalatable. So even here lots of things are
only apparently good.

*

**Ruth Schwarz, b. 1926**                                        *Tapiau*

The prison was already overcrowded when we were admitted. Men and
women were kept separate. At mealtimes, too. We saw our father three
more times here. We saw him for the first time when the men arrived
in the prison courtyard a day after us on the trucks from Löwenhagen.
We were allowed to move freely around the building, and looked
through the windows into the internal courtyard, where we could see
the men who had just arrived. There we spotted our father. He looked
terrible. The men were treated far worse than us women. Who knows
what he could have been through?

We were shocked by the thought of what these old men must
have endured. After only a few days of subjugation, they were completely demolished; humiliated, partly by blows and torture under
interrogation, hollow-cheeked, unshaven, run-down and completely
apathetic. And one of them was our Papa. That was the first encounter.

Then for a few days we saw and heard nothing more of him. We
were able to see him for just another minute when we went to eat in

the courtyard. He called to us from a hole in the cellar, and when we asked, 'How are you, Papa?' he said, 'I have terrible diarrhoea.' Then Mutti said quickly, 'Do you not have any charcoal down there? You can eat that, it helps!' Then we had to move on again. We saw him once more in the same way, and he told us quickly that the charcoal had helped. That was the whole of our conversation, given our haste. More was not permitted, and even that was forbidden.

A few days later I saw him again, and that was definitely the last time. It was a sad sight. About ten men, in five pairs, pulled the handcart behind them out of the camp. All run-down, miserable and a picture of resignation and hopelessness.

*

### Edmund Wilson, 1895–1972 (London)

When I had just come to London in April and was taken one evening by English friends to dine in a first-class restaurant, I ordered 'roast duck' as a dish that sounded attractive and normal. I noticed, however, that the Londoners approached the menu with a certain quiet wariness, and that none of them selected duck. The duck, indeed, when it came, turned out to be disappointing: it consisted of little dry and tough slivers from a bird that seemed incredibly thin for even a poorly-fed barnyard fowl. The other day, when I was walking with G. through one of the narrow streets near Holborn, we found ourselves inhaling a foul stale smell, and, looking round, saw a little market, on the shelves of whose open windows were laid out rows and rows of dead crows. That was apparently all they sold in that shop.

### Paul Valéry, 1871–1945 Paris

I'm astonished, reading Robert d'Harcourt – *Goethe et l'art de vivre* – to encounter a lot of 'phobias' and manias common to Goethe and me – with certain significant differences, of course. But the number and energy of the common features are striking.

My *hand* is very similar to his (cast at the home of Abbé Mugnier), and both are very different from Victor Hugo's. But what contrasts: the sense of order, the art of withdrawing etc. I can do none of that.

It would just be interesting if one were to produce a careful list of differences.

Addenda. While reading, I encounter aspects of Goethe that occur *in my Faust*, but of which I knew nothing before I wrote it down.

Same with the appearance of the pupil in *Lust* and the big scene in Act II. I don't see how I can interpret these striking similarities that I have with Goethe in ego-aesthesia, while it seems to me that in other respects he is uncommonly like Gide. Plants, insects, flight, practised attitudes, pupils etc.

Perhaps there are *chrononomical* resonances. I feel more and more eighteenth century… For a month I have been intoxicating myself with Voltaire (letters).

### Hans Friedrich Blunck, 1888–1961              (Greben, Holstein)

A letter. Someone wants to improve the world and particularly present-day Europe by educating people about the form of the tetrahedral atom. Start of the healing therapy? (One of his headings: 'the primal image required by the present of the unifiedly tetraedically structured C-atom as the supreme nuclear and key principle of the world-view reuniting Europe'). As the author is a well-respected PhD., one started reading seriously.

The days are unspeakably difficult. The heart won't right itself and is to stay fresh for the tasks that lie ahead. A good thing the house doesn't have lots of mirrors!

Attempt to distract myself with Stifter's *Nachsommer*. But in these times those extremely detailed descriptions are unreadable, and it is also unbearable to think of the wonderful Vienna described in it, and about summer in Austria, about all the time and room that the people had down there, and about the destruction of those days. […]

Gustav Frenssen has died. Philosophically we were very remote from one another, as compatriots good and close friends. He brooded away his last years in solitude. Lucky for him that he doesn't have to experience these days as we do. […]

Yesterday one of the English newspapers set the tone. 'Air Force Major Bell declared that it was his philosophy that all Germans, women and children, should be killed, and that he could think of no greater pleasure than to excel in that respect.'

I could not think of a German voice that could have produced such an inhuman utterance, I have never heard the like in the whole of the war.

*

**Martin Cranz, b. 1926**            *prisoner-of-war camp near Dülmen*
The crammed army trucks roared northwards, headlights on full beam, through the eastern Ruhr. We had to hold on to one another to keep from falling overboard on the bends, which was to be avoided. The convoy stopped near Dülmen. All around stretched meadows and fields, along the road two dilapidated townhouses interrupted the rows of poplars. Agitated soldiers told us to get out, here in the open fields. Barbed-wire spirals as tall as men met our frightened eyes, we had to force ourselves through a chaotic wire sluice-gate into a field – crushed beneath the feet of tens of thousands, or was it fifteen thousand men who filled this pen, as if for a count of beasts for the slaughter? Night darkened and it rained, hesitantly at first, then emphatically, then remorselessly. In the middle, the prisoners pushed their way together, they stood packed together with me in the centre. More and more were gathering, to keep their bodies dry and warm, and then someone started singing, two, three followed – then all of them, a hundredfold, a thousandfold: nursery rhymes, folk tunes, *Heimatlieder*, a monumental chorus, moved by painful longing and aching hope. In the grey light of midnight the plinth of humanity fell silent, broke apart, some of the people leaning against each other sank on to the soaking ground. The rain went on falling until morning, and then continued for the whole of the day.

**Gerhard von Rad, 1901–71**    *Bad Kreuznach prisoner-of-war camp*
That was the time when all jokes had vanished from the men's lips. Cursing took the upper hand instead. As a soldier you get jaded about juicy, bawdy rants; but the cursing, and what it's about – I mean feeling helpless and impotent, a tooth-gritted, wild rant against an all-powerful fate – the noises sounded as they came from some infernal abyss. And

when these crowds of people massed together, whether in the queue for food or maybe because 20 pairs of socks or 10 pairs of underpants were being handed out, or when storming a tent with room for 30 people at the most, the onrush reached demonic proportions. I often found myself thinking of those paintings by the old masters, of the fall of the damned, of those falling human bodies, those distorted faces and knotted arms and hands, reaching out to each other for support and, because no one has any purchase, only dragging each other into the depths. Here a truly godforsaken dimension opened up, and we were all clearly on our way to the end where that apocalyptic vision of the Bible and that of the old masters stands. It was one of the most important experiences of my time in the camp, to see these last, extreme possibilities on man's journey, of which the Bible speaks openly but which we theologians have always tended to avoid, confirmed as naked reality.

**Philipp Schasset, d. 1983**    *Remagen prisoner-of-war camp*
Before lying down for the night, we went one by one – someone always had to stay in the hole as guard – to the latrines, where all the misery of the masses was revealed on each visit. The days were spent on all kinds of trivial things, unilluminated by even a single exhilarating glimmer of hope. Always with our coats on our shoulders or properly dressed, collars up, hands in our pockets, hat-flaps mostly down too – we stood shivering like that, drenched and trembling, still brooding: what's going to happen, what comes next, how long will it be?

**Franz Bittkowski, b. 1915**    *Bad Kreuznach prisoner-of-war camp*
Very cold, clear moonlit night. 'Big wash' in a jam tin. Queued three hours for water. Queuing for provisions for several hours every day.
     Wonderful sunset. Beautiful day.

*

**Lance Corporal Karl Friedrich Waack, b. 1921**    Grabow
Back via Karstädt–Wittenberge–Pritzwalk to Neustadt/Dosse. Unloaded there and march to Grabow near Freyenstein. Because the company has only a few vehicles, only the oldest are allowed to go, we

younger ones have to march. – In Grabow I get a chance to play the organ in the village church. In the audience are some concentration camp inmates being taken to the west under SS guard. They sleep here in a pub hall, and can move quite freely.

**A doctor, d. 1945**                                    **Wittstock an der Dosse**
The flow of people through the town is ebbing. Great crowds trekking north. About 1,000 female concentration camp inmates march through the town, a pitiful sight, young girls and old women, some of them barefoot, some in slippers, even some with one foot bare, the other in a shoe. In the camp for foreigners outside the town there are 300 Jewish women who are supposed to join the procession.

At 3 in the afternoon a sergeant comes with his sister and urgently asks me to come and help him with the military hospital train on the Berlin-bound tracks outside Wittstock. I go there with Charlottchen and find another grim, sad picture of collapse. In the cattle truck, on very little straw, crammed together, so that you have to be careful not to stand on any wounded, are about 700, most of them seriously injured. There's no doctor on the train, just a nurse. No bandages, no tablets, no medication. They are calling for help from all the trucks. I am dragged with some difficulty into a cattle truck. A picture of misery: blind in both eyes, one leg amputated, shot to the lung, coughing blood, hectic appearance. A woman shot in the arm. Next to her, her child with a bullet in the back and the beginning of scarlet fever. A 16-year-old South Tyrolean, both legs amputated. A corpse covered with blankets. People with their arms amputated. A bullet in the temple. Average paralysis, the catheter, which has been inserted, doesn't work, it's probably blocked. The urine bag is full to bursting. Horrible! I have the most serious cases brought to the military hospital. Together with Charlottchen and the nurse on the train, I bandage up the cases most in need. All the bandages are seriously soaked, the patients stink. It looks like gangrene and pyocyaneus. Lots of the wounded don't even have shirts on their backs. They're just covered with a blanket. Charlottchen gives morphine injections.

It's physical torment, bandaging people on my knees in these terrible conditions. Not a drop of water. I'm drenched in sweat. Everywhere the injured are shouting. We are to hurry, as the train is to be driven to the station and the tracks need to be cleared. Those hours between 3 and 8 have put the image of collapse most vividly before my eyes. No leadership left. Like these wounded, the whole nation is being led towards its downfall, towards suffering and misery. In comparison, defeat in the Great War was child's play.

Foreign Minister v. Ribbentrop has checked in to the Deutsches Haus in Wittstock. This means that Wittstock has become an island of apparent safety. As I learn later from Hoffmann, he talked to Frank and the lieutenant from the Wehrmacht fitness camp for almost an hour. 'He can't do foreign policy at the moment.' So he exchanged only banalities with the three of them. He says all is not lost. All rumours about disagreements between the Allies, Germany wooing America, all the rumours circulating at the beginning of the week are invented, a pack of lies. The Vlasov Army has come to nothing. Timoshenko's army is an invention: 'The German people would have to hold out for three months, then there might be a chance of being saved. And yet Germany will not be defeated!'

**Bertram Bietz**          **on march from Sachsenhausen concentration camp in the direction of Mecklenburg**

The columns aren't marching any more, they are just dragging themselves forwards. For the weak and the laggards the question 'How will it end' is solved. Shot to the head! We only have one intelligence-service gun left to defend ourselves with. Slow down, let us be together for a long time in the last hour between freedom and death!

Those arms that still have strength become a place for the weak and the sick to die. Solidarity! Passing her probationary exam once more.

Herzberg – Altruppin – fleeing Wehrmacht columns, tanks – cars – stretch of refugees – horse-corpses by the side of the road, and the murdered of Sachsenhausen, that is the picture on 25 April 1945.

The mute accusers lie by the roadside in their striped robes of honour.

Mothers, fathers, brides, sisters – who did you think of last? Oh, if you only knew in Dortmund, Paris, Utrecht, Brussels, Milan and Belgrade, what is happening in these days and hours. – Oh, Germany! We traitors, underminers of the Wehrmacht, agitators and criminals of state, we still bear the... [missing]

**Ernst Niekisch, 1889–1967**                    **Brandenburg prison**
The gunfire was getting closer by the day. The shelling of Brandenburg
intensified, the Red Army forced its way via Brandenburg out towards
Görden and occupied Landesanstalt Brandenburg, a mental institution
ten minutes from the prison. The German troops were to the west
of the prison, meaning that it was in no-man's-land. Shots flew over
the prison. Plainly these were only the vanguard, the Soviets seem
to be waiting for reinforcements. The director of the institution
suddenly changed his attitude. He established a council of prisoners
which was to be canvassed for its opinion. Now the Protestant vicar
stepped forward. One had the impression that he was sucking up to
the prisoners and trying to push the director into the background.
The prisoners' council demanded that civilian clothes and luggage
be distributed to the prisoners. But that demand got us nowhere. On
25 April, however, it was ruled that the cells of the political prisoners
should no longer be locked up during the day.

**Strategy meeting**                    **Führerbunker, Berlin**
Hitler: I think the moment has come when the others will, out of
an urge for self-preservation, confront this proletarian-Bolshevist
colossus and Moloch, which has grown beyond measure. If I were
cravenly to run away from this, the consequence would be that the
others would try to form a kind of neutral line in southern Germany,
and that would be all. National Socialism would have been removed,
and so would the German Reich. If I strike successfully here, and hold
the capital, perhaps the hope will grow among the English and the
Americans that they might be able to confront this menace side by side
with Nazi Germany after all. And the only man fit to do it is me.

**Staff Lieutenant Franz Kuhlmann, 1905–89**      **Stralsund–Berlin**
After a lengthy flight we made out the capital below us, unmistakable
because of the blazes and the dark glowing zones, partly caused by the
last air raids, but probably also from the recent bombardments by the
Russians. It was a gruesome picture with apocalyptic overtones.
    For some reason the pilot couldn't risk landing immediately, and
then at last we descended. We slid out of the plane on to the runway

and went crashing wildly into each other. At the same moment a loud, sharp command rang out: take cover! To the bunkers!

Nearby we saw a huge concrete bunker, which we reached at a run. The military air traffic controllers were in the bunker. [...]

After a certain amount of waiting, an SS-Sturmbannführer appeared. He greeted me, and said he'd been ordered to take us to the Zoo bunker. When I objected that I'd been told to go straight to the Reich Chancellery he said slightly condescendingly, 'Well, leave that to me. You will get to the right place.' We then marched eastwards with him, towards the military road, but were repeatedly forced to take cover, as the sky was full of Russian fighters.

Our SS guide accompanied me to Mohnke's command post, which was in one of the bunker spaces under the Reich Chancellery. He told me I could report to the General; then he himself disappeared. SS General Mohnke, the commander of the citadel, was clearly very interested in our arrival, as I was able to tell because we all received a great deal of attention and interest that was completely out of proportion to the fighting power that might have been expected from us. He inquired very precisely into the number, weapons and training of my soldiers, and was clearly impressed, as they were officer candidates, though he was plainly disappointed by my unit's lack of equipment. Overall he seemed benevolent and genial, until I made the gaffe of telling him I had orders to report to Hitler in person. Then his friendly tone suddenly changed: he said it would be even better if every little commander wanted to report personally to the Führer.

Mohnke gave me instructions to lodge my soldiers in the cellar of the Foreign Office for the time being, and to keep myself ready for deployment and await further orders. [...]

Over the next few hours we were completely ignored and kept in the dark. That was all the more surprising because the shelling of the Reich Chancellery was becoming increasingly fierce, and the soldiers of the Red Army – as we learned from some orderlies – were making progress in their advances on the citadel. I think a night had passed when I was urgently summoned to the telephone by my adjutant. On the phone was Admiral Voss, who was representing Grand Admiral Dönitz in the Führerbunker. In an ungracious voice he said to me, 'I have just learned that you have been here for some time. You were ordered to report to the Führer as soon as you arrived. Why did you not carry out that order?' I explained to him that I had been brought initially to Brigadier Mohnke, but he had thought the idea of reporting to the Führer was absurd. To which Voss said, 'Aha! Well, come to the Führerbunker straight away! I'll be waiting for you by the doors to the entrance.'

I immediately set off. You had to climb out of a cellar window at the Foreign Office into a courtyard, cross a patch of garden that was under heavy enemy fire, and then climb down through side entrances into the subterranean labyrinth that connected the Führerbunker and the big bunker under the Reich Chancellery. I was in full military uniform, steel helmet on, my sub-machine gun over my shoulder, etc., and was very surprised how easy it was for me get all the way to Hitler fully armed. The sentries were satisfied with my explanation: 'I've been summoned to see the Führer.'

Admiral Voss welcomed me on the steps leading to the bunker. After announcing myself I wanted to give him an explanation for my previous behaviour. But he waved my words away and just said, 'Afterwards – first I want to introduce you to the Führer.' We went down the stairs and into the big conference room. There was a big table right beside the entrance. On it, legs dangling, sat Reich Minister Goebbels. He was chatting to General Krebs, the Chief of Staff, who was sitting at the head of the table. As we entered the room, Goebbels immediately came towards me as if electrified, asked with great interest about my soldiers, about our numbers, weapons, etc. But suddenly he broke off and said to me, 'Please report to the Führer.'

While Goebbels was questioning me, I had seen an old man in civilian clothes standing at the end of the room beneath an arch leading to another room, and was deeply shocked to realize it was Hitler himself. I announced myself, Hitler shook my hand and the first thing he said was, 'You have come to hell!' Then there followed something like a quick interrogation. But what Hitler said sounded so strange and disconnected that I was completely at a loss. At that time I had no idea how poor Hitler's health really was.

Voss was plainly trying to soften the impression he sensed I was getting, by making his own interventions in the questions and answers. But Hitler's complete degeneration couldn't be hidden from me. His body had collapsed in on itself, his hands and legs were trembling violently, and much of what he said sounded as if he was speaking in a state of feverish delirium. I still remember fragments. So often he would say something like, 'Oh, these Berliners, these Berliners!' or, 'One would need a Hanna Reitsch!' At the time I knew nothing of the events that had played out down there, and couldn't make head or tail of the scraps that I was hearing.

Then Hitler dismissed me, shaking hands with me again, and I climbed the bunker steps with Admiral Voss once more. Although I was profoundly shaken, I said nothing to Voss about my impression. He didn't mention Hitler's condition either. But I knew that he had noticed my discomfort. Then he gave a few hints that there had been a plan to smuggle larger navy units to Berlin. The attempt had failed, and we were the only ones who had managed to get through.

A few hours after I had been with Adolf Hitler, a delegate of Reich youth leader Axmann came to see me. He and I were to discuss how the members of a Hitler Youth training course that had been held in Potsdam but had been surprised there by the rapid encirclement of Berlin by the Red Army and transferred to the Palais Hess on Wilhelmstrasse in Berlin, along with my young officer cadets, could be deployed for the defence of the Reich Chancellery and the Führerbunker. Before I could authorize this acquisition, I asked to take a look at the boys, and was shocked when I saw a group of 12–15-year-old children before my eyes.

I refused to let them be deployed, but even today I can't forget those boys standing in front of me, pleading over and over again, 'Staff Lieutenant, please take us! We are willing and able to fight for the Führer!' They were probably deployed by SS Brigadier Krukenberg, and by chance I was able to witness Goebbels gathering these boys around him again over dinner on 30 April, to say goodbye to them, and award the Iron Cross to many of those who had distinguished themselves in service.

*

**Lothar Loewe, b. 1929**                                                **Berlin**
While a unit of the Hitler Youth and French Waffen-SS volunteers
defended the Karstadt department store in Neukölln, suffering heavy
losses, our staff, the fortress anti-tank unit, received an order in the
early evening to transfer the command post to the deep bunker of
the supreme command of the army on Fehrbelliner Platz. At a rapid
pace, under violent artillery fire, we left Tempelhof in our vehicles.
On Gneisenaustrasse we skirted ruins, craters made by grenades and
overhead tramways hanging down. In the underpasses on Yorkstrasse
the supply trucks of the 'Müncheberg' tank division were parked
bumper to bumper. Soldiers had begun steering burning trucks into
the side streets, where they exploded.

The deep bunker in the inner courtyard of what is now the
Wilmersdorf district offices on Fehrbelliner Platz was an emergency
military hospital full of cadres, wounded men, and lots of women with
children from the surrounding area. We let out a sigh of relief. The
bunker was bomb-proof, an electric light was burning, the taps were
on, we could wash, there was warm soup for us for the first time in
days, and we immediately fell into a deep sleep on the mattresses.

**Artur Axmann, 1913–96**                                              **Berlin**
On 25 April 1945 there were Red Army units in Zehlendorf,
Schlachtensee and Nikolassee, and they advanced towards the western
city centre. Soon they had also reached the Heerstrasse and the
Kaiserdamm, where our duty station was. Just in time the head of our
organization office, Otto Würschinger, had deployed Hitler Youth
leaders and boys in position to fight off the attack. [...] The first Soviet
attack was beaten off. The first dead and wounded were on our side.
Stammführer Schlichting was killed. Otto Würschinger himself took
command. Bannführer Moses was seriously injured. [...]

When I was in my office the phone rang, the line was still intact.
A call from the Führerbunker. Secretary of State Dr Naumann was
on the line. 'What's going on there?' he asked, in response to the
banging and crashing that he heard down the receiver. I explained our
situation. 'You can't possibly stay there. I'll call back.' He called back
a short time later. He had spoken to Hitler in the meantime, and told

me to move my command post to the party Chancellery. That was in the government district, 64 Wilhelmstrasse, diagonally opposite the Führerbunker. We couldn't leave our injured and girls in the duty station. We took them with us.

**Julia Tremayne, b. 1903**                                          **Sark**

I would so like to be in London. I wonder if it is very much damaged and altered. We have also heard all our armies have linked up and Berlin is surrounded, if it is true the end cannot be far off.

**Strategy meeting**                              **Führerbunker, Berlin**

Hitler: I have said: it is not as if I have a completely stable front in southern Germany and a glacis and am refusing to leave Berlin purely out of wilfulness. I see how things are developing. All my attempts to steer tactics are simply in vain. In the defence of the Rhineland as well as in other places, insane, disastrous errors have been made. All the plans I elaborated failed simply because the ground was repeatedly pulled out from under them due to the high-handedness of the lower commanders.

**Albert L. Kotzebue, US lieutenant, d. 1987**              *on the Elbe*

Our initial meeting with the Russians was very formal. We exchanged salutes and shook hands. I explained to Maj. Goloborodko through Kowalski that we were an American patrol […] and that I had been instructed to arrange a meeting between the American and Russian commanders as soon as possible. The time was 12:30 p.m. […]

Within moments, we all became more at ease, smiling and exchanging compliments. While we waited for the regimental commander, the Russian photographer had us pose for a few pictures. […]

The CP [command post] was in a large farmhouse. A banquet table had already been set. Everyone was in the festive 'Spirit of the Elbe', a spirit of comradeship, mutual sacrifice, happiness, and relief that the war would soon be at an end. Maj. Gen. Vladimir Rusakov came in shortly. We toasted the late President Roosevelt, President Truman, Prime Minister Churchill, Marshal Stalin and 'everlasting friendship' between us all.

**Alexander Olshansky, Red Army soldier**           *on the Elbe*

When we stood facing one another, we were at first rather monosyllabic with embarrassment. During the fortification we had smeared ourselves from head to toe with mud, and our uniforms were frayed from crawling. Our Allies looked clean in comparison, although like us they were unshaven.

The Americans were surprised that we weren't wearing helmets. We told them we'd taken them off before the raid. They're good at defending you when you're sitting in the trench, we said, but in a raid you're exposed to full-sized bullets and splinters. A helmet that slips over your eyes and obstructs your vision is only a nuisance. And it's too heavy.

The Soviet and American soldiers greeted one another as comrades-in-arms, as fellow fighters, and exchanged a firm handshake.

After Kotzebue had radioed his staff to tell them about the meeting, he sent some of the soldiers back with the report. They left in two jeeps. He kept eleven men and three trucks with him.

For the Americans the war was over, but we continued the attack on Dresden and Prague.


**Konstantin Simonov, war reporter, 1915–79**           *Torgau*

I still have photographs taken on the Elbe, showing us together with American soldiers and officers, and in my desk drawer I keep souvenirs from that time; nickel-plated American insignia, which I swapped for the officer's stars that I took from my spare shoulder patches.

I remember the great joy I felt at that time, a joy that was not yet burdened by doubts and fears.

I remember lots of things, but in the notebooks I still have from those times there is nothing about it.

*

**Edwin Chapman, British soldier**           *north-west Germany*

*To his parents*

Dear M & D

The weather has been dry again during the last three days, although it is not as hot and sunny as it was last week.

The other night the chap here, who is a game and poultry merchant, gave me peewits' eggs to eat. They were quite good.

Yours with love

Edwin

## Wilhelm Bodenstedt, postal official, 1894–1961        Breslau

Again no mail from Wifey; on the other hand I know that all mail was flown out of Breslau today, so that my Wifey will probably get lots of mail from me next Sunday, which I will be very, very pleased about.

The battle here is almost unstinting; it's on fire in the west: Alsenstrasse, Zehnerstrasse, etc. It's 10.30 p.m. now. We just had a visit from the pilots, and the lads rained down explosive bombs very close by, so that our doors blew open. Goodnight, my Wifey.

## Akim Popovichenko, Soviet officer        *Austria*
*To his family*

Dear Verushka, dear Vodik, dear Dinochka!

Now spring has really arrived. The apple trees, the pear trees, the cherry, apricot and peach trees are in blossom. How beautiful it is all around, how ill it sits with the life I'm leading at the moment.

Dear Verushka! I've now been at the front for almost two years.

Of course I will not come home the same man as I was. The war has left its mark on me. Perhaps I will be more tender, perhaps more coarse, certainly older, although no one who sees me thinks I'm over 30.

Kitten, I still haven't sent off my parcels. It's a real shame. I have about 100 kg of silk alone – that's 500–600 metres, and then wool and other fabrics. Life and happiness are the things that count, everything else will sort itself out.

I received your dear letters. I never thought you could be unfaithful to me. Never! That would be stupid of me. And if I joke about such matters now and then, that's how you must receive it: as a joke. We two have developed an attitude to life that has grown out of a number of difficult experiences, it would be idiotic not to trust one another. I am no longer afraid of physical betrayal, although our relationship to one another would hardly stay the same even if I were to find out about it ten years later. I don't think I'm jealous, but I've been through too much, I've seen too much of this world and the people in it, of all that repellent cheating, of flattery and lies, of that damned deceit.

How would I feel writing you such flattering letters for almost two years, if I, like many others, had a companion here? Where then would be the great soul of which you write so often, for which you so yearn? No, Verushka, such a thing will never come to pass.

Goodbye. Warm kisses and hugs.

Your Kima.

**Mariela Kuhn, b. 1909**   (*Oxford Military Hospital – Head Injuries*)
Went to the eye clinic to visit Berna – just managed to say goodbye as he was being taken to the German prisoner-of-war field hospital in Watford. He was afraid to go, blind as he is, to leave against his will a place he had become used to. I accompanied him down the stairs to the car, with only a dressing gown over my pyjamas; he was clutching his belongings, a pitiful sight. A friendly little sentry with a gun in his belt and a sub-machine gun over his shoulder and a lady ambulance driver took him off in a small car.

Roehl is much better, he reads and looks well; an average German, an average person all round; he is neither excited nor depressed about the news, battles in Berlin etc., his attitude and his way of putting things are: 'You have to take life as it comes.' He has no toothbrush or toothpaste, it looks as if these provisions have been suspended for prisoners of war.

Johess from Ward M4 died on the 24th. I don't even know if that's his real name, it might have been Johannes Hess. The name goes with Field Post Number 11339, I'll try to find out more about him and contact his family.

**Ruth Klüger, b. 1931**                                    (*Straubing*)
And one day there they were, the Yanks. The weather was fine, spring had arrived, they'd taken the city by driving up in their tanks and jeeps, and there had been no battle for Straubing. The long horror story that my life has been, those seven terrible years since Hitler's troops marched into Austria, they too without a fight were suddenly over. We were at

our destination. We had never planned beyond this moment. The three of us went into the city centre, looked at each other in bafflement and wondered, 'What now?' My mother summoned up her best school English, which incidentally turned out not to be too bad, walked confidently up to the nearest American soldier, an MP who was directing traffic on that street corner, and told him briskly and to the point that we had escaped from a concentration camp. I didn't understand what he said, because I couldn't speak English at the time, but his gesture was unmistakable: he put his hands over both ears and turned away. My mother translated. He had had enough of people who claimed to have been in camps. You found them everywhere. We were no different.

The April sun warmed my skin. From now on I could wear short sleeves, and it didn't matter if anyone noticed the concentration camp number; I could call myself by my real name as well. It would remain an unforgettable day, but I was glad we had freed ourselves, and didn't need much more from the victors, because the hour of liberation, which I had so long yearned for, and which I had fantasized into a big party in my imagination, had fallen rather short. Here was my first American, and he was holding his hands over his ears.

So one thing was certain: this war had not been fought for us.

### Alfred Kantorowicz, 1899–1979                    *New York*

In April 1945 the western world has 'discovered' the existence of concentration camps in Nazi Germany. A cry of horror is running through the press of these democratic nations. They could have become aware of all this twelve years ago, from the thousands of reports from escaped victims, from books backed up by documentary evidence – the Brown Book [*Braunbuch*], for example. If they hadn't ignored the truth back then, this war with its thirty million dead and the devastation of Europe might have been prevented. We all warned them: look around, this is how it starts; the first victims are the good Germans themselves, you will be the next if you don't hurry to help them. Now that it's all over, the bloom of Europe is rotting partly in the camps and partly in the battlefields. Now they are 'discovering' that Nazis act like Nazis. It won't bring the dead back to life.

\*

**Joan Wyndham, 1922–2007**                    *Watnall, Nottinghamshire*
Yet another hellish concentration camp, Dachau, has been found – we liberated it yesterday. The Russians and Americans have finally met up on the Elbe and joined forces.

**Franz Ballhorn, 1908–79**          *Sachsenhausen concentration camp*
We stagger down rainy streets and paths, sometimes creeping rather than marching. The dead, the dead… their names whirl up again and again like long-fallen leaves.

Many of them have shoes that are falling to bits. They have bound them with twine and wire, which come loose along the way, so that they go on staggering half barefoot. Coats and trousers hang loose in rags around their creaking joints and bones, no flesh on their ribs. To the right and left are bullet-riddled corpses in the mud of the street and in the ditches. Their wide-open eyes are washed by rain, their thin, dirty hands are sunk in the mud. They bare their teeth horribly at the sky. No cross will ever lead their grieving wives and mothers to their final resting places.

We don't weep, we don't curse, we don't mourn. Our faces are hard to recognize in our ashen skin. Between our pointed, protruding cheekbones our dead eyes lie like dark, muddy holes. The last days that lie behind us give us no grounds to believe that we are still alive. No one speaks, no cry rings out. We are weary to death, defeated, half-starved, pitiful figures looking for a handful of leaves somewhere, a bundle of straw and rags to lie down and die on. We gasp away, bent over, feet dragging. Here and there a grey, ruined figure crouches some distance away, spraying blood and mucus. Sometimes another falls over and lies there, writhing in terrible pain. The bullet to the head is the bitter conclusion.

One should be able to scream. But tongues and vocal cords are paralysed. It will be a while before we can speak, cry, roar, shriek again, shrilly, so that it freezes the blood of those who are supposed to hear: the inexpressible despair of our souls and bodies.

Will we never be normal people again? This age has taken us like a piece of filth in its bloody fists and slapped us into horror, into sadism and madness.

One creeps forwards on all fours, pale in horror at the coming end. No one pays attention, not even the man standing nearest. Each one knows only himself, only dully feels his own torment. His terrible suffering numbs him, day and night.

How good it is that you at home do not know how terrible it is for us to drag our torment through the long hours. Your poor, weakened, fearfully listening hearts would shatter.

## K. A. Gross, 1892–1952                    Dachau concentration camp

Morning mass is so well attended that the chapel is filled to capacity. In vain they try to close the door on those standing outside. It keeps opening again, and each time a stream of cold morning air floods in, clutching the necks of the praying priests as if with frosty hands. Sunk in prayer, no one looks back. The litany in honour of St Mark, whose feast day is being celebrated today, is like an expedition through the earliest days of Christianity; poignantly the conjuration of the Apostolic champions and martyrs rings out time and again: 'Sancte Petre, Sancte Paule, ora pro nobis!' – the chain of martyrs is unbroken, and this soil too has drunk the blood of those who have, unnoticed, sacrificed their lives for the sake of faith.

Communion! A solemn moment! They all kneel respectfully to receive the sacrament. Each one bows deeply when the priest walking along the rows passes him the consecrated bread. Then – again a sight of touching profundity – they hug and give each other the fraternal kiss. For all its simplicity, this noble form reaches deep into the heart. [...]

What has played out before our eyes throughout these days are the last twitches of a terrible fight to the death. One unit after another is closing down. [...] Hartmann, in charge in Ljubljana, tells me that today the porcelain factory is packing its last figures. Farewell, you Seydlitz cuirassiers, farewell, you flag-bearers, busts of Hitler and bears, you candle-holders, pots and cups and other fine china objects. Stay well, like the Übermenschen, the virago and the Cerberus, under whose protection you may continue to live out your fragile existence in the new brigands' lairs of the Tyrol.

*

**Hella Jacobowski**                    **Schloss Wudicke, near Rathenow**
The country road is full of refugees, most of them from Berlin. In cars and horse-drawn carts, on bicycles and on foot, an uninterrupted stream drifts westwards. We ask where on earth they want to flee to, because the war will come after them anyway. They all want to cross the Elbe, at Tangermünde there is supposed to be a slight chance. Anywhere away from the Russians!

Many soldiers are on the road, including many with only one arm or one leg and with bandages. And this sorry crowd, trotting listlessly along, now westwards, now eastwards, is to defy fate at the last minute! Only a troop of young SS men speaks loudly of 'moving to Berlin' and 'defending the homeland', where Hitler himself is supposed to be leading the fight for the city, and Goebbels too is said to have been committing some sort of heroic deeds, or at least making heroic statements. The poor lunatics! Now, they will hardly get as far as Berlin, because everything, even the last main road, has been closed.

In Trittsee, a very cosy teatime. The atmosphere there is much warmer and friendlier.

**Gertrud Bayer, b. 1909**                                    **Berlin**
In the forest opposite our house, there is a camp with a combat unit that plans to fight its way through to the west. Can I join them? I bury my jewellery in the garden.

When I went to have some real coffee with the Haeberleins in the afternoon, I talked to the soldiers there. They had civilians with them, people who had fled from already occupied areas of Berlin, who were able to give vividly horrific accounts of what had happened to them. One young girl was quite numbed, had hardly a stitch on, and the soldiers organized clothes for her from an empty house. The fighting unit, which came from the east, has been ordered to march on to Hamburg. After consulting the Major, they agree to take me along 'at my own risk'!

**Private Herbert Nürnberger**                          **near Berlin**
Shortly afterwards, it must have been perhaps 23–25 April, we were suddenly told that anyone capable of marching was to turn up with

as little luggage as possible, they were setting off for Berlin!! And I saw something from the window of our room that I haven't forgotten: a group of old men half in uniform marching by down below with 'antediluvian' shotguns, one of them with what we might have called 'a humpy back'!

So the march really was bound for the west or the north-west. I had brought a wooden chest from home, which I swapped for a rucksack; such things were already lying at the edge of the road. But suddenly there was a pause, and our procession was halted by SS men – and that was the end of our westward march!

\*

**Strategy meeting**                                 **Führerbunker, Berlin**

Hitler: What was I going to use to hold the south against the west? You see, it's the same everywhere: a name implies a certain order. Wherever there is a name, a personality, order prevails. As long as there was a personality in Italy, there was a certain order there. Under Colonel-General Heinrich Vietinghoff the demoralizing influences have become stronger again. Those are the know-alls that Clausewitz warns about, people who always describe the easier way as the more intelligent. In fact that easier way is the more stupid. And then there is false intelligence. There is no doubt for me: the battle has reached a climax here.

If it is really true that differences are arising among the Allies in San Francisco – and they will arise – then a change can only come about if I deal the Bolshevik colossus a blow at a particular point. Then the others will perhaps be convinced that only one person is capable of halting the Bolshevik colossus, and that is me and the party and today's German state.

If fate has other plans, then I will vanish as an inglorious refugee from the stage of world history. But I would consider it a thousand times more cowardly to commit suicide on the Obersalzberg than to stand and fall here. Let no one say: You are the Führer.

I am the Führer for as long as I can really lead. I can only lead by sitting on a mountain somewhere, but to do that I must have authority over armies that obey. Let me win a victory here, may it be ever so difficult and hard, then I will also have a right once more to remove the sluggish elements that are constantly creating obstructions; then I will work with the generals who have proved themselves. Only a heroic attitude can allow us to survive this most difficult of times.

*

### A flyer from the 'Werwolf Oberbayern'
Warning to all traitors and henchmen of the enemy!

The Werwolf Group of Upper Bavaria warns in advance all those who want to help the enemy, or threaten or deceive Germans and their families who remain loyal to Adolf Hitler. We warn you!

Traitors and criminals against the people will pay with their lives and the lives of their whole clan. Village communities who sin against the life of our people or show the white flag will suffer a devastating retribution sooner or later. Our revenge is deadly!

The Werwolf.

**Herbert Steiner**                                    **(Koprein, Carinthia)**
The Sadounik family from Koprein near Eisenkappel in Carinthia was murdered by the SS on 25 April 1945:

Franziska Sadounik, née Slopst, b. 26 January 1868
Katharina Sadounik, née Dobranc, b. 25 April 1901
Lukas Sadounik, b. 6 October 1906
Anna Sadounik, née Haberc, b. 15 June 1909
Franziska Sadounik, b. 4 February 1932
Albina Sadounik, b. 11 February 1938
Viktor Sadounik, b. 8 April 1941
Mirko Sadounik, b. 8 April 1944
Gottfried Sadounik, b. 4 August 1944
Stanislaus Kogoj, b. 13 November 1935, neighbour's child
Adelgunde Kogoj, b. 28 January 1942, neighbour's child

The family had supported partisans.

**Pastor August Ganter**                    **Ewattingen, Black Forest**

On the morning of the new day, Wednesday 25.4, as on the two
following days, those who wished to take communion met at the
pastor's invitation in a quiet and remote corner of the slope. There,
after communal prayer, they received the body of the Lord. Above
this communion feast there lay a deep seriousness, which can hardly
be forgotten by any of those who took part in it.

**Field Marshal Wilhelm Keitel, 1882–1946**              **near Berlin**

Early on the morning of 25.4 I went back to the front and first sought
out Gen. Holste at his command post. After finding out about the
situation from my corps, I spoke to Gen. Wenck on the phone and was
informed that he had moved his army command post again. I gave my
view of the situation to Jodl to pass on to the Führer. Gen. Wenck and
his attack personnel had fought their way through to the lakes south of
Potsdam, although on a very narrow front that looked like a pointed
wedge. But he lacked reserves and additional impact, because stronger
parts of his army were involved in intensified fighting around the
Elbe crossings (I lack a map to identify the locations more precisely)
north of Wittenberge, so that he could not free them for the attack on
Berlin and a combined operation with the 9th Army, which obviously
consisted only of remnants. The 12th Army was too weak to perform
both tasks.

In this situation I authorized Gen. Wenck to face up to all the
dangers on the Elbe front, and at least to free a division for the main
task in the direction of Berlin, and to report this decision to the Führer
by radio himself with reference to me.

Towards midday, when I wanted to drive through the small town of
X (I can't remember the name without a map), about halfway through
Brandenberg–Nauen, some troops blocked my path, explaining that X
town was being attacked by the Russians, and was under enemy fire.
As I could not hear the sound of fighting, I drove on into X town.
In the marketplace a 'Volkssturm' company had dug and occupied
a trench, 1 m deep, barely 11 m from the houses opposite. Nothing
was known about the enemy except that an attack on the town was
expected. I told the company commander about the nonsensical nature

of his measure, called the company around, delivered a brief address and ordered the company commander to take me to the commandant of the town.

On the way there, at various points I saw artillery pieces of all kinds (field howitzers, infantry cannon, 3.7 m flak) placed on limbers in courtyards, clearly hidden from the view of the planes, and tow trucks and crews standing idly around. Intermittent rounds from an enemy battery seemed to be targeting the edge of the town.

I found the commandant in a remote house issuing orders to about 10–12 officers who were gathered around him. He was an active pioneer officer who was not only surprised by my appearance, but also thrown into confusion. He told me that he had ordered a decampment and the blowing up of the bridge at the eastern entrance, because the enemy was about to attack the town. I only shouted at him, asking him if he had lost his mind, running away in response to a few shots of long-range enemy fire. What had he seen of the enemy, where had his combat reconnaissance force gone, what had they reported, and why were those cannon standing around all over the place in the courtyards of the town? I fetched the whole company out of the house, went with them to the road out of town, where the enemy was supposedly about to attack; there was nothing to be seen apart from some missile craters. Under my supervision the order to defend the town was given, the artillery pieces put in position, and the Major moved into a command post from which he could survey the wide open plain, where the enemy was nowhere to be seen.

I told him that the abandonment of the town would cost him his skin [...], that I would visit him again the next day and expected to find a well-organized defence. He was to report my intervention and the orders I had given him to General Holste immediately via motorcycle messenger. I drove along the retreat route planned by the brave commander, and found columns several kilometres long of formations of all kinds and the baggage trains already decamping, whole columns of vehicles, piled high with rifles, machine guns, ammunition and so on. I stopped them all and sent them back to the town, under the leadership of some elderly military police officers that I'd managed to collar. [...]

In the late afternoon I went back to our camp at Neu Roofen and prepared my flight to Berlin for the following night. As Jodl had already informed the Führer by phone, I did not make a personal phone call, given that I was about to fly to the city. Unfortunately the Reich Chancellery forbade me to land at Gatow airport, because it was already under enemy artillery fire. The military road between Charlottenburger Tor (Technische Hochschule) and Brandenburger Tor had been set up as the runway for aeroplanes to launch and land, and from nightfall onwards for flying in transport Junkers with all kinds of ammunition ordered by the Reich Chancellery or the commanders in Berlin, and also the landing of 2 SS companies which have volunteered for duty. My own inbound flight was set for just after midnight so that I could take off again before daybreak. From 24.00 hours I waited at Rheinsberg airport for an order to take off. Instead, however, what followed was a categorical refusal because a fire in Berlin had swathed the Tiergarten in such a layer of smoke that landing would have been impossible.

Even a personal phone call didn't help; I was told that because of this veil of smoke many planes had crash landed, so the runway wasn't free. So my plan had failed. While negotiating with the Reich Chancellery again after my return, about flying in at daybreak, I was informed of the Führer's personal prohibition, after Colonel General von Greim had been injured the previous evening, during the last of the daylight.

*

**Emil Barth, 1900–1958**                    *(Haan, Rhineland)*
This is also a part of the aforementioned healing process: that I, since it has been under way, have felt only slightly inclined to take note of outward events as a chronicle. I am concerned only with all that is connected to this healing process – enough and more than enough, of course! It is a far-reaching process, and its ardency confirms me in my old conviction that man, as long as he is in the prime of his life, is great both physically and spiritually.

To mention one extreme instance: is not the night, as it falls once more, silvery and velvety, giving of itself with silence, with voices of immeasurable silence and breathing, as it drips from all the stars with sleep's sweet oblivion, and pours itself on rivers of dreams through the sleeping breast – is it not like one physically related to me, one from whom I was long parted? A most delicate body, woven from starlight, aeons of time, eternities of space? Not the veil only of myself, but itself the substance of myself? Or the oak up on the windy hill, many hundreds of years old, that I used to pass almost daily for over a year, but hardly ever without feeling the pang of the wound that it was outside of me: is it not part of me once more, standing there and turning green? A zone very much my own, where it stretches its mighty branches and bears within it nests of sky? And so it is with many things. Even the clear-up tasks in the street appear to me primarily, directly, within this aspect of healing and restoration of something of my own; although, as I know – because it is not noticeable from outward signs – certain bearers of the local tyranny have been put to this work, which they must feel as a humiliation (while it might be an opportunity for them to humiliate themselves having understood their active share of guilt in the terrible game of our national tragedy). But in order to look at that, I need a particular impulse of consciousness, such as that produced by the appearance of a familiar face from whose features the foolish arrogance of power has now fled. Incidentally, this work will be finished within a few days, as far as the high street is concerned; most of the anti-tank barriers have been cleared away, the cars, fired on and burned out or cleared out by looters, the shattered rifles, the jettisoned steel helmets and belts and whole mountains of scattered ammunition all collected, and only the party building, cleared out in fury, from which an armour-piercing missile was fired, and the burnt-out ruins of two houses near the city hall, which went up in flames in the first night, will for a while serve as reminders of the crucial hours of that unforgettable Monday. But even those stains and marks are quickly placated by the green of the old lime trees that curves its crepuscular gold arch across the street in such a timely manner; and when I go to my father's house for an hour in the afternoon or towards evening, I walk beneath that green arch embraced in peace sweeter than any I have felt before, and which I would never again have thought possible.

*

**Ray T. Matheny,**
**American prisoner of war, b. 1925**                    *Braunau am Inn*

We passed through several small villages and towns. In one town,
Altheim, I believe, a couple of our men managed to buy some ice
cream, but the supply was short. In the same town an enterprising
father offered his daughter for a few cigarettes or Reichsmarks a
'throw'. There were several love-starved Kriegies [POWs] waiting
their turn. Billy and I made snide remarks about the men standing in
line, and they clearly felt some embarrassment at their conduct. Such a
crude experience was not what I looked forward to.

On the outskirts of Altheim we stayed in another barn that night
and rested there the next day. Along the road sometimes Austrian
women set out baskets of apples or carrots for us. In one small town
the women threw chunks of bread down to us as we marched by.
We blessed these women as they doled out small amounts of food,
but I couldn't help but wonder if anyone had been as kind to the
Hungarian Jews when they had come through their town. There
was a general fear among the civilians because the German armies
had already abandoned them. The civilians probably treated us kindly,
at least in part, in hopes it would affect their fate when the war was
over.

**Arthur Thomas Scales,**
**British prisoner of war**                    *on the run near Regensburg*

However, our fourth day in the forest finally dawned. [...] During
that morning and afternoon, we lay perfectly still, not daring to move,
although any movement by us would not have been heard above the
deafening noise of the guns, it was important, however, that we did not
shake the bushes beneath which we were sheltering.

There was plenty of activity during the late afternoon, and we heard
the German soldiers trailing their machine guns behind them, running
along the track 7–8 yards from us. While they were passing we kept our
heads down, although I did see one of them as he tore past, carrying a
light machine gun.

Five o'clock – things seemed quieter – no machine-gun fire – the artillery guns firing each 3 rounds every 15 minutes.

Then, in the distance we heard a loud rumble which increased in volume, until we realised it was that of a tank. We kept well down as the monster rumbled past on the same cart track. As the sounds diminished, we whispered to one another, asking whose tank it might be. We decided that it must be the Germans pulling out.

Still only the artillery fire and rifle shots. 5.45 p.m. the sound of an approaching car was heard and to our astonishment turned up with the screeching of brakes. We could not see through the bushes but it was only about 20 yards from us. Then we heard someone speak – we glanced quickly at each other. Had we heard correctly? Emmott looked at me and making no sound formed the word, 'Americans?' with his lips. I replied in the same way, 'I think so'.

The car moved off and about 100 yards along the track stopped again.

Then we conversed in whispers – all of us thought we had heard the words, 'Headquarters', spoken with an American accent, but could not be completely certain.

We wanted to crawl out on to the track to see if they really were Americans. However, Emmott said as he was senior in rank he would go. Shepherd insisted on going with him.

Emmott withdrew a small Union Jack from his pocket, and pinned it to his cap. We whispered our 'Good Luck' as they both crawled through the undergrowth.

The moments that followed seemed an eternity. What our thoughts were at that time I cannot remember, but this moment meant that after 5 years in captivity we should be free or… !!

We heard the two crawling through the bushes – branches snapping, stones moving under their feet. Then we heard someone shout, 'Don't shoot. British prisoners of war.' After that there was a horrible silence, and then for one terrible moment I thought I heard the German word, 'Nein'.

We four listened to catch the words spoken by the man on the cart track.

Emmott was the first to return – his face wreathed in smiles – closely followed by an American soldier with a Tommy gun slung over his shoulders.

We were all terribly happy, but no one knew quite what to say. We all shook hands with the Yank and said, 'Thanks a lot'. It was hard to realise then just what that moment meant, but I know I felt as though an enormous weight had been lifted from my shoulders. Out on the cart track we all crawled, and there I saw my first jeep. Standing by the side of it were 5 GIs, who ran forward to meet us and warmly shook our hands. They gave us chocolate, tinned meats, biscuits, candy and some delicious hot coffee from a Thermos.

One of them contacted his Squadron's Headquarters by wireless, and reported his find, and asked for further orders. He was asked if the area was cleared, and upon giving the answer in the affirmative, received instructions to bring us along to H.Q.

We all piled on the jeep. Ten of us including the crew. We bumped and rocked over the stony ground through the forest, till finally we came to the road upon which many tanks and armoured vehicles were advancing towards the enemy. We came to a village where from every house fluttered a white flag. Their occupants, standing in the doorways, looking very soured. We arrived at a very large house and drove into the yard.

Here we met the officer in charge, who asked us about our experiences and gave us tea and, to our great astonishment, white bread – something we had not seen for over 5 years. At first we thought it was cake, but the Lieutenant laughingly assured us it was bread. The house had obviously belonged to an influential person, being wonderfully furnished and decorated.

The GIs were busy looting the place before the arrival of the Military Police, who usually followed close behind the spear heads. They told us to take anything we wanted, but we were so delighted to be free, nothing else seemed to be of any value.

**A. J. East, British prisoner of war**          *Stalag I VB, Mühlberg*
Today, Bill, Reg Fox and I set off to sight-see Mühlberg, although Reg had to return owing to indisposition.

Hundreds of looters with stolen bicycles, prams – even dolls' prams

– carts, babies' cots, etc., all loaded with booty were returning. A few German migrants were also on the move.

The streets of the town were littered with rubbish and excited crowds were rushing around with red-eyed German civilians looking at their houses from the outside.

Apparently, the method employed was to follow a soldier who would stop at a house or a shop, bang on the door, which would be quickly opened by a German Frau. She would plead a little, but would be quickly brushed aside by dirty little Eye-Ties, followed by other nations, including British. A plague of locusts have nothing on a loot-crazy rabble.

The camp padres were attempting to prevent the worst of the vandalism.

Bill and I with our noses in the air walked through the streets as far as the 'Hafen', which is a canal running from the Elbe to the town, which had large barges moored to the quayside.

[...]

Although our pride forbade us to join in with the general looting, it allowed us to enjoy the fruits of others who had brought plenty to the barrack. We now have bacon, preserved fruit, honey, milk, jam, onions, rhubarb, ersatz coffee, butter, rice, macaroni and other odds and ends.

There was great excitement tonight when a jeep containing Americans drove into the camp. There were prolonged cheers and excited kriegies [POWs] loaded on to the car which drove up the main road and back.

The officer declared he was as happy as we were to be here and thought that we should get away by road transport very shortly and cigarettes would be brought in. We all went to bed very happy, although I am afraid that many were worse for wear after riotous living since liberation day. All through the night there was a long 'sick' parade.

### Karla Höcker, 1901–92 (Berlin)

Unreal evening at Gründgens': small, barricaded basement room, candlelight, champagne. For a few hours it's as if the war had moved further away. Discussions about what's to come. Scrullo says something curious, something that affects us all. He says, 'It was our destiny always to have to be "against", and we would have had such a gift at being "for".' By that he means: I could have been enthusiastic for humanity, for intellectual freedom. For much else besides. 'For this here? – Nooo!' Geri says, 'A new form of life will be found, we, who have been successful, can do without outward possibilities for happiness. Profession, art – we've lived through it all, we have fulfilled ourselves to a certain degree. Perhaps we will now catch up on other possibilities of human experience...'

Gründgens says in something of a murmur, '– and I will have to portray nothing but SS men.' Again and again, in spite of all his superiority and irony, the obsessive nature of the actor, who *has* to act, breaks through – the one for whom a life without theatre is unthinkable. 'Of all my roles I would only accept two again. Even Hamlet – good Lord, if I could act him now!'

Later a grotesque scene in the kitchen. Gründgens fetches tinned sardines, ready-made liver pâté, and we eat, by soft candlelight, greedily and happily at the kitchen table, as if it were the fulfilment of this curious day. [...]

We talk about what is to come. About people acting in plays in basements, without costumes, in tents – but they will act. New things will develop. In opera, Geri says, grand performances will disappear, there will be a return to chamber orchestras, there will be experiment. Scrullo, sceptically: 'Yes, if they allow us to experiment!' The big question. In this new world, do we still have a right to exist? Will we be able to think, live, eat, act and portray that which is demanded of us? The inviolability of the person has been fundamentally destroyed!

Gründgens smiles as he turns a champagne glass in his fingers: 'Before them, we have lived out all that struck us as beautiful, right, perfect, we set up models and examples. But I'm afraid we will be held to account for all that we have said and done under coercion. We will be held responsible for things of which we are innocent.' Then, in an attempt to make the situation look ridiculous: 'We are in fact, like the Hen in the station in Morgenstern's poem, we are "not built for it". It isn't our style. We have to experience all this, but it doesn't suit us.'

**Lieselott Diem**                                    **Eichkamp, Berlin**

Young soldiers in flight and in retreat are coming through here, breathless from running. They are escaping through our gardens to get back to the city. Poor children – young as they are. The Russians are supposed to be at the station – everywhere there is agitation and fear. We wait. Everything will happen calmly. If only the fight were over soon. We still don't know anything more…

In the early afternoon we dare to leave the house, and the whole of Eichkamp is out and about, fetching water and shopping. There is meat, dried milk and bread. I walk past the Zettelmeyer house, the wife is miserable and downcast. There was a Russian tank on Eichkampstrasse, and one woman was shot, others wounded. On the way home heavy fire again, and a tank flies into the air towards the forest, a bright, glowing rain of shrapnel.

Towards evening my husband suddenly arrives – released at last! He's profoundly gloomy about everything, but we're happy to be together. Now we will find many things easier to bear. Many people have fallen beside him today, hit by artillery fire or bombs – fate has been kind to him, as so often.

Sleep isn't easy, as the cellar is so small. We – Carl and I – first try to do it in the dining room on the floor – impossible, as from one o'clock the hail of bombs sends plaster raining down on our faces. We lie on the floor down below – my husband is exhausted.

**A doctor**                                                   **(Berlin)**

Hanged soldiers in Berlin, with signs around their necks: 'I was too cowardly to defend my wife and children.' There is hysteria to be read in those texts.

Dead people, when they are hanging, aren't people any more. Through the bend in the neck, the crookedness of the head's angle, and the slackly hanging limbs, that which makes a human being is eradicated.

**Strategy meeting**                              **Führerbunker, Berlin**

Hitler: Even in earlier times the Asiatic storm could not be broken by everyone surrendering, but somewhere it must be halted. We ourselves have experienced how difficult it is to negotiate with Molotov. We were at the peak of our power at the time. Here stands the Asian Khan who wants to conquer Europe. England understands very clearly that Bolshevism is going to go on eating beyond the points already reached. This is the decisive battle.

If I win this battle, I promise myself nothing for my own personal name. But then I will be rehabilitated. Then I can remove a number of generals and subcommanders, including those in the SS, who have failed at crucial points. But to all those I have reproached for stepping down, I myself must set the example of not stepping down.

It is also possible that I will perish here. But then I will have perished respectably. That would still be better than sitting in Berchtesgaden as an inglorious refuge and issuing useless orders from there. This so-called 'southern fortress' is not self-sustaining. That is an illusion. The armies down there are fragmented. There is simply nothing to be done in the south.

*

**Hans Heischmann, 1906–90**　　　　　　　　　　　**Tempelhof, Berlin**
It has been claimed for some days that we have reached a ceasefire with America and England, and that now the Americans will fight with us against Russia. Who believes that? It's obviously a deliberate rumour to cheer up the soldiers and the civilian population and bolster their resistance. Some people are also suggesting that an army of German tanks is on its way from the west, and that we will only have to hold out for another 24 hours and everything will change. I am willing to believe that the west is being laid bare to save the capital of the Reich, but not that anything about the final result can be changed. Every day I see our troops outside the window. No war can be won with them. But the possibility remains that there are still reliable troops in the main line of battle.

After going to the Aeronautical Preparatory School three times the day before yesterday without meeting anyone, I tried again yesterday, again with the same lack of success. However, somebody must have been there, because 1) the barracks pub was open and 2) a search revealed that the ball of fat, about 6–8 pounds, had disappeared. I was about to go home without setting foot in the barracks, when I saw Herr Müller from the house opposite standing outside the front door. I had a chat with him; then there was an air raid siren. Of course Herr Müller wanted to 'inherit' something as well, but I told him straight away that it was out of the question. We didn't want to do any looting. But then we climbed in through an open window anyway, so that I could show him the provisions. We also fed the abandoned bunnies with turnips from the cellar. A shame, a shame, we both said. These supplies of potatoes, turnips, sauerkraut, red cabbage, bread, noodles, semolina, sugar and so on! And now it was all going to fall into the hands of the Russians! The locker of one of the boys who had been on sentry duty was searched, as a rotten smell was coming out of it. And lo and behold!, a big haunch of pork, already half rotten, was revealed! And, oh joy!, a big pack – 10 pounds – of dairy butter. We decided to share them both and take them away before they went off completely. Perhaps the meat could still be used. We stowed the butter away, then decided to borrow two loaves of bread lest the Russians get hold of them. When we were coming back from the cellar, we heard voices, and lo and behold!, Frau Krause had come with another woman, a laundry basket in her hand, to save some more food. Now at least there was an authorized person there who could allow us to take food away. And that was what she did; because the Russians were expected to invade over the next few days.

Frau Krause opened the downstairs supply room, and there was nothing there but sacks of sugar, salt, flour, semolina, and lots of pea sausage, powdered egg, vinegar, ersatz coffee, artificial honey, crisp-bread, soup spices, etc., etc. We packed everything we had room for and what I was able to bring home. Herr Müller lent me his handcart so that I could take about a hundredweight of food. However, the real prize was a whole leg of beef that I still had hanging in the storage cupboard so heavy that I couldn't even lift it. The storage cupboard was locked, and we couldn't find the key, but I crawled in through a side entrance and cut off bit after bit of the meat and passed it out to the women. In the end the rest of the leg was carried out. The meat was portioned out; Herr Müller had the lion's share. I brought about 8–10 pounds of meat home. And 4 loaves of bread, 10 boxes of crispbread, 6 packs of artificial honey, about 10 pounds of sago, the same amount of semolina, 5 pounds of sugar, a few packs of coffee substitute, a bag of noodles, a bag of dried onions, about 10 pounds of flour and 5–6 pounds of ham. It was a pretty good haul. At the same time the sirens wailed alternately air raid warning and all clear, and there was a lot of activity in the sky. I was delighted when I got home in one piece and without being stopped. I was soaked through, not from the rain, but from sweat; because of course I'd hurried as fast as I could.

**Hertha von Gebhardt 1896–1978**                    **Wilmersdorf, Berlin**

Rumours, rumours. We live on them as if on slightly rotten food, we have nothing else. The fears that haunt us and constantly reappear in new forms are more distressing even than the state that *exists*. Can one trust all one's housemates? Does anyone still have weapons? Will we get the armour-piercing missile and the artillery piece we've been promised into the house? Then God have mercy on us! Secret consultations. We'll have to reckon with soldiers or housemates who want to shoot here. We are all children of death when the house is being defended. Can we risk flying white flags already? General view: too soon.

Another big danger: all the U-Bahn stations are supposed to be blown up. If that happens here and we have no warning, it'll be the end of us all. If we are warned, it'll mean leaving the cellar – and then where will we go? So we repack the last of our belongings over and over again: from the necessities to the absolute necessities, in smaller suitcases that we can carry.

New rumour: the Russians in Steglitz are very friendly towards the civilian population. It's only the houses that are being used for military purposes that the cellar community has to leave, and with their hands in the air. Packing again for that eventuality. At Renate's suggestion: briefcases, very small suitcases that can be hung over both shoulders with straps or belts, so that the hands can be raised.

The cellar community are now much more friendly towards one another. Everyone helps each other, does each other favours. We've finally got used to living twenty to a room, letting air and light through the iron windows, but generally it doesn't last long, because we have to barricade everything up for safety again, and feel our way around in the dark by the light of the few candles. The darkness is desperate for me, I can't find a thing, I bump into things all over the place, I get indescribably depressed. The electricity has been off for good today. The U-Bahn has been closed now – is it going to be blown up?

Exhausted soldiers keep drifting by, it's impossible to know where from and where to. Wounded men drag themselves past.

Heavy bombing in the afternoon. Eight hits on this block alone. The air raid shelter has held out impeccably, all the flats above us are terribly badly damaged. 8 Gerolsteiner slightly damaged, hits to the cellar, our cellar still accessible and intact.

Evening: we no longer realize what danger we've been in. What we've just been through is the worst so far. We were slung around, a flame shot into the room from the burning stove, clouds of dust and mortar came through the window frames. I can't let Renate leave my side now – we're only calm when we're close together.

**B. N., b. 1921**               **cellar of the Propaganda Ministry, Berlin**
I'm in demand, there have only been two girls here until now, and aside from their duties men come to them with all kinds of requests like sewing on buttons, darning etc. You feel you're needed here, and I'm glad to be near Jochen.

Today another danger was added to the others: Soviet bombing raids. It was so unsettled during the night that I only lay down to sleep in the cellar at about 3 o'clock. Early on I secured provisions for the men, tidied everything at home and then headed townwards with a full rucksack and a shopping bag. My progress was slow, I kept having to take cover. Sometimes I said to myself, it's madness, and was close to turning round again. But then I thought of Jochen. I'd promised to come back, so I battled on. At Kaiser Wilhelm Platz I was picked up by a truck, stopped on the way by shelling, everybody out, then on over rubble and broken glass, till you couldn't see or hear a thing. I walked the last stretch from Möckernstrasse and sighed with relief when I reached my destination – I wouldn't like to do that journey again.

I'm being a secretary, a seamstress – as required. I enjoy it. Even though I can't discuss private matters much with Jochen – we are close to one another. I often have to look at him, and I feel as if I'm growing fonder of him from day to day.

We just said a quick goodnight. I'm lying on a mattress near the telephone exchange with blankets in the cellar, where we girls are sleeping, outside you hear the detonations of falling bombs – my daily routine during the war!

### Strategy meeting                                    Führerbunker, Berlin

Hitler: I see a chance to repair history only if I can succeed somewhere. Also bear in mind the repercussions of our defeat on the English. If we successfully defend Berlin today, and there are certain signs of an anti-Russian mood, they will see people with the appropriate foresight standing up to this colossus. They may then say to themselves: if one went with Nazi Germany, one might be able to face the colossus.

Goebbels: It would also be encouraging in the other direction. If Stalin sees this development in the mood of the western states on the basis of a German victory in Berlin, then he would say to himself: I'm not going to get the Europe I imagine. I'll just bring the Germans and the English together. So I'll throw in my lot with the Germans and reach some kind of agreement. Frederick the Great was once in a similar situation. He too got all his authority back at the Battle of Leuthen. If the Führer shows that this is possible, that one can stay, and that by staying one can win a battle, then these executions will have an instructive purpose and not a depressing effect.

Hitler: For me personally it's simply unbearable to have other people shot for things that I'm doing myself. I didn't come into the world just to defend my mountain retreat.

Goebbels: If matters in the south-west had been different, and there had only been a battle for Berlin like the one for Breslau, then I would have insistently argued against you coming to Berlin and turning it into a matter of prestige. But developments have now turned this battle for Berlin into just such a matter of prestige. The Führer has decided to stand up to the Russian enemy, and he has summoned the German people of Berlin to their last act of allegiance. This situation must be fought through now, in one way or another.

Hitler: There was no dilemma for me here. It is my only chance to restore my personal reputation.

Eventually the power of the Great Asian Khan must be broken. Back then it was the Battle of Vienna. Now it is the battle for Berlin. When Vienna was liberated, the whole of the Turkish forces were not broken straight away. It took years. But it was a beacon of hope. If the Viennese had cravenly surrendered then, the Turkish forces would have advanced still further.

*

**Friederike Grensemann, b. 1924**                                    **Berlin**
In the days leading up to 25 April you could hear the thunder of cannon. It was an uninterrupted rumble. I was becoming more and more frightened. In the evening the sky looked red in the east, and every now and again it lit up with bright flashes. Our almond trees had already blossomed, and so had the tulips, and the lilac was on its way. When all of a sudden lots of German tanks appeared on Berliner Strasse, I cut everything down and decorated the tanks with it. But what was there left to defend?

We'd been joined by Dirk's former Jungvolk leader Ingo Körner and a comrade of Wolfgang's, both already dismissed from the army. Then there were the two girls from next door to the Sturms', so there were seven of us sitting in the Lautenbachs' music room. They had a white grand piano, and there were chairs standing casually around. Ingo was a terrific pianist, and amidst the wail of the missiles he started playing Franz Liszt's *Hungarian Rhapsodies*. The missiles hit the house opposite, and were bound to hit us at any moment. I will never forget that end-of-the-world mood as long as I live. No one said a word, no one cried, only Ingo played. No one who hasn't experienced that could imagine it. Then there was also the sound of the anti-tank fire, and also machine guns. It was over! We would either snuff it or leg it. We decided to leg it, each man for himself towards the Kurfürstendamm.

**A woman**                                                    **Berlin**

Wednesday, 25 April 1945, afternoon.

To recapitulate: at about 1 o'clock in the morning I climbed from
the cellar to the first floor, and slumped on the widow's couch again.
Suddenly a violent fall of bombs, then the flak rages. I wait, I'm so
drunk on sleep, nothing matters. The windowpane was already
broken, wind blows in with the smell of fire. Under the bedclothes
I have an idiotic feeling of security, as if the sheets and blankets were
made of iron. And bedclothes are supposed to be so dangerous. Dr H.
once told me he had to treat a woman who'd been hit in bed, and the
particles of spring had penetrated her wounds so deeply that they were
almost impossible to get out. But the moment comes where complete
exhaustion wins out over fear. That's probably how the soldiers at the
front slept in the dirt. [...]

With a bucket in each hand I wandered through the blossoming
bowers to the pump. The sun shone so warmly. A long queue at the
pump, everyone worked the handle themselves; it moved heavily,
squeaking. Back the quarter of an hour's walk with buckets spilling
over. 'We are all fair burdenable she-asses.' (From Nietzsche, I believe.)
People are still jostling outside Bolle's because of the free butter. At
Meyer's there's an endless, dark-coloured queue consisting entirely of
men; they're selling schnapps there, half a litre per ID card, all available
kinds.

I went to fetch water again. A sudden fall of bombs on the way
back. On the grass in front of the cinema a column of smoke and dust
rose up. Two men in front of me threw themselves flat in the gutter.
Women ran to the nearest house doorways and down the stairs. I came
down after them, into a completely unfamiliar cellar without lights of
any kind. I brought the full buckets with me, otherwise people would
steal them from you. Down in the black darkness a terrified heap of
people, strange. A woman's voice groans: 'My God, my God...' And
silence again. [...]

When I returned once more from fetching water, the widow sent
me to find out what was happening in the meat queue. A lot of
angry shouting there. It seems that the delivery of sausage and meat
is constantly being delayed. This annoys the women more than the

whole war right now. That's our strength. We women always have the most obvious things on our minds. We're always happy when we're able to escape brooding about things to come and immerse ourselves in the present. At the moment sausage occupies the most important place in these minds, and distorts their perspective about things that are big but far away.

Back to the cellar at about 6.00 in the evening. Couldn't go on lying quietly up there, got scared as there were direct hits nearby and thick chunks of plaster fell on my blanket. I dozed away down here until Henni came from the baker's and reported that there's been a direct hit in the pharmacy. The owner died straight away. Whether from shrapnel, the blast or a heart attack it wasn't immediately possible to tell. Henni says he wasn't bleeding. One of the three black-clad women stands up and asks with elegantly pursed lips, 'So, how'd the fellow peg out?' The word 'shit' trips lightly from our tongues. We speak it with satisfaction, as if we were expelling our inner waste just by saying it. We approach the coming humiliation through our language.

**Arno Pentzien, guard**                                    **Zoo, Berlin**

The battalion commander informs me that I can go back to the battery. We set off and after walking around for a long time we find the battery in the Volkspark. Everyone was asleep, and I went to the artillery tractor position to see the boss, who immediately ordered a change of location. At about 10.00 a.m. the whole unit heads west. Ivan is firing fiercely at the houses again. The poor civilians! After a short journey we set up, to our surprise, in Berlin Zoo. We park our vehicles under the trees less than a hundred metres from the big flak tower. We don't have much time to look at the zoo. There's a lot of noise here, and we immediately dig foxholes for ourselves. The heavy flak gun in the tower is firing at targets in the air and on the ground. I lie down beside my foxhole and immediately go to sleep, in spite of the noise. At about midday I am woken by a terrible explosion, and even before I've woken up I'm lying in my foxhole. Russian bombers attack both flak towers. As not every bomb strikes its target, some of them reach us, but luckily there are no casualties. [...]

Some of the bombs fall into a big basin with pelicans and other water-birds in it, barely 20 metres away from us. This causes a massive shower which, since it's very hot, doesn't feel unpleasant at all. But at the same time the big birds that were slung into the air by the explosion fall back down dead in places. A big brown bear in a cage is bleeding badly from its shoulder, and growling and roaring with pain. Luckily our car is ready, and we leave this sad place very quickly. By the entrance an attendant sits in a little pointed bunker. I call up to tell him that his bear has been hit, and we set off towards the hospital. I'm so tired that I go to sleep on the seat in my car, and don't even hear the bombs falling around us. We had two more casualties from this shelling.

**Strategy meeting**                                    **Führerbunker, Berlin**
Goebbels: It seems important to me that for as long as we are not relieved from outside, we must keep our area of defence around Berlin as big as possible.

Hitler: The more cramped we are, the worse it is – the Allies will have drawn a demarcation line on the basis of diplomatic agreements. But the Russians certainly aren't thinking about keeping to them. I remember what it was like in the winter of 1940. I didn't go into war against Moscow on a whim, but because I knew on the basis of certain information that an alliance was being prepared between England and Russia. The question was whether one should strike or wait until one's hand was eventually forced.

I did meet Molotov back then. The Russians hadn't achieved any overwhelming global successes. They had been defeated in Finland. Then they had occupied a few territories. In the Polish campaign they waited until we were far beyond the agreed demarcation line. Then came our campaign in the west, in which we enjoyed a massive victory. The French hadn't expected that. The power of the Great Asian Khan must be somehow broken. It was the greatest victory in the history of the world. Then came our Luftwaffe's various demonstrations against England. And in the midst of this situation Molotov made monstrous demands on us.

*

**Lieutenant General Adolf Galland, 1912–96**          **Riem, Munich**
Germany's destiny was being fulfilled during these days. On 25 April
American and Soviet soldiers shook hands at the Elbe. The last defence
ring around Berlin would soon be broken through. The Red Flag flew
over Ballhausplatz in Vienna. The German front in Italy was collapsing.
And the last of the 2,755,000 tonnes of western Allied bombs that had
been dropped on Europe fell on Pilsen.

Around this time I summoned my pilots and said to them, 'The war
is lost in a military sense. Even our dedication can do nothing about
that… I'm fighting on because this deployment of the Messerschmidt
Me 262 has captured my imagination, because I'm proud to be one
of the last fighter pilots of the German Luftwaffe… Only those who
agree should go on flying with me…'

By now the harsh reality of war had definitively resolved the
question 'Bombers or Me 262 fighter pilots', and the latter had been
proved superior. The leadership in Berlin and elsewhere was completely
preoccupied with itself. Numerous authorities which had previously
argued for the distribution and deployment of jet planes had stopped
functioning or could no longer be heard. Bombers, reconnaissance
planes, ground attack pilots, night fighters and various operational test
units supplied to us along with our missing Me 262s now delivered
their planes to us. We were being supplied with turbos on all sides. In
the end we had a total of 70 planes.

*

**First Lieutenant Fritz Radloff, 1916–89**          **Westend, Berlin**
The night is quite quiet. The Russians scatter a few bombs, but not
many. The sun rises at about 3.45; 25 April is beginning. It's going to be
Westend's big day. The section still has five new batteries: Gartenfeld,
Plötzensee, Ruhleben, Westend and Grunewald. Just before 4 o'clock
the first orders to fire come in. Zilch holds his calculator pad on his knees,
Drews stands by the map, and I have the commander shouting in my
ear. The battle is being fought fiercely along the whole front. From the
Schiffahrtsweg in Spandau, from the Tegel Bridge to the Jungfernheide
dam. The enemy crept through to the Hinkle Bridge during the night,

and is planning to fight on to the S-Bahn embankment. As soon as the order to fire with trapezoidal sights has been given, the output values are issued to the cannon. Boom! Boom! Boom! The blasts ring out, the grenades whirl through the air to their target. The pioneers are asking for support fire, the lookouts at the front demand fire, the section gives orders, sometimes we don't know where to shoot first. The armoury sergeant leaps in, 'we've got to set up barrels, they're too hot!' The gunner next to him shouts, 'Cartridge compressor!' The Cäsar has a jammed barrel, sometimes we're just firing with one, but we're still firing. [...] There's barely time for a cigarette, hour after hour passes like that. The air is filled with the drone of shelling. Planes frolic above us, open fire from above, bombs, air battles, but we're not distracted by that, we fire, fire, fire! My two squadron leaders are already hoarse, the orders are coming so thick and fast.

At about 10 o'clock the pioneer liaison officer, a lieutenant colonel, brings us the following situation report: 'Enemy gathering to attack in the Jungfernheide. Counter-attack from Spandau at 11. From 10.45 until 11 heavy fire on XY area with all available barrels.' That's a mammoth task. I speak with the commander, and we're given another twelve barrels to add to the four we have already. At 10.45 to the second we unleash our deadly fire, blast for blast, shell for shell! In rapid clusters the shells leave the barrels, the earth trembles, impossible to hear a word. We're swathed in smoke and fog, all hell has been let loose. There! The red flares! The agreed sign to stop firing. Now the counter-attack begins, so, off you go, pioneers, God be with you, force the Russians out! Our best wishes go with you! We did what we could.

There's a new focus of activity at the Tegel Bridge. That's where the enemy is trying to cross with their tanks. The Gerstenfelde battery is in mortal danger. The lookout sits in the Siemens Tower and gives us the coordinates. This assault is turning into my heaviest of the whole war. We're homing in, firing at pinpoint targets, better and heavier than on any firing range. Bravo, bullseye! A tank is on fire! Keep going, keep going! Cluster after cluster out of the barrels! We've got to do it! The second tank is on fire, the crew climb out. Two lines to the left, 100 metres away, fire! Blast after blast, the shots strike home, the enemy loses one tank after another. And then the order: cease fire, tank retreating! With this order I climb on to the edge of the cannon and three times my men shout Bravo! New coordinates come in! And already it's going off again, no one is weary.

Down in the south, in Grunewald, things are looking bad. We have to turn our guns by 180 degrees and support the Grunewald battery. They've got 2,000 rounds of ammunition down there. Everyone not deployed at the cannon unloads ammunition. Round after round leaves the battery. Turn 90 degrees again, the village of Döberitz is under attack, fire support for Döberitz. Then my staff sergeant comes back from the pioneers. The counter-attack has collapsed, Jungfernheide is broached, the enemy has reached the embankment! We fire, fire and fire, all to no avail. It's impossible! And now it's time to defend Jungfernheide, everything we've got, the enemy must be pushed out! The assistant gunners are performing superhuman feats, drenched in sweat and covered in soot they stand by the cannon loading round after round, no one falters, it's a fierce duel, you or me! If you keep going, then so do I [...]

When the last cannon leaves the position at around 9.00 p.m., I head for my car to drive up Königsplatz on a reconnaissance mission to the Reichstag. I don't know what awaits us there! The commander just told me on the phone, 'What you and your battery are doing to defend the Reich capital is terrific. God will reward you!' The battery advances slowly along the Reichsstrasse, stopping repeatedly, taking cover and then setting off again. I myself drive on in my car, reach the east–west axis, swerve to avoid the anti-tank barricades, tell them a heavy anti-aircraft battery is coming, avoid bomb craters, shrapnel whizzes past my head, but I have to keep going. Keep going, because the battery's at stake. So I reach Tiergarten and I'm passing the Victory Column when a murderous rain of bombs comes wailing down. I'm thrown out of my car, I land next to a tree, things rattle and burst, just behind me a munitions store goes up, new bombs fall, columns of smoke rise up, the ground shakes, incredible explosions, dirt and red-hot iron fly through the air. Boy, you've found yourself in hell, I think. Just a good thing that the battery's still a way back, it mustn't come through here now. So it's off to the car and back! Easier said than done. The rain of bombs is coming down steadily, is my vehicle still intact? If not, I'll have to go on foot, because the battery would be irreparably lost here. So off we go! As a blast right next to me subsides, I get up, head over to my car. I run towards it twice, twice I'm thrown back by the blast, the third time I manage to get in, 2nd gear and accelerator down, all in a matter of seconds. The engine roars, and I pelt along the east–west axis, towards my battery. I reach them at the Knie and manage to get them to stop… Thank God, it's done. Sweat runs down my forehead, my reconnaissance officer gives me a cigarette, a brandy is passed from the back of the car, that feels good, I'm glad I've reached the battery again, the men are glad that I'm back with them.

**Senior Lieutenant Kroemer**                    **Tempelhof airport, Berlin**

In the morning we're standing at Tempelhof airport. Russian artillery is firing steadily. Of the eight Berlin defence sectors we're now holding sector 'D'. The combat commandant is at the Aviation Ministry. Our main forces are concentrated on the Karstadt multi-storey building and the Sarotti chocolate factory. Instead of infantry backup we've been sent cobbled-together air raid units. Behind us we've still got civilians appearing, trying to escape the artillery fire. They're carrying meagre little bundles, what's left of their possessions. Every now and again the injured soldiers try to get back to their families. But most of them stay because they're worried about being caught by kangaroo courts and hanged as deserters.

The Russians are blazing away with flame-throwers at the houses. The screams of the women and children are terrible. At about 3 o'clock we've only got just over a dozen tanks and about thirty armoured personnel carriers left. These are the only armoured cars in the whole Wilhelmsplatz Command. The chain of command is unclear, because orders from the Reich Chancellery are repeatedly coming in via Erich Bärenfänger . Tanks are being ordered to other flashpoints in the city, from which they don't return. It's only down to the steadfastness of General Mummert that our division isn't being sent to the slaughter today. There are hardly any vehicles left to transport the injured.

In the afternoon the artillery is transferred to the Tiergarten. There's very little ammunition left. Around the Tempelhof administrative building it looks as if all hell has broken loose. Shouting, grenade explosions, shells from the Stalin organs. The cries of the wounded, the noise of engines and machine guns. Above all this are patches of smoke, the smell of chlorine and burning. In the streets the bodies of women who were killed trying to fetch water. But also a scattering of women clutching anti-tank grenades, Silesian women filled with a wild thirst for revenge.

**Strategy meeting**                                    **Führerbunker, Berlin**

Hitler: [Molotov] insisted that we set up bases at the entrance to the North Sea on Danish soil. Even back then he was making claims on it. He was demanding Constantinople, Romania, Bulgaria, Finland, even though we were the victors at the time! So how is this man Molotov going to respond to the British and the Americans now, with such victories and after the catastrophic bankruptcy of the Allies. And now there's the Asian conflict as well. In America sober reckoners will be saying; What are we even doing here? Preparing capital investments, perhaps? But we won't find any profitable markets here. Our raw material is in China. But on the other hand we don't want Russia to go to war against Japan. They're saying: We'll sort out Japan on our own.

Goebbels: If the Soviets advance as far as the Elbe, including the Protectorate [of Bohemia and Moravia], the Americans will retreat and let the Russians take over. Only 20 to 25 British divisions will be left. Pacifist and armchair Bolshevik propaganda will spread among the British troops. Stalin will militarize his territory, including the German part. He will wage a propaganda war against the western powers because they have destroyed the cities. He is a better propagandist than the British.

The Soviets can pull out all the stops. Within a very short time there will be another conflict here. I can't imagine there is an intelligent Englishmen who can't see that.

*

**An SS man**                                    **Neukölln, Berlin**

Our men advanced as if on manoeuvres, leapt from door to door and fell upon the Red snipers hidden on the upper storey here. The tanks behind them spewed fire and flames and barely gave the enemy infantry the opportunity to fire effectively. Our attack gained ground, but then we suffered a severe blow. A unit that had been held in reserve arrived at Neukölln Rathaus, thought they were safe and stayed in the street in march formation. At that moment a whole salvo of Russian anti-tank missiles hit that very street corner. Shaken, a moment later I counted the corpses of fifteen young soldiers on the blood-spattered tarmac.

To our right and left the situation was increasingly confusing. As we cleared the reconquered area of Russians, we should really have been bumping into neighbouring squads. Instead, there were Russians on every side.

In the end a curious order reached us from the division: if the attack hasn't yet begun, then stop and wait for new orders. Otherwise do your best. So we would then have retreated three hours after a successful attack. In fact, however, there was no front left to us either on the right or the left or behind us. So I wondered what we were supposed to do now, and decided to stop our advance for the time being, but to take special care not to be cut off. The Rathaus thus became the centre of resistance, and a group of Hitler Youth were sent to us as reinforcements.

**A doctor**              **prisoner-of-war hospital, Neukölln, Berlin**

I spent a lot of time by the window of my observation post. In the street I saw women with shopping bags, hunkered soldiers moving along the buildings, armoured vehicles and motorcycles drove past. There was not a German plane to be seen, only Russian ones. Light anti-aircraft fire could be heard from Tempelhof airport. On the right a cloud of smoke hid the two 80-metre towers of the Karstadt department store, which loomed above the district.

The fighting edged closer, on the left-hand side particularly there was the rattle of machine-gun fire. The Russian attack seemed to be coming from two directions; in a straight line along the canal towards

Tempelhof and along the Ring to Hermannplatz. Lots of smaller units passed the hospital towards the centre of the city. These were the signs of an impending German collapse.

We hoped the fighting would stop soon, because our difficulties were mounting from hour to hour. 300 sick prisoners of war had to be treated, the water supplies were running out, and what were we to cook with? The situation of the seriously ill patients was particularly bad; they lay crammed together on stretchers or thin mattresses on the floor of the cellar in almost total darkness. Medical treatment and even the simplest hygiene was almost impossible. The cramped conditions were further intensified by the presence of many wounded Germans civilians, who were in no state to leave the field hospital after their initial treatment.

The operating theatre had had to be abandoned long since, and we made do with a former supply cupboard, where we performed amputations on an old wooden table with a mattress on it. The doctors worked without gloves, antisepsis was almost impossible, and the instruments were inadequately sterilized. It was no longer possible to change operating overalls and hand-washing was becoming a problem. The paraffin lamps were empty and the last candles used up. Luckily we had managed to find two bicycles with dynamos, and their two lamps – the pedals were turned by hand – provided enough light to operate by.

**Edmond Michelet, 1899–1970**    *Dachau concentration camp*
Suddenly an image from an operetta: a group of French Waffen-SS from the 'Charlemagne' Legion, who claim they have been accused of being deserters from the Russian front in a German court martial, march delightedly into Block 24. I walk over to them. They all look outrageously young and proudly display the red, white and blue insignia beside the SS death's head on their shoulders. Luckily for our morale, their Red Cross parcels had arrived. Auboiroux can't calm down. He would like to send these French SS men to the German VIP block. Sadly that isn't within our power.

**Strategy meeting**                                    **Führerbunker, Berlin**

Hitler: Now we are seeing the provisional peace treaty which Lloyd George once predicted. At the time Lloyd George explained in an essay that the peace of Versailles will be untenable and is insane. England is destroying the European equilibrium. It was a classically prophetic essay by Lloyd George.

\*

**Alexei Zaporozhets, Red Army soldier**                    *Berlin*
*To his girlfriend*

Hello, Dear Dora!

I send you, my love, these greetings, from... Berlin!

Yes, yes, from the capital of Germany, Berlin. Berlin is burning, all that is left of it now is ruins. Women and men cry in the streets as they walk eastwards. Let them cry, they have been laughing for almost four years. The whole of Berlin is in ruins, we are advancing steadily. For now I am healthy and cheerful and I love you deeply and truly.

When will we see each other? Soon, it would seem, but... as long as everything goes well.

I kiss you warmly

Your Lyosha

**Pyotr Zevelyov, Red Army soldier**                       *Berlin*

Dear Mamochka, Papa, Shura, Taya!

We are heading towards the centre of Berlin. Everywhere there is shooting, fire, smoke. The soldiers run from house to house, fighting their way across the courtyards. The Germans are attacking our tanks from windows and doors. But our tank-drivers under General Bogdanov have chosen a clever tactic: they are driving not down the roads, but down the pavements, some are firing cannon and machine guns to the right, others to the left, and the Germans are running away through windows and doors. In the courtyards themselves our supply-service soldiers are distributing food to the starving people of the city. The Germans are emaciated and completely exhausted. Berlin is an unprepossessing city – the streets are narrow, there are barricades everywhere, defective trams, cars, barely any people in the houses, everyone's in the cellars.

The mood among our privates and officers could not be better, we already see the day of victory in front of us.

Everyone here is pleased that you are already sowing grain. How I would love to be planting potatoes, tomatoes, cucumbers and pumpkins with you in our garden.

Goodbye, I kiss and hug you

Your Pyotr

## Ilya Krichevsky, Red Army soldier, b. 1907    *Berlin*

Three men, two correspondents and I, received the latest assignment from the editor on 25 April, when the fighting was becoming fierce and our soldiers had to fight for every building, every floor. This was all different from ever before, and we felt that we too would soon be facing special challenges.

We were supposed to join the 52nd Guard Division, but only had a vague idea of how it operated. While searching for the desired regiment we stopped in the building of a third-rate cinema. The place was crowded with soldiers relaxing after the battle. What was striking was what a good mood they were in. They still faced challenging and dangerous battles with the enemy, but they all drew confidence from the knowledge that the war was really coming to an end.

In one corner of the foyer something curious was happening. An elderly German stood at the bar of the former buffet, doing a thriving trade in some kind of lemonade. But to judge by the mood everyone was happy with the deal.

Warmly welcomed, supplied with lemonade, we decided to collect material about the best of these soldiers. Unfortunately I only had enough time to draw a single fighter, and there were so many great faces around. Everyone watched, and I would have liked to continue, but our editor's commission was still hanging over us. So we said goodbye and went on walking down the endless streets of Berlin, which echoed with gunfire. [...]

My last conscious impression fixed in my memory an incredible crash, a blinding fireball and a dull blow against my head.

When I came to, and struggled to open my dirty, sticky eyes, I tried to understand what had happened to me. I had a particularly loud roaring noise in the right half of my head, as if a bell were ringing right next to it. I wanted to get up, but I felt pain everywhere, as if I were being put through a mincer. [...]

Unfortunately I didn't own a watch, so I couldn't tell how much time had passed. I was worried about my comrades. I only had one option: to look for the regimental headquarters; I hoped I might be able to find a clue to their whereabouts there. A private soldier helped me get to the right place, on a parallel street. That last bit of the journey was extremely difficult. My head spun, my legs gave way. [...]

Only several days later did I find my way back to the division newspaper's editorial office, with the help of my editor. My appearance there was unexpected. My companions, who were alive and unhurt, had reported me dead.

In those historic days each one of us did what he could, it wasn't the time to think of one's own poor condition, and a day later I was making my way through the burning streets of Berlin once more, my portfolio of drawings on my back.

**Erna Saenger, b. 1876**                                                **Berlin**
Addi's birthday – where is she? And my boy, where are you? They're shooting all night! What is being without electricity, without gas, without water compared to this attack on home and Fatherland? I couldn't reach the morning watch – the bullets are flying – the infantry is firing. 'We are in the hands of the Lord and we want to stay there.'

**Strategy meeting**                                         **Führerbunker, Berlin**
Hitler: If we retreated so shamefully from the world stage, our lives would have been pointless. Whether one goes on living for a while or one does not is of no consequence whatsoever. Sooner end the battle honourably than go on living in shame and dishonour for another few months or years.

*

**St Georgen Parish Congregation Cemetery     Prenzlauer Berg, Berlin**

Name: Frika N.
Date of birth: 4.9.1923
Profession: Wife
Date of death: 25.4.1945
Notes: Suicide

Name: Heinz N.
Date of birth: 26.12.1913
Profession: City inspector
Date of death: 25.4.1945
Notes: Suicide

Name: Johannes H.
Date of birth: 3.1.1891
Profession: Bank manager
Date of death: 26.4.1945
Notes: Suicide by shooting

Name: Gertrud H.
Date of birth: 18.1.1897
Profession: Wife
Date of death: 26.4.1945
Notes: Suicide by shooting

Name: Gisela H.
Date of birth: 17.11.1923
Profession: Office manager
Date of death: 26.4.1945
Notes: Suicide by shooting

Name: Nikolaus v. R.
Date of birth:15.4.1889
Profession: Interpreter
Date of death: 26.4.1945
Notes: Suicide

*

**Traudl Junge, secretary, 1920–2002**          **Führerbunker, Berlin**
[Frau Goebbels] barely had the strength now to face her children
calmly. Spending any amount of time with them was such a monstrous
burden to her that she burst into tears afterwards. She and her
husband were now mere shadows, and already doomed to die. [...]
When I walked past the nursery door, I heard the six children's clear
voices singing. I stepped inside, and there they were sitting on three-
tiered bunk beds, holding their hands over their ears lest they put one
another off in their three-part harmony. Then they cheerfully wished
one another 'goodnight' and at last fell asleep. Only the oldest, Helga,
sometimes had a sadly knowing expression in her big brown eyes.
She was the quietest one, and sometimes I think with horror of how
that little child's soul felt in its deepest depths the hypocrisy of the
adults. [...]

We still joined Hitler for meals. Only Eva Braun, Frau Christian,
Fräulein Manziarly and myself. There is now no subject interesting
enough to divert us. I hear my voice like a stranger's. 'Do you think,
mein Führer, that National Socialism will return?' I asked. 'No.
National Socialism is dead. Perhaps in a hundred years a similar idea
will come into being, with the power of a religion that crosses the
whole world. But Germany is lost. It was not mature enough and not
strong enough for the task I had set it,' the Führer said over our heads,
as if to himself. I no longer understood him. [...]

Over in the bunker rooms of the New Reich Chancellery there
was the most terrible confusion. The men staying there were von
Below, Fegelein, Burgdorf, Krebs and Hewel, and Flight Captain Baur
and Oberführer Rattenhuber, who were longing for their Bavarian
homeland. They were, apart from me, the only ones who came from

Munich. Then there was Admiral Voss, a few unknown staff officers and Heinz Lorenz from the press. Bormann, with his staff, had his quarters there somewhere. Exhausted Volkssturm and Wehrmacht soldiers were living in the long corridors. A field kitchen kept them supplied with warm drinks and soup. Sleeping figures lay all over the floor, helpful women ran among them, and refugees, girls and nurses, Reich Chancellery employees, intervening where it was required. A makeshift operating theatre had been set up in one of the big rooms. Senior Dr Haase, who had been bombed out over at the Charité, worked day and night, amputated, operated, bandaged and helped where he could. The beds, which had been set up wherever possible, were no longer numerous enough. Soon there were no shirts, no underwear left for the wounded. [...]

The long corridor that led under the ground from the Reich Chancellery to the Führerbunker had already been shot apart in many places, and the thin ceiling had collapsed. Hitler wanted Frau Christian and me to be near him even at night. A few mattresses were spread out on the floor of the little conference room, we slept in our clothes for a few hours and outside the half-opened door the officers Krebs, Burgdorf, Bormann lay in chairs, snoring and waiting for the Wenck Army! Instead all hell broke loose above us. On 25/26 April the firing reached its climax; shots crashed without interruption, and each individual one seemed to be aimed directly at our bunker. [...]

Everyone everywhere was smoking a lot, whether the Führer was there or not. The dense swathes of smoke no longer bothered him, and Eva Braun stopped hiding her 'vice'. Sometimes a weary reporter came to us from the front. The main battle line was moving closer and closer to Anhalt station. Now it was the Berlin women and children whose cries we thought we heard when we went up and looked out into the flames and smoke. We heard German women being used as targets by Russian tanks, and again the only way out we could imagine was death.

When I think back today on the exclusiveness and gruelling precision with which everyone constantly discussed the best possible way of dying, even I can't understand how it is that I am still alive. [...] 'I do not want to fall into the hands of the enemy, either dead or alive.

When I'm dead my corpse is to be burned, to remain undiscoverable for all time,' Hitler decreed. And as we mechanically took our meals, without noticing what we were eating, we talked about the most thorough and certain ways of dying. 'It's best to shoot yourself in the mouth. Then your skull explodes, and you don't notice a thing. Death is instantaneous,' Hitler explained to us. But we women were horrified at the idea. 'I want to be a beautiful corpse,' said Eva Braun, 'I'm taking poison.' And from the pocket of her elegant dress she drew a little brass capsule containing a phial of cyanide. 'Is it very painful? I'm so afraid of having to suffer for a long time,' she admitted. 'And if I'm prepared to die a heroic death, it should at least be painless.' Hitler explained to us that death by this poison was completely painless. Through the paralysis of the nervous and respiratory system, death would occur within a few seconds. And that 'comforting' knowledge led me and Frau Christian to ask the Führer if we too could have such an ampoule. He had been given ten of them by Himmler, and when we left him after dinner, he gave us one each, with the words, 'I'm very sorry that I can't give you a nicer farewell present than this.'

### Friedrich Helms, bank director, 1883–1955    *Wilhelmshorst, near Potsdam*

My eye falls on my neighbour's garden fence: I am astonished to see a white flag protruding from it on a long pole. I am about to rage about this measure, which has never even been countenanced hereabouts, when the rumour rushes along the street that Russian armoured cars have crossed the village into the town and are now negotiating its surrender.

Waving the white flag! No, at first the thought was unthinkable. However, the general pause soon made way for feverish activity. Soon various forms of white were fluttering on houses, from windows and skylights. Here it was a handkerchief, there an apron on a walking stick, even a child's nappy appeared on a garden gate. A long, half-polished curtain rod hung with a cushion cover torn on one side, on which I could still read the letters M.T. near the nails, was our sad sign of defeat. […] All along the streets, house after house flew the white cloth of surrender, at least of this place, and, was it my imagination or fact, it almost seemed at first as if the flapping of these 'flags' was an over-hasty sigh of relief by the individual.

**Eva Richter-Fritzsche, artist, 1908–86**                    **Pankow, Berlin**
We are in no-man's-land. Arrivals of Russian and German soldiers in turn define an everyday that has descended into chaos. Here it is the individual case that characterises events and shapes opinions. And since yesterday our world here has been divided clearly and decisively – although the walls of home still bind us.

There were a few hours yesterday that cast a bright light on all human relationships. It was one of the longest days of my life, and had it been the last I would have been beyond hope.

**Margit Röhrich**                                                   *Berlin*
At 12.00, Russian invasion! School was occupied, us in the cellar, we didn't comply with Russian demands – at gunpoint – and they didn't shoot. We were in disguise.

*

**Matthias Menzel**                                                  *Berlin*
It's ages before morning comes. When it does, the first Soviet soldier is standing in front of us: a fair-haired youth of about seventeen, in a thick greatcoat, his clumsy pistol in his hand, his sub-machine gun over his back. He studies the watches, studies the women, studies the distilled water bottles that stand in the corner. A first incredulous, almost embarrassed smile darts around the cellar when he refuses to believe that the young woman painter is thirty-five. […] Now the visits to the cellar are never-ending. Young people and older ones go in and out; those straight-backed in stature and burly chaps; clear, vital faces and rugged Mongols. They come, wave their pistols about, ask for weapons and soldiers, search and go. We've stopped closing the doors. They have used the last bombs of the war, and have blown the windows off their hinges. The cellar is a bedroom, sitting room and reception room for the many who set foot in Berlin like this. They are the front-line warriors. I can't help thinking of the German soldiers, their victory and

trophy processions... Were we any different? Is this not just another category of front-line war, informed by the rough structure of the east, chiselled by the expansive power of the steppe, grown out of the nature of the bigger and less comprehensible mass of humanity? A monstrous procession of battles marks their features, a march of thousands of kilometres, a march of wrath, of rage, of retaliation.

They replace one another ceaselessly: the rough, the vicious and the ones with the smile of children. The victors go through the open doors. That is the primordial right of war. In the evening the rumours spread from house to house that women are being smiled at and looked for, women in whatever shape. And they, the women, race fearfully up and down the stairs, hide their faces with scarves, hide themselves, black face and eyes, want to stop being beautiful. Anything strange, any-thing sudden, anything violent frightens women, who have been living their lives without love for years. They hunger for silence. But every victory comes with the blare of shawms.

**Ilsetraut Lindemann, b. 1923**                *Falkensee, near Berlin*
Survived a day and a night of Russian occupation. Now it's past 8.00 p.m. and I have myself sufficiently under control to collect my thoughts in writing. I want to try to report on things one at a time. After the first Russian column had passed on, the baggage train came with all its appurtenances. It was of course unavoidable that there should have been unpleasant events in many places. [...]

But the fear was largely unjustified. Here they were *all* friendly, with one exception. He was thoroughly intoxicated, and his comrades brought him to his senses and took him out into the fresh air. The first batch stayed with us in the cellar for over two hours. Unfortunately communication was very poor. But we agreed that we are peaceful, good people and don't want war. They were very suspicious because they have had such grim experience of our soldiers.

No sooner was the first batch out than trucks came rolling up and their occupants moved in. It was like a pigeon loft. The senior boss with his staff stayed in our house. There were about eight people in all. But the men kept coming in with reports and orders all night. It wasn't very easy. But the officers were so decent, they gave us a large part of their food. Bacon, pork legs, tinned sardines, etc. There was an interpreter there, he was very valuable. Because otherwise there are so many misunderstandings that give unnecessary cause for concern.

But by and large everyone still has anxieties about those traits that exist in every nation. But the officers are keen-eyed and see off everything within their power. As I said, we have to be glad *so far* that we've survived like this. Hopefully it will be a peaceful night. I want to head for the cellar straight away. Mutti and Omi want to sleep upstairs. They desperately need to. Their nerves are stretched to breaking point. May God continue to protect us.

**Max Peuschel, 1905–81**                          *Tegel, Berlin*
A 'commissar' and two Russian soldiers appear in the air raid shelter in the early morning. Children are given bread and butter. Russians behave decently, eat, smoke and soon move on. They soon found 'friends' in the house. The adolescent daughter of one of the residents bows and scrapes to them. In the street someone tried to steal my watch, but it wasn't good enough for them! Herr Stephan (who also lives here) talks about looting near the prison.

Groats and glucose are being distributed to everyone in the building. At P's we can get cheese with ration cards. Russians passing through are handing out jam.

**Strategy meeting**                          **Führerbunker, Berlin**
Hitler: I have considered the situation of East Asia. If the Americans are at all interested in gaining anything from this war, then the war must somehow prove to be useful for them. It can only do that if they

1. destroy as much as possible in Europe. Then it will take European industry the next ten years to build itself up again, and during that time it will not represent competition.

2. America must maintain East Asia as a long-term profit market. And the Americans should fight now for the freedom of the Dutch and British colonies, only so that other people do business and the Soviets are in China and Manchuria.

It's all insanity! The Americans are calculating too! The change that has just taken place is a deep-rooted regime change. If history comes to a standstill here, what are the consequences? The consequences, on the assumption that we actually continue to exist and that we really beat the Russians and give him a shove without collapsing – the consequence is that the Americans say we want to concentrate on East Asia and secure a massive long-term profitable market in this huge area of half a billion people, including Korea, the Philippines and Manchuria.

*

**Theo Findahl, Norwegian journalist, 1891–1976**    *Dahlem, Berlin*
We must have dozed off, because at about half past twelve we suddenly started out of our half-sleep. Heavy truncheon blows against the house door. 'Open up! Open up!' Ada Norna rushes upstairs to open the door. The Russians! A second later it's as if the cellar is swarming with soldiers. In fact they are only three or four men, while others are stomping around in the rooms upstairs. The Red Army – an exciting encounter. The Russians in their soil-brown uniforms; black, dusty as always in a battle, armed to the teeth, look keenly around. We smile involuntarily with relief, the battle for Dahlem must be over, the Russians are already here.

'Finnish,' says Ada Norna.

'Norwegian,' I say. 'No Germans in the building.'

The Russians want to check that we are telling the truth, they check our passports and start searching the house. Two stay sitting downstairs in the cellar, an officer and his adjutant – an NCO? – I don't know the insignias of the Red Army, but the two young people have finer uniforms than the others, with lots of decorations and medals: the Red Star, the Order of Stalin, the Order of Lenin on their chests; the other Russians potter about in the villa, now we hear them in the dining room, now they go up the stairs and into the bedrooms on the first floor, now they're already up in the attic.

'Water,' says the adjutant, who speaks good German. 'We want to shave.' We fetch water in a bowl, the officer throws off his coat and the adjutant starts soaping his face with great skill. 'White collar?' asks the adjutant. We seek one out. He asks Frau Norna to sew it to the inside of his uniform collar. Frau Norna fetches needle and thread, puts on her glasses and fits the collar on tightly so that a narrow white edge stands out over the rim. The young officer wants to look his best for such a solemn occasion as the conquest of Berlin. The minutes pass. It's very quiet in the cellar. They've finished their ablutions. New soldiers come and go, no one speaks. The adjutant looks around the cellar, which is full of cases and boxes.

'Weapons?' he asks, eyes gleaming.

'Food for four people!' he demands next. Frau Norna makes some sandwiches.

'Schnapps!' The villa's wine cellar consists only of a few bottles of poor-quality Slovakian white wine, and the bottles on the shelves are filled with boiled water. We uncork them and drink a little first, to show that they aren't poisoned, and let him try it. He wrinkles his nose. 'Weapons?' he asks again, pointing to a box in a corner. 'Open it!' We open one case after the other, and he rummages through everything like a customs official, but doesn't take anything for himself. Everything would have been fine if Frau Norman hadn't stored boxes belonging to friends in the villa, which is, after all, under the protection of the Swedish embassy. She has no key for the suitcases, and doesn't know what's in them.

If one of them held a revolver we would be lost. The adjutant breaks the suitcase open with his sword. 'Yours,' he says to Ada Norna, and throws all kinds of women's clothing at her, dresses, underwear, lengths of silk. 'Yours,' he says to me, and throws suits and ties into my lap from an amply filled suitcase, obviously the reward for looking after them. The last box that he opens is unfortunately full to the brim with wine and spirits – French champagne, fine cognac, Mosel and Rhine wine of good vintages, liqueurs; a small fortune. If we had been their most bitter enemies, we couldn't have set a more cunning trap for them, or exposed them to more dangerous temptations. The Russians beam from ear to ear. 'Schnapps!' – at last, at last! A bearded ginger-haired boy who has chosen a pair of light blonde stockings as his private trophy from one of the other people's suitcases, fills a tin mug with champagne and looks sceptically at the bubbling fluid, a strange drink for him, but his first sips make him soft as a puppy. The champagne foam pearls like light spume on his stubble, he smiles like the sun. 'Good,' he says, and swings the cup, 'Ver' good. War no good.'

As if by magic the news of the alcohol seems to have spread all around the villa; one Russian soldier after another stomps in and wants to grab a drink. The mood continuously rises, now there's a party going on here, and they decide they want to wash themselves. In the cellar 'dining room' there are six fellows soaping their faces, laughing and messing about and splashing our valuable water supply around the place – they are very different in appearance, and we immediately learn from this that the Red Army has a very diverse recruiting base. The most agreeable one is a fat fair-haired middle-aged chap with a kind face, who repeats over and over again: 'Voina (war) nix gutt, Berlin kaputt. Gitler kaputt' (Russians can't pronounce the letter H). The least agreeable is the brash, German-speaking adjutant, who started out so prettily, reassuring us that he believed in God, but who has a sharp tone and is only too willing to start fingering his revolver if he doesn't get an answer quickly enough.

'Help, help!' cries a voice from the next-door garden, perhaps a wounded soldier? 'The Germans are swine,' the Russians say, 'they don't look after their wounded.'

It's increasingly jolly in the cellar, the box is big, the goods first class. Some of the Russian soldiers are thoroughly inebriated, and start dozing off. The adjutant maintains order and sends them upstairs from the cellar. With the bottles wedged under their arms they climb up the stairs to the second floor to lie down on the beds. 'Help, help!' cries the voice from the next-door garden. We sit there, unable to do anything. The hours pass. A new day dawns slowly. The Russians snore.

*

**Dr Schmidt, bank director**                    *Lichterfelde, Berlin*
The first Russians enter our house at about 8 o'clock. Machine guns at the ready. Question: watch? Parabell? (Pistol). German soldiers here? 10 minutes later the next troop arrives. Again the same questions, above all, very menacingly, the demand for watches.

Then over the course of the morning things really get going. A troop has fetched the two wine cupboards out of my cellar and smashed them open in front of the house. I anticipate terrible things. Luckily a car drives up and takes most of it on board. But there's enough left here to get lots of people drunk. One of them has drunk almost a whole bottle of brandy on his own and lies senseless in my front garden. At Frau F.'s house they start a carousal with my wine. Soon we hear piano-playing. It goes on like that. One troop after another. Always the same question about schnapps and watches.

A field kitchen turns up by the entrance to our garage, and people start setting up home in our laundry. They fetch potatoes out of all the cellars, they have everything else already.

One comes with our neighbour's chickens, roasts them for two officers, who then sit at our table in the dining room. We have to accompany them and are told to join in. With that, they bring brandy from my cellar, Hennessy. They like that, the Rhine wine is rather contemptuously rejected; nix good, nix strong.

We have our first conversations, one or other of them speaks a little German. Threats against Hitler, of course, who has covered peace-loving Russia with war. But now Berlin will be kaputt in a few days, and then the 'voina' will be over, and they'll be going home. That is repeated often, but equally often the reference to the scandalous deeds carried out by German soldiers in Russia. [...]

All day the troops scour the houses. In my house I can hear them smashing doors and furniture. As the next day teaches, I heard correctly. Suddenly a terrified Frau F. comes running into our house from across the street with her sister-in-law. So it's true that the women aren't safe. I hide both of them in the boiler room for the time being. The cook from the field kitchen soon starts dropping hints, he talks away at me and points at Eva. We look like two decent men confiding our fears to each other. They promise nothing will happen.

At 11 o'clock we withdraw back into the air raid cellar with the wives and children and shut the iron door, as agreed with one of the men. I cobbled the words together from a little dictionary and he understood 'close door'. When we've been lying there for 10 minutes there's a knock at the door. Outside a murmuring voice: come, come. After consulting with Schütz we open up. The cook! What does he want? He has brought a big plate of cooked meat that we're to eat.

We say we're too tired and would rather sleep. He goes. Ten minutes later he tells us he wants white flour to cook chops. He gets it, and disappears back into his kitchen. I reassuringly tell my friends, who are almost quivering with terror. But then in the night there are no more disturbances apart from a salvo of German shells nearby and the shattering of our windows.

### Gert von Eynern, 1902–87                          *Nikolassee, Berlin*

The San Francisco conference begins today! When and how will we ever find out anything about it?

Rohrer calls from Zehlendorf West. He drove across at about 6 this morning. Unfortunately he isn't asked for more information – how many tanks, infantry too, in what direction and what density.

We are alternately in the cellar, in the house, on the floor. Several fires nearby, a house near to Röhl the butcher burns to the ground, others towards Schlachtensee-Bunker and Machnow.

Clip-clopping horses. A coach full of Russians (fur caps), another one, a third, laden with sacks. The baggage train of a unit being sheltered here? Or a baggage train already departing? They turn by the garage at number 8 and move on again.

Ruth reports a single Russian in the garden of no. 8. We're standing rather hesitantly in the dining room when he knocks at the back door. Where Brügelmann? (Up on my balcony, unaware of anything.) Gretel and Ruth and I are to go to the cellar, Gretel sets off agitatedly soon after I do, and a short time later we're joined by Ruth. Then Brügelmann, who had come to find Ruth, was sent upstairs again, then the soldier had come to him and been given his watch. And left again.

We consider going upstairs, but instead decide to eat the potato salad with garnish in the cellar, with brandy. From 9 we go to sleep there, in spite of lots of rifle shots and firing from a mortar set up not far away. Some nearby shots had broken windows by the back stairs. In the afternoon a shell did some damage to no. 9 and no. 8. Brügelmann beat E.W. at chess.

**Frau Speer, d. 1968**                    *Zehlendorf, Berlin*

We understood that we were really Russian when the sun rose, and that was around about 4.30. Then a strange life started up outside, a loud clip-clopping and knocking at the door, we heard saws and axes at work, strange voices in a very strange language. Then we got up quietly and made ourselves ready. The women were sent to the upstairs rooms and told to stay quiet. The street was full of Russians, going in and out of all the houses. I watched with interest. Sibylle did the same from upstairs. Back in the garden the Russians were strolling about but not trampling anything, even though they were climbing over the low fences and getting from one house to the other like that.

The weather was beautiful. I was wearing my green suit, the one that I haven't taken off during the day, probably for 14 days, and Sibylle's green headscarf. When I started clearing up in the kitchen, the first Russian looked through the bars and said, Hei! That was probably supposed to mean 'Heil'. He laughed affably and so did I, and he walked on. The troops look fabulous, incidentally. Nothing but tall chaps with immaculate kit.

Some time had passed before I suddenly noticed that some of them were standing on the broken garden steps and wanted to enter the room. I called to them, and they came to the kitchen window and cheerfully came down the little steps. I told them to watch out and not to knock over my water barrel. They were very careful.

Sibylle's budgerigar was in the dining room. What a delight! One of them in particular started talking to the bird and playing with it. The other looked raptly at the Holbein family. The first was a small, dark Tartar type with a huge sub-machine gun, the other very pale blond, with a beautiful rifle that he rested on. Then they went into my room, and the little dark one sat down on the sofa. On the table was a tiny pack of cards belonging to Sibylle. He picked it up straight away, said something about 'children', and shuffled the deck and looked at me pleadingly and clearly wanted to have it.

Then he looked at my books on the table, there happened to be one by Bernard Shaw: *The Intelligent Woman's Guide to Socialism and Capitalism*, or something, it was called. They chattered about that for a long time. I asked the dark one what insignia he was wearing, and they explained to me that it meant membership of the NKSW = SS, they said. I was hoping we would have a lengthy conversation, I wasn't scared at all. They asked me if I was Polish. And then they peered at my handbag, but were a bit embarrassed and didn't go near it. They asked if there was a man in the house, and then found the Luftschutz helmet, and seemed furious about that, but understood my explanation. They then scratched off the swastika on it with a nail and announced really angrily that 'that was it'. Then they went out of the front door, 'to street'. The other residents had been quiet as mice. That was my longest conversation with Russians.

When most of them had left I went outside with Conradus to take a look. Everything was in a state of wild excitement. The women all wore black headscarves and looked like nuns, and when I heard all the things that had been done, my knees gave way. At first no one would believe me that everything had been so calm here. It was incomprehensible, and at first I didn't understand either. There had been looting everywhere, everything had been rummaged through, the men threatened, the women and girls had been raped, it must have been terrible, particularly in the courtyard. Herr Fernau was dead, so was Herr Erkelenz. I went home in a quite different state of mind. There I found Sibylle and had a direct word with her. I advised her to look as smart as possible, her hair nicely combed, and to be friendly. From my observations that could only be useful. Thank God she was so thin as well. We were to be very careful, she was to hide as much as possible, but if anything did happen, under no circumstances was she to make a tragedy out of it! Then we played halma all day and set out games of patience.

From that point on I didn't open the door if anyone hammered at it. It didn't happen very often. The door struck me as solid enough. The Russians were forbidden to force their way into the houses. We wanted to take a risk, and we were right. We did have anxious minutes when they stopped for a long time outside the door, but then in the end they always went to our neighbour, who was usually more stupid and opened up. They didn't come from behind anyway because there was so much damage at the back, and they avoided houses like that. Basically it isn't very hard to get on with the Russians if they aren't drunk and you're not scared. It would probably be perfectly easy if we could communicate. They're very sweet-natured, they share what they have, but they also take what they feel like taking on the spur of the moment, whether they can use it or not. They have quite primitive notions about that. Not a trace of morality. They're always charming to little children. I just say this in passing, because there's lots one can say on the subject of children. Our first Russian day was now over, meaning that the worst of it was.

**Peter Bagh**                                    (*Babelsberg, Berlin*)

When the battles on the other side had subsided, things livened up on our street. A Russian major with retinue viewed the houses and gardens from the street and sent a sublieutenant and ten men who wanted to know if our attic was a suitable place to set up a lookout post. I brought the sublieutenant up, he thought the attic was suitable and sent two men with phones up there. When he heard that I spoke Russian, he and all the others gathered around the circular table in the dining room, bringing with them wine and cigars from German Wehrmacht stores, and soon we were engaged in the liveliest conversation. They had problems with the Dutch cigars at first, because they tried to smoke them with their white wrappers still on. It was from them that I first learned about the mobile gas chambers that the Nazis had used as a means of mass extermination in the east. At the time I didn't believe their reports. In response to my remonstrances about the looting, rapes and murder that the Russian troops were supposed to have committed after crossing the German borders, they explained that after crossing the Oder they had been under the strictest instructions to avoid committing such crimes. If we learned of any such abuses we were to inform them immediately. The guilty parties would be shot on the spot. I concluded from this that the crimes that the Russians had committed in East Prussia, Pomerania and Silesia were part of Stalin's policy, as brutal as it was deliberate, to encourage the troops to behave violently and drive the German population as a whole to flee. Our conversation lasted until well into the night, when the Russians fell asleep on their stools, in their armchairs, on the sofas, on the floor, wherever they happened to be, without bothering us in any way. Early the next morning they had disappeared, as had the guns that had been going off in our neighbour's garden.

**Vladimir Kovanov, Soviet field surgeon, b. 1909**   *Blankenfelde, near Berlin*

Our medical unit was in Blankenfelde outside Berlin. Right nearby there was a German field hospital that had already been occupied by our troops. My boss, Colonel Tarasenko, ordered me to visit the wounded lying in the hospital.

'It's possible that among the wounded there are uninjured Fascists who will shoot us in the back,' he said to me. After half an hour we reached the field hospital. Our sentry was standing by the front gate. The sentry warned us: 'A captain from our counter-intelligence service has just arrived.' So we marched to the main entrance. We were still on the steps of the front building when a shot went off inside, and we dashed to the entrance hall. We were met by our captain, his arm dangling lifelessly. I quickly used my handkerchief as a tourniquet for him, and the captain said quietly, 'What an idiot! He should really have been shot down on the spot, but I couldn't do it, both the chap's legs have been amputated...' At that moment an old German military doctor ran up to us. It was the head of the field hospital. His whole body quivering, he tried to explain to us that his patients didn't know his hospital had been occupied by the Russians. That's why the German officer fired at the Russian captain with the pistol he had under his pillow when the captain entered the ward.

After I had treated the captain's wounds in the operating theatre, assisted by the German doctor, we did the rounds of the wards together. In every ward we were received by a doctor and a nurse, who told us the basic facts about their patients. They all made a huge effort. We visited all the wounded like that. My companion kept a pistol at the ready under his white coat. We found no unauthorized patients.

**Emmi Z., housewife, b. 1893**   *Karlshorst, Berlin*

A horde of Russians stormed into the stairwell and we all had to do it. Even little Inge, who was just 8 years old, I knelt down in front of the soldiers, it did no good.

Later we had to cook for them, they didn't like the gravy boat.

**Strategy meeting**                                   **Führerbunker, Berlin**
Hitler: It could be that the isolationists will say: American boys can only fight for American interests. Why should the Americans die for non-American purposes? In all those countries there's no democracy at all, for example Romania, Bulgaria, Finland. The Americans are going to withdraw from here and hurl themselves at East Asia, obliging the Russians to stay here because they cannot leave us free, so the Russians won't be able to get involved in East Asia.

\*

**Walter Schellenberg, 1910–52**                            **(Flensburg)**
The next day, 25 April, I had Standartenführer Bovesiepen summoned to Flensburg. First I showed him my special power of attorney with Himmler's signature, which said, 'As General Schellenberg is acting on special instructions from me, his orders are to be obeyed without question.'

Now I explained to Bovensiepen that all concentration camp inmates of Danish and Norwegian nationality without exception are to be handed over to Sweden. I added that I planned to travel to Copenhagen the next day to discuss the political situation of Denmark with the Extraordinary Minister and Plenipotentiary in Denmark, Dr Best.

After that I asked him to make preparations for this meeting. The chief purpose of the journey was to stop all death sentences from being put into effect.

**Mopsa Sternheim, 1905–54**                            **(Ryd, Sweden)**
Ravensbrück. And then, one fine day, on 23 April 1945, the Swedish buses outside the camp. Bright white trucks with the Swedish cross on them. Those wonderful lads from the Swedish Red Cross who swamped us with cigarettes and cakes and helped us out – who didn't shout or jostle. [...]

And now here. Folketspark – the People's Park, a little park for the people of Ryd, on the shore of the lake and surrounded by forest. [...]

Everything's organized, it's terribly hygienic and there's nothing dreamy about it.

130 Frenchwomen are crammed together into a ballroom. I'm in the little room next door, with four other patients. The window looks out on to the lake. The lake and the forest are as flat as the whole country, and lots of bright blue sky. A beautiful sky, with no depth and no secrets, a hygienic sky.

Beside me are four elderly survivors. Peaceful, chatty. And me with my fluttering nerves and not fully conscious.

\*

### Adolf Hitler, 1889–1945                    Führerbunker, Berlin
*To Alfred Jodl*

A quick implementation of all the relief attacks in the directions ordered is urgently required. The 12th Army must advance along the Beelitz–Ferch line and immediately continue the attack in an eastward direction until it unites with the 9th Army. The 9th Army attacks towards the west along the shortest route and establishes a connection with the 12th Army. After the unification of the two armies the important thing is to turn in a northerly direction, destroy the enemy units in the southern part of Berlin and establish a broad connection with Berlin.

### Charles de Gaulle, 1890–1970                    *Paris*

Philosophers and historians will later argue about the reasons for this stubbornness, which is leading a great nation to its complete collapse, a people that is guilty and needs to be punished, but whose destruction will be lamented by the intelligentsia of Europe. As far as we are concerned, at the moment we can do nothing but double our efforts side by side with our allies, to bring things to an end as soon and as completely as possible.

### Erich Weinert, 1890–1953                    *Moscow*

To the men and women of Berlin!

Compatriots! The hour has struck. The end is here. Not the end of Germany, as Hitler and Goebbels tried to tell you, but the end of their murderous and incendiary rule. This end could have come earlier, before our homeland became a theatre of war. It lay in your hands. But until five past twelve you allowed these rogues to chase you into the fire. Now our Berlin is a pile of rubble.

You have put up with it for twelve years now. It began with arson, murder and deceit. Hitler had the Reichstag set on fire and thus gave the signal for war against the liberal forces of Germany. Berlin was caught unawares, before it could collect its strength to resist. And arson, murder and deceit remained the means with which the bandits ruled until the very last day.

Hitler means war! – that was our tireless warning when the man-servant of the armament companies set about taking control of state power. But Berlin let things happen to it rather than going on the attack. By then it was too late. Anyone who got in the way of the brown-shirted menials was silenced. Thousands lost their home, to wage from abroad the battle against those who had dishonoured their fatherland. [...]

Berliners! The war is over. Berlin is in ruins, but no one now will hang his head. May will not forget to blossom, even over ruins.

New life begins with the last shot, with the last bomb. What has happened can no longer be changed. But from now on every stroke of the hand or the hammer will not mean death and destruction, but will serve construction, peace and life.

Times will be hard before life in Berlin resumes, before every Berliner once again has his roof over his head, his workplace, his daily bread. But with every working day the oppressive burden that the cursed days of Hitler placed upon your shoulders will grow lighter.

Order will come from chaos. Our torn, deracinated, deluded nation will once again, on the basis of the law, feel free and safe. The honest workers of all classes and philosophies will come together into a truly democratic community.

And Berlin will once again lead the country. To work, compatriots!

**William L. Shirer, journalist, 1904–93**                *San Francisco*
As Berlin lay dying in the flames and blood of the war that started there nearly six years ago, we saw in this splendid city today the first step taken on the long road toward an organized peace.

The conference of forty-six United Nations got off to a good start. The opening ceremony was simple, but like the simple things often, very moving. Here in a resplendent Opera House, built as a *War* Memorial, were expressed all the hopes we have of peace. In Berlin, a maniac's hopes of world conquest were being buried in the debris of a once great city, here in this beautiful community along the ocean we call Pacific, more decent hopes were being born.

Everyone seemed to feel it. I have never seen diplomats – fellows who usually are rather proud of their cynicism – so solemn as they are today. They all knew – you seemed to feel – that they dared not fail this time in the job of getting an enduring peace.

There was a very symbolic little touch at today's formal opening. Along the great stage, behind the speaker's rostrum, a group of GIs, men and women representing all of our armed forces, stood at attention under the flags of the forty-six United Nations. They were youngsters. They had seen war at first hand. Some had been wounded. There were no officers. They were just average Americans – average American citizens – in uniform. It is these Americans, who have fought the war, who now insist on building for the peace so that they and their children won't have to go through this mess of war ever again.

**Grete Paquin**                                    *Geismar, near Göttingen*

The relaxed atmosphere of grateful freedom is making way for a vague fear. Many things are happening that I would not have believed. Thus for example the editorship of the only newspaper has been taken over by a man whom many of the people of Göttingen have known to glitter with every political colour. He drinks wine with Americans, his house was not confiscated while old democrats were thrown into the street. University matters seem to lie in the hands of people who, to put it mildly, have been through several political transformations. I wouldn't be surprised if the old Dozentenführer [leader of the university lecturers] were to turn up again and explain that he'd only joined the SS to keep worse things from happening. Such things happen and are believed.

Among the ordinary people one can experience the same thing. A fat master baker who answered with a loud 'Heil Hitler!' when I said 'Good morning' recently explained to his customers, 'At last I can breathe. For years the Gestapo was standing at my back with a revolver.' Sophie at the Institute, who wanted to fight the 'plutocrats and parsons' after the final victory, explained, 'We've already thought about joining the church again.'

What's going on there? Isn't this just the confusion of the first moment, and do these things cleanse themselves, or must we learn that certain people always float to the surface like corks in water? To some extent we can withdraw inwards and try to give an example with our lives, but many people are already embittered, and in view of public injustices it takes character to remain relaxed.

*

**The German Red Cross Tracing Service, 1989**
Subcommittee for the Tracing of Children – 2,697 – male
   Surname: unknown
   First name: unknown
   Assumed date of birth: 20.4.1943
   Found: in April 1945, seriously injured by the Kleinhammer forestry building near Königswusterhausen
   Clothing: unknown
   Description: blue eyes, dark fair hair. Birthmark on his back.

*

*Spring*

Man forgets his spirit's cares,
But spring is in blossom, and most things are glorious,
The green field spreads out magnificently
The stream flows brightly beautiful.

Trees cover the mountains,
And glorious is the air in open spaces,
The far vale stretches into the world
And tower and house rest against the hills.

Your obedient servant
Scardanelli

Friedrich Hölderlin

O taste and see that the Lord is good.
Blessed is the man who trusteth in
him.
DAILY READING: PSALM 34: 8

Die ofen heizen
Dee aiefen hitesen
Light the stoves
STARS AND STRIPES,

DAILY GERMAN LESSON

**Adolf Hitler, 1889–1945**                    **Führerbunker, Berlin**
*Wireless message to Alfred Jodl*
  1. Where Wenck spearhead?
  2. When due to attack?
  3. Where 9th Army?
  4. Where Holste group?
  5. When due to attack?
  Sig. Adolf Hitler

**From the Wehrmacht report**
The heroic fight for the centre of the Reich capital is continuing with
undiminished intensity. In fierce battles in the streets and houses
troops of all parts of the Wehrmacht, Hitler Youth and Volkssturm are
holding the centre of the city. A shining symbol of German heroism.

    The enemy, who has broken through Anhalt Station, along Potsdamer
Strasse and in Schöneberg was halted by the brave defenders. Flying
units have dropped ammunition over the city again, at great sacrifice
to the crew.

**Klaus Mann, 1906–49**                                               *Rome*
Still working on the article and waiting for marching orders to set off
for Germany. Evening with Hans Brinitzer, here from Caserta.

**Rolf Hädrich, 1931–2000**                          **Hermsdorf, Thuringia**
Today there was skimmed milk.

*

**SS-Standartenführer**
 **Dr Ernst Günther Schenck, 1904–98**              **Führerbunker, Berlin**
Night – 12 hours before Hitler's suicide: […] We must have been
waiting for a few minutes, then Hitler, alone, came out of the door that
closed off his accommodation bunker and greeted us from the bottom
of the stairs with the words 'Forgive me for getting you out so late.'
Haase reported, and I saluted. […]

 I had never before stood so close to Hitler; the man was not a
shadow of the one shown in millions of pictures. He was wearing
a grey frock coat with the gold embroidered insignia and the Iron
Cross on the left side of his chest, and long black trousers; but the
man in that outfit had collapsed in on himself to an alarming extent.
I looked down at a bent back with protruding shoulder blades, from
which he lifted his head almost in torment when he spotted Haase.
A mountain rested upon him and made it hard for him to climb two
more steps. The eye that he turned to me stared painfully. It no longer
shone, the white was dark, no expression stirred in a face in which bags
beneath the eyes testified, compellingly and revealingly, to a lack of
sleep. Deep-etched lines ran from the wings of the nose to the corners
of the mouth. The mouth remained closed, the lips pressed together.
The movement with which he demanded my hand and shook it was
a reflex. […]

 In an almost toneless voice he said he wanted to thank us for
taking charge of the wounded. He climbed on to the step where I was
standing. Inches away from me, I could see that the lunar landscape
of his ravaged face was a pale yellowish grey. A handshake for Sister
Erna, and a puppet-like further step up to the second sister. We had

said nothing, but she was troubled and agitated, overwrought and hysterical, she started repeating what she had heard a thousand times: '*Mein Führer* – faith in the final victory destroys all foes – *ein Volk, ein Reich* – eternal allegiance – Heil.' Hitler stood in front of her and looked at the agitated creature. Haase, who had been standing behind him, reached for her arm. She broke away from him, crying, almost shrieking. [...] I thought the outburst was unseemly, but Hitler had come across someone who still stirred something within him. He said dully, to no one in particular, 'One should not try cravenly to escape one's fate', and turned away.

He slowly went down the steps of the spiral staircase, past Haase, to whom he waved to go with him. An orderly opened the door to his rooms and closed it when the two men had stepped through.

*

### Fritz Hochwälder, 1911–86    *Zurich*
*To Georg Kaiser*

Dear Herr Kaiser,

I have not been in touch because until now I have seen no opportunity to join you in Ascona. But as I am on fatigues from 14 May for four weeks, I would like first to speak to you – if I may. [...]

I saw your *Raft of the Medusa* here – unfortunately the production was inadequate. The piece will survive the decades once all the nonsense studied now with such care and effort has long been forgotten.

It is curious how indifferent I am to the events of the day, for which I've been waiting for twelve years. [...]

Warmest regards

Your Fritz Hochwälder

### Oskar Kokoschka, 1886–1980    *Dartington*
*To Josef P. Hodin*

Dear Hodinus, thank you for your article, which I don't wish to complain about, as long as you take up the tender pen-strokes that I have added to clarify the matter.

Painting political pictures in England doesn't just mean complaining about the Nazis in Germany. Anyone who lives in safety here could do that. Instead one must tell the people here that the difference between Nazis and democracy does not lie, or not only, in insular delusion. I know there are the famous 'degrees in which we differ'. But first of all Fascism is not yet dead, and then the differences between here and there can become even less pronounced over time. We are constantly trying to pursue the process of making it so. Our leader Churchill helps.

So if you have time, please include my quiet whispers in your opus and show your Swiss and Swedish friends that I am not a 'refugee' but a person in full possession of his critical faculties. I wish you a good recovery and still more Armageddon.

Yours O. Kokoschka

## Richard Strauss, 1864–1949　　　　　　　　　　*Garmisch*

On 30 April Garmisch was occupied by American troops. At 11.00, after some major had declared my house suitable for billeting, a Major Kramers turned up and, ignoring any protests, started to clear out the house including my sick mother. Richard [Strauss's grandson] didn't want to let me protest, lest I get worked up, but I went to the car and told the young major only my name as composer of *Rosenkavalier* and *Salome*, whereupon he immediately remembered his manners and shook hands with me and in two minutes everything was resolved. [...] I gave everyone my picture and finally played the Rosenkavalier waltz: in short: successful self-defence via the intellect!

\*

## Factory buyer Joseph Lewis, b. 1907　　　　　　*Birmingham*

Events in Germany are happening at a great rate, and if we can trust the papers, particularly these last evenings, Himmler has decided on an unconditional surrender to the British, the Americans and the Russians, and if all goes well, this will be the week of peace.

**John Colville, 1915–87**                                    *London*
The newspapers are full of 'Victory any minute now', and so indeed
are we all. But opinion remains sober and I doubt there will be the
same jubilation or the same illusions as in 1918.

**Harold Nicolson, 1886–1968**                               *London*
It has snowed again very hard during the night and the lilac is weighted
with great puffs of snow looking very odd. It is very evident that
we shall accept an offer of surrender from Himmler and that it may
come at any moment. Meanwhile the news of Mussolini's murder is
confirmed. He was caught near Como and murdered.

**Adolf Hitler, 1889–1945**                    **Führerbunker, Berlin**
*Political testament*
   Since 1914, when I deployed my modest strength as a volunteer in
the First World War forced on the Reich, over thirty years have passed.
   During those three decades all my thoughts, my acts, my life have
been devoted only to love and loyalty for my people. They gave me the
strength to make the most difficult decisions that any mortal man has
ever faced. During that time I have exhausted my capacity for work
and my health.

                                *

**Major General Wilhelm Mohnke, 1911–2001**  **Führerbunker, Berlin**
7 in the morning
   I stepped into his bedroom with my documents. He was sitting on
a chair beside the bed. Over his pyjamas he wore a black silk dressing
gown; his feet were in black patent leather slippers. [...]
   The man seemed to be very collected, and to have slept well – which
of course he hadn't. Admittedly on his left-hand side his limbs were
trembling. [...]
   Now Hitler asked me precise questions. The first was: 'Mohnke,
how long can you hold out?' I replied: '24 hours, mein Führer, no
longer.' Then I described the situation to him. The Russians had
reached Wilhelmstrasse, they had entered the tunnels of the U-Bahn

under Friedrichstrasse and even advanced under Vossstrasse, most of the Tiergarten was in their hands, and they were fighting on Potsdamer Platz, 300 metres away from us. Hitler listened to this quietly and with great concentration. [...]

Now, after we had discussed military matters, he began to talk to me about politics. It was probably the last of his many monologues. The basic idea that he outlined to me that morning was: the western democracies were decadent and would not be a match for the young, fresh nations of the east, for whom rigid leadership like that represented by the Communist system was exactly the right thing. The west would be subjected. The tone in which he expounded on this thesis was relaxed and detached. Shortly after 7 I left him again and returned to my position.

**A telephonist**                                      **Führerbunker, Berlin**
He looked broken, burnt-out, lost. We had realized long ago that he had no choice but to kill himself, and we waited for the stormy conference of 22 April with a feeling of nervous anticipation for the shot with which Hitler would bring matters to their conclusion. In the stillness of that morning – the only sound the quiet hum of the fans – I found his brooding silence particularly oppressive, indeed uncanny; I quickly withdrew back to the little telephone switchboard beside the engine room.

**Otto Günsche, adjutant, 1917–2003**                **Führerbunker, Berlin**
I greeted him; he was completely calm and his voice had its familiar tone when he said to me, 'I don't want the Russians to display my corpse in a panopticon. Günsche, I expressly order you once again to ensure under all circumstances that nothing of the kind can happen again.'

*

**Edward Perry Morton, US officer, 1894–1954**                *Palermo*
I have just returned from a visit to Catania and Taormina. Catania is a seaport and is a surprisingly beautiful city at the foot of Mt. Etna,

built on the remains of an amphitheatre that must have looked like the Colosseo in Rome. But it was Taormina that rewarded me for the four or five hour trip, for Taormina is one of the most delightful vacation spots in the world. It is an improved model of Laguna Beach and Carmel with a superb Greco-Roman amphitheatre thrown in. A picturesque sea coast, rich in both historical interest and natural beauty, extends to both north and south; and in the Badia Vecchia, Taormina has one of the most beautiful Gothic exteriors in the world. Trim of black lava from Etna, in the most artistic design, is superb.

### Paul Valéry, 1871–1945                                             *Paris*
What could be more repellent than Mussolini's death? Everything about the matter is mean; he and his murderers. His weakness in the face of death, the corpse being spat on, the display.

   Milan – what horrors!

*

### Martin Hauser, sergeant in the British army, b. 1913         *(Italy)*
Mussolini has been shot in Milan by partisans who had recognized and arrested him on his flight to Lake Como and, after a short trial, executed him. So died the founder of Fascism – 'Il Duce' – shot in the back as a traitor in the main square of Milan, on the same spot where anti-Fascists had been murdered a short time before.

### Alexander Vishnevksy, Soviet field surgeon               *Ussuriysk*
Reports have come in that Mussolini and some of his ministers have been executed in Milan by Italian patriots. So Italian Fascism is coming to an end.

   I still vividly remember an evening many years ago, when Gorky came to us and told us about the Fascist system in that country.

### Richard Falk                                              **Lauterbach**
No one knows for certain what is happening on the fronts, nor what is happening in politics. The only German stations still broadcasting are Hamburg and Munich, although we can't pick them up on the wireless.

The official foreign stations are noticeably reticent. All the louder are the foreign propaganda broadcasters. Rumours are circulating that Göring has relinquished his official duties 'because of a heart condition', that Himmler offered the unconditional surrender of the Wehrmacht to the British and the Americans, but not to the Russians, that Reich Education Minister Funk is forming a new government with General von Brauchitsch as War Minister, that Mussolini was arrested by Italians at Lake Como, not far from the Swiss border, and shot soon after, that his corpse was put on display in Milan and could be viewed by the people.

### Rachele Mussolini, 1892–1979                                      *Como*

Then I was separated from my children and brought to a little cell in the prison where there were already other women, and still others were constantly arriving. My own arrival was barely noticed in the general excitement. Hardly anyone looked at me, as they were all telling the story of their arrests. Only one woman looked at me, her eyes widened, and she cried, 'Are you here?' I waved at her to be quiet, and she started crying quietly. News slowly came in about what was happening outside. At regular intervals we could hear the horrible sound of names being called out followed by shots. Then there was a pause in which the wheels of a cart creaked, and then another name was called.

The tragedy continued like that all night. The young woman who had recognized me was desperate about her husband, who was being held prisoner in the same courtyard, and each time a name was called she clutched the bars, crying hysterically. […]

Another prisoner was a poor concierge who had been arrested after being reported by a youth. She was accused of having found a room for a Fascist several months ago. I felt almost calm in this general tragedy and the others asked me in amazement, 'Yes, and you? You're not crying? Haven't you left anyone behind?' But when the pain is so strong, it is paralysing.

**Friedrichsfelde Central Cemetery**                              **Berlin**
Margarete B.
  Frankfurter Allee 177
  Suicide (poison)
Hans B.
  Frankufrter Allee 177
  Suicide (poison)

*

**Bruno Hoenig, Luftwaffe auxiliary, b. 1928**        *near Koblenz*
It has become clear to me that my views, desires and ideas don't fit in
with these times. I like to feel contented, and I hate today's pomp and
pretence. I'm also too open and honest. I can't be nice to someone
while inwardly thinking that he's worthless. But then I'm also bossy
and rather coarse and like it when people praise me a little. Perhaps
I would have got on better with the Biedermeier period or the days
of the Hanseatic League. But I'm living now, and I have to engage
with my times. It's simply that I'm in favour of a Führer state. In
my view a democracy is nonsense. The church is also a structure
ruled over by a single individual. I love Germany above all, and will
use all my strength to see to it that it is strong and powerful once
again. A Christian, nationally and socially governed state, run by a
single person, is my ideal, and may I one day live to experience such
a state.

*

**Winston Churchill, 1874–1965**                              (*London*)
PERSONAL AND SECRET MESSAGE
TO MARSHAL STALIN
   In the absence of a signed instrument of surrender, the four
Powers will have to issue a declaration recording the defeat and the
unconditional surrender of Germany and assuming supreme authority
in Germany. A draft text of such a declaration is before the European
Advisory Commission and I would ask you to send urgent instructions

to your representative on the Commission so that a final text may be settled without delay.

## Joseph Stalin, 1879–1953                                    *Moscow*
PERSONAL AND SECRET MESSAGE
TO THE PRIME MINISTER, MR W. CHURCHILL

I have nothing against your proposal for publishing, on behalf of the Four Powers, a declaration establishing the defeat and unconditional surrender of Germany, in the event of Germany being left without a normally functioning centralized authority.

The Soviet representative on the European Advisory Commission has been instructed to insert in the preamble to the declaration, the draft of which has been submitted by the British delegation, an amendment laying down the principle of unconditional surrender for the armed forces of Germany.

## Dwight D. Eisenhower, 1890–1969                            *Rheims*
*To Field Marshal Montgomery*

Dear Monty:

All our plans have agreed on the tremendous importance of anchoring our flank on LÜBECK as quickly as possible. I know that you fully appreciate the importance of this matter in the mind of the Prime Minister. I note in this morning's briefing that the front around STETTIN is, as we anticipated, growing fluid. This re-emphasizes the need for rapidity. While I realize that you are straining every nerve to move as quickly as you can, I want you to let me know instantly if any slowness on the part of the US CORPS assigned to your command might hold up your plans for a day or even an hour. I am informed here that the additional logistic support promised your Army Group is fully forthcoming. This HQ will do anything at all that is possible to help you insure the speed and the success of the operation.

As ever,

(Sgd) IKE

**Wilhelm Pieck, 1878–1960**                                    *Moscow*
Dear Comrade Khvostov!

  I am sending you a copy of the list of comrades who are to be called to Moscow for a one-month course before being deployed on behalf of the country. This list is passed on by Comrade Ulbricht of the cadre department.

**Wolfgang Leonhard, b. 1921**                                  *Moscow*
On 27 April we were summoned once again to a short meeting with Ulbricht.

  'Everyone prepared, everything ready?' he asked. It was the first time I had seen Ulbricht smiling and friendly.

  'We plan to fly on 29 or 30 April. Before then we have a farewell party at Wilhelm's. Only one more practical matter...' He opened his briefcase and took out a bundle of banknotes, which were distributed among us. 'This is a thousand roubles for each of you, for minor acquisitions' (a sum that already far exceeded the then monthly wage of the average worker). But the distribution of money was not yet over.

  'And now each one of you also receives two thousand German Reichsmarks for the first exercises in Germany.'

  Again we received freshly bundled, freshly printed notes – this time Marks of the Allied Occupation, which had been produced by the Americans. We had heard of this occupation money, but it was the first time we had seen it.

  There was only one thing that wasn't yet clear to us: was our imminent journey a short visit, a quick briefing, or would it be 'for ever'? I was about to ask, when I remembered that now more than ever the important thing was to avoid doing anything 'contrary to the party line'. I didn't ask, but assumed it was a quick briefing, and we would soon be back in Moscow.

**Nina Aralovetz-Kovshova**                                     *Moscow*
*To her boyfriend*
  Dear Borenka! Hello!

  I congratulate you on the 1 May celebrations. For the first time in several years one is really aware of the festival in Moscow. There is a prevailing mood of joy, because you are finishing off the Fascists far away. Our troops have joined forces with those of the Allies. And the most important thing is that our Red Army is in Berlin!!! Our dearest wish has been fulfilled. *Our* army has taken Berlin!! Now let's celebrate! The festival has burst in on us!!

Borenka! Yesterday the blackout in Moscow was lifted. Now Moscow is ablaze with light again. Even on the second evening I didn't lower the blind. The room is fine and even in a particular way quite cosy, and it's bright, even at night. The floor has been scrubbed till it gleams. There are white tablecloths and runners everywhere, and white covers on the beds. There are pirogi on the table! A real feast, in fact!!

I can hear the second salute of the day. This time it was for Rokossovsky, for a whole series of flattened German cities. The other is for the 1st Ukrainian front, for Ostrava in Moravia. It's now only 11 o'clock in the evening. Another salute might be fired at midnight. It happens sometimes.

I have become so 'slack' as spring has progressed, I get tired easily and need to take breaks. At the same time I have enough work and worries as it is, I couldn't do it all on my own. All that standing in queues!! But now, with this holiday, we've been spoilt as never before. There were lots of delicious things, everyone got a double portion of sugar and so on. The people should be allowed to breathe easily a little now. They've earned it three times over. If only the war were soon finished, then everyone would feel less anxious. If one can't bank on being able to see one's own loved ones again, then one can celebrate for the others, who were meant for the happiness of seeing their beloved, longed-for, dearest ones again and holding them in their arms. What great joy that is!

Events are now advancing with giant strides. Today we read with great satisfaction that Italian patriots, without shilly-shallying for long, and without consulting anyone, have executed their rogue of a 'Duce'. So he didn't end up waiting for his trial in a sanatorium. He would probably have run away from the sanatorium anyway. So those fellows did the right thing! They managed without 'advice from above'. Now we have one less monster in the world. But – only one less for now! And how many others are still creeping around? We fought and fought for goodness and justice, and that's how it must be, now and in times to come!! Until we see each other again soon, Borenka! Stay well and healthy!

Your friend N.A.

**Arseniy Golovko, Soviet admiral, 1906–52**                   *Kola Bay*

The new convoy arrived today. It was preceded by an intensified search for submarines, in which five British corvettes, our Catalina and big anti-submarine aircraft took part. According to reliable evidence the planes sank one submarine and severely damaged another.

**Adolf Hitler, 1889–1945**                   **Führerbunker, Berlin**
*Political testament*

It is not true that I or anyone else in Germany wanted the war in 1939. It was wanted and started exclusively by those international statesmen who were either of Jewish origin or working for Jewish interests. I made too many offers to restrict and limit armaments, which posterity will not be able to deny for long, to be held responsible for the outbreak of this war. Also, after our disastrous First World War, I never wanted a second against England or indeed against America. Centuries may pass, but from the ruins of our cities and artistic monuments hatred will constantly be renewed against that people that must ultimately be held responsible for everything: international Jewry and its helpers!

*

**Hildegard Holzwarth,**
**seminarian, b. 1928**                   **Hermannshütte, Sudeten**

Tomorrow is 1 May, Labour Day. It is a national holiday for the German people. How will it be celebrated this year? I don't know. Diary, how good it is that I have you at least! It is so terribly sad, standing before such an unspeakable end to the war. We have held out for six years. In spite of our defeat it will not have been entirely pointless. Oh, the events of the war could knock one down.

My father is going through the most terrible torment. How deeply we love the German people. What will happen to them? The thought is like torture. The whole of my father's great life's work has been destroyed. We allowed ourselves little at home, and only ever saved.

The roar of cannon from the front is getting closer and closer. Even now, as I write, it is rumbling away outside. I used to be so afraid. If only it were all over! At the same time, we must be grateful that it is the Americans who have come to the Sudetengau [German administrative district] and not, as feared, the Russians. We have only one hope. Our present enemies, the western powers, will not look on as the whole of Europe becomes Bolshevik. We must make common cause against Bolshevism. Everything else must fade into the background. We Germans have long acted as an outpost of Europe. We can do it no longer. Everything is breaking down here. The soldiers and the girls just want to live life to the full.

Many officers don't take their responsibilities and their rank seriously enough. Everything is chaotic and panic-stricken. Here are the typical signs of collapse. The people's resistance is broken. We have been overpowered. There are fierce street battles in Berlin. The Führer is alone there. We tremble for his life.

The Duce has been murdered by Italian partisans along with 17 followers. Dreadful! The great men are all perishing now. On the opposing side the greatest warmonger, Roosevelt, is dead. Is that not almost a miracle? The new President Truman (Harry) is certainly not too bad. Perhaps with his help we will soon engage the rite of sacrifice of the white race against the yellow. This inevitable clash has come close more quickly than one [text breaks off here]

**Alisah Shek, b. 1927**  **Theresienstadt concentration camp**
Austrian government, Soc. Dem. 6, Communists 3, Citizens 2, Christian Social 2, President – Renner.

And what about us? We have been waiting for six endless, unbearable years for this moment. And now everything has become so shabby and has lost its halo, because it's all so superfluous and futile. Everything is going round in circles. Those who destroyed us saved the last scraps and still want to be celebrated. Everything, everything is so futile. We sit here and watch: the worst thing they have done to us, is to rob us of reality, of the concept of reality. We know only a tormented, fear-filled world of cruelty, in which we are the victims of events, objects. And dreams. And what lies between, the only thing capable of being reality and being lived, is darkness. They blindfolded us for so long, and now we are blind. We are fading away in the eternal flight between dream and cruelty on the rocks of reality, swathed in eternal night. It's too late for everything. What is left with a point in all this pointlessness? Things are revealed in all their pointlessness. And now of all times, when we hoped to live, after dying endlessly between the ages of 12 and 18.

**Erich Kessler, b. 1912**          **Theresienstadt concentration camp**
Since yesterday afternoon I have had diarrhoea and therefore eaten nothing all day but old bread. Afternoon did not feel well, so did not carry out my tasks.

*

**Annemarie Hedinger**                          *Brünn, Moravia*
It's been clear for three days. The Russians are staying, the Czechs have the upper hand, and between these two victors there are fierce disagreements. The Czechs have the illusion that they are now in charge. Their victimization of us Germans is multifarious and arrogant. The Russians are annoyed by this, because if they hadn't defeated the Germans, Czechoslovakia would always have remained in the shadows, because – the Russians say irritably, from the little man to the officer – what have these people done to liberate themselves? They have put up with everything, they have lived better than the Germans, they have made no sacrifices and now want to act like the men in charge. But there's nothing to be done about that, and the common decisions are threadbare and conceived and implemented more radically by the Czechs than the victorious powers had intended. In the Czech camp they agree that they must humiliate us, and will in the end get rid of us. We lived side by side for centuries, peacefully, albeit critically. The Germans were cultured, and built up the economy and industry and ran them well. Czechs who responded positively to the construction and administration were given leading roles; their ethnicity was never

turned into a source of contention, on the contrary, many cultural aspects were mixed up and blurred and can no longer be assigned to any particular group. Even in the years of the protectorate, hostility and arrogance towards the Sudeten Germans never appeared. The Germans from the Reich, who had never had the experience of living in a border area, couldn't empathize with this situation and introduced unease rather than decent values. It was so shattering for me that two such spirited, maternal, tolerant peoples as the Czechs and Germans should have sought to die in such an undignified manner.

### Harald Simon, private soldier, b. 1927       (Moravia–Prague)

The month of April was approaching its end. Nowhere did I see germinating seeds, nor birds, nor cats nor any other creatures. It seemed as if even the animals had fled.

Again we had cleared a position during the night. Weary and dirty, we reached a town. I saw a sign: 'Ruederswalde'. Somewhere in Moravia.

We occupied a trench on the town's edge. Supported by artillery, tanks and the particularly feared, low-flying ground-attack planes of the 'Ilyushin II' type, the Russian infantry attacked. Long red flames licked from the firing cannon of the aircraft. The sun shone on this inferno from an immaculately blue sky.

Then shot caught me in the face. I was suddenly engulfed in total darkness. Someone shouted through the noise of battle, telling me to hold on tight. He gripped my hand. I felt a belt. Later I lay on my back on a cart, and my feet dragged over the ground. At some point I was given injections. Then I was in a train. Later someone took off my dirty uniform. I felt warm water, then a bed. Everything around me was still in darkness. I asked what was wrong with my eyes. A nurse said my left eye was destroyed, but I still had my right, and an eye specialist was bound to be able to sort it out. Thank God, the darkness was only temporary. I longed for an eye specialist. There was none here. The doctors had fled, apart from one dentist. He tried in vain to relax my lockjaw. Every day a nurse pulled splinters of bone from my face. In a hand-out of tobacco I received eighty cigarettes. Even though I couldn't smoke, I was pleased by this incredible bounty, and kept feeling around for the four packs on my bedside table. One day they weren't there, and they never reappeared. That brought it home to me that defencelessness represents a temptation to morally weak people, because it makes it possible to do evil without risk to oneself.

**Manfred Klein, Waffen-SS officer, b. 1926**                    **Slovenia**

On 30 April the regiment, probably the whole division, was withdrawn from the front line. The regiment staff was moved to Gnas, five kilometres west of Bad Gleichberg. With our radio transmitter we occupied the village school, on the market square. The next day a member of the regiment who had deserted was picked up again. The division's summary court-martial passed sentence immediately: death by hanging. The sentence was carried out the following day. At the appointed time, about 1.00 p.m., the regiment appeared in the marketplace. A gallows had already been set up. But there was some hesitation, the regiment marched off in formation and was allowed first to watch a film. After the end of the film show the troops returned to the marketplace. We radio operators didn't have to join in, but watched from the windows of our radio station. The criminal, hands cuffed behind his back, had to climb on to a small handcart below the gallows. When the noose was laid around his neck, the court officer stepped forward, read out the sentence and asked the condemned man if there was anything else he wanted to say. He did not react, so after a short pause the court officer said, 'He who fears death in honour, dies in shame.' The handcart was pulled away, and the condemned man now hung on the rope, but barely any lower than before, because he was still standing on the cart. He died a horrendous death. He drew his legs up for a long time, and actually choked and strangled on the gallows. A sign was hung around his neck with the inscription: 'I am a traitor. I received the punishment I deserved.'

During the night I observed a few officers who had come drunk from the inn. They walked up to the gallows, one of them struck the hanged man from the side with his stock, whereupon the man turned on his own axis. This was a great source of amusement to the drunken men, who yelled with laughter.

*

**B. R. Cowles, British captain**  *Bologna*

In the afternoon I organised a rat hunt which went down very well indeed. Two rats were caught.

Later played cricket for the Troop and afterwards nearly made ourselves ill eating a huge pile of freshly picked strawberries.

The Italian variety is very small but the flavour is O.K.

In the mess the day finished playing cards. Not very keen on this but at the moment I don't seem to be able to settle down to some serious reading such as my *Maths for the Million*.

At the moment at R.H.Q. they are working on release groups. Makes one very disinterested in army life which is now very much a short term matter.

**Benedict S. Alper, American soldier, 1905–94**  *Rome*
*To his wife*

Dear Sweet E–

You mean to tell me that people are *still* going into the army? Fantastic – here all we think of is when do we go home, now it's in its final hours. Good about Musso – tried and executed at the hands of those whom he had betrayed. I like the way they are doing things up there: an industrial society is used to working cooperatively and in a disciplined way.

Now that it's so close, it can't be too long before we're together, darling. The end makes everything that went before worthwhile, some- how – all the heartache and loneliness and guilt and worry – it's all suddenly worthwhile, like convalescence after sickness. The world's alive, and most of the people in it, despite millions that have died so we may live. Tom Lloyd dropped in and left a note: 'it's beautiful weather all over the world today.' I guess that's just about it. We have lost time together, my sweet, chances to make love, but not love itself, that is, if anything, stronger than it was. Surely we will never take each other for granted again, and I promise not to be inconsiderate ever again, or angry, or any of the silly things I have kicked myself for so many times since.

I love you and we are forever ours – Bups

**Boris Marchenko, Soviet officer, b. 1904**                    (*Austria*)

I came back from Vienna yesterday. I have travelled around a lot and seen a lot of things, but never before have I seen such a place. It isn't a city, it's just a dream. In comparison with Vienna, Budapest is a shitheap. It's interesting that you can go in any direction you like, and everywhere you will come upon corners more beautiful than any you have seen before. I also had to look for a particular unit. I was told it was in the courtyard of the Austrian palace. So I went there. It's beyond words. I didn't find the people I was supposed to find, but I was told that there was an imperial cellar there with a lot of wine in it. I went there. I walked about a kilometre and a half under the ground and finally reached my goal. I'd never seen anything like it before. The driver and I took as much of a wine that was over 15 years old as we could fit into the car. Basically you can't even call it wine, it's something quite extraordinary. You toss-pots should try it some time.

I also went to the opera house. The part at the back has burned down, but it's still a remarkable building. In a word: I'm wild about Vienna. Who would have thought I would ever get there. Oh yes, I forgot to say that in Vienna they celebrate holidays the way we do. Red flags hang from the windows. The people are very accommodating, and if you ask someone the way a group of five to ten people immediately gather, and they all try to outdo each other in helping you. They speak German and are amazed that I can communicate quite easily in the language. In a word: I would like to stay here and take a good look at all this beauty. Warmest kisses to you and Nika.

Yours, Borya

**Akim Popovichenko, Soviet officer**                    (*Austria*)
*To his wife, Vera*

Verushka, you really are so unlucky. The parcels that other people sent off at the same time as I did arrived long ago, and you're the only one who hasn't received anything. I sent the first parcel to the T. G. Shevchenko address. I've told you that and sent you the receipt and the dispatch date, so check with the district communications office in Smela. The thing I regret most is the leather for new boots. The rest doesn't matter. Although there were stockings for you in there as well.

I've sent you another four parcels, my friend the deputy editor Yasha Bibergal gives them to you. He has no relatives and no one he can send anything to. You can consider his parcel as belonging to you, just leave him the 3.5 metres of grey wool. He has asked for it. And the other parcels you receive from him you can open up and take out everything apart from the 10–20 metres of crêpe, he wants to come and collect those if he survives and if he ever has the chance to come and visit us.

He's a Jew, but he isn't a Jewish Jew. He's really a fine chap. That's all. I look forward to seeing you soon, my love!

Your Kima

**Vasily Vasilyev, Red Army soldier**                             *Berlin*
*To his wife*
My dear!
Best wishes for the First of May – the feast of spring and victory. With Himmler's first rehearsal Germany has shown that it doesn't want to capitulate to the Soviet Union, but is willing to surrender to England and the USA. That is telling. It is no longer just a matter of trying to provoke division between free people, but at the same time a confirmation of our power, our *special power*.

We can be proud of that!

Germany is being forced to its knees.

It would now be particularly appropriate to remember the words of Lenin and later those of Stalin about the instigation of the imperialist war and its possible and inevitable consequences!

It all happened as they said it would. Look at the Balkans! Look at the Poles! Look at Europe, where everything is in motion and for now also in confusion.

Leninism has passed a test in the hailstorm of battles and fighting whose like the world has never seen before, battles on a huge scale and with terrible consequences. The Fascists wanted to lord it in Moscow. Now they know the place as prisoners. We, on the other hand, don't want to go to Berlin, but now we are there as victors.

That's what the reality looks like.

**Adolf Hitler, 1889–1945**                    **Führerbunker, Berlin**
*Political testament*
   Three days before the outbreak of the German–Polish war I proposed
a solution to the German–Polish problem to the British ambassador in
Berlin – to keep it under international control, like the Saarland. That
offer cannot simply be denied either. It was only rejected because the
leading circles in English politics wanted war, partly because of the
business to be had from it, and partly driven by propaganda organized
by international Jewry.

*

**Wolfgang Soergel**                    *(prisoner-of-war camp in Scotland)*
On 20 April Jena and Saalfeld are occupied, General Patton with his
US tank army, coming from my university town of Leipzig, reaches
the outer districts of Chemnitz. Where will you be? Will they force
their way into our house in Rabenstein, into our forest…

   *'again the woods smell sweetly, the hovering larks lift the heavens
   with them…'*

and again it is April, and Hitler's birthday appeal is being broadcast
from Berlin, a man whose madness is apparent to everyone, even
the most unsuspecting, grey-leather-clad U-boat crews who want to
believe nothing else, who are lying [at anchor], even they are wondering
whether Adolf Hitler is a sick man or Satan himself.

**Paul Gross, b. 1925**    *Florence prisoner-of-war camp, near Tucson*
On orders from the main camp at Florence on 30 April 45 I had to
go for a personality test. My journey took me via Safford, through
magnificent mountain landscape towards Globe, via the Coolidge
Dam past great plains with cacti to the main camp at Florence. There I
was led to the main administration building, to an American sergeant
who spoke fluent German. I had to give him my details, which he
typed on to a form. When I was asked about my unit membership
I didn't mention that I had been with the Waffen-SS. When he had

typed everything up, he took from the drawer the same form that had been completed in France just after I was taken prisoner. This form included details about my membership of the Waffen-SS, the elite Nazi unit. After studying the form he threw it in the waste-paper basket. A great relief to me, as he could probably tell from my grateful goodbye.

**Dr Hans-Georg von Wick, 1907–64**        *Crosville prisoner-of-war camp, Tennessee*

*To his wife*

My darling! My thoughts fly always, always to you, anxious and concerned. Where will they try to find you? In our beloved Verden, now a battle zone? Were you able to stay there in the days when the front ran through Verden and the fighting was there? And what must you and our little ones have endured! May God protect and preserve you, and let you be healthy! That is my most fervent prayer. I can't tell you with what feelings of fear and anxiety I have thought of you particularly over these past few days. Here I am sitting in peace and safety, hands tied, while you, my dearest ones, must go through such difficult times! What will have become of our house? As long as you still have a home! Otherwise the loss of material goods is so irrelevant, as long as you are uninjured and we will see one another in good health again one day, and be able to start our lives together once again. If only I could know how you are, my only darling, my brave, beloved wife!

Again and again I imagine your fate and dream up new possibilities, in despair because I cannot help and support you.

My darling, as long as you and the children are well and you have survived it all! I cling to that hope. With much love!

**Walter D., b. 1921**        *Maxey prisoner-of-war camp, Texas*

Americans and Russians have clashed in Torgau. Himmler is supposed to have offered to surrender to America and England. Russia has imposed a new government in Vienna. England and America refuse to recognize the government. The Russian Foreign Minister Molotov has been called away to the conference in San Francisco.

That is how things stand in the last days of April. Germany has lost the war. These words are unimaginably hard to write. But it is the truth. We have lost.

### Ethel Inglis, clerical worker, b. 1908                     *Glasgow*
There are bitter remarks about the fact that the German prisoners of war are getting twice as many rations as the civilian population. They are getting the same rations as the British troops. The Americans are always being praised for knowing how to deal with the German civilian population. We are paying for what we take away from them, while the Americans just demand this and that.

'We are too soft.'

### Lieutenant Rudolf Palitza                                 Onigo
30 April was another hard day's march that looked very much like flight, according to the motto 'Every man for himself'! Infantrymen on foot had it easy because they were advancing inland in the shelter of vineyards and trees. All horse-drawn and motorized vehicles were exposed to uninterrupted fighter plane attacks, and the losses were correspondingly high.

I was relieved of all duties and left to my own devices, and had a lot of time to observe the remains of a defeated army flooding back, only 200 metres away. Luckily a low layer of cloud prevented the fighter-plane attacks. Everyone was pushing northwards, even motorized vehicles and guns, but mostly there were disorderly crowds of private soldiers many on bicycles and individuals on horseback. When the column thinned out, I joined it and arrived at Onigo in the evening, where friendly locals even offered us a place to sleep. It was on the first floor, so I carried my bicycle up there and tied it to my leg. The night was calm, but the caravan moved on early the next morning.

### Karl Koch, Wehrmacht radio operator                      Castelfranco
We are marching. My ankles are rubbed raw, my socks have holes, my shoes are falling apart. In this terrible Italian heat my feet are stuck in leather, day and night. No bath to take the sweat away. And the lice, the lice! Yank and Tommy come after us inexorably. We can barely sleep. In the afternoon there's a downpour. A bunch of soldiers let

me on to their big cart, covered with a large tarpaulin. At last I can sit a little, drenched to the skin as I am. And spare my aching feet for a while.

In Castelfranco we have to go over a crossing, on one side of which the Tommies have stopped far in the distance. Evening is already on its way. We get over the crossing at great speed, unit by unit. We're counting on a sensible response from the enemy! If the partisans had involved us in a skirmish here, we would certainly have found ourselves up against the Tommies as well. Who knows what would have happened? And now the Tommies are arriving on our left, up ahead!

### Fritz Köhler, private soldier                                    *Bassano*

The Italian partisans want to hand us over to the Americans, but they are persuaded to let us move on. But they warn us about their 'colleagues' higher up in the mountains ('red' partisans)... My comrades and I don't have any great desire to be shot down at the eleventh hour, and having heard this warning from several directions I decided it would be better for us to hand ourselves over to the Americans. As it later turned out, that was correct, because hardly anyone got through... Before the partisans lead us to the American camp we are given bread and wine. Then we start our march into captivity.

### Thilo Koch, 1920–2006                                           *Mione*

Travelling along Route 42 we reached Edolo on 30 April. From here it's only about 30 kilometres as the crow flies to the Swiss border. It was with some difficulty that I persuaded the two comrades with whom I was trying to escape not to take this opportunity to make the break. I was afraid that we would be accused of surrendering as deserters, and I didn't think the Swiss would grant asylum to German soldiers.

So we stayed with the long snaking line of soldiers moving over the beautiful Tonale Pass, where the trees were already blossoming, on the pleasant Strada Nazionale 42 towards Bolzano. At Lago di S. Giustino our commander suddenly decided to lead his unit into a cul-de-sac, as I later noted on the map. Now we travelled strictly northwards on a small side road and only stopped in the little mountain village of Mione because the road ended there. In front of us, around us, nothing but mountains and forest.

## Mayor Walther Bringolf, 1895–1981                *Schaffhausen*

In the time from 21 to 30 April the crush of refugees mounted to such a degree that it exceeded all expectations and hence all arrangements. Some matters had to be improvised, and on certain days it was simply no longer possible to subject all refugees to disinfection. Whole transports of Russians, perhaps 800 to 1,000, were simply treated at the station, then put on railway trucks and transported into the interior of the country. There were days when we had no covered accommodation at all. All the tents were occupied as well by now, even at night. The refugees came from a great variety of nations, European and non-European, and apart from the Germans all were starving or dressed in rags, or bore the mark that the Nazis had branded on them. So they drifted daily through the streets of the town in long processions. A German Volkssturm column or whatever it might once have been turned up with a big vanload of butter, bacon, jam, bread and fruit. When I asked the meaning of this truck, the German group told me, 'These are our supplies. We bring them with us. Because in Switzerland you have nothing to eat.' I took this on board without further comment, confiscated the vehicle and passed the food on to our kitchen, so that everyone can benefit.

\*

## Helmut Smend, 1894–1984          *Remagen prisoner-of-war camp*

Of course we staff officers stuck together, moved through the pathways between the crowds of people until we found a little free space where we could stop for a while. The situation could not have been more hopeless. In the chill of April, without any shelter, unimaginable! One could easily perish. And then on top of everything it started raining.

A large group of men moved along a broad strip by the barbed wire to relieve themselves. And every day that strip came closer and closer to the inmates of the camp. My kit, and particularly my new uniform coat, really came into its own now. The others were wearing their old uniforms, which were far less sturdy, and long boots made of thin leather that had immediately turned soft.

Well, they couldn't get me down as easily as that. As long as it was raining, even if it lasted all night, I stood on the spot and thus got less wet than anyone else, only on the top of my uniform. But that makes for a long night!

We stayed here for two weeks. Luckily the weather improved, or at least it turned dry, otherwise we would all have perished. We lay around all day and throughout the night as well on the bare ground. Many had dysentery. Everywhere you saw soldiers in civvies, who had been picked up on the country roads, lying dead in puddles of water. There were hardly any provisions. Some bread was given out at the camp gate, but the way there led through the vast crowd of people. The soldiers who dispensed provisions had difficulty finding us again, as there were no points of reference in the swarm of men. You can't even blame the Americans, they didn't know what to do with these mounting crowds of people. And they didn't dare simply send the soldiers home, either.

**Philipp Schasset, d. 1983**          *Remagen prisoner-of-war camp*

Our soldiers stood by the camp fence 70 metres away, swapping watches, rings, medals and decorations for cigarettes, biscuits and jam. Hunger and hardship lowered the prices, and good watches swapped hands for 20 cigarettes, only 3–5 cigarettes were offered for a golden wedding ring, for a fountain pen only a few biscuits. Who could blame the comrades, who might have had to spend the day shivering in the cold, the mud and the rain, perhaps without coats, blankets or tarpaulins, who often didn't get dry for days, for scraping the barrel for something to raise their spirits!

The days creep slowly along. All around us in the sick bays a great many people are dying of exhaustion, particularly the young, and those in the special compounds marked 'dysentery' or 'typhus'. They too are all lying on the bare muddy floor in big hospital tents. Conditions in the latrine trenches are wretched, there is indescribable misery. Death gazes from the eyes of so many!

One 25-year-old non-commissioned officer must have suffered

from barbed-wire madness. When I was observing the exchange negotiations at the camp fence, I noticed this young man climbing first through the inner fence and then immediately through the outer fence, and then starting to run towards the little bridge. But the American sentries had already noticed the running man and now started firing at him. Very agitated, we called to him to come back, but he didn't hear us, was soon hit and fell dead to the ground. The Americans enjoyed this shooting a great deal, and clearly didn't waste any thoughts on their very active involvement in a perfect tragedy, because, rather than shooting, four or five men could have caught the fugitive. In the dark the American sentries fired thoughtlessly into the camp as well, for instance if a group was cooking something over an open fire, because supplies turned up very late in the day.

*

**Gerhard von Rad, 1901–71**    *Bad Kreuznach prisoner-of-war camp*
We had seen for a long time that the camp was constantly growing; as far as the eye could see, posts had been hammered in and barbed wire stretched over them, and then one day our whole camp ground was cleared. You can imagine what it was like, before the 80–100,000 men were distributed around the camps higher up, which took a whole day. Much was different in the new camp. There were only 10,000 of us, and this number was divided into hundreds (platoon), of which ten men (a group) were always located side by side. This arrangement was a kindly one. Now you had your particular circle of neighbours, you also had a group leader and a platoon leader. So the horrible chaos was to some extent diminished.

Around now I began spending time with Anton Schlotter, an even-tempered, monosyllabic brewer and farmer. First of all we set about digging a proper hole in the ground. Our only tool was the lid of a jam jar, so the work advanced slowly; in fact we never actually finished it, because new improvements were always being applied. The hole itself was about one metre deep and one metre wide, and had a tunnel-shaped recess at one side to accommodate outstretched legs. It was very cramped. Two of us side by side could only lie crammed close together in a very particular way; if one of us wanted to turn around, he woke up the other one so that he could turn over completely. Still, it freed us from the unbearable cold. If we were lying in there and had laid a piece of cardboard over the whole from inside, it could get quite warm. Admittedly the roof didn't do much to keep out the rain. As the clay ground didn't absorb anything, the water ran into our hole from all directions.

*

### Erich Kästner, 1899–1974                              Mayrhofen

Vorarlberg is already occupied, they say, and the enemy is approaching Innsbruck! If that is the case, our army in Italy, if it uses the Brenner Pass, will run straight into its arms. The Steiners are worried about their daughter. Viktl is in the Stubai Valley, where her fiancé, one-armed, is in the field hospital. The parents fear they might get caught up in the possibly bloody confusion at the Brenner Pass.

Recently someone, somewhere in the mountains, met the inmates of an invalid field hospital that had been hastily cleared and moved because of the approaching enemy. The one-legged soldiers, balanced on crutches, journeyed 'on foot' along the country road in single file. There would have been trucks, but there was no petrol. The heroes had to hobble for twenty kilometres!

Invalid field hospital, mutilated amputees, enemy approach, front realignment – the fussiness and delicacy of the new loyal German vocabulary will soon keep the philologists busy. The 'euphemism' chapter will be a long one. The wolf in Grimm's fairy tale ate chalk to soften his voice before he devoured the seven kids. The linguistic geologists will have to examine the new cretaceous age.

This morning the pupils of the teacher training institute based in Strass had to leave the inn. The landlord and the new tenants were in a hurry. The new tenants? A group of general staff. Everywhere regimental staffs without regiments and division staffs without divisions are looking for picturesque boltholes. They are unemployed now, they are commandeering remote lodgings, sleeping late, breathing in the mountain air, updating the chronicles of their troops, destroying ambiguous documents, discussing the situation, coordinating future answers to awkward questions and, as they wait to be taken prisoner, having a batman iron the white flag in the kitchen. It was a mute day. It wasn't only the Munich transmitter that kept its mouth shut. The foreign stations were silent too. What had made the various languages speechless? Were they broadcasting speeches at an international congress of Trappists? Lies on the radio, coarse and refined, can be interpreted, but a big silence throws up mysteries.

**Ruth Storm, 1905–93**                                      Schreiberhau

The last weeks have been full of harmony. My husband was able to stay here. The Bosnian horse Minka from Paula Busch's stud in Mühlatschütz is in our stable with the filly Buschy. By crossing with Haflingers I wanted to breed a tough and modest mountain pony. Now those plans are at an end; the Haflinger stallion from Tyrol won't be able to get here. But I still have the two mares! The two of them frolic on the high mountain peaks with sweeping, floating movements, the wild spring wind playing in their dense manes and long tails.

Their noble Arabian heads with delicate, mobile ears, often sniff the air of the distant landscape; the old posture of the steppe animals, they drink in the air. Often I listen to the creature's beating pulse to forget the terrible events.

The day is full of work, but the war sometimes lets us forget the fate of our country. But will we be able to stay? Who knows? We are grateful for every day, we are still free!

**Clara Falckenthal, b. 1926**                *near Königswalde (Warthe)*

Today the Russians of the Landsberg garrison headquarters wanted to collect their roast for 1 May. They had set aside the last bit of young stock for the purpose, but they came in vain. During the night the gangs had taken it. All we have left are three foals, three horses and four cats.

Our heifer started calving on the 27th. The poor creature was in torment until the following noon, then we decided to stab her to death. We couldn't help her any more, because the calf was dead, it was a big-

muscled creature of about 60–65 kg. We had to distribute the meat to
117 people, to everyone now living in the mountain colony. We only
kept a haunch.

*

**Max Beckmann, 1884–1950**                              *Amsterdam*
Finished S. ghost. Started work on Fromel portrait. Afternoon Peky
again and evening. Worked too much. – Fighting on Potsdamer Strasse.
Mussolini dead.

Pour flattery on your spiritual wounds.
Flattery will heal the world.

**Barthold Fles, literary agent, 1902–89**              *New York*
*To Heinrich Mann*
Dear Mr Mann:
[...] Where *Untertan* is concerned, what would you think of the
new title: *Little Superman*? Not perfect, but not bad either; pretty
much in line with the book. The book will probably be published in
the winter. [...]
As always, yours, Barthold Fles

**Thomas Mann, 1875–1955**           *Pacific Palisades, Los Angeles*
Writing fluent on the chapter. Worked. After dinner the newspaper
about Mussolini's pitiful end. It now matters not a jot whether Hitler
is still alive or not. Himmler, in Denmark or Lübeck, the only one who
can announce unconditional surrender, and probably hopes to save his
life in the process. The wretched Ribbentrop is supposed to have been
taken prisoner by German 'partisans'. In Munich still battles with
snipers. Accumulated suicides among the Nazi top brass: the supreme
BDM leader General von Rang. Two Swiss to tea, correspondent
of the *NZZ* and the Swiss consul. About the imminent American–
Russian competition to rebuild Germany. In the evening read Busch's
memoirs. First edition of a new Frankfurt newspaper with the letter
from Bonn on the second page.

**Wilhelm Hausenstein, 1882–1957**            *Tutzing*

Slept passably throughout last night, woken now and again by loud explosions in the distance. Some of those explosions, I was assured, were caused by blasts that the German army thought it necessary to unleash in the frenzy of doom. It is telling that in an area where an agent of the devil has ruled for twelve, almost thirteen years, every last thing is being ruined: the devil's final balance sheet will be *Nothing*. It would be quite in line with the monstrosity of the dying system if the autobahns had been built only to be destroyed in the end.

The war seems to be over for our undamaged district. This afternoon the white flags were flown in the village. Negotiations for surrender to the occupying powers seem to have happened *very* quickly, as far as I can tell.

This morning three Hungarian Jews from Dachau camp begging at the door: indescribably wretched, figures of extreme misery, but polite; humanity, far from being crushed, was more apparent than it is in the bulk of people we've seen walking around in freedom around here over the past few years. The beggars took away what we gave them (cheese sandwiches and beer) to distribute it among their own people, who were *even* worse off.

**Adolf Hitler, 1889–1945**            **Führerbunker, Berlin**
*Political testament*

But I have also made it quite clear that, if the nations of Europe are again to be regarded as mere shares to be bought and sold by these international conspirators in the world of money and finance, then there is one people that will be held responsible, that is the real culprit in this murderous struggle: Jewry! I also left no one in doubt that this time not only would millions of the children of Europe's Aryan people die of hunger, not only would millions of adult men suffer death, and hundreds of thousands of women and children be burned and bombed in the towns, without the real criminal, albeit by more human means, having to atone for that guilt.

*

**Riemann**                                     *Rothenstein camp, near Königsberg*

Two days before the First of May the name Riemann was called out in the night. My brother Paul and I identified ourselves. We were led by a sentry to the main building, received by a major and asked if we could plant or arrange two big Soviet stars out of red flowers in front of the house by 1 May. I said yes.

With about 40–50 men, whom I was able to select the following morning, we started marking out two patches of green lawn to form two big stars on the forecourt. We planted one of them with red pansies and scattered the other with red brick dust. The major was pleased. After that my brother and I were able to move about rather more freely.

**Tamara Astakhova, Soviet sergeant, b. 1922**       *Frische Nehrung*

In April 1945 our division was near Frische Nehrung, not far from Danzig. I was keeping watch one night. Suddenly I heard creeping footsteps behind the house.

'Halt! Who goes there?' No one spoke. After a while I heard those cautious footsteps again. 'Halt or I'll shoot!' And I fired into the air. And then there appeared… our dear Starshina.

Apparently he was just trying to test my alertness, or seeing whether I hadn't gone to sleep at my post. And in his hand he was, strangely, holding a cooking pot. What for?

'Come on, Bashkirova, let's have a smoke,' he said. And he told me that in the cellar of a neighbouring bombed house a German family was in hiding. A woman with five children. The oldest boy was only 9. He had told the cook from the field kitchen so that the German children could have something to eat as well. But the cook's whole family and his little sons had been shot by the SS somewhere near Voltshansk.

'Let them come. They'll get a pan of boiling water in their faces. I'll feed them all right.'

After that our Starshina brought some food to the Germans in hiding every night. Illegally. Secretly.

**Michael Wieck, b. 1928**     (*Rothenstein camp, near Königsberg*)
We have the first deaths in our cellar, we drag them on to the pile of
corpses when we go out in the morning. Some are about to die. Some
are resigned, and have stopped collecting anything to eat. Others
immediately take their bowls. My spirits are declining from one day
to the next.

At one point a Russian asks if anyone here is a painter. I immediately
identify myself and am led to an officer. He smiles sceptically and gives
me coloured pencils and paper. I draw his profile as best I can. It isn't a
bad likeness, in fact, but he isn't convinced. Before I'm sent back to the
cellar he gives me another bit of bread. Something at least. [...]

Every morning at least one of them has died, and they're all glad of
the extra room. In fact it's getting gradually more spacious, but we're
still lying on top of each other.

**Dr Hans Graf von Lehndorff, 1910–87**     *Rothenstein camp,*
*near Königsberg*
In the morning they come for the dead. Several have died in the corridor,
one is sitting dead on the bucket. The others aren't so easy to find, as
even the living only react very slowly when you talk to them or nudge
them. Later, thirty-six corpses lie stacked up in the washroom more
than a metre high, all men. The women hold out for longer. Many are
almost naked. Other people have already appropriated their clothes as
protection against the cold. A very few of them still have papers. But
even these won't last for long, and later no one will be able to say who
has actually died here. [...]

All day new patients are being brought in, and there is constant
friction with the Russians, who aren't happy with anything. Fresh
consignments are constantly appearing, and there are women in
uniform as well. We no longer know where to hide.

As we can't accommodate all the dying on a single floor by any
means, about a hundred men are laid up at the top in the attic, a terrible
torment for all concerned. There are draughts, and rain is pouring in
through the open windows and the holes in the roof. When it's quite
dark again I go up there and find them all lying in every direction.
I hear quiet, meaningless talking here and there, sense vital spirits

gradually being extinguished. Some of them are certainly dead. I take off the coats and jackets from the dead and cover up the living with them.

From time to time I feel as if a voice were asking me, 'What are you actually doing here?' Yes, what am I doing here? What are any of us doing? But there's no point trying to find an answer. This isn't action in the true sense of the word, it's just occasionally being granted permission. And when I turn round in the door again as I leave the attic, my arms lift into the air as if of their own accord, to bless these dying men.

As the night wears on, the first of the twins is born by candlelight with help from me and Erika. Life goes on, as they so rightly say.

### Adolf Hitler, 1889–1945                                    Führerbunker, Berlin
*Political testament*

After six years of war which, in spite of all the setbacks, will one day go down in history as the most glorious and valiant demonstration of a nation's life-will, I cannot abandon the city which is the capital of this Reich. As the forces are too small to make any further stand against the enemy attack at this place and as our resistance is gradually being weakened by men who are as deluded as they are lacking in initiative, by staying in this city I should like to share my fate with those, the millions of others, who have also assumed the task of doing so. Moreover I do not wish to fall into the hands of an enemy who requires a new spectacle organized by the Jews for the amusement of their overheated masses.

*

### Paul Peikert, parish priest, 1884–1949                               Breslau

The sight that met me in the morning in the Church of the Redeemer was shocking. The southern wall of the nave and the presbytery was torn down; as were all the windows and doors; the roof was seriously damaged; some of the altars had been knocked over, including the high altar. Only the statue of Our Lady of Perpetual Help stood undamaged in its place. [...] With Diocesan Councillor Dr Brown we set about saving the Holy of Holies from the tabernacle of the toppled high altar. It wasn't easy to get to the high altar across the rubble, and the tabernacle itself was hard to open because of the pressure. The Holy of Holies could only be taken out of the bent tabernacle with some difficulty, and I carried it into the house chapel of the monastery and celebrated holy mass on it.

**Hugo Hartung, dramaturg, 1902–72**                                   **(Breslau)**
Last night I had to receive reports in the command post, and wasn't able to lie down in the office until about four o'clock in the morning. But sleeping was out of the question, because the shrill cries of a wounded man didn't subside until well into the day.

**Wilhelm Bodenstedt, postal official, 1894–1961**                    **Breslau**
Another bad night passed, and still life goes on. Already children are rolling their scooters over rubble and stones and woman are pushing their prams up and down in the streets, but they all know full well that the howling grenades could explode very close to them. They disappear into the dilapidated doorways just in time. Hurray! A letter from Wifey has arrived, dated 10.4, reaching me along various byways via an operations unit. No hairs, unfortunately. I was very, very glad of it. I answered the letter today. Well, goodnight, my Wifey, sleep well and dream of me.

**Horst G. W. Gleiss, schoolboy**                                      **Breslau**
The cellar rooms of our house which were still free are occupied by Waffen-SS on 29 April. [...] They keep themselves to themselves and fit out the cellars they have occupied like club rooms. They bring mountains of valuable carpets with them, hanging them around, and sleep in feather beds with pure white covers – hardly ever a night alone.

They bring with them a little bevy of saucy, well-built girls, and as their numbers aren't enough to give all the men delightful nights, partners are swapped briskly throughout the night. When I am off duty and can sleep at home, all that separates me from one of these love nests is a thin curtain and a wall whose wooden slats are nailed up with great gaping holes between them. I hear and sense a lot of things that are not meant for the ears of a boy my age. The erotic aural images presented to me every night as I lie in bed very closely resemble the soundtrack of a French pornographic film. I quietly think to myself: 'Now I know where these lads get their constant fighting spirit from. If the nights in the war are as hot as the ones on which I am allowed to listen in, then plainly it's worth keeping the war going for some time to come. Every day counts – or rather every night!' On the other hand, I think, these young lads have deserved the chance of a few fine nights after fighting the enemy out at the front for years.

Those are my thoughts, when the commotion from the next room subsides and I'm able to go sleep. I am, after all, at an age when one knows that the two people lying a few centimetres away from me aren't groaning because they're in pain, and aren't breathless because they're playing catch with one another!

### Thea Seifert, b. 1903                                                    Breslau
No one talks any more about many horrific matters, and some things look so simple when written down. But there were major difficulties, for example before the Kaiserbrücke was crossed, which could take hours because of the firing, the corpses had to be taken away on trolleys and, near the 'Schweizerei' pavilion in Scheitniger Park for example, buried in mass graves without coffins, just as soldiers and civilians have been buried on all parts of the promenade and around the city-centre churches. The many people waiting for their relatives will often wait in vain, because in most cases no records have been made, and if there have, the lists and inscriptions have been lost again.

And many refugees who imagine Breslau in its old glory will remember their beautiful, abandoned home, and still hope they will be able to return to their former comforts, but there has been nothing there for ages.

*

### Casimir Katz, b. 1925                                                    Lübeck
Our house was full to the rafters. My aunt in Berlin came about 14 days before the end, when the Russians had crossed the Oder. The wife of

the former director of the Lübeck Theatre, who had worked with us in the Berlin office, came and brought with her an eighteen-year-old miniature pinscher that was no longer house trained, as well as a cage with a Barbary dove. A short time later her husband, who had been called up to the army, joined us. An acquaintance who was a secretary in the Ordnance Office came, and a short time later her mother too, and then her brother, a frigate captain who had been separated from his unit at the end of the war.

**Lieutenant General Albert Fett, 1872–1963**      *Frankfurt am Main*
We took Mr and Mrs Bergmann into Fischer's room and a middle room.
Major Frankenberg is moving into our bathroom. His flat at 3 Melemstrassse has been confiscated by American troops.
8 a.m. registration of the Frankfurt population at police station no. 9. We are given papers.

**Dr Hans Lill, 1882–1970**                          *Würzburg*
Have been given my pass at last. 2 o'clock in the afternoon at Father Peter's Chapel. Stations of the Cross only slightly damaged, 2 roofs of the lodge burned down. Figures only slightly damaged, church unharmed. View of the city from the terrace terrible, everything as grey as a skeleton. I cried my eyes out!
Got 150 Marks out of the savings bank with some difficulty. Wages for May are temporarily going unpaid. Afternoon boring.

**Mayor Theodor Spitta, 1873–1969**                  *Bremen*
Visit from Knittermeyer. The library took seven artillery hits and has been severely damaged. [...] British soldiers lodged in the upper rooms. Protection against looting and stealing of things. In Knittermeyer's flat on the Osterdeich, which got through the war unscathed, twelve British officers are billeted. As a firearm is supposed to have been found, Knittermeyer goes there. Conversation with British officer. Knittermeyer says he is a philosopher and doesn't know how to use a gun; the British officer says German philosophers are in favour of war and guns, like Nietzsche. Knittermeyer refers to Kant's 'On Eternal Peace'. Conversation about war. Question on views of the

'Werwolf'. Knittermeyer rejects Werwolf; war only between soldiers. British officer: 'I am for the Werwolf'. They had, he explains, similar organizations in France, Holland and Belgium.

The looting by foreign workers is on the rise, systematically, street by street.

A lot of gunfire near Bremen.

**Adolf Hitler, 1889–1945**                              **Führerbunker, Berlin**
*Political testament*

I have therefore decided to stay in Berlin and, of my own free will, to choose death there at the moment when I believe that the position of Führer and Chancellor itself is no longer tenable.

I die with a happy heart, conscious of the immeasurable deeds and achievements of our soldiers at the front, of our women at home, the achievements of our farmers and workers and the work, unique in history, of our youth, who bear my name.

That I express my thanks to you all from the bottom of my heart, is just as self-evident as my desire that you should, because of that, on no account give up the struggle, but rather continue it against the enemies of the Fatherland, no matter where, true to the creed of the great Clausewitz.

*

**Dieter Wellershoff, b. 1925**                      **Gross Kelle, Mecklenburg**

It is deadly silent and dark, only the trees sometimes rustle in the wind. One might at such times shed the idea that a disaster is taking place all around, one familiar from the history books. I haven't even begun to deal with everything that is happening. I really can't even grasp it. The Germany that I have so loved is finished. Because it isn't just a war that's being lost. It's much more comprehensive and definitive, a loss of the whole of the imaginable future. I know just one thing, that I want to survive. I'm only nineteen years old. Everything should just be starting.

**Peter Neumann**                                             **Malchin**

We have to stop outside Malchin. Two young officers, still in pristine
uniforms, demand to see our marching papers. No one can produce
them. So we are disarmed: our carbines fly on to a big pile, and I set
down a hand grenade as well. We are led to a courtyard in the town,
because a new battle unit is supposed to be assembled here. A Major
or Colonel Wolf has appointed himself fortress commander and the
city itself a fortress that needs to be defended. But he seems to lack
authority. We quickly abscond, and meet stray unarmed soldiers all
over the place

**Lieutenant Vasilenko**                                   *(Neustrelitz)*

First we reached Alt-Strelitz. As the streets were mined we headed
along the railway embankment. There we were fired on. It wasn't
immediately possible to tell where the shooting was coming from.
The job had to be done, so I ordered the other tanks to drive along
behind me. Then I saw two heavy German tanks, 'Tigers', had taken
up position on the edge of the city of Strelitz and were firing from
there. Alt-Strelitz was already destroyed. So we thought we weren't
the first and expected to bump into our own colleagues. But when we
were fired at from the prison with anti-tank guns and machine guns,
we knew for certain that our comrades weren't there. Then an elderly
lady came along and showed us where the SS were hiding. Hitler Youth
were now firing anti-tank grenades at us as well. One of our tanks was
already on fire, then the next one too. The important thing now was to
act quickly and resolutely, lest we put our lives at stake unnecessarily.
From there we advanced to Neustrelitz. In the market place my tank
took a hit and started burning. I myself was wounded. A Hitler Youth
had let the tank go past and then fired at it.

**An unknown man**                                          *Neustrelitz*

The dawning of 30 April will always represent the most horrific day in
the city's history. Even though there was no longer any resistance and
the remaining residents quietly endured it all, the city was abandoned
to looting for a few days by Commander Rulenkow. The most terrible
scenes of horror were played out in the houses; all over the city the

cries of women being raped rang out. Men coming to the aid of their wives or daughters were shot. Many residents from every social circle preferred to take their own lives, poisoned themselves, hanged themselves or committed suicide in the lakes on the edge of the city.

It was only subsequently established that no fewer than 681 people had opted for self-destruction during those days. [...]

The fires began on 30 April. After a few days the old Residence Palace was entirely destroyed. The castle tower remained, hanging crookedly above the rubble. The old government building, the old Palais, the theatre, two of the noblemen's houses near the palace and about 40 houses, mostly near the railway station, on Strelitzer Strasse and the market, fell victim to the flames. All attempts to put out the flames were prevented by the Soviets. Two days previously the centre of Alt-Strelitz, about 4 km away and recently incorporated, had been almost entirely destroyed by fire.

**Francis Sampson, American cleric**                    *Neubrandenburg*

On 29 April we had a visit from a Russian general who praised our armaments and told us the Russians couldn't have held out if the Americans hadn't equipped them. Almost all the equipment we saw in Russian possession came from America. Even the Russian planes flying around were Bell Airacobras. After that we were visited by a commissar, who assigned us to be transported by American troops.

The Russian soldiers received a daily ration of vodka, and had also found German schnapps, so that most of them were constantly drunk. In this state some of them stole valuables from the Americans, particularly their watches, and forced them to dig them latrines. I looked for the Russian colonel in charge of the camp, but he was drunk too. Gradually we felt a lot less safe among the Russians than we had among the Germans, and didn't know exactly what to do. An old French priest who was with us as a prisoner asked me to go with him into town in the afternoon. He wanted to see how the German clerics and the Germans who hadn't been able to escape were getting on. I admired the old man's courage. Even though we were prepared from the worst, we were so shaken by what we saw that it cannot be captured in words. A few metres from our camp, in the forest, we saw a sight that I will never forget as long as I live. Several German girls had been raped and killed here. And some had been hung by their feet and their bodies slit open. Comrades had told me about similar things before, but I hadn't wanted to believe it. We stopped and said some prayers.

When we arrived where the lovely little town of Neubrandenburg had stood only a few days before, I felt as if I were looking at the end of the world and the Day of Judgement. Most houses were still burning, and the ruins of collapsed walls were piled up in the streets. A big group of Germans, men, women and children, was clearing the main street, guarded by a Russian soldier. Corpses lying about were ignored as long as they didn't obstruct the traffic. Hanging over some of the streets was an unbearable smell of burnt meat. The old priest didn't say a word; I only heard him sigh when we came across fresh atrocities. When he gathered his cloak and stopped by each body to say a quick prayer, he looked to me like a symbol of the church in a shattered world.

At last we reached a German parsonage and went inside. Part of the building had been destroyed by fire, and it had collapsed in many places. The vicar's two sisters were sitting on the bare steps. The vicar himself and his father crouched next to them, and their pale faces revealed the extreme agitation to which the people had succumbed. Three women huddled on a sofa. One of the sisters talked to the French priest and told him a horde of Russians had raped the three women and forced the vicar and his father to watch. The French priest asked them if there was anything he could do for them. But they shook their heads in despair. And I saw that they were close to losing their minds. They were in a state that was already beyond fear, and an expression of sympathy could no longer reach them. I was glad when we reached the camp again, because I was worried that the old French priest would fall ill.

*

**Léon Degrelle, Waffen-SS officer, 1906–94**          **Mecklenburg**

On 30 April 1945 I heard the startling news on Radio London: 'Himmler is negotiating a ceasefire!' The negotiations were, it seemed, taking place somewhere near Lübeck.

Fascist Italy had gone. Mussolini murdered with terrible sadism. His corpse hung feet upwards, like a dead piece of meat, right in the middle of Milan.

The main road to Lübeck gave an accurate picture of the situation.

All the way to Schwerin the stream of civilians and armies coming from the east surged, massive and noisy, the whole width of the road.

In Schwerin the streams of people flowed together.

Isolated behind slate-grey moats the ducal palace emanated the serenity of stones that had seen people and centuries pass. The rest of the city was drowning under the huge crowds of people from east and west.

There the immediately imminent end of the war in Germany became a thrilling reality for us. A stream of people surged along, fleeing from the Soviet tanks. A second stream of people was coming from the Elbe, escaping the English. Two Allied armies approached like two double doors closing. [...]

British planes swooped on the columns, from which ten or fifteen dense clouds of smoke rose a short time later. Petrol tanks burned. Tyres burned. Luggage burned.

From five hundred metres, indeed a thousand metres, you could see only a single, almost opaque blaze interrupted by explosions.

The ragged dresses of fleeing women fell from ruined carts. Endless columns were now in a state of confusion. My Volkswagen and that of my chief of staff had terrible trouble struggling through the rubble and fires. Every five minutes we had to drive into the city moat while the salvos from the low-flying planes rattled away above us.

The saddest sight was the wounded. The field hospitals in the area were cleared in great haste. But there were no field ambulances. Hundreds of poor boys with their arms or torsos in plaster, were sent on to the main road with their bandages. Lots of them were hobbling on crutches.

So on we continued to the Baltic, on foot, under enemy fire, through burning trucks and amidst unimaginable crowds of people.

**Erich Mende, 1916–98**                                                **Warnemünde**
By the time we decided to go to the city of Rostock on 30 April, we'd already been overtaken by a Soviet tank unit advancing from the south-east. The tanks had entered Rostock! The road from Sanitz to there was blocked to us. We managed to get past the city in our trucks, with the infantrymen on board, in our utility vehicles and in our bicycle units. These bicycle units tried to get past Rostock to the south, unnoticed by the Soviet tanks. They all waited for one tank column to pass through, before crossing the Rostock road before the next one arrived, and finally headed on towards Bad Doberan. Our utility vehicles and trucks couldn't do that, of course. So we went off the beaten track and reached the exit for the harbour on either side of Warnemünde. The refugee ships still anchored in Warnemünde harbour were about to leave. From the railway ferry towards Gedser there was constant commuter traffic heading north. One ship after the other, obviously filled with refugees and civilians from Rostock or Warnemünde, had right of way. We were required to wait until all the ships heading northwards had left the harbour. When we were waiting here with about 1,200 soldiers at the junction outside Warnemünde, a curious procession of about 400 to 500 people came towards us in very striking clothes! Striped prison clothes! We soon worked out that they were from a concentration camp.

**Walter Wendel, 1928–98**                          **RAD camp, Schlutup, Lübeck**
The English were nearby, and we wanted to reach them. The streets were full of soldiers, all on foot. We all wanted to get to the British, no one wanted to get to the Russians! Our RAD association gradually dissolved, and the RAD leaders couldn't do anything any more. There were 'Zivilpolen' [Polish civilians who had been forced labourers] standing outside all the villages, and they took everything from us. I had a watch I'd been given by my brother Ewald, and I'd already taken it off my arm and put it in my pocket just in case. But the Zivilpolen simply reached into our pockets and took everything out. When we

reached a big field we saw that the English had set up a prisoner-of-war camp there. And then I saw that the English had taken the little boys, some of them even weedier than me, and cut their trouser legs off above the knee. 'What are children doing among soldiers?' the English kept asking. Now we too became prisoners in this big field. People were sleeping in tents. [...]

Every day we got a few biscuits and a thin soup, and the English themselves didn't have anything more to eat! But there were too many of us, thousands of soldiers. I can't get over the fact that we survived, 16 years old and so little to eat.

\*

**Ernst Thape, 1892–1985**            *Buchenwald concentration camp*
There are preparations for 1 May in the camp. This matter throws up some interesting questions. All the nations are parading under their national flags. So, the German committee is now busy with the question of what the German flag should be. On behalf of the Social Democrats I put forward the colours black, red and gold, and suggest that we might do something like the Yugoslavs, who put a five-pointed star in the middle field of their flag. The suggestion was such a surprise that no one voiced an objection, and the decision was simply postponed. Today they've found their tongues again and told us that the majority of camp inmates, all of whom are Communists of one kind or another, objected so strongly to the Weimar Republic that they wouldn't tolerate black, red and gold. Instead they wanted a red flag with a five-pointed star, the symbol of the struggle against Fascism.

I discovered, and expect I will do so again in today's evening session, that all other socialists and anti-Fascists will show their national symbols and don't give a thought to the internal political arguments that were often played out under those symbols. The French march under the tricolour without anything added to it as naturally as the compatriots they were fighting against. The Belgians, the Dutch, the Italians, they all do the same. The Austrians who resisted the Heimwehr [the Austrian paramilitary home guard], whose colours were red, white and red, and who were put in concentration camps by them where they are now still surrounded by barbed wire, still carry the red, white and red flag as international Communist Marxists. The only ones in the whole of Buchenwald, among more than a dozen nationalities, who are unclear about their country's colours, are the Germans. In Russia a 'Free Germany National Committee' was set up under the leadership of a German general, but the national colours that any schoolchild would immediately recognize as German, and which were always flown in the struggle against the Fascists, cannot be shown.

We are in the minority here and cannot impose our will.

In the name of my friends I call for the following order of priority:

1. We apply black, red and gold on the flagpole of the Germans. Black, red and gold with the five-pointed star, not because we want it, but because we think it correct as a sign of our membership of the anti-Fascist front, to avoid any misunderstanding. If this demand is considered unsustainable, then I request
2. that the German flagpole be left empty to show openly that the Germans have no flag. As that too will probably not be accepted after the previous discussion, I suggest as a solution that
3. a simple red flag be flown and only if that too is rejected can I do nothing if the Communist majority in the German committee decides
4. to fly the Red Flag with the five-pointed star on the national flagpole of the Germans.

**K. A. Gross, 1892–1952**          **Dachau concentration camp**
I subsequently took a look at the daily Bible quote and hurried to write it down along with the explanatory text and the weekly saying, just as, yesterday morning, when we still had no idea of the force of the surge of events and the significance of this Sunday's cantata, the wonderful words of Pastor Rackwitz were read out at the beginning of the service. 'Sing unto the Lord a new song, for he has done marvellous things!' That was also what the boy Hiob said repeatedly in the last week, when his situation was so terrible that nothing could be done

for him. He had been chosen twice for transport; even the doctor had agreed to his being sent away, and it seemed that only a miracle could have saved him, and then the miracle took place. He is still with us, and is able to celebrate the feast of liberation with us. An unforgettable experience of the loyalty of those who stay loyal even to the disloyal.

Ah, he would so love to rejoice with all his heart, but grief overwhelms him when he thinks of his fatherland, which has been brought low. But how? Cannot Germany too enjoy the fruits of this victory? Quite certainly, one must go to the heart of things. If those who have now been completely dashed to pieces had emerged victorious, would that not have been the greatest misfortune, indeed a terrible defeat for Germany? Because the descent would have been completed in victory. Our arrogance would have sealed our final fall. But when God faced us in his wrath, HE demonstrated his goodness to us, which wanted once again to grant us room to repent. HE allowed us to share in the victory of those who defeated us. Might Christ's generalship prove superior before the whole world? So chin up, my brother, you may weep with those who weep, but at the same time laugh with the victors as one of their own – practise this, Boy Hiob, it is the most precious skill of all!

*

**Navy Lance Corporal Klaus Lohmann, 1910–2002   (Travemünde)**
I was allowed to preach in Travemünde again. The church was very well attended, many of my colleagues from the reading group and the Bible circle were there. I preached joyfully on John 6: 67–69. (1. A crucial question, 2. A cordial answer, 3. A philosophical confession.)

In the afternoon I go for a walk with my friends again. After that, to church together, where a musical vesper is taking place. Very beautiful organ music, solo and choral singing. Music from the time of Bach and also some modern pieces. In between, a reading from the scriptures and prayer. That contemplative hour makes one feel so much better!

In the evening I go for the last time to the parsonage, where I have spent so much time over the past few weeks. It is so hard for me to say goodbye! May God protect those dear people and their house!

**Cathedral Chaplain Fritz Bauer, b. 1913**            **Würzburg**
Prelate Werthman, acting as pastor, and Dr Winkler the chaplain
are celebrating today at the main altar, so I go to the side altar in the
Elisabethenheim. Then Dieter from Haug Monastery comes and asks
me to creep with him into the cellar of his house. We find nothing
left there but ashes. A lovely Madonna statue lies in the gravel where
Semmelstrasse turns into Handgasse. Her head has come off. Luckily
I find the head and put it beside the statue.

**Isa Vermehren, b. 1918**            **(Niederndorf, Austria)**
The radiant spring morning the following day brought us all together at
nine o'clock for the Episcopal mass in the village church. To this hour
of complete salvation belongs one of the most profound impressions
of this whole journey. Not only was each one of us freely able to satisfy
a personal wish by once again going to church, it was also a source of
private delight for each individual. More moving still was the revelation
of the same inner attitude in each person, as formed within us all by
our fate over the past months and years: the attitude of sacrifice and
gratitude, the attitude of respect and worship. In this the equality of
all human beings as children of a single God found expression, and
with it came peace. It was a monumental and profoundly engaging
hour, as children of all nations on the threshold of liberation came to
receive blessing and peace from the hand of the church! From that first
hour the boundlessness of mercy left a glimmer of devotion in many
hearts for a long time after, until our last restraint dissolved into pure,
benign joy – 'Henry, the coach is breaking!' – 'No, sire' – Now the
last iron wheel came off, and hearts exhaled in freedom never before
so savoured.

**Victor Klemperer, 1881–1960**            **Unterbernbach, Bavaria**
Once again we have a great feeling of relief and gratitude (gratitude to
whom?) for having actually survived that danger, incredible and yet
mundane. It wells up in us still, but over it, from hour to hour, there
settles all that *guaio* – even for those less sorely afflicted it would be a
real misfortune, as it is for those of us who are hardened, and in the end
not merely hardened but battle-weary and literally demolished – all

the misery of our situation: the cramped and primitive conditions, the dirt, the ragged clothes and shoes, the lack of every single thing (like shoelaces, knives, bandages, disinfectant, drink…).

**Adolf Hitler, 1889–1945**                                      **Führerbunker, Berlin**
*Political testament*

From the sacrifice of our soldiers and from my own unity with them unto death will spring up in the history of Germany the seed of a radiant renaissance of the National Socialist movement and thus of the realization of a true community of nations.

*

**Anni Antonie Schmöger, schoolteacher, 1889–1994**           **Munich**

On Sunday we went to holy mass at 7 o'clock, so that if there was an air raid warning at least we would have received the host. Shortly after the holy transformation bombs suddenly fell, and the sirens sounded shortly afterwards. I hurried to the door with a number of others, but then turned back again, as I hadn't yet taken communion. After the blessing my sister and I left the church immediately and hurried home. […]

A few white flags were already flying in our street – my heart bled, for which person of character does not love his fatherland and feel sorrow when the Americans will soon march singing through his city's victory gate?

**Hella Reidt, 1901–78**                                             *Halle*

Today we were shaken by a bloody event. Hartmut Blume, 15 years old, found an anti-tank grenade while looking for firewood behind our garden. He handled it, and the propelling charge shattered his thigh horribly.

Frau Schneider found him lying helpless and alone, and came straight to me, and I went with Frau Maschmann, who happened to be with me, to the place where the misfortune occurred. The sight of the poor fellow, who was fully conscious, made me feel ill, his leg looked so shredded. It was scorched to the bone. Rüdiger and young Schneider dashed to the doctor on their bicycles, but Garber didn't come. Then I sent for Poschmann. He came sluggishly along in half an hour and said he couldn't do anything, the boy needed to go to hospital straight away. Now the boys dashed to the town hall and the Red Cross nurse. The community had no vehicle at its disposal, so Rüdiger and Frau Schulz had no option but to call an American ambulance. It stopped immediately, and the crew declared themselves willing to take the boy straight away. They got there very quickly, and bandaged the poor boy who had been lying on the ground the whole time without making a sound. His leg was expertly placed in splints, and Frau Blume was even able to drive with him to Halle.

### Dr Walther Kaldewey, 1896–1954         *Osterholz, Bremen*

It's as quiet as the grave today [...] The more one asks around, the clearer it becomes that the English have behaved badly, with certain exceptions. They have taken my car and tyres, all the instruments from the compasses case, they have destroyed medical apparatus in the institute, many handkerchiefs are missing. In the flats of the population after the withdrawal of the billeted soldiers it has largely looked disastrous, everything thrown into chaos, furniture used as firewood, even though wood was available in other places. Cameras are very much in demand: above all, of course, compact cameras, internationally first-class pieces of German craft. The wealthy are enriching themselves on a poor nation. Many cases of purely wanton destruction were reported all over the place. That the victim is chiefly the little man is now giving most people pause for thought. It is also now becoming apparent how objective our news service was. Everyone yearns to receive German news, because we are constantly forced to acknowledge how unreliable, contradictory, rabble-rousing and irritating the enemy news service is.

Most people are slowly beginning to shake off the shock of the first few days, and to go on believing as before in our good cause, all the more so when we take cognizance of the rudderlessness of the enemy.

Our bedroom is usable again. We all sleep in it. But the other rooms in the flat are not yet usable.

**Franz-Rudolph von Weiss,**
**Swiss Consul General, 1885–1960**                      *Cologne*
In the afternoon I received a lovely visit from my old friend Baron
Waldemar von Oppenheim, who used his first trip to the larger area
around Cologne to pay us a visit with his wife. It was truly shocking
to hear what that family had to go through during the six months
when they were in hiding in Cologne, often close to starvation, without being able to find an air raid shelter in the many heavy air raids
on Cologne, always fearing that they might be found alive, which
would have meant certain death. For someone standing outside it is
impossible to imagine the suffering of this respected family. Before
the invasion by the Americans, the mother of Frau Oppenheim was
arrested by the Gestapo in spite of her American citizenship and taken
to Brauweiler penitentiary. From there, even though she is 75, she
had to travel the 100 km to the penitentiary in Siegburg, but had then
to be left behind for lack of time. As I have already mentioned, the
Oppenheims' castle at Schlenderhan was left in such a terrible state by
the American troops that it is simply impossible to describe the state
it is in.

**Robert Bauer**                                  *Heilbronn*
Walk through the industrial zone. Severe battle damage everywhere.
All major factories totally destroyed.

On the corner of Wilhelmstrasse and Cäcilienstrasse a black and a
white soldier are playing handball with two German boys. In other
places too children can be seen playing games with the soldiers.

On the other hand one also hears increasing complaints of threats,
looting, robbery, actual attacks and Russian and Polish workers harassing women. They move from house to house in groups, particularly
remote smallholdings and vineyard cottages, and recklessly, heedlessly
take everything that isn't nailed down. It's a real scourge. Unfortunately the police have no power to do anything and have to look on
in silence.

The Bismarck monument is undamaged. Unmoved, the 'Old man of
the Saxon Forest' looks out over the bombed-out city and the ruined
bridge. One might think that his gaze is even harsher and gloomier

because of the terrible effects of a policy which deviated from the path he had shown: keeping and securing peace with Russia.

**Grete Dölker-Rehder, 1892–1946**                    *Neumühle*
'A mighty fortress is our God, A bulwark never failing. Our helper He, amid the flood of mortal ills prevailing.' The enemy is so far behaving with great rectitude [...] Despite the curfew, there was a big pilgrimage to Ratzenried. The tanks had driven off again, the place was guarded only by former French prisoners who had been armed, and who behaved in a calm and friendly way. They had opened an enormous food store in the brewery there, and distributed the goods to the people. It didn't look nice, the way they threw those precious things into the crowd, and how greedily the people grabbed for them, tore them from each other's hands and trod them into the dirt. We thought it was undignified. I was ashamed when I ended up carrying away a box of Nestlé's milk powder , which was held out to me even though I hadn't asked for it. But that's how unprincipled five and a half years of war has made us. You might think our experience of this great tragedy would only ever be tragic, when in fact there is no shortage of sober or even grotesque events.

We know practically nothing about the wider world of politics, newspapers stopped coming ages ago – radios have been handed in, so we must rely on contradictory rumours. Hitler is said still to be fighting in Berlin. Himmler is supposed to be negotiating with the chairman of the International Red Cross, Bernadotte.

**Adolf Hitler, 1889–1945**                    **Führerbunker, Berlin**
*Political testament*
Many of our bravest men and women have resolved to unite their lives with mine until the very last. I have begged, and finally ordered, them not to do this, but to take part in the further struggle of the nation. I implore the heads of the army, the navy, and the air force to strengthen by all possible means our soldiers' spirit of resistance in line with the National Socialist cause, with special reference to the fact that even I myself, as founder and creator of this movement, have chosen death over cowardly resignation or even capitulation.

*

### Alexei Kalinin, Soviet captain, b. 1911                    *Berlin*
*To his wife*

Greetings to all of you from Berlin!

Yes, Murochka, we are already in Berlin, we are fighting in the suburbs here and will soon take the city from the Fritzes. And only here, Murochka, have we come fully face to face with the lives of the Germans. They are all fatally similar, they are thin and pale, not rich, of course, and the workers suffer terribly from hunger. We go into a place – and they are frightened, they tremble, but after ten minutes they see that we are not monsters, and then they ask, without the slightest embarrassment, for bread or something to eat; they are well dressed, but they stand in the street and ask our soldiers for bread (silk on the outside, shit on the inside, as our people say). As soon as our kitchen begins supplying the soldiers, the German civilian population, both men and women, come running with bowls.

Murochka, you ask in your letter why you aren't receiving any parcels – I don't know either, Murochka, I've sent you three. Tomorrow is 1 May, and I shall sign off this letter to you, and meanwhile the guns are thundering here, they're making things good and hot for the Fritzes, you actually feel sorry for the lads, there's no time to sleep, we're hammering and hammering away at them, luckily we have no shortage of cucumbers.

So goodbye for now, my love!

I kiss you warmly

Your Lyosha

### Akim Popovichenko, Soviet officer                    *(Austria)*
*To his wife*

Dear Verochka!

Best wishes for 1 May. Let this be the last May Day that we cannot celebrate together.

Today at last I have succeeded in sending two parcels of valuable items to your address. Two to three new ones are already prepared, they are no less valuable than the ones before, now I have enough for another with silk and wool. In the parcel that we are sending to your address in Yasha Bibergal's name there is black wool fabric on the top, and there are also two pieces of dark blue cloth, women's fabric, all of that belongs to me, the rest to Yasha, and everything else belongs to him. In the parcel in my name, of course, everything belongs to me. I won't list everything that's in it, because there are so many silk and wool fabrics, I can't remember how many metres of what, and I don't want to rack my brains over the colours. When it all arrives you'll see anyway, and if it doesn't then listing everything would be pointless anyway.

There are silk stockings for you, I think about eight pairs, all new of course, then two silk ladies' blouses, one is light blue and the other pink. If everything I've sent to you and everything I still hope to send you arrived, then you would be the richest woman in Smela. I mean that quite seriously. It would be very annoying if I were to enrich not you, but someone else. I'm sure you haven't even dreamed of the kinds of materials I'm sending you, not in your whole life. I'm sure that at least some of it will arrive, and if nothing at all arrives – I'll come myself!

Goodbye. I hug and kiss you warmly.

Your Kima

PS Write to Vadya in Kiev or via the district recruitment office. Writing through the army takes a long time and is pointless.

**Pyotr Zevelyov, Red Army soldier**                    *Berlin*
*To his parents*

Mamochka, Papa, Shura, Taya!

Decrepit, scruffy, often completely exhausted German soldiers and officers are laying their guns down everywhere in the streets and squares, and giving themselves up in droves as prisoner to our troops. The Germans are flying white flags on many houses. Right at this minute I see two Hitler officers walking with lowered banners and no guns from the Tiergarten Park towards the Brandenburg Gate, near which there lies a pile of guns, and crowds of German soldiers and officers are standing.

Many of us have already learned to speak German, and many Germans can already cobble together a few phrases of broken Russian.

The last paradox of all: I am writing this letter and looking through the window, as one of our soldiers and a German soldier take turns drinking straight from a bottle of schnapps, gesticulating and talking about something or other. Amazing! You can hardly imagine this triumph of ours now happening in Berlin.

Please pass my greetings and best wishes to all our relatives. Hoping to see you soon, your Pyotr.

Berlin, Unter den Linden

*

**Friedrichsfelde Central Cemetery**                                   **Berlin**
Martha M., b. 1904
 Wilhelmstrasse
 Suicide (poisoned)

Willy M., b. 1901
 Wilhelmstrasse
 Suicide (poisoned)

Brunhilde M., b. 1930
 Wilhelmstrasse
 Suicide (poisoned)

Helmut M., b. 1933
 Wilhelmstrasse
 Suicide (poisoned)

*

**Lieutenant Hans Kranich, 1919–80**                         **near Jägernburg**
What did we have to say about the situation? Nothing! Perhaps the artillery officers spoke about what was happening, but we didn't. There were bound to have been the wildest speculations: Frau Pätzold (Marie Pätzold) had said at the first meeting that we were perhaps letting the Russians into the Reich deliberately. She was cross about it:

now they're making our soldiers fight and die, and then you have it: it was just a joke – the Russians are our allies. Officers often mentioned secret contacts with the Bandera partisans who were achieving fabulous victories over the Soviets in the Ukraine, with the support of German military advisers. I had placed great hopes in the Russian (and Tartar etc.) units who wanted to fight side by side, but one hears suspiciously little about them.

**Captain Arthur Mrongovius, 1905–92**                                    *Linz*
In the Russian general I encountered an extremely cultivated, sophisticated man whose confidence I soon won. In the presence of a translator, a very intuitive woman of German–Russian origin, I had many deep conversations about God and the world with Mikhail Meandrov, and I had no doubt that like so many of his officers he hadn't joined Vlasov's Russian Liberation Army out of opportunism or for materialistic reasons, but out of the genuine conviction that Stalin's rule was leading the Russian people to their ruin. In those days he placed all his hopes in the Americans, and could not imagine that they might hand him and his troops over to the Soviets, which was then what happened to the whole Vlasov Army – and like Vlasov he would pay for the support he gave to an attempt to remove Stalin's rule by being hanged on the walls of the Kremlin in Red Square in Moscow.

This general also revealed great circumspection when a transport of concentration camp prisoners arrived one day. Meandrov persuaded the SS guards to release the prisoners, swathed in their striped prison uniforms, and they scattered in droves all over the surrounding area, throwing up the danger that these half-starved people might die by their own hands on the farms of the local population. That everything went off peacefully was down entirely to the negotiating skill of Meandrov, who was able to persuade the villagers that it would be for the best to take these people in and feed them for the time being. Incidentally, this was the first time that I found myself face to face with something I had previously known only from hearsay, and to which I had lent no credence: the boundless misery of the concentration camp villainy. But I always assumed that Hitler was not the man ultimately responsible for it.

**Adolf Hitler, 1889–1945**   **Führerbunker, Berlin**
*Political testament*

May it, at some future time, become part of the code of honour of the German officer – as is already the case in our navy – that the surrender of a district or a town is impossible, and that above all the leaders here must march ahead as shining examples, in faithful fulfilment of their duty unto death.

\*

**Marianne Goerdeler, 1919–2011**   **Austria**
On 30 April 1945 […] we were transported out of Dachau concentration camp. That evening has etched itself unforgettably into my memory. Today it seems to stand for all the misery of those days. This time the windows of the bus were uncovered, and the guards were palpably nervous. We drove into the dying day. The sun, low in the sky, illuminated a ghostly scene with its sharp beams: for an hour we drove past marching, no, dragging columns of prisoners. Those emaciated figures of misery seemed countless, degraded into numbers, with their shaven heads and in their grey striped prison uniforms. Even in the bus we heard the hard tread of their wooden clogs, half dragging, half marching.

There was a cruel absurdity in the picture; in the middle of the chaos of collapse and dissolution they were still organized and ordered in rows and blocks under the command of their guards. Dead prisoners lay by the roadside, either been shot or having died of weakness. Where were the others bound?

**Frau Gretka, b. 1925**   **Tünzenhausen**
While I was staying at the little farm, one afternoon just before the Americans arrived, I had to cycle to a farmer some distance away, to fetch a so-called calving rope, because one of the cows was calving.

On the way there I found myself in the middle of quite a large column of strangely dressed men: grey and blue or grey and green (I can't remember exactly) striped uniform and headgear. Their faces grey, gaunt, as if they were dead. A baker's wife ran into the house and came back out with her arms full of bread, which she threw into the crowd. I stood wedged in between with my bicycle. The men pounced on the loaves like hungry dogs. The accompanying guards fired into the air, as they wouldn't otherwise have been able to keep control of the situation, and shouted terrible things at the baker's wife. She shouted back, in good Bavarian style. The men actually smelled mouldy. After the shots were fired they fell back into the rank and file. I was completely confused and didn't know what was going on. I pushed my bicycle on and saw a man squatting by the roadside, trousers down, doing his business. A guard with his rifle under his arm beside him. The man covered his face with his arm out of modesty as I walked past. Today I know that they were concentration camp inmates from Dachau, who were being taken somewhere in the last few days, God knows where.

**Willy Sägebrecht, concentration camp inmate**        **on the march**
The long, long death march began... It was very cold in those April days. Rain day and night. We marched in drenched clothing; a cloud of fog had formed over the long grey marching column of thousands of concentration camp inmates. We were tormented by hunger and thirst. We used every opportunity to slake our thirst. The SS fired on us. Many dead lay where they fell. When we passed by a potato field, we pounced on it in great numbers, to supply ourselves with raw potatoes. Here again the SS shot down many of us with rifle salvos. Various prisoners tried, when they left the field by the side entrance, to get away in the shelter of shrubs and bushes. The marching column was secured on both sides by motorized SS men with dogs. During such escape attempts, many concentration camp inmates were also killed. Many of the comrades died on the march. We prisoners were so weary and exhausted that many of us couldn't go on. But everyone who fell back into the back rows and couldn't keep up were shot in the back of the neck.

We supported the exhausted prisoners as long as we could.

**An unknown concentration camp inmate**                    **near Bad Tölz**
Next morning the march continued in the direction of Bad Tölz. The
Germans formed the first marching blocks each of about 1,000 men,
then came the Jews and last of all the Russians. On the march we could
already hear the rifle and machine-gun fire of the front not far behind
us. All the bridges and roads had already been blown up. We learned
that some of the Russians had already fallen into the hands of the
Americans, and others had been shot dead by the death squads.

Individual comrades now tried to make their escape when darkness
fell, although many lost their lives. Volkssturm and Werwolf killed
most of them with bullets to the back of the head. The road we walked
was in turn drenched with the blood of the murdered. Dead and dying
lay by the roadside, a picture of horror and nameless misery was being
played out before our eyes. Hopelessness and despair took hold of
many comrades.

Then, at around midnight, they drove us into a gorge and, when
they saw we were about to light a fire, opened up their rifles and
machine guns on us. It was bitterly cold that night, rain and snow
drizzled down on us, and we had to spend the night outside without
any shelter.

**Max Mannheimer, concentration camp inmate, b. 1920**     *Poing*
On 28 April 1945 the order comes to clear Mühldorf concentration
camp. Goods wagons stand ready for us on the platform. I am very
emaciated and have to be led straight from the sick bay to the wagon.
Five weeks of typhus has left me very weak. Leaning on my brother, I
reach the wagon. I feel I've reached safety – I'm in shelter. After a few
hours the transport sets off. The accompanying crew consists not only
of SS but also members of the Wehrmacht. That reassures us a little.

We stop in that little station. We notice that we're heading west.
We stop for a long time in Poing, not far from Munich. On the
next platform there is a train full of anti-aircraft gunners. Suddenly
a siren goes off. Our guards, who were surrounding the train, have
disappeared. A low-flying air attack fires at the two trains. We flee
the wagons and run into the fields. Can it be true? Is the war over? At
any rate we don't plan to get back to the wagons. Some of my fellow

prisoners die in the air raid. Now, at the last minute, including a friend of ours. An engineer from Prague. He's survived for five years. In vain.

Freedom doesn't last long. Suddenly we're encircled. The sentries fire over our heads and drive us back into the wagons. The transport drives on. It's 30 April 1945. We stop in the open countryside. From a distance we can see a long motorized column. Our guards have disappeared. We open the wagons. The gateway to freedom. A few hundred metres away an American military column is driving along. We are free. We still can't grasp it. I'm too weak to leave the wagon.

Beside the train the Americans set up a provisional field hospital. Two orderlies take charge of the patients and lay them on camp beds. Wash them. Give them tonics. Ambulances arrive. The most serious cases are to be brought to a hospital. We are human beings again. We can go to hospital without being afraid. We are free.

*

**Edgar Kupfer-Koberwitz, 1906–91**   *Dachau concentration camp*
The news arrives in dribs and drabs, lots of comrades visit me – I hear a lot, I try to sound people out as best I can, and from what people tell me I receive the following picture: when the Allies were on the way to Dachau, at one spot they found a pile of 400 prisoners who had been shot and killed – massacred. Later they found another pile of about the same number. In Dachau they then found a train filled with corpses, including massacred prisoners, about 2,000 or more – they say some of them were even lying in open wagons. The Americans are then supposed to have gone into the surrounding houses of the SS and killed everyone they found. – Is it true? It seems not quite certain to me. –

White flags waved from the towers and various other places in the camp. – But when the Americans approached the camp they were fired on by the SS. – Supposedly – I say: supposedly, however, the agreement had been made that Dachau camp had to be cleared of all SS by Friday 27 April at 12 noon, and the white flag was to fly everywhere. – The white flag was flying everywhere, but the SS didn't keep their word, they were still there and firing in spite of the white flag. – Then, and because of the corpses that were found everywhere, the order is said to have been given to shoot down every SS man found in the camp grounds, regardless of whether he surrendered or not. – That, of course, puts things in a very different light. –

All over the camp the flags are flying from every block in the colours of all the countries represented here. – Where can they have come from? White fabric, – fine: canvases, bedsheets – but the other colours? Did the comrades find them in the SS stores? –

I saw the street through the wood fence. – Dachau, as always, lots of inmates walking along the camp road, but they're walking, they're not dragging their feet, they're walking more freely, more confidently. – Some group or other marched on to the parade ground – but it isn't marching like before, everything is more relaxed. The colourful flags are flying, otherwise it's the same as ever and… at the same time it isn't. – There's something in the air, – something very special lies over everything, the whole atmosphere almost reminds me of that of a quiet funfair.

But what I can't see, what I only sense: the corpses of the SS are lying around everywhere, – they haven't been cleared away. – Why not?? – It makes me sad, and I think of the stolen shoes, watches and the like. – But then I think that after all the terrible things that most of us have experienced, after all the diabolical and barbaric things that have happened, it is in fact a good sign for our comrades that none of them is attacking the corpses, that they are being left in peace.

You might also think that people would be furiously kicking the corpses or otherwise unleashing their fury on them. – But it's encouraging to think that there is apparently no one among us who develops and expresses emotions in such a bestial way. –

The roar of the cannon can still be heard. – Munich is said not to have fallen yet, – it's as I thought. –

American soldiers come to the camp to look at us. – A group of them were led to a block. – In the washroom lay 50 corpses that had died, starved, exhausted. – One of the officers started crying when he saw that. – Strange to think of a man coming from battle, who sees corpses all the time, an officer in the middle of war, crying at the sight of our dead. – But I know that, – I know what our dead look like, so shocking that even the tears of a warrior are understandable. –

Apparently a division of film journalists came today and took shots of the cheering inmates and the dead SS, the camp and so on. – Of course these shots are authentic, but they would have been most authentic at the moment of liberation. – But the shots the soldiers took, at the very first moment, I'd like to see those – how authentic must they be! – […]

An international committee of prisoners has been set up. – Former SS members from other countries who lived among us as inmates have been identified. – The prisoners themselves found that out among themselves. – The accused were led away and handed over to the Allies. – They are in the bunker and will face the courts in their own countries, – ex-comrades. – Former capos, block staff and others have been dragged out, the ones who have a lot on their consciences. – That was done by large groups of inmates who were all able to testify to the shameful acts of the ones being led away. – They are said to have been shot immediately, – I can't check whether it's true about the shooting. – There are supposed to have been lots of them. – A big clearing-up operation is starting up. – It must be terrible now to have a bad conscience, even for a prisoner and particularly for him. – What a bitter fruit life will be for them. […]

There are already radios in many of the blocks. The Americans bring them to us, they take them when they find them in the SS area. –

The food… – Yes, I nearly forgot to mention it: we are now getting thick soups, – the bread ration has gone up. – There are tinned meats, half a tin each for dinner. – It's still camp food, camp supplies, – the tinned meat is from the Wülfert canning factory in Dachau or other SS supplies. – For us it's a feast – Everyone smiles blissfully when the food arrives. How must the population of Dachau be faring? – They were always so good to us, they gave us what they had and helped us where they could, – the SS were the ones they couldn't stand. – I hope they don't have to pay for the deeds of the SS, I hope the name of their nice little town won't bring them misfortune because it also gave the camp its notorious name. – I worry about it. –

**Johann Steinbock, pastor, b. 1909**     *Dachau concentration camp*

The misery of our homelessness wasn't lifted straight away. It was explained that we were going to be taken to the barracks of the SS camp. But they first had to be cleaned and furnished. The Americans kept wanting to photograph and film the wretchedness of the camp, and more and more visits and commissions came to be shown the original state of the camp. So we have to stay living a Gypsy lifestyle together for a while. Immediate release from the camp to home isn't yet possible, first because there's been spotted fever in the camp for a few months, leaving around a hundred dead every day, so there will be quarantine for a few weeks, and inoculations will have to be given, and secondly because there are no means of transport, the trains have stopped running and there are no cars available as yet. We are to stay until the individual governments send means of transport. A number of foreigners and criminals had left the camp during the first excitement, and had done some damage to the SS camp and the plantation and caused mayhem in the surrounding area. So the Americans have also set up sentry posts around the camp. [...]

Every barrack and almost every room was in search of a radio and a typewriter. Anything the SS had left behind was requisitioned. From all the windows at all hours until deep into the night music and a hubbub of voices now rang out. There was almost the danger of the oppressed suddenly coming into their own: if people had previously talked, rightly, about SS big shots, one would now almost have been tempted, because of the behaviour and the feudal-looking furniture fetched from the SS rooms to some of the committees, to think in terms of 'big shots' in the camps again. In the end the committees weren't given very much power and strength anyway.

The Yugoslavs were particularly recognizable from a distance by the Tito stars on their caps. At their celebrations the repeatedly chanted cheer of 'Tito, Tito, Tito' filled the street. But, for me it was too reminiscent of the formerly familiar Italian cries of 'Duce, Duce'.

The Germans were the only ones without a flag during those days. Some individuals among the various different nations didn't at first want to see them represented on the international prisoners' committee. But the more insightful referred successfully to the fact that the Germans present in the camp were victims of the Gestapo and the SS just like the other nations, and so a German committee was formed as well.

### Emil Barth, 1900–1958                     *Haan, Rhineland*

In the street, members of the occupying troops are distributing the *Kölnischer Kurier*, a newspaper published in German by the American army. As the foreigners are very fond of children, are very childish themselves, and as their posts and billets are hence constantly surrounded by children, they let the little ones help with the distribution too, our unsuspecting German children, who have no idea what a legacy of shame and misfortune they have been given in life, and what an awful rag they are so eagerly holding out to the grown-ups. Because it is awful, in the full sense of that word; there is something of the awfulness of the voice with which Cain asks after his brother Abel, or that mythical list of misdeeds which will, according to the faithful, be shown to the sinful on the Day of Judgement. It contains eyewitness reports and photographs from the concentration camps […].

I may have spoken to a good two dozen people today, and no one, man or woman, was stirred by anything but these revelations of the horrific crimes that have had their infernal seat in the power circles of the German Reich over the last twelve years. 'If it's all true…' said some, trying to cling to a hint of hope; but in truth they had stopped doubting, and their hesitant reservations were outweighed by the unspoken: 'Then… woe betide the lot of us!'

### Jutta, schoolgirl                     *Verchen am Kummerower See*

I can't describe the shouting that went on in the streets and in people's homes. My father hid me in a hayloft, but brought me back down a short time later because he thought it was dangerous there too. And so it was: ten minutes later the Russians climbed up, and poked their bayonets into the hay in search of women. They were the troops who had spent weeks lying in the bogs along the Oder, and now they pounced on us like wild animals and vented their fury. Many of them were drunk. I have suffered terrible anxieties, and experienced terrible things myself. My parents couldn't protect me.

**Irma von Blanck-Heise, b. 1916**                                    *Ahrensberg*

When things calmed down, we went back to the stable. It looked desolate there. The Russians had slit open our cases and bags, and my rucksack too, and tipped out the contents on the sheep-dung; they'd pocketed everything that struck them as valuable. Among what remained I found my precious brilliant brooch, an old gemstone whose gold rim had also disappeared, and my husband's green suit. [...]

In the meantime the Dutch tried to make friends with the Russians they met, crying, 'Hollandski, Hollandski, friends!' But the Russians didn't understand a word, and just replied, 'Hollandia nix gut – Uri, Uri!' and took all their watches and other valuables from them.

In the meantime a completely ragged-looking, long-unshaven man came into our stable. He proved to be a released Polish prisoner who spoke barely any German. Although everyone else was repulsed by him, something impelled me to approach the man and tell him that he could stay with us. I gave him my husband's suit, and from our big cooking pot, which was always full of tasty porridge, I gave him as much as he wanted to eat. He stayed with us, and over the next few hours he was to be our best protection against the Russians who kept forcing their way into the stable.

**Erich Zimmermann, musician, 1900–1987**                    *(Heubude)*

Every day Grandma Paula had to fetch water from the pump at the first farmhouse on Rieselfeldehaussee. She found some plates for us there, and various bits of leftover food. The most precious was a very big, fat beef-heart from a pickle barrel. When she had cooked it in our iron oven, we all devoured it with relish. The heart muscle meat and all the pickled rancid fat was probably the ideal food for our starving state. The daily walk for water and searching the abandoned farmhouses was always an anxious undertaking for Grandma Paula, and it was always with great apprehension that I awaited her return. Even though the whole area was completely deserted, Russian soldiers still prowled around every now and again. Once she met a Russian officer who asked her what she was doing. When she showed him what she had collected he let her go, and she looked pitiful enough anyway. Everyone in our miserable camp looked so wretched that it was no wonder the Russians left us in peace as soon as they had flushed us out.

**Ella Kossol**                                                              *near Stolp*
One night an old, kind and jovial-looking Russian came to our little room in the company of a very young boy, told us to lie down and seemed only to want to talk to us. He told us, as far as we could communicate with one another, that he too had children the age of our little ones at home, and that he hadn't seen them for many years. Nodding sadly to the children, they left us soon afterwards.

**Andrei Filin, Soviet lieutenant, b. 1918**                        *East Prussia*
Another day and we were on the march again. I lay on a horse-cart and held my pale face towards the warm April sun. Glorious!

Then all of a sudden I saw a German woman running across the field about half a kilometre from the road.

'Please, stop, Red Cross, Red Cross, help...' she called to us.

I halted my men.

As far as we could understand, it was about her father, fatally wounded by a bullet from a Russian soldier. Our regimental commander opposed any attempts to rape German women.

'The war would have been over ages ago if we hadn't behaved like Asiatic savages in East Prussia. Now German kids aren't defending their bloody Führer or their Nazi fatherland, but their mothers and sisters. And they will do so to the last bullet. For every soldier who can't control himself there are holes of every calibre peppering the fence. And they're all a hundred per cent clap-free.'

Colonel Pyatov gave me a translator and we ran to the house. Unfortunately the old man was already dead.

It turned out that an armed Russian soldier had forced his way into the house and demanded schnapps. He had been given the schnapps. Then he saw a young girl in the house and wanted to rape her. The old man stepped forward to protect his granddaughter and got a bullet in the belly.

We found the drunken Asiatic from the NKVD troop, who usually advanced behind the fighting units, 3 km from the house in a little forest. He was sleeping the sleep of the just. Our colonel gave the murderer his pistol with a single bullet in the barrel. 'I give you five minutes, my lad, be brave. In five minutes I'll help you as I would help a coward.' The shot rang out a few seconds later. We put it down to suicide.

*

**Hans-Heinrich Beerbohm, harbour commander**        **Stralsund**
At a strategy meeting for all the officers of the 1st Navy Training Detachment on the Dänholm, at midnight on 29 April, I received an order from garrison commander Zollenkopf to sink the sailing school ship *Gorch Fock* lest it fall into Russian hands. It was completely unrigged, the sails were in the sheds on the Dänholm, and there was no ship's engine on board as it was being overhauled in a wharf. The crew had gone on land. Lieutenant Commander Kahle had been redeployed. At between 1 and 2 in the morning I ordered my staff sergeant, Bauer, the director of the boat harbour on the Dänholm, to take a motor-yawl with a fireman to the sailing boat, which was moored near the Drigge peninsula in the middle of the stream. The drain-holes were opened so that the water could rise quickly into the ship. Blowing it up was important, because the Russians were on the opposite shore, on dry land, and would have reacted accordingly. The day before they had fired with artillery at a train of barges and sunk some when they had tried to escape under the long railway bridge on the northern channels to Sassnitz.

**Antonina Romanova,**
**forced labourer, b. 1927**        *Alt-Neheim farm, near Greifswald*
We were put up in three sheds: Poles, Ukrainians and we Russians. We had to work every day, in all weathers. Mostly in the field. On 30 April 1945 we had planted potatoes. I carried a big basket full of potatoes with a strap around my neck, it was sunny and warm outside. All of a sudden we saw white sheets being hung out of the windows of the farmer's three-storey house. We couldn't understand it. The beds had been aired only two days before. And then all of a sudden a few wildly

galloping horsemen appeared. It was a Red Army reconnaissance patrol.

'Where are the Germans?' they asked. – 'All gone.'

My God! We surrounded them, we pulled them down from their saddles, we kissed the boots of our liberators, their stirrups, we stroked their horses, we were drunk with joy. It was probably the happiest minute in the lives of all these forced labourers.

After this reconnaissance our troop then headed west. Tanks, horse-carts. We stood by the roadside, waved to our soldiers and wept with joy.

**Soya Romanova,**
**forced labourer, b. 1934**          *Alt-Neheim farm, near Greifswald*
The day of 30 April 1945, when we were liberated, will always be etched on my memory. As long as I live it will be the most glorious day of celebration. I had to suffer so many terrible things in the months of bondage. As a child I wasn't allowed to be put to work on the farm. I had to sit in a shed for days at a time with the eight-year-old Ukrainian boy Ostap, who didn't understand much Russian and always cried when his mother was away. I always did everything I could to comfort him.

But these were trivial matters compared to the bullying I was subjected to by Erich, a member of the Hitler Youth. This red-haired brat, tall and weedy, who was four years older than me, was more than a sadist. He lived in a detached house with his mother, who, like other German women, had done some sort of work in the farmer's house. Every day he lay in wait for me in some remote corner and beat me mercilessly, sometimes with a thick stick. He strangled me and said as he did so, 'You savage wolf of the steppes, I'll make sure no monsters creep from your c—t.' I understood German very well, children find languages easy, but I didn't know that word.

Two things completely poisoned my childhood in the war: the bombing raids – even today the memory terrifies me – and Hitler Youth Erich, damn him to hell.

**Anna Popovskaya, forced labourer, b. 1926**   *Gärzig, near Dessau*
We saw no sign of a liberator in the little village. All of a sudden the
farmer told us that from now on we were all free, and had to gather
at an assembly point the following day. Anyone who wanted to could
take a bicycle. With the money we had saved (we earned 4 Reichsmark
a month) we bought second-hand clothes from a shop. I was still
wearing some of those in 1950 after I completed my studies. That was
how we were repatriated to the Russians. We were sent home on a
freight train transporting dismantled industrial equipment to the
Donets Basin. Five of us had been driven from our village in 1943 and
four of us returned home. One girl had married a Pole and stayed in
Poland. A few months after our return we started thinking of going
back to Germany. At least we had had plenty to eat on our farm, while
at home we spent many years starving.

**Adolf Hitler, 1889–1945**   **Führerbunker, Berlin**
*Political testament*
    Before my death I am expelling the former Reichsmarschall
Hermann Göring from the party and depriving him of all rights which
he enjoyed by virtue of the decree of 29 June 1941; and also by virtue
of my statement in the Reichstag on 1 September 1939. I appoint in
his place Grand Admiral Dönitz, President of the Reich and Supreme
Commander of the Armed Forces.

*

**Dmitry B., Soviet bomber pilot, b. 1918**   *Berlin*
We set off three times to bomb Berlin.
    The last mission at the end of April 1945 was unforgettable for
me. Our target was Tempelhof airport, where lots of fighter planes
and fighter bombers of the German Luftwaffe were supposed to be
ready for action in hangars. The cloudless sky, glorious weather, green
fields and blossoming gardens down below. Even from our altitude of
5,000 m we could see every little house.
    From Küstrin some fighter planes were supposed to give us cover.

But we couldn't see them. All right, we thought, the war was practically over, and the enemy's air force had been paralysed. If a confused German fighter plane turned up, our tail gunners would surely be able to shoot him down. So we went on flying without cover. Everything all around in dense, black clouds of smoke. It was impossible to make out the sky or the earth. A real inferno over Berlin. Everything was in flames in all directions, and smoke rose up to the sky like thousands of chimneys.

Normally we dropped the bombs from 4,000 m, this time we went down to 1,500 m because we couldn't see the target. Only sometimes did a wing of another plane appear on either side of us, dart past, and then once again there was nothing but black clouds and an incredible cacophony in our headphones. At last we had reached our target and dropped our payload.

When we had gained altitude again we suddenly saw that a wide strip of German soil below us, from the Havel to the Oder, was in flames and smoke.

**Paul S., businessman**                    *Lienewitz, near Potsdam*
Lots of activity at our farmhouse. We were sitting in the kitchen warming ourselves. Then a few Russians came and asked us if they could cook. General 'yes'. Then it got going: margarine dumplings, a bucket of dripping, meat and everything you can imagine. For lunch there was liver and onions. We had to join them and eat as much as we could. In the evening, noodle soup with a lump of beef, any amount of bread and fried fish (caught with hand grenades) swimming in fat.

As I write, infantry bullets are whizzing past the window. That doesn't bother veterans of the front. We're in clover here. The commandant told us especially to eat anything and as much as we wanted. And that's what we're doing.

It's about to get dark. All of a sudden the Stalin organ starts up. You won't know that gun. It's indescribable. Some primeval animal with a thousand throats. A terrible roar. The organ sends out death and destruction. And on the Leipzig Autobahn triangle a few crazy SS men have a gun post. Yesterday they had 182 dead, 72 wounded, and 35 want to go over to the Russians. 15 of their own people have been shot from behind. Tomorrow it's 1 May.

Yours, Papi

### Hermann Kasack, 1896–1966                              *Potsdam*

When I was with Anne in our front cellar on Monday morning, discovering that many of my book boxes and the manuscript parcels from my publisher had been torn open, but mostly untouched, we were called upstairs because two Russians had turned up. [...] One of them, one Guards Major Yermakov, spoke a little German. He had made some regretful remarks about the state of the flat when he came in, but added that the Germans had behaved no differently, in fact rather worse, in Russia. When my wife, Maria, retorted that only a few of the German soldiers had acted like that, he replied harshly, 'No, all of them.' He added that the Russian population in the war zones had had to endure worse cruelties. 'By the way,' he added pointedly, 'the Germans normally like order.' Of course we understood this nod. He was stocky of build, with an intelligent, expressive face. It was only in the afternoon that we discovered that he was the deputy city commandant of Potsdam.

### Carl Diem, 1882–1962                                      *Berlin*

Then the Russians came. One after the other came into our house with their machine guns raised, searched it from top to bottom 'for weapons' and took whatever he pleased. Above all watches, rings etc. We let some rings go, and hid the others. My wife had cut my eldest daughter's hair – she was 14 at the time – and made her wear trousers; she walked around as a boy and no one paid her any attention. My 12-year-old sat in the dark corner of the cellar, clutching a big doll, and also remained unharmed. My wife stood in the street and refused to be drawn in by any cries of 'Come, woman.' I was regularly searched, one or other of them tried to intimidate me by putting his gun to my chest. Some of them fired at the radio, shot the telephone to pieces, fired past my head, but if you showed no fear they held back, and probably my books were my best defence. As my whole study was full of books on all sides, they took me for a great scholar. They asked me about my job. 'Professor' and 'physikultura' were familiar and respectable terms. A few words of Russian that the family had learned before came in useful. Our old cook, 'Mashka' as they called her, didn't stand on ceremony. Any men who got through into the kitchen, she pushed back out with her bare hands. Without my knowledge an NCO put a sign on the door to say that this important doctor was to be left unmolested.

One day in the garden when a group of people asked me what I was, I showed them the high bar and pretended to do a pull-up. Then I had an unexpected gym team, and everyone wanted to do the same. Everyone wanted to play volleyball at our house, and in the end we received a particular patron saint in the form of a Siberian nomad who discovered the Kirghiz pictures in my book *Asian Equestrian Sports* and was quite wild about them. He turned up every few hours, always bringing something to eat, a pot full of pea sausage or a loaf of bread or sweets for the girls. When drunken soldiers came he pushed them back out, and when his column marched off at last, he paid us a sincere farewell visit.

### Elisabeth Ditzen, 1868–1951                              *Carwitz*

Monday, probably the hardest day of all. Very early in the morning a driver came with our lieutenant from the previous day, who was now quite altered. He waved my 'good morning' dismissively away. The driver was probably of a senior rank, he was very angry that we wouldn't give him a watch. Woman not lie, he said to Suse, then he went to the garage. They wanted to have the car, Frau Burlage's, but the battery was missing, it had been given away. [...]

Then in the afternoon a horrible time began for us, particularly for Suse. One horde after another appeared with rifles, horsewhips, swords. Again that terrible word rang out: Uhrr, Uhrr. We could only point to our two alarm clocks, but they turned them down. Then the rummaging began in every room in the house. It looked indescribable afterwards. Every button in the sewing box, all the craft materials were examined, things were pilfered from all the cupboards and suitcases. It was probably a shame that so many suitcases had been brought here. [...]

The young Russian who took my dear husband's watch stared at me as he left and suddenly shook my hand. Before, he had wanted to throw another stone at my radio, but Suse said: Germany is so broken anyway, please don't! So he didn't.

## Adolf Hitler, 1889–1945                                     Führerbunker, Berlin
*Political testament*

Before my death I expel the former Reichsführer-SS and Minister of the Interior, Heinrich Himmler, from the party and from all offices of state. In his stead I appoint Gauleiter Karl Hanke as Reichsführer-SS and Chief of the German Police, and Gauleiter Paul Giesler as Reich Minister of the Interior.

Göring and Himmler, quite apart from their disloyalty to my person, have done immeasurable harm to the country and the whole nation by secret negotiations with the enemy, which they conducted without my knowledge and against my wishes, and by illegally attempting to seize power in the state for themselves.

In order to give the German people a government composed of honourable men – a government which will fulfil its pledge to continue the war by every means – I appoint the following members of the new Cabinet as leaders of the nation: [...]

Although some of these men, such as Martin Bormann, Dr Goebbels, etc., together with their wives, have joined me of their own free will and did not under any circumstances wish to leave the capital of the Reich, but were willing to perish with me here, I must nevertheless ask them to obey my request, and in this case place the interests of the nation above their own feelings. By their work and loyalty as comrades they will be just as close to me after death, as I hope that my spirit will linger among them and go with them always. Let them be hard, but never unjust, above all let them never allow fear to influence their actions, and let them set the honour of the nation above everything in the world. Finally, let them be aware of the fact that our task, that of continuing the building of a National Socialist state, represents the work of the coming centuries, which places every single person under an obligation always to serve the common interest and to subordinate his own advantage to this end. I demand of all Germans, all National

Socialists, men, women, and all the men of the armed forces, that they be faithful and obedient unto death to the new government and its president.

*

### Ivan Kovchenko, Soviet staff sergeant, b. 1927 (Berlin)
The battles for Berlin were characterized by particular toughness and resistance on the part of the Germans. Sometimes one had the impression of facing a fresh army rather than a weary one. The enemy refused to give up an inch of land without a fight. Our 5th Division shock troops broke through the enemy lines of defence on the outermost ring around Berlin relatively quickly, and on 22 April 1945 our battalion fought fierce street battles inside the city, while we advanced slowly from the north-east to the city centre. Everything was on fire. We spared nothing, and no ammunition, just to advance another few metres. It was even worse than in Stalingrad. The ferocity of the battles is borne out by the fact that over half of our officers and the men of our battalion fell in Berlin. And before the attack we had one hundred per cent strength.

### Lothar Loewe, b. 1929 Berlin
On the morning of 30 April we were in Sophie-Charlotten-Strasse, when three Russian tanks suddenly rolled in, firing in the direction of Kaiserdamm. Felgentreu and I fled through the hallways and basement passageways of a house into quite a big cellar with a little window on to the street. On the lieutenant's orders I got the anti-tank grenade ready to fire, with my visor raised. I hit the second Russian tank. The tank stopped, gave off smoke for a few seconds, and then there was an explosion 20 metres away. In a blind panic, in the gunpowder smoke from the grenade recoil, I had instinctively thrown myself to the floor. I think I was shuddering with fear. Felgentreu pulled me up and said very calmly, 'Come on, lad, let's get away through the backyards, Ivan isn't going to wait...' We escaped towards Schlossstrasse and crossed Bismarckstrasse under fire from grenade throwers. This was a disturbing experience, and I didn't feel any great desire to fire at Russian tanks again.

**Patrolman Arno Pentzien**                                        **Berlin**

At last, after driving for hours, we manage to take up position at dawn near the Westkruez in the Lietzensee Park. We billet ourselves on some civilians, who welcome us in. Everyone is very frightened. But we don't get much peace. The railway tracks are behind this house front, and the Russians are in the houses beyond the tracks. There are snipers over there, who fire at any movement on this side. In front of us on the tracks there's a very weak Volkssturm battalion. We take our rifles and fire at the Russians, who are working their way across the tracks. After an hour we have disabled nine Russians. But the worst is yet to come. Meanwhile a Russian has set up an AT-gun position on the third floor of the house opposite and is firing briskly at us. There's also a grenade launcher. Our chief patrolman Fricke, who wanted to fire back, was shot through the chest and was now lying in the stairwell. We quickly brought him to a nearby field hospital. Luckily he had only been shot in the lung.

**Willi Damaschke, teacher, 1892–1957**                          **Berlin**

9.30 a.m.

Last night we suddenly had to 'move'. For many hours we'd been standing in a hallway and now upstairs we've broken through a library door: I walk along the rows of books: August Winnig, *The Book of Science*, Felix Timmermann, *The Hernat Family*, Wilhelm Scholz, Regina Holderbusch, etc. etc. How differently I would stand here in times of peace. It's on Ravennee-Strasse. I was once a guest of the industrial magnate Ravennee at Schloss Marquardt near Potsdam. You were able to visit me then. Now I'm in a Ravennee-Strasse, in the midst of infernal fire.

I hope we'll get out of here again.

I'm writing this in the rooms of the library. In my right coat pocket I have a bottle of 'Haase-Köm', from which I warm myself from time to time.

A wretched life!

I'd like to get back to the house, but the courtyard's under heavy fire.

*

**St Georgen Parish Congregation Cemetery**   **Prenzlauer Berg, Berlin**

Name: Johannes H.
  b. 3.1.1891
  Bank manager
  Suicide by shooting
Name: Gertrud H.
  b. 18.1.1897
  Housewife
  Suicide by shooting
Name: Gisela H.
  b. 17.11.1923
  Office manager
  Suicide by shooting
Name: Bruno M.
  10 years, 1 month, 21 days
  Schoolboy
  Shot by own mother
Name: Gisela M.
  9 years, 1 month, 4 days
  Schoolgirl
  Shot by own mother

*

**Jacob Kronika, Danish journalist, 1897–1982**   **Berlin**
For many hours it is completely impossible to leave the bunker. The shooting has turned into an uninterrupted barrage. There are a lot of hits outside. The bunker itself is shaking violently. They're probably fighting on the east–west axis, at Zoo and Tiergarten stations, as well as in Charlottenburg. We now have the feeling that 'our' corner of 'Fortress Tiergarten' will be the last battlefield of Berlin.

In the afternoon, in a pause in the shelling, there is an opportunity to dash over to the embassy. Most of the SS men have made themselves scarce. There are only a few privates and a lieutenant left in the building. There are sentries outside. But of course that isn't for the protection of the embassy! The sentries are gazing tensely across at the Tiergarten. They too are waiting for the first Russians. But their feelings are different from ours.

Because a water pipe has been damaged at the legation, we have to be careful with the water. So far we've taken it from the boiler room tanks that Carl far-sightedly filled before the battle for Berlin began. The Germans haven't discovered our secret water supply. But otherwise they've tracked down everything drinkable and edible within the embassy walls!

**Theo Findahl, Norwegian journalist, 1891–1976**    *Dahlem, Berlin*
The Russian lads have left before I come down to the ground floor, and have made everything neat and tidy; the only objection one might raise about our fleeting guests is that they made a terrible mess of the toilets. It's more unpleasant than it sounds, because there's no water in the pipes. Water has now become a genuine problem. We like to laugh about the little washing water butts shown to the tourists in old castles, but now I learn that you actually can wash your face clean even if all you have is a little cup full of water; to shave all you need is the remains in the bowl. When you think of the amounts of water that people use in the course of the day at the heart of civilization in places like New York, it seems like an unimaginable waste. Luckily we have enough wood and coke to boil as much water as we need. In the next-door garden the Russians have set up a field kitchen; they're constantly cooking lamb, baking aromatic, powerful rye-bread loaves, and are not shy of sharing with people who ask for food.

**A woman**                                                    *Berlin*
From eight o'clock, the usual bustle through the open back door. All kinds of strange men. Suddenly there are two or three of them there, pressing themselves around me and the widow, trying to grab us, greedy as foxes. But usually one of the ones we already know comes and helps us to get rid of the strangers. I hear Grisha warning them off by mentioning Anatol's name. And I'm proud that I've actually

managed to tame one of the wolves, probably the strongest of them, so that he keeps the rest of the pack away from me.

**Dr Schmidt, bank director**                    *Lichterfelde, Berlin*
Yesterday afternoon we fetched Frau L. and her two lodgers, Herr Kä. and Herr Za., both Telefunken employees, out of the cellar and buried them. All three lay in the same room, amidst the bedclothes, laundry, scattered plates and clutter. Simple shots to the head, terrible pools of blood. Getting them out was an unbearable task. I said the Our Father by the open grave. [...] While this was going on Bolshevists prowled through the parks and watched what we were up to. The grave is in the Kod.'schen Garten [a park]. I couldn't do anything about that; it had been more than half started by strangers when I got there. [...]

After the terrible agitation of the first few days the reaction is now becoming palpable. I feel as if I'm broken, body and soul, every limb feels shattered, and in my head there's a dull void. I stare at the blossoming trees in the garden, they are somehow unreal. Can nature go on blossoming and growing and dressing itself in its finest spring raiment, if all around the human beast scorns the whole of God's creation!? What is the meaning of it all? It must have some meaning! But I can't find it – everyone is tired of life, we envy the dead their peace. If poison were distributed somewhere, the people would come streaming by in droves and fight each other for it!

**Adolf Hitler, 1889–1945**                    **Führerbunker, Berlin**
*Political testament*
I demand of all Germans, all National Socialists, men, women, and all men of the armed forces, that they be faithful and obedient unto death to the new government and its president.

Above all I charge the leaders of the nation and those under them to scrupulous observance of the racial laws and to merciless opposition to the global poisoner of all peoples, international Jewry.

Given in Berlin, 29 April 1945, 4.00 a.m.

Adolf Hitler

Witnessed by: Dr Joseph Goebbels, Wilhelm Burgdorf, Martin Bormann, Hans Krebs

\*

**Plonzstrasse Cemetery**                                    *Berlin*
Gerhard N., b. 1914
    Rüdigerstrasse
    Suicide by shooting
Ilse N., b. 1914
    Rüdigerstrasse
    Suicide by shooting
Irma N., b. 1944
    Rüdigerstrasse
    Suicide by shooting

**A Soviet soldier**                                         *Berlin*
Dear mother

All the terrible, unrepeatable things that have passed before my eyes in recent days will never disappear from my memory.

It is hard to imagine such a possibility, but the eyes and ears confirm something that the intellect refuses to believe.

I drove into Berlin for the first time at 9 o'clock in the morning on 23 April. [...] Hanging on the fences you could see, as a kind of tribute to the day, the hastily thrown-up inscriptions in German: 'Berlin bleibt deutsch – Berlin stays German' etc. (an irony of fate – all German magic spells and prophecies are bursting like soap bubbles). After that came the big houses. Tiled roofs again, mansards again, here and there a detached villa sprinkled in among them, leftovers from far-off days, when the suburb was still a remote village. There is a lot of rubble and rubbish in the streets. The German soldiers have taken a considerable amount of trouble to construct all kinds of obstacles and barricades, but none of it could prevent our advance.

By the time we entered the suburbs, the battles had moved into the centre. At first it was very bleak, but then all of a sudden the residents turned up too. Very threadbare, clothes of poor material, worn-out shoes, pale, gaunt faces. But their appearance turned out to be rather better than the actual state of affairs. Shamelessly, with hungrily gleaming eyes, with wretched, forcedly smiling faces, women, men and children came towards us and asked for bread and something to eat. When I remember all this, even today it brings tears to my eyes. It was a sad spectacle, this march of hungry, frightened people. Then came the looting of the department stores by the Berlin population. The crowd charged through shattered shop windows and doors torn from their hinges. Old men staggered under the burden of the sacks of food that they'd managed to grab hold of, old women tore tins of food from the hands of children. […]

I can be proud that the first road signs in Berlin in the Russian language were written by me. Not somewhere in the back of beyond, but in Berlin. The tram-wires have been torn down in some streets, and white Berlin tram cars stand around wherever they happened to be caught up in the storm of war.

**Adolf Hitler, 1889–1945**                    **Führerbunker, Berlin**
*Private testament*

As I did not consider that I could take responsibility, during the years of struggle, of contracting a marriage, I have now decided, before the closing of my earthly career, to take as my wife that girl who, after many years of faithful friendship, entered, of her own free will, the practically besieged town in order to share her destiny with me. At her own desire she goes as my wife with me into death. It will compensate us for what we both lost through my work in the service of my people.

*

**Hertha von Gebhardt, 1896–1978**              *Wilmersdorf, Berlin*

The looting of the shops has begun. It isn't the Russians who are doing it – although perhaps here and there they are – but mostly our fellow country-folk. Indescribable scenes wherever goods were to be found. The women hit each other, scratch each other, pour oil over each other, smear each other with jam, pour away good flour, good food, drag everything away by the hundredweight wherever they can. Revolting. Small shops have been looted, like Fräulein Sander's shop with its bras and rolls of thread. The stock in the shops is disappearing. There's no stopping it now.

There were three Russians at Hefter's on Breitenbachplatz, they called Frau E. over, and one of them took her into the cellar and then generously gave her the whole shop by way of thanks. There wasn't that much left in it, but she came running in: 'Children, one of you heat up some water for me, all the rest come with me!' We didn't know what was going on; then it became clear: we dragged away a big haunch of beef, a huge bowl of jam, various foodstuffs. In the end the decision is made to cook communally. Frau P. will cook, everyone adds whatever they have to the meat, noodles, fat etc. The haunch provides two fabulous meals. Huge bones to be boiled down. It took two of us to carry them. I couldn't have dreamed that I would be marching along from Breitenbachplatz to Rüdesheimer Platz carrying on my shoulder a haunch of beef that didn't cost anything, just a woman's willingness to have intercourse three times. […]

New Russian encampments all around us. Pigs are being slaughtered in the Laubenland, car after car dashes past, Wilmersdorf has never heard so many car horns or such clattering of hoofs. Long columns of refugees in between, with little carts full of their belongings, or a few bundles in their arms.

### Friederike Grensemann, b. 1924                    *Mitte, Berlin*

One of the house residents died on 30 April. An old gentleman. He was wrapped in a carpet, cobbles dug from the courtyard, a pit shovelled and in with the poor fellow. He had survived it! The toilets were full to the brim, and the flush had stopped working. The water was slowly running out. On the opposite side of the street from us there was still supposed to be a pump. Eva and I wanted to try and fetch fresh water. We tried to crawl along the Ku-Damm with a bucket, but didn't get far. The Russian tanks were coming. When I was standing by the entrance to the cellar I was hit by a piece of shrapnel from a shell, it whizzed past my right lower arm. You could still see the scar ten years later.

There were a lot of groaning wounded people lying in the cellar, it was almost unbearable. The famous Stalin organs wailed over Berlin, everything was burning and smoking and there was the sound of crashing. The Russian infantry were getting closer, house by house. It could only be a matter of hours, and then they would have us. People

were saying: now they're in no. 217, now 215, no. 213 and then...
Funny, it's all over 31 years ago, and I can write it down as if it was
yesterday. I was just 20 at the time, I'm 52 now, and I still see it with
the same eyes.

Just before the Russians came into our house, 211 Kurfürstendamm,
the chief staff physician said to us, 'You don't need to worry, I'm part
of the "underground movement" and have papers, nothing will happen
to us!'

The anti-tank grenades from the courtyard had already been taken
away or blown to pieces, the doctor said, 'Anyone who owns a gun
either give it to me or leave the house *straight away*!' I had my pistol in
my coat pocket, and what was I supposed to do with it? I'd promised
Dad that I would shoot myself if the Russians came! Was I supposed to
do that now? I was afraid of my own courage! Was I supposed to leave
the house? Impossible, then I might as well shoot myself. It was very
hard to decide! I hesitated. The pistol in my hand in my pocket was
threatening and enticing. I crept into a corner, took the pistol, with the
safety catch still on, and put the barrel into my throat! Filling it with
water is even more effective someone had told me. I've never forgotten
the minutes that were supposed to decide my life or death back then.
I stared into the courtyard, where the big rubbish bins stood. One of
them had been turned upside down to take the guns that some people
still had and put them in at the bottom. The idea darted through my
head: perhaps the Russians won't even get me, perhaps they aren't as
we've been told – the *Untermenschen*? The minutes sped past, what
was I to do?

I opted for life. I quickly ran outside and threw my pistol in the
rubbish bin.

And on it goes! The Russians came into our house! The underground
doctor was the first who had to give the Russians his leather jacket
and his wife her mink coat! The Russians probably couldn't read his
papers. At first we were furious, then gloatingly pleased!

The Russians came into our house, into the cellar. One of them
was probably in charge, because he issued the orders to the others in
Russian. Imagine the cellar like this: like a corridor 10 m long, 1½ m
wide. The individual cellars of each flat led off it, about 2 m x 4 m.

All full of suitcases, beds, all kinds of luggage, etc. There was quite a big room at the end of the corridor. In it there was straw, where the wounded lay. Germans and Russians, more or less seriously wounded. Then came the order: everyone out (into the 'corridor'). No one said a word, everyone's heart was in the pit of their stomachs. The man in charge was a big fellow, a Mongol! He ordered that all the cellars be searched, bayonets were stuck into every bed, every mattress and every piece of luggage. Such confusion! The feathers flew, and everything fell in all directions. The Russians stank of schnapps. One of the horrible men lifted my face up with a finger under my chin. As he did so his schnapps bottle fell on the floor. Smashed! I thought, I'm bound to be shot now! But I wasn't.

When they had left our cellar, there was only an awkward silence among us, even our 'underground fighter' didn't say anything more.

In the house next door the Russians had flushed out a store of tobacco, but there was no time for them to do anything about it, because for them the melee was still going on. The Zoo bunker was still putting up a fight. Of all places, I had to seek refuge in the area where the very last of the fighting was still going on! But the store of tobacco attracted our attention. It was just across the courtyard. So we looted the shop; after all, we had nothing left to eat. So since that day I've smoked, like a chimney.

**Eva Richter-Fritzsche, artist, 1908–86**          *Pankow, Berlin*
We're surrounded by crashing and roaring. The sunshine is sulphurous, always buffeted by haze from the flames. In between, April rain and hail showers, dark bales of cloud alternate with flickering flashes of light. There isn't even anything familiar about the weather any more.

Last Wednesday – so after those people were killed on Tuesday – all the residents of Elsa-Brandström Strasse were forced outside. They had to leave the church – men, women and children – and go with a Russian tank that was setting off from there to put down a centre of rebellion in the Gartenkolonie. There were fatalities and injuries among the unhappy civilian livestock.

*

**First Lieutenant Fritz Radloff, 1916–89**                    Berlin
The Reichstag full to the rafters with blind-drunk Russians. Where
ten have been shot, twenty new ones arrive! It's terrible. Hand
grenades and pistol shots rain down from above, the underground
passageways and vaults echo with anti-tank grenades and rifle fire, in
the end everyone is shooting at everyone. Suddenly, at the southern
entrance, there's chaos, shouting, hand-to-hand fighting! The Russians
are trying to force their way in. We need reinforcements. Everyone
with a working pair of legs, you're needed. In 20 minutes the situation
is under control. At about 2 in the morning a figure comes shouting
wildly from the direction of Kroll-Oper, hands in the air: 'Don't shoot,
don't shoot, German doctor!' What was going on?

It's a German senior staff physician who had been used by the
Russians as an intermediary to force the Reichstag to surrender. An
ultimatum is given for 10 o'clock tomorrow, otherwise the whole
building goes up.

**Ilya Krichevsky, Red Army soldier, b. 1907**               *Berlin*
The battles in Berlin were coming to an end. Our army had worked
its way close to the Reichstag. The joyful excitement was reaching its
peak, everyone knew that the taking of this last bastion of the Fascists
meant definitive victory over Hitler's Germany.

But it wasn't easy to take the Reichstag. The remains of the
once fearsome Fascist army fought desperately. The building was
transformed into a fortress. And yet – in the end it was done. The
announcement of the victorious storming of the Reichstag spread like
lightning through the whole army. Everyone wanted to know who
was the first to enter the Reichstag, and who had planted the victory
flag on top of it.

**Klimenko, Soviet lieutenant**                              *Berlin*
When the 79th Artillery Corps had conquered the Reichstag, my
division was put up in the building of Plötzensee Prison; the Wehrmacht
soldiers taken prisoner within the area of the Reichstag and the Reich
Chancellery were brought there.

**Yevgeny Khaldey, Soviet war photographer**      *Berlin*

It was about eight o'clock, the Reichstag was on fire. I climbed on to its roof with the Russian soldiers and handed one of them the flag. At last I found the point where the burning Reichstag could be seen, with the burning houses as well as the Brandenburg Gate in the background. I knew that was it.

**Adolf Hitler, 1889–1945**      **Führerbunker, Berlin**
*Private testament*

What I possess belongs – in so far as it has any value – to the party. Should this no longer exist, to the state; should the state also be destroyed, no further decision of mine is necessary.

My pictures, in the collections which I have bought over the course of years, have never been collected for private purposes, but only for the extension of a gallery in my home town of Linz a.d. Donau.

**Rummelsburger Strasse Cemetery**      **Berlin**

Fritz H., b. 1894
  Caprivi Allee
  Suicide

Wilhelm M., b. 1905
  Geusen Strasse
  Suicide by shooting

Erich P., b. 1893
  Siegfriedstrasse
  Suicide (hanging)

**Staff Lieutenant Franz Kuhlmann, 1905–89**      **Reich Chancellery,**
**Berlin**

On the afternoon of 30 April, it may have been between 3.00 and 4.00, I was on the way to some groups of my soldiers who were supposed to be defending the northern flank of the Reich Chancellery. I was about to leave the big bunker to cross the Kohlenhof to the path that leads up to the Führerbunker, when one of my staff sergeants spoke to me and asked me to go with him to the so-called Green Room in the Reich Chancellery. I followed him, and thus became witness to the farewell party that Goebbels had organized for his Hitler Youth members. His wife, Magda Goebbels, came too, as well as almost all the Minister's children, secretaries from the Führerbunker, some civilians I didn't know and cadets from my unit. I too was immediately asked to sit at a long table, had a dish of pea soup set before me and saw the Minister sitting diagonally opposite me in lively conversation with some Hitler Youth members. My staff sergeant was sitting in a different room next to Frau Goebbels, and some of my cadets had taken the younger children on their laps. After dinner, accompanied by a concertina, Hitler Youth songs were sung and, at the Minister's request, the old fighting songs of the National Socialists. In between, Goebbels said a few words and awarded the Iron Cross to a row of Hitler Youth who had come in from outside, who had already destroyed some Russian tanks with anti-tank grenades.

I was able to observe Goebbels very carefully, and saw the tears running down his cheeks at the old fighting songs. There was a curious atmosphere in the room, very hard to describe, which no one among the crowd of participants would have been able to escape. Everyone felt somehow that this was a farewell for ever, the end of a world for which millions had fought and shed their blood, and that all the sacrifices had been in vain.

The fierce, relentless bombing outside, all the dead who couldn't even be granted shelter, the singing in here, all the very young faces that were already marked by the terrible handiwork of war, then the innocently playing children – it all created an atmosphere that was ghostly and unreal, and yet will continue to have its effect throughout the lives of those once gripped by it.

**Adolf Hitler, 1889–1945**                    **Führerbunker, Berlin**
*Private testament*

It is my most sincere wish that this bequest may be duly executed.

I nominate as my executor my most faithful party comrade, Martin Bormann.

He is given full legal authority to make all decisions. He is permitted to take out everything that has a sentimental value or is necessary for the maintenance of a modest simple life, for my brothers and sisters, also above all for the mother of my wife and my faithful co-workers who are well known to him, principally my old secretaries, Frau Winter, etc. who have for many years aided me by their work.

I myself and my wife – in order to escape the disgrace of deposition or capitulation – choose death. It is our wish to be burned immediately on the spot where I have carried out the greatest part of my daily work in the course of twelve years' service to my people.

Given in Berlin, 29 April 1945, 4.00 a.m.

(Signed) A. Hitler

Witnesses:

Martin Bormann

Dr Goebbels

Witness:

Nicolaus von Below

## SS-Sturmbannführer Erich Kempka, 1910–75      Führerbunker, Berlin

It was about midday on 30 April 1945. The shells of the Russian artillery were incessantly striking the area around the Reich Chancellery and the government district. The battle was becoming increasingly fierce. Houses were collapsing with thundering crashes.

The 'Führer' took his leave of the people who were still there. He shook hands with each of them again and thanked them for the work they had done and for their personal loyalty to him.

The secretaries, Frau Junge and Frau Christian, as well as the dietary chef were invited to lunch. Adolf Hitler's wife sat next to him. As in his best days he tried to conduct the conversation informally, and to address each of those present.

When this last meal was over and the three ladies had already withdrawn, the 'boss' called them in once more through his adjutant Günsche. He and his wife stood at the entrance to his antechamber. He took his leave from the three ladies again. Frau Hitler hugged her husband's long-term colleagues, and shook hands with each of them as she said goodbye.

**Heinz Linge, valet, 1913–80**              **Führerbunker, Berlin**
I looked at the man I had served devotedly for over a decade. He stood
there stooped. His lock of hair fell – as always – into his now pallid
brow. His hair was grey. He looked at me from weary eyes and gave
a sign that he was about to withdraw. It was 3.15 in the afternoon. I
stood to attention and gave my notice for the last time. Outwardly
relaxed and in a quiet voice, as if he were just sending me into the
garden to get something, he said, 'Linge, I'm going to shoot myself
now. You know what you have to do…' I performed my bow. Hitler
came two or three weary steps towards me and shook my hand. For
the last time in his life he raised his right hand in the Hitler salute. A
ghostly scene. I turned on my heel, opened the door and walked to the
exit of the bunker, where his bodyguards were sitting about.

**Otto Günsche, adjutant, 1917–2003**         **Führerbunker, Berlin**
In tears and extremely agitated, she [Magda Goebbels] asked me to let
her in to see Hitler one last time. I told her the Führer had already said
goodbye and no longer wanted to be disturbed, but I would try once
more. I went into the little antechamber and knocked on the door of
the living room. Hitler came towards me – there was no sign of his
wife – and asked me brusquely, 'What do you want?'

'Can Frau Goebbels talk to you again?'

'No, I don't want to talk to her any more.'

But at that moment she had pushed past me into Hitler's room. She
pleaded with him to leave Berlin; it was still possible, she said. Hitler's
categorical 'no' brought the conversation to an end. He was visibly
displeased by this incident. After a minute or so Magda Goebbels had
left the living room again and withdrew, weeping.

**Traudl Junge, secretary, 1920–2002**         **Führerbunker, Berlin**
Suddenly a shot rings out, so loud, so close that we all fall silent. The
noise echoes through all the rooms. 'That was a direct hit,' Helmut
exclaims, and has no idea how right he is. Now the Führer is dead.

**Artur Axmann, 1913–96**                    **Führerbunker, Berlin**

We looked at one another in silence. Then Dr Goebbels asked, 'Wasn't that a gunshot?' A moment later Otto Günsche appeared and reported, 'The Führer is dead.' It was about 3.30 p.m. I followed Günsche into Hitler's living room with Goebbels and Bormann. We stopped in the doorway and raised our arms. Hitler lay dead against the wall facing us, in the right-hand corner of a small sofa. He was wearing uniform, long black trousers and a field-grey coat with the golden party insignia and the Iron Cross 1st Class. His torso was tilted to one side and his head had fallen slightly backwards. His face and forehead were remarkably white. A thin trail of blood trickled from both temples. His eyelids were almost closed, his lower jaw pushed slightly to the side. His left arm lay alongside his body, his right hung down the arm of the sofa. There were spatters of blood on the cushion. The pistol lay on the carpet. The fact that his lower jaw was pushed to one side led me to assume at first that death was caused by a bullet fired into the mouth. Later I learned from Otto Günsche that Hitler had shot himself in the right temple. Eva Hitler sat next to him in a dark dress. Her eyes were closed and her mouth slightly open. Her body showed no sign of violence. She looked as if she were sleeping. Eva Hitler had poisoned herself.

*

**Heinz Linge, valet, 1913–80**                    **Führerbunker, Berlin**

Adolf and Eva Hitler were sitting on the sofa. Both were dead. Hitler had shot himself in the temple with his 7.65 mm pistol. The 7.65 and his 6.35 pistol, which he had kept in reserve in case the larger weapon failed, lay on the floor beside his feet. His head was turned slightly to the wall, there was a pool of blood on the carpet beside the sofa. His wife sat on his right. Her legs were drawn up on the sofa. Her contorted face revealed the manner of her death: cyanide poisoning. Her features showed that her teeth were clenched. The box in which the cyanide had been lay on the table.

**SS-Sturmbannführer Erich Kempka,**
**1910–75**                           **Führerbunker, Berlin**
Dr Stumpfegger and Linge carried Adolf Hitler's corpse, wrapped in a
big dark field blanket, through the antechamber. The face of the 'boss'
was covered to the base of his nose. Under his hair, which was by now
very grey, lay his forehead, the waxen pallor of death. […] I quickly
bent down and placed Hitler's left arm closer to his body. His hair
flapped unkempt in the wind.

**Staff Sergeant Hermann Karnau**        **Führerbunker, Berlin**
An officer ordered me to leave my office. […] I did so, and went to
the officers' mess. Half an hour later I came back. The door to the
Führerbunker was locked. I came back and tried to get through the
emergency exit that led into the garden of the Reich Chancellery. When
I reached the corner between the elevated bunker – that was a sentry
post – and the actual Führerbunker, and when I was level with it, I
suddenly saw a petrol-soaked rag being thrown. Before me lay Adolf
Hitler on his back and Eva Braun on her belly. I established precisely
that it was him. I went back and informed my comrade Hilger Poppen,
although he didn't believe me. Half an hour later I came back. I could
no longer recognize him, because he was quite burnt. I spoke to Erich
Mansfeld, who was on sentry duty in the tower at that point, and he
confirmed: here – there lies Adolf Hitler. He is on fire. I left that place
[…] and on the steps I met Sturmbannführer Stedle, who confirmed
to me that the boss was burning behind the house in the garden of the
Reich Chancellery. At about 8 o'clock I was at that spot again. […] I
saw that Hitler and Eva Braun were by now so burnt that their striking
bone structure could still be seen. Whether more petrol was poured
on these remains between 6.00 and 8.00 p.m. I don't know, but when
I returned there at around 8.00 p.m. the individual flakes were already
flying in the wind…

**Otto Günsche, adjutant, 1917–2003**      **Führerbunker, Berlin**
Sergeant Tornow, Hitler's dog-keeper, was completely drunk, and ran
around in the bunker of the New Reich Chancellery shouting, 'The
Führer is dead, every man for himself!'

**Martin Bormann, 1900–1945**                    **Führerbunker, Berlin**
Adolf Hitler ⅄ [Rune]
   Eva H ⅄ [Rune]

*

**William L. Shirer, journalist, 1904–93**                    *San Francisco*
Berlin is finished, and Germany, and Nazism! The war is just about
over. But we learned here in San Francisco today how difficult it is
going to be for the nations that won the war, at such a terrible cost,
to work together for the peace. For the first time the unity of the big
powers, which did almost all the fighting, was publicly broken. And
over a strange issue.

We, whose late President and former Secretary of State had been so
critical of the fascist pro-Axis military clique in Buenos Aires, insisted
that Argentina be admitted to the United Nations. The Russians,
flaunting in our faces every bitter word Mr. Roosevelt and Mr. Hull
had uttered about Argentina, asked for 'a few days' delay' to enable
the conference to think it over. We insisted on a vote – today; as if you
could run the peace any more than you ran the war with 'majority
votes'; as if the Russians and everyone else didn't know that we could
always garner the twenty or so votes of the South Americans (who did
not fight in this war), and the British the votes of the Commonwealth
nations (as well as India, which is not even an independent state,
though it is a member of the United Nations).

Ed Stettinius demanded his vote, and got it – a thumping majority
for America's insistence that fascist Argentina be made a member of
the United Nations it had done everything it could to wreck.

Home in a bus, with Walter Lippmann, both of us too depressed to
speak.

*

*Spring*

When spring comes to life from the depths,
Man marvels, and new words strive
From spirituality, joy returns
And songs are solemnly sung.

Life arises from the harmony of the seasons,
The nature and the spirit may go always with the senses
And perfection is One in the spirit,
Much is found so, and most from nature.

Your obedient servant
Scardanelli
24 May 1758

Friedrich Hölderlin

Thou, even thou only, knowest the
hearts of the children of men.
DAILY READING: I KINGS 8: 39

Ihr seid geschlagen
Eer zite ga Shlahgen
You are defeated
*STARS AND STRIPES*,
DAILY GERMAN LESSON

**Winston Churchill, 1874–1965**                          *London*
The war against Germany is over. [...] Advance, Britannia. Long live
the cause of Freedom. God Save the King.

**Harry S. Truman, 1884–1972**                       *Washington*
General Eisenhower informs me that the forces of Germany have
surrendered to the United Nations. The flags of freedom fly all over
Europe.

**Joseph Stalin, 1879–1953**                            *Moscow*
Comrades! Compatriots, men and women! The Great Day of Victory
over Germany has come. Fascist Germany, forced to her knees by the
Red Army and the troops of our Allies, has acknowledged her defeat
and declared unconditional surrender. [...] Being aware of the wolfish
habits of the German ringleaders, who regard treaties and agreements
as a blank sheet of paper, we had no reason to believe their words. Since
this morning, in pursuance of the act of surrender, German troops in
mass have begun to lay down arms and surrender to our troops. This
is no longer an empty scrap of paper.

**Charles de Gaulle, 1890–1970**                                          *Paris*
The war is won! Victory is here, the victory of the United Nations, and
that is the victory of France.

**Post-mortem examination of the corpse of a man**          *mortuary,*
**disfigured by fire (presumably Hitler's corpse)**     *Buch, Berlin*
The remains of a male corpse disfigured by fire were delivered in
a wooden box (length 163 cm, width 55 cm, height 53 cm). On the
body was found a piece of yellow jersey 25 x 8 cm, charred around the
edges. [...]

On the body, considerably damaged by fire, no visible signs of
severe lethal injuries or illnesses could be detected.

The presence in the oral cavity of the remnants of a crushed glass
ampule [...] the marked smell of bitter almonds [...] and the forensic-
chemical test of internal organs which established the presence of
cyanide compounds permit the Commission to arrive at the conclusion
that death in this instance was caused by poisoning with cyanide
compounds.

*

**Sir Basil Henry Liddell Hart, 1895–1970**                  *(London)*
On September 1, Hitler launched his forces into Poland. Two days
later, Chamberlain was pushed into declaring war on Germany. Six
hours afterwards the French Government, more reluctantly, followed
suit. Thus the train of European civilisation rushed into the long dark
tunnel from which it only emerged after six exhausting and devastating
years. Even then, the bright sunlight of 'victory' proved an illusion –
the crowning illusion of the Western peoples.

**George F. Kennan, diplomat, 1904–2005**                    *(Moscow)*
I cannot recall that I felt any great elation over the end of the war
in Europe. Like everyone else, I was glad that the bloodshed and
destruction of the battlefields was coming to a close. I had never
doubted the necessity of the total destruction of German Nazism.
But I could derive little comfort from the circumstances in which the

war was ending. It was clear to me, as already stated, that no tripartite collaboration for the governing of Germany would be workable. Yet we Americans were continuing to base our plans on dreams of such collaboration. We had made no realistic plans, and had come to no adequate agreement with the British, for the establishment in the Western zones of the constructive and hopeful sort of order by which alone, it seemed to me, one could hope to resist effectively the political pressures which the German Communists, with Soviet support, could be expected to bring to bear. Meanwhile, tales were reaching us in depressing abundance – in some instances from decent members of the Soviet armed forces, themselves disgusted with the behaviour of their comrades – of the wild brutalities and atrocities being perpetrated by a portion of Soviet troops (rarely the fighting men themselves, more often the rear echelon people) as they made their way into Germany and other areas liberated from the German forces. Was this, I wondered, the sort of victory we had hoped for? Was the price not such as to make a large portion of the victory unreal?

### Alfred Kantorowicz, 1899–1979                    *New York*

As of today the long overdue has become official. I chose the night shift, sent my young reporters out to join the victory celebrations in the streets of new York, and stayed on my own with my notepad in the newsroom listening room. It's good to be alone today. So that's all behind us. Still, twelve years. Twelve years that accumulated the crimes of a thousand years. I'm trying to get an idea what it must be like over there right now, but I know that any idea of a million-fold reality must be a failure. I don't yet dare to go on thinking. Beethoven's Fifth is being broadcast from somewhere. The hymn of victory? There is no victory. At the end of this war there are only the defeated.

### Elsbeth Weichmann, 1900–1988                    *(New York)*

The war is over.

It was a warm May day. I was standing in Time Square when the neon letters on the *New York Times* building beamed the news of the total capitulation of the Germans into the dense crowd. Loud cheers broke out. I could hardly hear it. Knees trembling, I sat down in the nearest café. Excitement made way for the certainty that from now on a new phase of life had begun for the world and probably for us too, a phase for which we had yearned for years, and which had now become possible. What horrific destruction is yet to come, what constructive forces would be wakened, and what disappointments would shatter all the hopes now coming into being?

In the evening, after work, we carried our unease outside, to Broadway, to the noisy hubbub of people, all cheering and noise. Visions of a world destroyed and now in need of rebuilding drove us up and down Broadway several times. The signs didn't look good. The Red Army was in Berlin, the gifted tactician, the great leader of the western world, Roosevelt, had died, the economies of all the belligerent countries were bled dry. What forces, what will to rebuild, what power relations would now be put in motion?

*

### A radio broadcast                                              *Paris*
Report from Paris from the end of the war in Europe 8'
Siren/bell ringing                                                  3'25
Cheers/Report (Fr.) from Place de la Madeleine
Marseillaise (sung by the crowd)
Cheers, including 'Vive de Gaulle'

### Aimé Bonifas, 1920–93                        *transport through France*
At midnight we arrive at Maastricht station. While we are being handed hot soup, a group of young lads and lasses fills the platform, dancing a conga. No one sleeps as we arrive in Belgium. Liège and Namur, draped in bunting, greet us in our mother tongue.

The journey continues amidst the fervent enthusiasm of the population who see the phantom of war withdrawing. At about 10 o'clock in the morning, on 8 May, our train crosses the French border. First French station Givet, a lovely little homely town, symbol of the Fatherland to which we are returning. One must have suffered as we have, far from French soil, to understand how bound to it one is. Nuns from the convent hurry over, and then Red Cross workers with milk and soup. The crucial thing is the great satisfaction: France hasn't forgotten us.

Early in the afternoon we're in Charleville; the administrative formalities for our return to France are performed. One small note: deportees receive preferential treatment. I inform the military security police about a German woman who is trying to smuggle herself into France under a false name.

**Flora Neumann, b. 1911**                               *transport to Belgium*

We were brought to a French prisoner-of-war camp. We both looked so sick and thin. We heard shots and thought it was the Germans, but this time it was shots of joy: the war was over! The Germans had surrendered. We hugged, no one could grasp it. We were brought to Belgium with other POWs by rail. Now I thought I was going mad, because the rails hammered away in my head: 'Is Berni alive?' I couldn't switch off. In Auschwitz I couldn't weep. No, after the liberation, I lost my nerve. Nora tried to reassure me.

Before we crossed the border into Belgium we were given an injection. They were probably worried that we might spread diseases.

*

**Chobaut, archivist**                                          *Avignon*

Official Victory Day. […] Of course last night and today have been one great booze-up. How petty we were in our actions, gestures and thoughts in the face of such a great event. But the joy was not as spontaneous and unbridled as in 1918, and there was more joy on display at the Liberation on 25 August 1944. People are jaded from suffering so much for so long.

**Fernand Picard, engineer**                                      *Paris*

Today we plunged into the Paris crowd, which is drunk on the joy of victory. From the Gare St Lazare to the Place de la République we followed the stream of people flowing along the whole width of the Boulevard, draped with the Allied colours. An incomparable spectacle, in which a whole crowd communicated in one great burst of relief and liberation. All generations mixed in with this great flood, constantly growing as fresh crowds arrived from the suburbs. Women carried very small babies in their arms, sometimes lifting them up to show them to the Allied soldiers. White-haired old men, emaciated by five years of deprivation, rediscovered the enthusiasm of their young years. Elderly women with strange hats in the style of the 1920s pushed their way to the kerbs to show their joy. The young boys and girls in colourful clothing, with blue, white and red ribbons and cockades in their hair, jostled their way into the American jeeps and trucks. They were shouting, beside themselves with joy. Allied soldiers of all ranks and nations brought a variety of colours and shapes and sizes to the whole thing: the khaki and beige of the Americans, the greyish blue of the RAF, the bluish black of the navy, the field caps and helmets of the GIs, the beige berets of the British, the cheeky caps of the young American girls, the kepis and caps of the French officers. They too mixed their joy and songs in with the indistinct hubbub of voices in this surging tide of humanity. It calmed sometimes, so that one could hear what individuals were calling out, or what kind of military music was coming from the loudspeakers hung in the trees. On Boulevard Haussmann the British soldiers, stimulated by whisky, were stopping cars outside their hotel doors, just for fun. They raised their arms, in the armbands of the Todt Organization, in a Hitler salute. Puppets of Hitler and Pétain dangled in a shop window on Boulevard Poissonnière. Amidst a noisy concert of horns, jeeps and trucks laden with flag-waving, cheering young people made their way down the middle of the street, right through the crowd who picked up the songs in chorus. A moving picture of the joy of a whole nation letting itself go for a day. And yet, in the expressions of that mass celebration I didn't find the enthusiasm of 11 November 1918 or 14 July 1919. I remember that kind of intoxication that gripped the people of Paris during those days. They burst open the gates to the Invalides and took possession of the looted cannon to pull them through the capital. The events of those last twenty years, the broken promises, the disappointed hopes, have stripped the French of their proverbial lightness. All of those who came down from the suburbs today to celebrate the victory of the Allied armies and the end of barbarian rule held within their joy the memory of all the disappointments of the past and the fear of the difficulties of the future. In 1918 the Parisians were celebrating not only the end of the war, but also of what they saw as the war to end all wars. Today no one yields to that illusion. They are all clear that the times ahead will be hard and full of threats, that we will have to fight to preserve not only peace but also our place among the great nations.

There is no longer an idealist who speaks of general happiness and eternal peace. The difficult negotiations in San Francisco, the opposition between Russian and American imperialism that is constantly making its appearance, the condescension with which we were treated not only in Moscow but in Washington and London as well have pushed aside a lot of illusions that were dear to us during the wonderful days of Liberation in Paris. We hold ourselves erect, but the path ahead is difficult, and the tasks that await us are hard: the reconstruction of the army, the re-establishment of a unity destroyed by political and religious feuds, the rebuilding of ruined towns and villages, the modernization of our antiquated economies, the repression of egoism, of the deceptive voices of the easy life. No one nowadays believes the old idiocies that calmed our worries in 1918: 'The Boche will pay!' – 'The Allies united for ever' – 'Law and freedom will determine justice in a peaceful world'. The crowds now adorning the boulevards of Paris demonstrated their joy over the capitulation of Rheims. But they did it with moderation, without extravagance and without false hopes, like a nation matured by the hard lessons of experience and reason.

### Claude Simon, b. 1913 (Paris)

While the Liberation of Paris in August 1944 was a cause for effervescent (and sometimes brazen) expressions of joy, 8 May 1945 was, strangely, almost a day like any other. [...] I remember that in the evening I left my flat with the intention of taking part in some expression of relief, of victory; but the streets of Paris, still unlit, were quiet and deserted. I went back towards the centre, thinking that something more or less spectacular might be happening there. I wasn't the only one: the rue de Rivoli, at the Tuileries end, was full of people walking at random through the darkness like myself, in a kind of confusion, in silence, with no shouting or singing, as if the end of this terrible war, in which the French, as they were entirely aware – in spite of such ludicrous proclamations as 'Paris and France have liberated themselves!!' – had received such a small, poor share, had left them disoriented, uncertain and baffled by the problems before them. It was bewildering, ghostly and dark, as if the weight of a million dead were weighing invisibly down upon the crowd.

\*

**Ekkehard Wagler, b. 1925**          *Rennes prisoner-of-war camp*
Allied victory celebrations.
   Continued exegesis, Matthew; Evening prayer John 2: 12–21.
   'Nietzsche lecture' by Schütting.

**Alexander Kern, b. 1911**          *Rennes prisoner-of-war camp*
The night of 8–9 May 1945 in Rennes prisoner-of-war camp, France. At close of day we are startled by unfamiliar cheering – 'victory frenzy' of all ranks of Americans, but not only them, also their 'satellites', their 'auxiliary troops' in the watchtowers, the Polish guards, and above the city of Rennes there is a big firework display, rockets hiss into the sky, Bengal fireworks light up whole blocks of flats. We understand from what people are shouting that they are celebrating the surrender of Germany, their great victory. Just as we are about to get out of the tent, shots are fired from the watchtowers, hitting the paths between the tents not far away: the jeering, drunken Polish sentries are using the hated 'Nemitzkis' as target practice. If any of us shows his face outside the tent or in the latrine he gets warning shots from above – no one gets hit! We clutch our heads: the Yanks, the English, they've all stuck their necks out, they have a reason to celebrate. But the French?? As *victors*? 1813 – 1870 – 1918 – 1940: one defeat after another. Is this some sort of amnesia?! After the shaming total defeat in 6 weeks in May/June 1940, the ceasefire? And now they are a *victorious* power?

**Ulrich Maier, b. 1927**          *Orléans prisoner-of-war camp*
8.5.1945. Feeling terrible. I can hardly stand upright for a short time. In the sick bay I got 2 tablets and a piece of wood, which I'm supposed

to burn to make charcoal and then eat it. That was all they had. So I'll fast for another day.

How was I supposed to make charcoal when all fires were forbidden in the camp? I chucked the bit of broom handle in the corner and made my way to bed, creeping on all fours by the end, where a violent fit of weeping brought some relief. I weighed only 99 pounds, a weight that I haven't even nearly exceeded in the meantime. They called the illness that almost all of us suffered from dysentery.

*

**An unknown man** *Reigate*

Today is V.E. Day. Last night it was announced at 9.00 on the News. We went to bed and slept with my curtains drawn back. I don't know why! But it seemed to symbolise the beginning of peace somehow.

It was a lovely May morning early, and they rang me up from school to-day – the Vicar of one of the Dorking Churches was holding a service for our children at 10.00 a.m. So I hurried up and tried to catch an early bus. […]

When I got to Dorking it was past 10.00. I hurried up the hill getting frightfully hot and clammy and perspiring profusely as usual! So I felt less peace-like when I got into the Church where the service was just finishing with a prayer and God Save the King in 3 verses!! and having no hymn book, as usual could only sing the first and hum the second and third!!

[…]

I forgot to say (I think) that on Sunday last the tomtits began building in their new box that I put up a week before in place of the old one. I think they are well away in it. So I hope they are preparing also for a long era of unclouded peace in it too!!

So many people have been saying 'everyone ought to go and see the films of the Concentration Camp horrors'. I can't help feeling that some of them take a morbid interest (I cannot say pleasure) in them, and that for imaginative people it is quite unnecessary.

**Mrs B. Hubbard**                                              *West Sussex*

The wireless programme here brought home to me the facts and feelings of VE Day by the descriptions of the London crowds – the sound of their cheers: outside Buckingham Palace + in Whitehall. Here, in our peaceful home, we've been out of the war for 18 months and at first it's hard to 'get it': but the other locals who have never been any nearer to the war than this seem to take it very seriously.

The Robinsons have a pathetically ambitious arrangement of bunting draped outside their house: Mrs K. drew my attention to it rather apologetically, saying they'd kept it since the coronation + 'it needed pressing'.

Hendley hoisted 2 flags on his flag pole, the Union Jack and the Goodwood Golf Club. Unfortunately since lunch time it's been still + warm so the flag hangs limply down… There's an <u>enormous</u> flag between Hillmans' and Gibbons' lodges however, pulled smartly taut.

I heard the declaration of war at Upton, in my bath. Now here on this sultry afternoon, the peace. Now it's 11 p.m. + vague sounds of rejoicing in the distance: cheers and snatches of song + occasional bangs that sound like fireworks.

**John Colville, 1915–87**                                      *Floors Castle*

Tuesday, May 8th, was V.E. Day. Mary and I lunched with the Balfours at Newton Don where we played bridge and listened to the Prime Minister announcing the end of the war against Germany. In the evening, after attending a packed service in the kirk, we went into Kelso to see the great bonfire. Mary, being recognised, was clapped by the populace.

I spent the days shooting pigeons, browsing in the magnificent library (chiefly on Captain Gronow's memoirs) or walking with Mary by the Tweed and through the glorious country round Floors. On Friday, May 11th, we bicycled over to lunch near Coldstream with Elizabeth Dunglass […] and then went with her to see Lord Home's remarkable rhododendron wood at the Hirsel. Returned to London by train, arriving at Mulberry Walk at 11.30 on Saturday, May 12th.

## Lord Alanbrooke, 1883–1963                     *London*

May 8th. V.E. Day. A day disorganised by victory. A form of disorganisation that I can put up with. [...]

At 4.10 p.m. left War Office for Buckingham Palace where I was due at 4.30 p.m. A meeting of War Cabinet and Chiefs of Staff with the King. I crossed Whitehall with difficulty, through Horse Guards, battled my way down the Mall and came into an impenetrable crowd outside the Palace. However, with much honking and patience we gradually got through and arrived in good time.

P.M. was very late and insisted in coming in an open car!

At last P.M., Bevin, Woolton, Lyttelton, Morrison, Sinclair and Anderson were gathered, in addition Cunningham, Portal, Ismay and Bridges. The King made a very nice little speech of congratulation, finishing up with a reference to the Chiefs of Staff as that organisation of whose real part in securing the success of the war probably only those present in the room had any idea.

We were then photographed, first all together, and then only the King, P.M., and Chiefs of Staff.

We then left for the Home Office where a balcony had been prepared on which the P.M., Cabinet and Chiefs of Staff were to come to see the crowd in Whitehall and to be cheered by them. A vast crowd stretching from the War Office to Parliament Square. Then back to War Office to finish off work.

## Lord Moran, physician, 1882–1977               *London*

The government's warning to housewives to lay in bread for VE day has not worked according to plan, and there were bread queues everywhere as I made my way to the House of Lords this morning to hear the P.M.'s broadcast on victory over the enemy. There was not a seat vacant in the Library: I found partial support against one of the ladders which serve the upper shelves.

At three o'clock the loudspeaker gave us the Prime Minister's speech from Downing Street. It was a short, factual statement, arranged by a man of letters, though the ending had a tinny sound.

'Advance, Britannia. Long live the cause of Freedom. God Save the King.'

The peer next to me (I could not put a name to him, for all sorts of unfamiliar faces turned up for the occasion) thought it strange that there was no allusion in the speech to God. There was, however, no doubt in Winston's mind to whom the credit was due.

I asked John Masefield what he thought. 'I'd rather,' he answered, 'have the honest utterance of Winston than the false rhetoric of a lesser man. Lloyd George might have gone in for this rhetoric.' Lincoln, I argued, would have struck a deeper note. Masefield agreed; but added that he was a man of deep piety.

*

**Nursing Sister Maud Cole, b. 1888**     *nursing home in Somerset*
A thunderstorm greeted V.E. Day, but was over before I went to join the longest fish queue I remember. People depending on the fishmonger to call, in outlying districts, were probably disappointed. I met Mrs E. – who was worried about Russia's attitude. There were lots of people in the village. The butcher was putting up his shutters, and our grocer's shop was packed to the doors. Glad I went last night. As I reached the greengrocer's the shop was being closed in a few minutes so I only just got the potatoes. After doing odd household jobs I took some fish down to Mrs W. – who, like Mrs E. – was worrying about Russia. I missed the 1 p.m. news. After lunch (fried fish, boiled potato; mock trifle) and sharing the clearing up I went to clean the church brasses etc., glad to be able to make an act of thanksgiving there to the accompaniment of the Victory peal ringing out from the tower. H. went to the Thanksgiving Service this evening while I sat with U. She reported the church was unexpectedly packed, and an organist had to be found at the last minute, and the planned simple service elaborated somewhat. We could hear church-bells ringing while listening to the broadcast service of Thanksgiving. The Archbishop's address was uninspiring. After I had gone to bed a klaxon horn, sounded to resemble an air raid warning, gave the signal for the lighting of local bonfires. We only saw two, but heard the crackers exploding. Panic reigned in the two neighbouring fields in each of which a horse was grazing... (I did not see a nearby mansion, now a temporary school,

flood-lit. We heard that there was dancing in the village street…) The King's speech at 9 p.m. was one of this best… Spirits are higher now…

**Charlie Draper**                                                                                    *London*
Everybody was just going mad and dancing and singing in the streets. Me and my mates had a few drinks and I ended up in the pool in Trafalgar Square. I think it was one of those occasions when I thought, 'Well, they didn't get me', and I was lucky to survive it and I thought, 'Well, that's it, I'll have a good drink and celebrate the fact that I'm still alive.' I must have ended up in St James's Park that night, sleeping there, because that's where I found myself the next morning.

**Joan Wyndham, 1922–2007**                                                          *London*
We were all of us on the earliest morning train we could take.

A crazy man in our compartment kept insisting that it was all a hoax – the war wasn't over and we were now actually at war with the Russians! It wasn't until the train got in and I heard the first church bells ringing that I finally knew that it was true. Arrived at Nell Gwyn House to find Mummy and Sid already celebrating with a bottle of sherry, in spite of having been up half the night with excitement and a terrible thunderstorm. Roosie, Sid's teddy bear, was sitting in his usual cradle with the Union Jack tied to one paw. Outside, the church bells were ringing like crazy.

[…]

Mama has prepared a celebration lunch from a recipe she's heard on 'The Kitchen Front' – an awful mixture of offal and oatmeal – not a howling success, but the tinned fruit salad was OK, and after it we brought out a long-hoarded bottle of gin.

[…]

Later that evening we decided to brave the West End. Mummy and Sid, who both remembered scenes of rape and wild debauchery from World War I, put on the most unseductive clothes they could find, with heavy, man-proof trousers – everything in fact bar a couple of chastity belts.

There was wild excitement in Trafalgar Square, half London seemed to be floodlit – so much unexpected light was quite unreal. There were people dancing like crazy, jumping in the fountains and climbing lamp-posts, and dull red glow in the sky from bonfires which reminded us of the Blitz.

Most of the pubs seemed to be running out of booze, so I took them both to the York Minster where red wine was flowing in torrents. Behind the bar was Monsieur Berlemont, his magnificent moustaches practically standing on end with excitement. We sat at a little round corner table [...]. A French sailor kissed Mummy and changed hats with her, taking her little brown velvet cap and giving her his with a pom-pom on top. Very embarrassed, she hastily rearranged her hair, pulling it over her ears. She never could stand people seeing her ears, although they are perfectly nice ones.

[...]

We were all fairly unsteady by the time we left Soho and headed for Piccadilly, fighting our way slowly through the crowds towards Whitehall, where we had heard Churchill was appearing. Everyone was singing the old songs, 'Roll Out the Barrel', 'Bless 'em All' and 'Tipperary', and dancing in circles. [...]

We linked arms and slowly made our way towards Whitehall – when we got there we were packed in like sardines. Everybody was singing 'Why are we waiting?' and 'We want Winnie' – a few people fainted but suddenly all the floodlights came on, sirens wailed and there he was on the balcony making the V sign, just like on Pathé Gazette.

He made a wonderful speech but I don't remember very much of it except for the bit where he said, 'Were we downhearted?' and we all yelled, 'No!' Then we sang 'Land of Hope and Glory' and I think we all cried – I certainly did. It was one of the most exciting moments of my life.

Limped home with my stockings in ribbons, the whole sky ringed with searchlights.

By now we were desperately hungry but alas, there was a note from Kate: 'Dear Madam. Went to do for Mr Houselander after I saw you this morning and he gave me a jug of rabbit stew for your dinner. Looked a bit off, so threw it out – thought I saw it move! So sorry, there's some powdered egg in the larder.' We made some rather nasty omelettes, drank cocoa and went to bed as it was after midnight.

Luckily Sid now has her own room upstairs, so Mama no longer has to climb over her every time she wants to have a pee.

Slept on 'campy' in the bathroom – a wonderful day.

### Miss B. J. Fisher                                          *London*

In the evening I went with a church youth group up to Victoria Station and from there we walked to Whitehall. There was a huge crowd waiting outside the Ministry of Health, as we learnt afterwards, to see the Prime Minister, Mr. Winston Churchill; all we saw was a floodlit balcony with people in the balconies either side. We walked, or rather pushed, up Whitehall to Trafalgar Square where there were tremendous crowds. Nelson's Column was floodlit from all angles. There were terrific bangs going on all round us, and at times it was some job trying to keep together. From Trafalgar Square we walked along to Leicester Square and through there to Piccadilly where everyone was absolutely jammed. We stopped there for quite a while and watched a girl climb a lamp standard on the top of which a couple of Air Force chaps were sitting. The girl eventually reached the top and waved her hand to the crowd who gave her three rousing cheers.

We then carried on past the Regent Palace Hotel into Regent Street, then into the Mall but we were unable to get very close to Buckingham Palace, the crowds were so thick. On we went into St. James' Park and across to a large bonfire around which many people were having a sing-song – we all joined in. Hanging on to each other we went through the Park and eventually came to Big Ben which said five minutes to twelve, at one minute after midnight the cease fire came into force officially so we waited and heard the hour strike. As twelve struck there was a sudden hush, then Auld Lang Syne and three mighty cheers.

As we moved on to Westminster Bridge there was a terrific din of ships' hooters, all different ranges of key, in fact a real hullabaloo!

An extremely enjoyable evening which would not be forgotten.

### Harold Nicolson, 1886–1968                                *London*

V.E. Day. Lunch at the Beefsteak. [...] I then enter the House. The place is packed and I sit on the step below the cross bench. I see a stir at the door and Winston comes in – a little shy – a little flushed – but smiling boyishly. The House jumps to its feet, and there is one long roar of applause. He bows and smiles in acknowledgement. I glance up at the Gallery where Clemmy [Churchill] should be. There is Mrs Neville Chamberlain there instead. And thereupon Winston begins. He repeats the short statement he had just made on the wireless ending up with 'Advance Britannia' and then he lays his manuscript aside and with more gesture and emphasis than is customary to him, he thanks the House for its support throughout these years. He then proposes that we adjourn to the Church of St Margaret's Westminster. The Speaker then leaves his seat and the mace is fetched before him. He is in Court Robes with gold facings to his gown and his Chaplain and the Sergeant-at-Arms are also in full dress.

We file out by the St Stephen's entrance and the police have kept a lane through the crowd. […] We then have a service – and very memorable it is. The supreme moment is when the chaplain reads out the names of those Members of Parliament who have lost their lives. It is a sad thing to hear. My eyes fill with tears. I hope that Nancy does not notice. 'Men are so emotional,' she says.

We all go to the smoking-room. Winston comes with us. Passing through Central Hall he is given an ovation by the crowd. They clap their hands. A tiny little boy, greatly daring, dashes up to him and asks for an autograph. Winston solemnly takes out his glasses and signs. He then pats the delighted little boy on head and grins his grin.

I have difficulty in getting to the Travellers afterwards as all the roads are closed. I eventually get there by going round by Berkeley Square. In the downstairs room we listen to the King's speech at 9. The words are excellent and he does not stammer too badly.

*

**Paul Winkler**                                      *Giesdorf, Lower Silesia*
Tuesday, 8 May '45, 3 o'clock afternoon, there was great delight among the Italians; there was singing and a band played cheerful tunes. I immediately went to them and learned that the Polish station had announced a ceasefire. The next day the Russian station announced the same thing.

**Hans Warren**                                                    *Holland*

8 May – VE Day. Everyone seems to be so cheerful, singing, playing, laughing, being generally over the moon. I cried for so long that I've got a headache now. I couldn't sleep for hours because of the searchlights moving back and forth, bright blue and white, piercing the night, low over the earth; flares going up, red, green, yellow and white; the endless foghorns of the ships: … —, … —, hoarse, high and vibrating. Girls came by, singing, in the middle of the night. They were singing the English songs that they'd been taught in lessons, and I lay there, biting my pillow, begging for sleep. I didn't want to hear the rousing sound of the soldiers and revellers.

**Horst Wilking, sailor, b. 1926**                                 **Rotterdam**

On 8 May 1945 I was on guard from 4.00 until 8.00 a.m. During that time, in the first light of dawn, a lot of bells started ringing in Rotterdam, even though it wasn't Sunday! There also seemed to be shooting somewhere in the city, and then on a warehouse in Katendrecht on the other side of the water (we were on our ship in St Jobshaven) we saw a red flag flying, decorated with the hammer and sickle! So that was it! The war was over, and our chief enemy could display his flag unmolested in a city still occupied by us.

I was still on guard until 8.00 – and it was very quiet on board, and in our dock. So I was able to go on thinking and decided to shoot myself once my guard duty was over. Because of my previous attitude to life I could see no chance of living, and death seemed to be the only way of masking that shame. When the time came, another thought flooded in. I had plenty of time to shoot myself; but it would be extremely interesting to know what happened next. That idea took root – and from then on I became my own spectator. And of course life went on.

**Max Beckmann, 1884–1950**                                        *Amsterdam*

Tuesday, 8 May 1945. A morning walk alone via the station. The English are coming in great numbers now, in tanks – trucks – the population are sitting on them too, cheering. – I went on working all day… Yes – life goes on as predicted.

*

**Bertolt Brecht, 1898–1956**                                        *New York*
nazi germany surrenders unconditionally. six in the morning on the
radio the president delivers a speech. listening i look at the blossoming
californian garden.

**Elias Canetti, 1905–94**                                          *(London)*
The crash of the Germans hits one harder than one might admit. It's
the level of deception in which they lived, the vastness of their illusion,
the blindness of their hopeless faith that won't leave one alone. One
has always despised the ones who glued together that revolting faith,
the few really responsible ones whose spirit was just enough for so
much, but all the others who did nothing but believe, and who in a few
years, with as much concentrated power as the Jews summoned over
millennia, had life and appetite enough really to want their earthly
paradise, world domination, to kill everything else to have it, to die
for it themselves, all in the shortest time, those countless blossoming,
abundantly healthy, simple-minded, marching, decorated guinea pigs
for the faith, trained for faith, more dressed up than any Mohammedan
– what are they now, in fact, if their faith collapses? What is left of
them? What else have they been prepared for? What second life could
they start now? What is left of them without their terrible military
faith? How much do they feel their impotence, when there was nothing
for them but power? Where can they still fall? What will catch them?

Perhaps, because we can't even take a breath, between this war and
the next, the latter will never come.

An invention that hasn't yet happened: undoing explosions […]

We've come from too much. We're moving towards too little […]
You can't breathe, it's all full of victory.

**Stefan Heym, 1913–2001**                                       *Bad Nauheim*
Over: German supreme command has surrendered, unconditionally.
VE-Day, the day of Victory in Europe, for which we'd been waiting
for so long, has arrived, the horror has passed. Sergeant S.H. slowly
gets dressed, then picks up his pistol, goes to the courtyard of the villa

and fires the whole magazine, one cartridge after the other, into the air. Outside the people run together, peer through the iron bars at the lonely soldier, who puts his pistol back in its holster under his shoulder and walks back to the house with a shrug; he will have a quick coffee, a sachet of powder in a cup of hot water, before walking across the park to the editorial office. Victory, victory means more work at first.

He is about to step on to the lawn, the spa lawn, the well-tended lawn, the gravel path around the patch of green is too long and too boring for him, and there are the two little boys there, five or six, charging about on the grass in the sun, when – God puts on his own spectacles – an official turns up, a kind of park warden or forester, in moss-green breeches, an equally moss-green jacket tight over chest and belly and the feathered little hat straight over his nose, and yells at the little boys.

Sergeant S.H. understands only 'Verboten!' and walks over to the uniformed man and plonks himself straight in front of him. He's wrong, he tells him, it isn't forbidden to play on the lawn, and would he leave the children alone. The man looks at S.H. through narrowed eyes, his lips tremble, he doesn't dare to contradict, he just points to the sign, a white painted wooden board, thirty centimetres above the grass: Verboten! Sergeant S.H. grins. Even that sign doesn't apply any more, he explains to the green man, the old order is over and finished, and from now on freedom prevails in Germany, and everyone is allowed to dance and sing, everywhere, new dances, new songs, and skip about on the spa lawn in the spa park in Nauheim, got that? And suddenly, in the tone that the man is used to: 'Attention! Turn! Go!'

The man complies on the spot, creeps away, shoulders bent. A world has collapsed, his.

But the boys have made off too, not over the lawn, but along the gravel path.

*

**Thomas Mann, 1875–1955**      *Pacific Palisades, Los Angeles*
Germany's capitulation is declared. Schwerin-Krosik and [illegible] were with Eisenhower, to sign the unconditional surrender to the three

powers. Döniz [*sic*] orders the return of the U-boats to their bases. This excludes the Prague unit that is rebelling and continuing the fight. Message to the German people: the enemy's superiority in terms of men and material obliges you to lay down your arms. Germany is to remain calm and start a new life. If the latter were meant honestly! [...] Report that the corpses of Göbbels [*sic*] and his family have been found. And that of Field Marshal von Bock. The German troops recently surrendering consist of 'magnificent', well maintained 'human material'. They have been spared and the Krupp factories sacrificed. – Is this the day, corresponding with 15 March 1933, when this series of daily entries began – a day most solemn in nature? What I feel is not exactly euphoria. Of course the present German government is only episodic, an instrument of capitulation, as Eisenhower couldn't leave Himmler in his tent. But incidentally this or that will happen *with* Germany, but nothing is said in German, and so far there has been no disavowal of Nazism, not a single word to say that the 'seizure of power' was a terrible misfortune, and to allow, to encourage it was a crime of the first order. The disavowal and condemnation of the *deeds* of National Socialism, inside and outside, the declaration of a desire to return to truth, to law, to humanity – where are they? The dull-witted conflict of emigration, envious hatred of me and my attitude also help to restrain my joy. – A certain source of satisfaction is physical survival. After the fall of France Göbbels [*sic*] reported my death; he couldn't imagine it any other way. And if I had taken Hitler's phoney victory to heart, I would have had no other option but to die. Surviving means: winning. It is a victory. Clarity about whom we have to thank for the victory: Roosevelt.

I wrote this in the morning and then continued with Chapter XXVI. After shaving went for a walk nearby. A lot of mail to read after lunch. Articles from the *Washington Post*, letters from Kerényi and from people issuing congratulations: letter from Monty Jacobs in London via the embassy about the birthday party to be held on 3 June in a London [concert hall], with English writers taking part. After tea dictated to K.: to Elmer Davis about Révy, to Knopf and Leiser. Truman and Churchill will announce the end of the Europe war tomorrow. There are celebrations in Europe, Rome, Oslo, Stockholm, Jerusalem.

But the fighting is still going on, supposedly because communication with the troops in Germany is a slow business, but probably in fact because the authority of those such as Döniz and Jodl is dubious and certain tank grenadiers, SS men and Hitler Youth simply refuse to obey. Neither do we hear anything about the disarming of the troops surrendering to Montgomery. It's also possible that the Russians are not happy about the mass surrenders to the Allies. The Russians did sign with Eisenhower in Rheims. Understandably, E. didn't yet want it published. Culpable haste on the part of the Associated Press.

*

### Svetlana Alliluyeva, Stalin's daughter, 1926–2011 *Moscow*

On 8 May 1945, when the end of the war was announced on the radio, I called Father; it was in the early morning, I was terribly worked up, the whole of Moscow was noisy and jolly, everyone knew about the victory already… 'Papa, congratulations on the victory!' was all I could say before bursting into tears. 'Yes, the victory,' he said. 'Thank you, congratulations. How do you feel?' I felt wonderful, like everyone else in Moscow that day.

We – my husband and I – invited all our acquaintances to our home. The rooms were crammed full, we drank champagne, danced and sang. The streets were brimming with people, I was scared to go out, I was expecting my child in two weeks. […] We were all in an elevated state, we were all so joyful in that May 1945.

### Ilya Ehrenburg, 1891–1967 *Moscow*

In the evening they broadcast a speech by Stalin. He spoke briefly and confidently, there was not a hint of agitation in his voice. He didn't address us, as he had done on 3 July 1941, as 'brothers and sisters', but as 'compatriots'. Outside there was the boom of a salute the like of which we had never heard before, the firing of a thousand guns made the windowpanes rattle. But I was thinking about Stalin's speech. The lack of any warmth made me feel sad, but I wasn't surprised. It was, after all, the Generalissimus who was speaking, the victor. What did he care for feelings? The people listening to his speech cheered

Stalin respectfully. I was no longer at all surprised by that. I had got used to the fact that there are people with their joy and their pain and somewhere above them Stalin. Twice a year you can see him from a distance: on the platform at the mausoleum... He wants humanity to march forwards. He leads people, decides their fate. I myself wrote about Stalin, the victor. I thought about the soldiers who believed in this man, about the partisans and hostages who ended their farewell letters with the words 'Long live Stalin'. [...]

Today, thinking back to the evening of 9 May, I could attribute to myself different, far more appropriate thoughts. I hadn't forgotten the fates of Gorev, Stern, Smusikevich and Pavlov, knowing that they weren't traitors, but honest, entirely clean people for whose removal, along with the liquidation of the other commanders of the Red Army, the engineers, the intelligentsia, our nation, we paid dearly. But I want to be perfectly honest: I didn't think about it that evening.

Everything about the words uttered (or rather: announced) by Stalin was convincing. And the salvos of the thousand guns sounded like an amen.

Probably that day everyone felt that an important hurdle had been taken, perhaps the most important one. Something is over, something new is beginning. I knew that life after the war would not be easy. The country is ravaged and poor, many strong young men have fallen, perhaps the best. But I also knew how much our nation had grown, I remembered the intelligent, noble words about the future that I had heard so often in bunkers and dugouts. And if someone had said to me that evening that we still had the Leningrad affair and the business with the Jewish doctors ahead of us, everything, in fact, that was revealed and denounced at the Twentieth Party Conference, I would have called the man a lunatic. No, I certainly wasn't a prophet. [...]

Everyone congratulated Stalin and sang the praises of the Red Army. And even so my heart would not be still.

And what will happen here after the war? I was thinking about that most of all. We need new methods of education: no snapping, no rote learning, no campaigns, but inspiration. Goodness and trust must be instilled in young hearts, and that fire that drives out indifference towards the fate of comrades and neighbours. And the most important thing: what is Stalin going to do now? [...]

On an assignment for *Red Star*, Irina went to Odessa, where the English, French and Belgians liberated by the Red Army were being shipped in. At the same time a transport of our prisoners-of-war arrived from Marseilles. There were some among them who had escaped the camp and who had fought in French partisan units. Irina said they'd been treated like criminals and immediately isolated; it was said that they were going to be kept in camps. For several minutes I wondered: is 1937 about to repeat itself? But logic kept playing tricks on me. I said to myself: back then we were afraid of Fascist Germany, that was why guns were fired at our own ranks. Now Fascism is defeated, the Red Army has proved its strength. The people have been through too much. [...] What was cannot be repeated. Once again I mistook my desires for reality and logic for a compulsory subject in the school of history. [...]

The last day of war... I never felt as connected to the others as in the years of that conflict. Some authors wrote good novels and poems at the time. But what was I left with? Thousands of articles that were all like one another, which only a very conscientious historian would be capable of reading, and a few dozen short poems. And yet those years mean a great deal to me. I suffered, hated, loved along with everyone. I got to know people better and love them more strongly than in the long decades before: so great was the need and the power of our hearts.

I found myself thinking about that at night too, when the fires from the rockets went out and the songs fell silent, when the women wept into their pillows to keep from waking the neighbours. I thought about suffering, about courage, about depth, about loyalty.

### Markus Wolf, 1923–2006                          (*Moscow*)

I spent the evening of 9 May 1945 in Moscow with my parents on the stone bridge near the Kremlin. During the gun salutes for 'Victory Day' we felt at one with thousands of cheering people whose fatherland had become our second home in the eleven long years of exile from Germany. At the sight of the bright exploding rockets reflected in the Moskva, there were tears of joy and many tears of grief. My father recorded his feelings in the poem 'Last Salute', which includes the line: 'Over is the war, gone the long night...'

**Gerhard Dengler, 1914–2007**                                          *(Moscow)*

Early on 9 May we – the members and staff of the 'Free Germany National Committee' – were summoned together into the big dining room by the Soviet commander. In a solemn voice he read us the official Tass communiqué about the unconditional surrender of the leadership of Hitler's Wehrmacht, which had taken place in Karlshorst, Berlin, the previous evening.

Now at last it was reality: that terrible, criminal war provoked by Hitler's Germany was over. All our efforts to spare Germany the fate of Stalingrad had been a failure. As in Stalingrad the Wehrmacht generals followed Hitler to the bitter end. But then the mood eased, and we hurried to the Soviet officers, shook their hands, congratulated them and hugged them. We, who had worked for a quick end to the war through the fall of Hitler since the foundation of the National Committee – through our newspaper and our broadcaster in the hinterland and with flyers and loud-speaker propaganda at the front – of course we felt this victory was also ours, because now the path really was clear for an anti-Fascist, democratic Germany. We were firmly convinced of that.

*

**George F. Kennan, diplomat, 1904–2005**                               *Moscow*

It was May 9, one day after V-E Day in the west, before the Russians, still suspicious lest the Germans continue resistance in the east even after surrendering to the British and Americans, consented to accept the fact that the war in Europe was over and to let their people know it. The news got about in Moscow in the very early hours of the morning of the tenth; and by daybreak a holiday mood so exuberant as to defy all normal disciplinary restraints was gripping the city.

The American flag was of course hung out from our combined chancery and staff residence quarters in the center of town; and from the National Hotel, wall to wall with our building, there hung the national flags of those unfortunate Allied representatives who had been unable to find premises of their own in Moscow and who still conducted their official activities (as we had done for several months after arrival in 1934) from their hotel rooms.

About ten o'clock in the morning, contingents of young people, apparently students, marching with songs and banners along the street before these buildings, spied the Allied flags on the National Hotel and burst into cordial cheers. Then, as they moved beyond the hotel, they discovered the Stars and Stripes, reacted with what appeared to be in most instances a surprised delight, stopped their march, and settled down to demonstrate before the embassy building feelings that were obviously ones of almost delirious friendship. The square before the building was commodious – it could have held two hundred thousand people – and soon our initial wellwishers were augmented by thousands of others, who joined in the friendly cheering and waving and showed not the slightest desire to move on. We were naturally moved and pleased by this manifestation of public feeling, but were at a loss to know how to respond to it. If any of us ventured out into the street, he was immediately seized, tossed enthusiastically into the air, and passed on friendly hands over the heads of the crowd, to be lost, eventually, in a confused orgy of good feeling somewhere on its outer fringes. Few of us were anxious to court this experience, so we lined the balconies and waved back as bravely as we could.

As a gesture of reciprocation, I sent one of our people across the roof of the National Hotel and procured from the hotel a Soviet flag, which we hung out together with our own. This produced new roars of approval and enthusiasm. But it did not seem enough. Being at that time chargé d'affaires (the ambassador was away), I thought it incumbent on me to say at least a word or two in appreciation. The balconies were too high to permit one to be heard; so I went down to the first floor and climbed out on to the pedestal of one of the great columns that lined the building. With me among others (for some cockeyed reason buried in the agreeable confusions of the day) came a sergeant of the military mission in uniform – a man who was, as I understood it, a preacher in real life. Our appearance produced new transports of approval on the part of the crowd. The police, who had been holding the people away from the walls of the building, and one party agitator who had obviously been sent to try to assume leadership of the people and get them to move on, were now good-naturedly shoved aside, and the crowd pushed over the little barrier that lined the sidewalk, and on to the grass plots at the foot of the building, so that they now surrounded the pedestal. I shouted to them in Russian: 'Congratulations on the day of victory. All honor to the Soviet allies' – which seemed to me to be about all I could suitably say. At this, roaring with appreciation, they hoisted up a Soviet soldier on their hands to the point where he could reach the pedestal. He pulled himself up into our company, kissed and embraced the startled sergeant, and pulled him relentlessly down to the waiting arms of the crowd. There, bobbing helplessly over a sea of hands, he rapidly receded from our view (and did not come back until the next day, I was told). I myself successfully escaped back into the building.

All day long, and well into the evening, this great crowd remained, waving and cheering, before the building. The Soviet authorities were naturally not entirely pleased with this situation, particularly because this was, as far as we could learn, the only place in Moscow where any demonstration of anything resembling these dimensions took place. A single polite though slightly suspicious cheer on the part of the crowd, accompanied by evidences of determination to destroy the 'remnants of fascism' (meaning any form of opposition to Soviet political purposes), might, one feels, have been considered in order, but certainly not this warmth, this friendliness, this enthusiasm, demonstrated before the representatives of a government of whose iniquities, as a bourgeois power, Soviet propagandists had spent more than two decades trying to persuade people. It is not hard to imagine what mortification this must have brought to both party and police. Without their solicitous prearrangement not even a sparrow had fallen in a Moscow street for twenty-seven years, and now, suddenly – this! Continued efforts were made to get the crowd to move on. A bandstand was even hastily erected and a brass band put into operation on the other side of the square. But it was all to no avail. The crowd stayed. We ourselves were even a little embarrassed; we had no desire to be the sources of such trouble on a day of common rejoicing. We had done nothing, God knows, to invite the demonstration, or to encourage its prolongation, once it had started. But we were even more helpless than the authorities.

\*

## Naval news service
Telegram 10.30
    To be broadcast on all wavelengths.
    Consent having been given to the unconditional surrender of all German forces, the sinking of ships and the destruction of military establishments and non-military facilities and establishments through-out all areas of the navy should be refrained from. Contraventions constitute a severe violation of the express will of the Admiral of the Fleet, and will bring severe disadvantages to the German nation.

## Eduard Adams, submariner                                    *Bergen*
Quiet during the day; I open my emergency supplies.

## Günter Bartelt, senior engineer                             *Norway*
That dark day, 8 May 1945, surprised us when we were in action on the sea. The general order was: no ships to set sail! All U-boats in the sea are to head for England! That was the first order we disobeyed. We turned round and headed with the ship that we were accompanying towards Farsund. We had been here many times before, and it was with a heavy heart that we now saw the sites of our former work in completely new circumstances. There was still the big old bridge that spanned the fjord, and still the squat little houses as before, but we saw everything through different eyes. The Norwegians had all of a sudden put up bunting. They were celebrating the end of the war in their way. We had no real idea of where things would go from here. First of all we moored beside a minesweeper, and burned all the important ship documents with the exception of the war diary in the ship's boiler. A few hours later we set off from Farsund towards Kristiansand and back to our flotilla outpost. A discussion with the head of the flotilla yielded the decision that all U-boats present – there were about 20 of them – should fire their torpedoes and send them to the bottom of the sea. In a quiet side

fjord we removed the noses from our torpedoes and let them all sink into the waves. The anti-aircraft ammunition had to be handed over and stored at the jetty. All viable U-boat units withdrew to a quiet side fjord and awaited further instructions. Hugely dejected, but also aware of having done our duty to the last, we waited. Now we were also able to think about ourselves. Stocks permitting, we changed into navy blue uniforms. If we were to hand ourselves over to the enemy, we wanted to do it with a proud bearing and impeccable appearance. Everyone set to cleaning and mending. [...] We had been on constant missions for a year, and had only ever worn the grey U-boat uniforms or leather kit. Now we saw ourselves in the blue uniform again. It was the preparation for a parade to commemorate leaving our U-boat lives behind.

### Adjutant Heinz Priesmeier                              *Kamakura, Japan*

We were ready for the surrender, and had made corresponding preparations. Then came 8.5.45. The Japanese Naval Ministry informed us officially that it had ordered the confiscation of German U-boats and ships in the southern seas and in Japan. All remaining naval stocks such as food, ammunition and money would remain in our possession. It also decreed that all members of the navy from Kamakura to Hakone were to be brought in for internment.

On 8.5 we were still the only duty station within the whole embassy area that had had radio contact with home from early May 1945 onwards. It was even through us that the German ambassador received his instructions from home. The Japanese interned us in a hotel in Hakone after the unconditional surrender.

Before we left Kamakura, on the instructions of my boss I had to make farewell visits in uniform, with our interpreter, to all the Japanese duty stations and authorities, and thank them for their kind cooperation. It was also my task to explain the bitter necessity of our surrender to the Japanese, and to wish them victory in their war, which was still going on.

The Japanese regretted Germany's fate, recognized our battle to the last and wished me all the best. It was a strange situation for me. I had never imagined that the war would end like that, amidst diplomatic conventions.

**Arseniy Golovko, Soviet admiral, 1906–52**               *Kola Bay*

8 May, evening. It's a terrible shame that I have kept the log very
sketchily, and in too compressed a form. The four years of constant
tension have passed in the blink of an eye. It's only now, looking back,
that we start to understand how far we have come, and that these four
years have cost me at least ten to fifteen years of ordinary peaceful
life. These four years have amounted to a whole era in the life of the
country.

\*

**H. St., tank soldier, b. 1925**                         *Courland*

We were roused from the loveliest sleep by the order that we had to
assemble at 4.00 p.m. The whole regimental staff was there at that time:
the senior officers, the reconnaissance platoon and the intelligence
platoon. The commander ordered us to turn round to face the open
square, and began his address with the following words: 'On this
fateful day…'

I thought, what's gone wrong now? And we were all completely
downcast when we heard of Grand Admiral Dönitz's offer of surrender.
The commander went on to say that there had been a ceasefire since
2.00 p.m., but the surrender was not yet complete. When the time
came, we had two options: one, that we allowed ourselves to be taken
prisoner, and be shipped off to Ivan; or that we battled on to Germany.
He was in favour of the second option.

Each of us dwelt on his thoughts.

Was it possible that Germany had surrendered? What had happened
to the years of victory? What was going to happen now? No one could
grasp it. But we must come to terms with it. We stood there now, over
1,000 km (as the crow flies) away from home. The bridges that led us
there were barred to us. Where was the proud German Wehrmacht?
Had it deserved this? Were all the sacrifices to be in vain? Our thoughts
took us back to front line. Yes, it was terrible to see your comrades
falling or being wounded next to you. Not that we weren't strong
enough to bear it. We were. But why did they have to shed blood?

**Gerhard Angerabend** *Libau*

The situation was becoming more critical by the hour. One ship after another was casting off, and in such a situation panic can break out unexpectedly among the people waiting, and that would have led to a disaster. During those hours the unbroken poise and discipline of German soldiers of all ranks were demonstrated once again in its most exemplary and overwhelming way. This wall of humanity stood mutely on the quay, not a single superfluous word, not a curse came from the lips of these men, who showed great self-restraint.

The sun was already sinking over the harbour when a steamer, the last one, moored in our dock, and the captain told me that he could only take 50 men with him. When almost all of us were on the ship, a sergeant came to me with the request to allow another 40–50 wounded soldiers on to the ship. The captain of the steamer had to turn down that request for safety reasons. Then I gave the order for the men of my division to clear out to make way for the wounded. A momentous order, because on the ship my men were already in safety, and who was going to give me and them a guarantee that another ship would come? The harbour was already empty. And yet they all came back to join me on the jetty. Brave German men who refused to leave their commander even now, and stood by him, even though they were aware that they might have missed the chance to go home. Some fearful moments followed, in which not another word was spoken, and in which all eyes were on me, with the mute question, what now? And then rescue approached. One of our navy's fast patrol boats had taken another round trip around the harbour, seen us standing on the jetty and taken us on board, after the commander had gone back to the flotilla collecting in the outside harbour of Libau to make room for us on his boat. After complete darkness had fallen, we were the last to leave the harbour of Libau and landed on the evening of 9 May in Gelting Bay in Schleswig-Holstein.

**A soldier** *Libau*

At about 6.00 p.m. we were driving towards Libau, when the truck came to a standstill. Everyone took his pack and his rifle and continued on foot. About 400 metres from the harbour everyone started running.

They called out to each other: 'Quick – the last boat!' Dramatic scenes played out in the harbour basin. Everyone wanted to get on one of those barges. Everyone was pushing and shouting. I clearly remember a petty officer shouting, 'Come on comrades, it's the last boat!' I jumped on to the barge just as it set off. So I may have been the last one to get out of Libau. I didn't experience the tragedies that were being played out there. I heard some shots, but I have no idea what might have been going on. People were running for dear life. All the thousands still in the harbour, and the comrades on the streets and paths to Libau: they couldn't get to the rescuing boats.

At about half-past nine in the evening the cutters, ferries and ferry barges assembled in the open sea and formed convoys to Schleswig-Holstein. Libau was ablaze. Five German transport planes were shot down by Russian night-fighters and plunged into the Baltic. There were about 200 people on our barge, crammed like herrings into the belly of the boat.

*

**Josef Potzgruber**                                    **Hela–Eckernförde**

When, on the evening of 8 May, the boots and barges arrived as punctually as they had done on previous days, we were already in our holes waiting to leap into action. When no order was forthcoming – yet again – we charged through the chest-high water to our already hopelessly over-full boats. Along with three comrades, I tried to grip the raised edge of the boat. Climbing on each other's shoulders, we helped one another and made it successfully into the boat, or on to the deck of the ferry barge. A little time later the small convoy set off, it might have been about 7 o'clock. It was a clear evening when we set off into the bay and on to the open sea. The news spread like wildfire that the ceasefire was coming into force at midnight. A cold shiver ran down my spine, given the thousands left behind, and my unexpected rescue at the last second.

**Fritz Bösel, senior helmsman, b. 1920**                              **Hela**

On the morning of 8 May I watched from our mooring through the glass and saw an incredible crowd of soldiers jostling on the piers, moles and quays, when the first boats, barges, lighters, fishing cutters and other vessels came into the harbour. Everyone who could be rustled up, anyone who could swim ran into the water and was taken on board. Small vessels kept coming in all morning. More and more of them, 50, 60, even more than that. [...]

We were assigned to convoys assembled according to speed. We took charge of protection and navigation. M 3109 and M 3108 took over three naval ferry barges of the 13th National Flotilla, laden with soldiers, including the head of the flotilla, a corvette captain as leader of the group. There was a spirit of optimism in our flotilla. All the boats were divided up into escort and security boats, mostly in pairs.

Our two boats were authorized to take on up to 120 private soldiers. In fact we loaded our KFKs (armoured fishing boats) up to the top of our capacity.

The men were loaded on in a disciplined way, quite unlike what happened in Pillau. A colonel came on board. A huge, coarse Bavarian of about 45 with a red face. He immediately imposed order among the soldiers. Later I allowed him to withdraw to my cabin. Convoys of small vessels left all morning, accompanied by security vessels of the 9th Security Division, from Hela westwards. Viable vessels full of soldiers were still arriving from the Vistula base. The last convoy of large vessels set off at about 1.00 p.m.

It was our turn at about 2.00 p.m. The leading ship of the 9th Security Division and a few minesweepers were left behind in Hela's military harbour.

We had covered over 300 sea miles as the crow flies to our destination, Flensburg harbour, at a rate of 7 knots due to the worn-out engines of the naval barges.

All we had to navigate by was a general map of the Baltic. We had no coastal maps for the sea areas that we were passing. When we had rounded the head of the peninsula in glorious weather we adopted a true course of 310°. The three heavy naval ferry barges clattered along behind our two armoured fishing boats.

We identified the vessels as the destroyers *Karl Galster* and *Friedrich Ihn*, a Z25 destroyer and T23 and T25 torpedo boats. The Grand Admiral issued the last offer to save what could be saved. We felt very melancholy as those last, light-grey, streamlined ships of the fleet that were still fit for combat sped past us level with Rixhöft, at the very spot where 6,000 people had found their seamen's grave at the bottom of the sea on board the *Goya*.

That night and the next morning the Baltic between Hela and Bornholm was scattered with ships of all sizes and types. From ferries to cutters, from coastal steamers to tankers, from harbour tugs to training boats, from vedettes to destroyers, and swimming in between them were lighters, barges, scows and open rafts, some of them in convoy. The Baltic had never seen anything like it. Luckily we had a calm sea. I was glad that we could divide our watch by three, thanks to the little senior helmsman. Still, I spent almost the whole night on deck. In the chaos you had to be incredibly careful that you didn't ram anyone; boats were turning up all over the place. All that 8 May we had been curiously left alone by the enemy. They probably thought they'd get us all eventually anyway.

### Corporal Alfred Pröbstle, b. 1922                                     Hela

Yesterday we were fired at by the artillery across the lagoon. The firing wasn't far away. Those shells must travel quite slowly. You hear the shot before the impact. We've absolutely got to get away from here, by our own steam if necessary. We've been pressurizing our lieutenant. We've threatened to leave him tied up in the dugout if he doesn't bail with the rest of us.

At midnight we're ready to do a bunk. Our lieutenant gave in, he's coming with us. There hasn't been an order, but we've got to get away. At the last minute the lieutenant receives the order: 'Every man for himself.' At 4 o'clock we march to the harbour. Unsuspecting infantry units come towards us. They're marching to the front on the peninsula. Incredible crowds of people in the streets of Hela and all around the harbour. In the harbour there are probably 20,000 people all crammed together. And there's the constant possibility of artillery fire or air raids. Very clear weather. If anything hit us here, the consequences would be appalling.

We're standing on a jetty when the artillery fire begins. Always twelve shots at once, calibre 17.5. But as we are practically standing in the water it just sends up a fountain. We run to a big freighter that is just taking people on board. Again and again, when we hear gunfire, we throw ourselves into the dirt. If those things land near us, at least we'll be lying down. Luckily all the shots fly over our heads. By the time we get to the ship, it's full. Still people want to get on. She has to cast off from the quay so that she's not stormed. One man climbs up the hawser that moored the ship to the jetty.

As there are no more ships we have to go back. We stand around in the harbour. Then a vedette pulls in. We ask what they're doing. They just want to fill their water tanks.

'Then we're going home, the war's over.'

The lieutenant and Oberdieck go to the commander of the boat, a naval sergeant, and ask if we can come along.

'As many people as we can get on the deck can come with us. No one's allowed below deck,' is the answer.

We're on board straight away. There are only twenty of us.

\*

**Corporal Eckart Oestmann, b. 1922**                              *Simani*

8 May dawns. Our lieutenant, Peter Braetsch, is with the staff receiving his orders. We have our briefing at 9 o'clock, and Lieutenant Braetsch delivers a farewell address. Half of us are selected to get away on a plane. They include Heinz Möller, our companion in suffering through the hard times, who is to go home because of his finger, injured by me. The rest are starting to destroy our work documents under the constant hum of the Russian war planes. Files, petrol, paper and much else go up in flames until we receive the order that all equipment is to be duly given up to the Russian troops, with whom the surrender is already being 'negotiated'. But our radio receivers make their way down to the bottom of the deep well we've dug. Air bubbles testify to their sad end.

From 2.00 p.m. the guns fall silent. The noise of the front, which wasn't very loud anyway, falls silent as well. A weird calm spreads over the sunny landscape. Then, in my bunker, I get a call on the phone that I always keep on hold, ready for orders from the staff. I pick up the receiver. Headquarters is calling all connected duty stations to pass on an order. I listen excitedly and take my last order of the Second World War. It is: 'From now on the Hitler salute will be replaced by the former salute in which the right hand touches the headgear. End.' It really is the end! I furiously throw the telephone in the corner.

Towards evening we get on the truck, after our Russian helpers have said goodbye to us. They probably face a darker future than we do. It's very hard for them to say goodbye; they were good lads.

The truck drives – well laden with supplies – towards Libau. We have no actual destination. We're just doing something to distract ourselves. We pass the anti-aircraft positions from which big white flags wave, and drive into town. The words and gestures of the people are hostile, but they don't dare to do anything given the huge number of German soldiers. After a few wrong turnings we end up in the harbour, where thousands of soldiers stand in the light of the setting sun, as if a camp service were being held. All eyes were fixed on the white curve of the harbour, surrounded by jetties. A fast patrol boat, overburdened with soldiers, is heading towards the sea. I'm standing on the brink of despair. Water ahead of us, the enemy behind us and no escape! I spend the hours in the bunker in the nearby dunes with Gerhard Polke and many others.

**Heinrich Keim**                                                    *Courland*

7.5.1945, last day in the Courland Pocket. As I know that my valuables will be in my possession for only a few more hours, I leave my wedding ring, my camera and my home address with a Latvian farmer. The future is as dark as night. The next day we hand over our vehicles, weapons and equipment to the Russians, and an interpreter tells us that from now on we are prisoners of war. The Russians can tell by looking at my epaulettes that I belong to a technical unit of the German Wehrmacht. I am separated from my company. I have just enough time to say goodbye to my comrades with a handshake, and wish them all the best for the future in the circumstances.

In the light of the setting sun I am led by two Russian sentries to a cemetery – and it is explained to me with lots of shouting and unmistakable waving of machine guns, that I am not to move from the spot. Night approaches, the sky is overcast now, and a fine rain is falling. Things slowly grow quieter all around. I'm not sure if I'm being watched. The loneliness and the feeling of being helpless in a foreign country take the mood right down to zero and make thoughts of sleep impossible. Then I take my blanket, the only thing I still have, and lie down between two graves. Even though I soon feel the cold, wet ground, I lie where I am so that my body can rest a little. Who knows what the coming day will bring me. In this semi-conscious state, I suddenly hear someone calling, 'Comrade!' In the dawn I see a sergeant I don't know. He must have spent the night not far from me in a similar position, having watched the sentries bringing me to the cemetery the previous evening. Now we sit together like two old friends, and yet each of us knows practically nothing about the other.

**Otto Faust**          *Szallias-Piz prisoner-of-war camp, near Riga*
In this camp I experienced the unconditional surrender of our fatherland. It was very hard for me. I joined this war as an idealist, a soldier and a National Socialist, and such fierce fighting has led to such a bitter ending. Some people were glad, particularly the gentlemen from the 'Antifa', the anti-fascists. Most of them were tramps, and I will never frequent their 'sort' again […] In the meantime I was physically so emaciated that in an examination I was categorized as 'without strength'. Apart from fetching food I wasn't allowed to do any work, there were lots of comrades who were much worse off than me, they were called dystrophics, they were underfed, and some of them died in the camp. Dysentery and oedema were the most common illnesses.

In May the surrendered troops came from Courland. They were still in good physical condition, they had good clothes and a lot of supplies with them. They were all confident that they would soon be released to go home, but that wasn't what happened.

\*

**Dr Hans Graf von Lehndorff, 1910–87**          *Rothenstein camp,*
                                                  *near Königsberg*

On 8 May we hear that the war is over. The loudspeakers ring out a
bit more piercingly than usual. In the halls a few sceptical German
soldiers are talking about the liberation from National Socialism
and the blessings of Bolshevism. Outside the commandant's door –
where can it have come from, in this wilderness? – an opulent flower
arrangement is being constructed. Otherwise we aren't really aware of
the final victory. The official food situation hasn't got any better. All we
have now are porridge and sometimes dried bread that is transported
in sacks. The field hospital has a considerable advantage over the rest
of the camp, however, in that it can fetch, prepare and distribute its
own rations. Otherwise patients and staff receive a tablespoon of sugar
every day.

What bothers us most is still the cold. In early May there have been
almost constant storms and rain, and temperatures at night are still
around zero. Most of the deaths are due to exposure at the moment. It
happens silently too. There's no sign of a fight to the death. Movements
become weaker from day to day, people still speak if you prod them,
but then you're glad when the time comes when you can take them
from the rows with a clean conscience and lay them on the pile in the
cellar that's buried every day, because there are a lot of people already
waiting for their empty beds.

It's only warm in the kitchens, one of which has been set up on
each floor. Iron ovens and stovepipes are fetched from the barrack
courtyards. The pipes are run out of the windows and the hole blocked
with cardboard. Anything that burns is used for fuel. The whole room
is usually full of smoke, particularly on the windy side, but the warmth
compensates for everything. Besides, we can now make the bread that
we've been breaking our teeth on edible. It's softened in water and
then toasted. Any other food is got hold of on the quiet. We spread
our bread with Vitamin B extract from a big tin which was found
opened on a rubbish tip by the tireless Erika. On an exploratory walk
around the former classroom of a barracks block that had just been

cleared Schreiner and I found traces of semolina, flour and rice that had been used as visual aids. We are as delighted as children about such unexpected booty.

The fence surrounding the camp is open in several places, and the gaps are only superficially guarded. Nonetheless, hardly anyone thinks of escaping. What we hear from town would not entice you to go there. Anyone seen on the road is picked up and set to work or sent to a different camp. And no one has the courage or the strength to carry on walking beyond the town boundaries.

A few days after arriving, with the help of Giese and Erika, I buried the twins, who had luckily soon died of cold, near the camp fence. Giese read a passage from the Bible and delivered a short speech. The rest of the dead are buried in quite a different way. The young chaplain Klein, who was assigned this difficult task because in the eyes of the Russians he must clearly be an expert at funerals, doesn't talk to us about it, even though we're living together. When I cautiously ask him if he could manage to say a spiritual word, he mutely declines. Once he lay there in silence for two days and Giese had to stand in for him. Then he described the process to me in the form of a confession: at the back of the field, near the fence, a long hole is dug into which the dead, fifty or sixty a day, are thrown, most of them naked, because clothes draw the men from the halls to the grave. It's the only way of managing without the Polish guards. As the men are all very weak, digging out the mud takes all day. And if someone collapses, it's hard to persuade the comrades to carry him back once the job is done. One's own body is quite heavy enough, and one is literally risking one's life if one makes any special effort.

### Michael Wieck, b. 1928                                    *Königsberg*

When Admiral Dönitz signed the surrender the Russians had an indescribable day of celebration. All day long they shot away with anything capable of firing. Everyone was relieved that the madness was finally over, and we could think about a new beginning at last. Racial mania and claims to domination had provoked a backlash that could not have been more destructive. The upshot of the dream of a world-dominating Greater Germany was Europe in ruins with a vastly enlarged sphere of influence for the Soviet Union.

From that day on I increasingly became the breadwinner for my parents. My father in particular was helpless in the face of the new living conditions that had made us all predators chasing too few prey. Now we had to use our senses and act nimbly. See, hear, deduce and have bright ideas – those were the life-saving qualities. Making oneself indispensable to the Russians, winning their sympathy, fixing something, a watch, for example, or a paraffin lamp. In return there was bread or porridge, rye or soup.

Mother had tendonitis from fetching water and was in terrible pain. In the evening I worked on a 'pede' – a yoke that goes over the shoulder – from which a bucket could be hung on either side. That made fetching water easier. That way mother was able to carry two half-full buckets without pain. But soon I myself was in a position to fetch the vital water from Luisenwahl. Father got used to being provided for by us, and started learning Chinese again. But even as an old man he should have been trying to contribute to our household in some way or other. The Russians now respect dignified-looking white-haired men, and give them administrative and organizational tasks. This has led to bitter arguments between me and Father.

**Horst-Harry Reuschel**          *Damsbrück stud, near Falkensee*

On capitulation day on 6 May and the victory parade on 8 May in Berlin, I too, another returnee to Damsbrück along with all the others, hosted the English flag on our stable. Klara had made it on Mother's instructions, and apart from the missing white diagonals it was genuine. I walked around wearing an American army cap with a British cockade fastened to it, and became considerably braver. I wasn't at all worried about chatting with the Russians now. A Russian, waving a pistol, wanted to steal our Polish pony, which we got through a 'swap'; I forced him to give a military salute in front of our flag and walk away. My 'force' consisted in saying in broken Russian: You Comrade? Vui Angliski ponemai, nix Germanski! Carasho slusheitye Tovarish! Su da Dosvidanye. [More or less: You understand English, not German! Listen well, Comrade! And goodbye!] Whatever happened, he saluted me or the flag. The horse was ours again. But I took a few blows as well! One time there was a Mongol lounging around rolling papiroski cigarettes on the back of a Polish pony, and I wanted to get him out of our meadow. My words had no effect, and neither did my gestures to his commander. He lashed out with a kind of nagyka [Cossack whip] and tried to chase me from the back of the horse, still lashing out. Luckily I was faster than him, and dashed full pelt along the paddock fence to next door's stud, where my Russian friend Alexei was commandant. Then he helped me and knocked the Mongol off the horse. The next day we were oiling our mowing machine, which hadn't been requisitioned, when suddenly this Mongoliski tapped me on the shoulder. Quite honestly I thought my final moment had come, and my nervous stomach probably dates back to those times, but it wasn't to be: grinning, he chatted on: you papiroski slutchaitye. [Would you happen to have papiroski cigarettes?] Well, he got not just one but two, so I had won, because from that point onwards Russian Polish ponies weren't allowed to graze on *Angliski Doma* [English estates].

*

### Hans Henny Jahnn, 1894–1959                     *Bornholm*

All morning, planes in the air. I assumed they were British ones, surveying the waterways. Unfortunately that turns out not to be the case. When I got to the farm I heard noises as if from a huge engine: the thunder of guns and the impact of the bombs. The columns of fire from the bombardment sprayed up from Rønne. It's been going on like that for at least an hour.

They might have been bombing Allinge as well. But we can't tell from here. We heard the sirens coming. So this is the first day of peace. And I can't see a single flag.

At three o'clock I heard Churchill's speech. It was short, 4–5 minutes. He gave a precise account of the surrender. I'd like to stress two points. The document signed yesterday has to be ratified in Berlin today, and will only come into effect tonight, at one minute past 12. Or to be precise: in the first minute of tomorrow. This explains the belligerent actions on the island. [...] It's becoming increasingly difficult to understand why the English haven't got here today.

[...] Tomorrow morning Russian troops are supposed to be turning up and effecting the disarmament. Because of my links with Germany I'm very gloomy about this turn of events.

11 o'clock. Officially ⅘ of Nexø and 70% of Rønne are supposed to have been destroyed, but no Danish dead. [...]

Officially 20,000 roaming soldiers from Courland are described as a danger to the island because they have neither food nor shelter. The Danish government has been requested, and is willing, to send ships with food supplies. There could now be more soldiers and refugees than inhabitants on the island. In Nexø an ammunition ship is in flames, and parts of it are exploding. So the fires in the town cannot be extinguished.

## Udo von Alvensleben, officer, 1897–1962                 *north Norway*

Our age is 'apocalyptic'. The whole civilized world is suffering from the consequences of the secularization of all cultural values and connections that have emeged over the past few centuries, since 1789. Our doubt is mountainous. How easily a constructive policy could have established the foundation for a cohabitation of nations under new, better conditions! But crimes are piled on crimes. The old Europe is collapsing. Will the coming generation be able to build a new one? In all that hopelessness may hope arise in secret among the few upon whom everything has depended in all ages. Will mankind, by turning just in time towards the eternal measure of things, save the world from self-destruction?

The Norwegians are starting to celebrate. On the night from 7 to 8 May St John's fires blaze all around. The files of the whole Wehrmacht are burned. It is done with grim joy. With the declaration of unconditional surrender by the Dönitz-Krosigk government the war is over. Processes like the ones in November 1918 are repeated, but how harmless defeat in the First World War now seems in comparison! The big ship that I saw sinking in my mind's eye on 1 September 1939 has now gone down.

I am surprised to note how things portray themselves to me with strange detachment and in a cool light. Taking the perspective of global-historical contemplation makes me see everything as if from too great a distance. The pain is pre-empted and burned out.

**Günter Bartelt, senior engineer**                                    *Norway*

Three soldiers from our naval base had to be arrested and sentenced. They had behaved in a very undignified manner and drawn up blacklists of superiors with whom they were uncomfortable. They had got so carried away that they tore their own uniforms apart amidst jeering and partying Norwegians in the streets of Kristiansand, sometimes even with their teeth. A naval officer firmly intervened and had the miscreants punished.

**Gerd Kochskämper, watch officer**                              *Copenhagen*

On 8 May 1945 all German ships in the harbour had flags flying from their topmasts. At 4.00 p.m. all German national flags were brought down as the surrender came into force at that time.

Shortly before, our commander delivered his last speech in which he stressed, among other things, that the crew of the training ship *Albert Leo Schlageter* and that of the auxiliary cruiser *Orion*, along with the merchant and naval ships of the merchant navy were to be taken across the sea for humanitarian purposes whose achievement would be fully recognized only in years to come.

**Ilse Vögerl, b. 1920**                                           *Copenhagen*

When the surrender in Denmark was over, the freedom fighters in the harbour area started firing at the ships from the houses. The armoured cruiser *Norma*, whose towers were bobbing prettily, was floating beside us, and we said to ourselves, 'I hope they're really firing.' We looked through the cross-hairs and were able to observe a war from close quarters. Our laundry steward was just that moment crossing the deck and took a shot to the thigh. The Danes had a great many dead, and the Germans fifteen. Then the Danish government came the next day and brought a wreath for the dead. Because they didn't agree with the freedom fighters starting something like that after the surrender.

**Thorkild Hansen , 1927–89**                                    *Copenhagen*

Incomparable summer weather, as if even the sun were trying to celebrate the happiest day for years. I lie outside on the lawn in my gym shorts and read *The Case of the King* by Johannes V. Jensen.

It's wonderful to feel your skin alternatively warmed by the sun and cooled by a gust of wind. I'm lying here with my winter-pale skin granted rebirth by the sun like the tormented earth. The others have gone into town to celebrate the day in City Hall Square, but I'd rather lie here and feel my joy alone. It's the old story: sooner be outside than feel outside. These days one wears an armband or else one stays at home. [...] I sit where I am as darkness falls. I see the light of the sky fading away down in the water, and making way for black darkness, the first star. I hear the birds stop singing. I feel the gnats, the cool air, the smell of forest floor. Then I get up and go home and sit down to write this. I can't force myself to go to bed. I sit by the open window just as I did yesterday. I tell myself that this is the second night, there wasn't just one. This is the second silent, holy night of peace.

### Knut Hamsun, 1859–1952                    *Nørholm, Norway*

I'm not worthy to speak of Adolf Hitler, and his life and deeds do not lend themselves to sentimental emotion. He was a warrior, a warrior for humanity and a herald of the gospel of justice for all nations. He was a reforming figure of the highest rank, and it was his historical fate to have to work in a time of unparalleled vulgarity that finally led to his downfall. That is how the average western European will see Adolf Hitler, and we, his true followers, bow our heads over his death.

\*

### Heimito von Doderer, 1896–1966                    *Oslo*

*Outside* • A pale, blue, windy spring day. Cheering, flags, banners, bunting, the streets densely lined with people. [...]

'*The Norwegians are to be congratulated.*' After quite a long stroll I come back to my room in the afternoon. I had to walk – and it was worth it, because I collected a hundred cigarettes, tobacco and cigars, all of which was suddenly distributed to everybody for free, a sign of the times in the precise meaning of the term! I had to walk, a long way, because the tram was too crowded, and was later suspended completely, because of the official victory and peace celebrations. All the bells were ringing, tens of thousands of flags were waving, the streets were swarming with people... I walked quite unchecked, a briefcase under my arm. Once a Norwegian worker gave me a friendly smile and waved to me, a wave of farewell, and another time I had a very polite apology from a young man for bumping into me in the crowd. That is Europe. These are the conventions that flourish only in free nations – by which I mean the ones in which the individual can live freely – and are so deeply rooted that alteration cannot loosen or tear them up. 'The Norwegians are to be congratulated', one might say with Robert Neumann, who wrote *With Borrowed Plumes* and who wrote to me with his own – after the publication of *The Secret of the Empire*: *A Novel of the Russian Civil War* – 'You should be congratulated on your novel.'

*Inside and outside* • And yet it's a torment: having to walk around in a German officer's uniform, in fact; signifying what one does not mean, having to see the bridge between inside and out, the bridge of reality, so completely broken, and experiencing the opposition between inside and out – one's own inside and one's own outside – sharply delimited with almost dramatic neatness, all this is a torment. Perhaps people pity me for something that I in fact find unendurable, and secretly respect me for a tragic dignity to which I cannot lay claim! Today a double life which I permitted brutal force to install within me – preferring, from the outset, to allow organized terror than to risk personal exposure – has become as crystal. Its edges and surfaces will not be as sharp and oppressive in many as they are in me; but some will be present, incomplete, admittedly, but outlined or at least suggested. One can become guilty through being patient. That, in the end, is how the totalitarian state enveloped man; and the culmination lies where what one represents no longer (to speak in Schopenhauerian terms) has any connection with what one is: only the bracket of that basic guilt through patience still holds the two together.

*Return of life* • Yes, I feel it: life is back, it will approach even me as an individual. The crystal that I spoke of metaphorically above must, once it has reached perfection, immediately shatter. – That was another good hour; my neighbour, a soldier I don't know any more than that, brought me a cup full of real coffee. – We are walking towards post-war captivity, a downgrading, life in a gloomy mass in barracks and between barbed wire once more... 'We': it comes to an end. The fakery is revealed. Now the correct term is: I. And I want to endure it.

*

**Léon Degrelle, Belgian Waffen-SS officer, 1906–94**      *Oslo–Spain*

It was perhaps half past one in the morning when I noticed an unsettling phenomenon. A big spotlight glowed behind us and searched the sky.

My heart beat faster.

In spite of all the celebrations we had been spotted.

Spotlights now shone very close to where we were. Others blinked far ahead.

Big rectangles of light stood out on the airfields. The runways gleamed.

Our plane flew as fast as it could to escape those damned lights.

But again and again other spotlights came on and followed us, as if trying to grab us.

Light sizzled along our wings.

The radio started crackling. Observers called to us from the Allied airfields: 'Who are you?... What are you doing?...'

We didn't answer, and flew faster and faster.

Belgium lay below me.

There was Antwerp, radiant in the first night of freedom regained.

I thought of our rivers, roads, of all the places where I had spoken, of the plains and the hills and the old houses I had loved so much. There, below the dark plane, was the whole nation, the nation that I had wanted to raise up, to ennoble and guide to the way of greatness... On my left I saw the lights of Brussels and the big black patch of the Forest of Soignes, where my long, beloved home town lay...

But how great is the misfortune of the defeated man, who sees his dreams trickling away! [...] I clenched my teeth when the tears started coming... In night and wind, pursued by bitter fate, I had my last encounter with the sky of my fatherland...

Lille lay behind us now. The spotlights of the airfields were still searching for us.

The further south we came, the greater was our hope of escaping death.

We approached Paris, which our 'Heinkel' flew over at a very low altitude. I could make out the streets and squares, which glowed as silver-grey as doves.

We were still alive! We flew over the Beauce, the Loire and Vendée. Soon we would be at the Atlantic.

But our planes were looking at one another with great concern. Certainly the danger of being shot down by Allied anti-aircraft units or night fighters was smaller now. But our fuel was running out.

The night was terribly dark.

I looked anxiously down. The glowing dial showed that it was five in the morning. A faint flow appeared in the darkness. I had recognized it straight away. It was the mouth of the Gironde. We were on the right course.

We flew along the sea.

We could just make out the surf on the beach. Far to the east it was lightening, almost imperceptibly.

The fuel level was heading more and more towards zero.

In the bluish glow of the instrument panel I looked at the worried features of the pilots.

The plane was flying more slowly, and coming down.

We flew past Arcachon. I lived there once, among the scented pines. The harbour was lit up as if for 14 July.

We flew along the gloomy stretch of 'Les Landes', in which the big lake of Biscarosse lay like a bright stain.

The 'Heinkel' was misfiring regularly.

One of the pilots gave us lifebelts. The fuel level had reached zero. We might crash into the sea at any moment.

With nerve-shredding tension I looked for what I took to be the line of the Pyrenees. A faint light glowed.

The mountain chains must be visible… We couldn't see them.

The misfirings were becoming increasingly audible.

In the south-east a pale blue chain stood out against the sky. It was the Pyrenees!

Would we be able to stay in the air until the Spanish border?

Driven onward by the storm, we had flown almost two thousand three hundred kilometres. We had to turn the plane on to the left wing and then on to the right wing to let the last litres of fuel run from the reserve tanks into the engines.

I knew the area around Biarritz and Saint-Jean-de-Luze. I could already make out the white notch of the Pyrenees at the mouth of the Bidassoa.

But the plane didn't want to go any further, it had almost dipped as far as the waves. We were to go down twenty kilometres before the Iberian coast.

For good or ill, we had to fire the red emergency flares: two navy boats came towards us from the French coast.

What bad luck! And there in the distance a lighthouse shone, a Spanish lighthouse!

The foaming crests of the waves and the surging of the sea, right below us, offered a strange vision in their willingness to engulf us… We still didn't fall. The coast came closer with its surf, its reefs and its dark green mountains, which had only just emerged from the darkness.

Suddenly the pilot pulled the plane steeply upwards, darted almost as steeply down again, tried to attract the last drops of fuel with the roaring engines, and then dashed over a rocky hill, flying off over a few red roofs making a terrible noise. We had no time to think.

In a flash we had discovered a short stretch of sand. The 'Heinkel', which had not lowered its landing gear, slid along the ground on its belly at two hundred and fifty kilometres an hour. I saw the right engine flying off like a fireball. The plane turned, plunged into the sea, sank into the wave and fell apart.

The water forced its way into the cabin and rose to our chests. I had five broken ribs. On the beach of San Sebastian excited members of the civil guard flew back and forth in heavy two-masters in front of the villas and hotels. Spaniards came swimming, as naked as South Sea islanders, to our stranded plane.

They hoisted me on to a wing of the two-engine plane and then into a small boat. There was an ambulance on the shore.

This time the war was really over…

I was alive. God had saved me. Even my injuries were a blessing.

I was to spend months in a hospital bed.

I had preserved my strength and my faith.

I had not had to experience the bitterness of falling helplessly into the hands of my enemies.

I remained useful as a witness to the deeds of my soldiers. I could cleanse them of the accusations of their adversaries, who have no feeling for heroism. I could give an account of their deeds on the Donets and the Don, in the Caucasus and in Circassia, in Estonia, in Stargard and on the Oder.

The day will come when the hallowed names of our dead will be called out with pride. The hearts of our nation will beat faster to those glorious stories. And it will recognize its sons.

Without a doubt we have been materially defeated.

We were now scattered and pursued around all corners of Europe.

And yet we could look towards the future with our heads held high. History weighs up the merits of men. Beyond all earthly imperfections, we had sacrificed our youth unreservedly. We had fought for Europe, for its faith and its culture. In an honest spirit of sacrifice we had remained loyal to the end. Sooner or later Europe and the world will have to acknowledge the justice of our cause and the purity of our devotion.

For hatred dies, stifled by its own base foolishness.

*

**Ilse F.**                                    *Lubovka camp, Soviet Union*
I wasn't working in the shaft any more, but outside in the 'otlatka', unloading wagons. At 5 in the morning we heard the ringing of bells. It must have been something very special. Later our foreman came to us and said 'Voina kaput', the war is over.

**Marlis Brink, b. 1927**                *Nizhni-Tagil camp, Soviet Union*
When the end of the war was announced on 8 May we all cried. Everybody hoped only that they would be going home soon.

**Bernhard Kuhn, b. 1891**        *prisoner-of-war camp, Soviet Union*
Our barracks commandant, a Pole who had no time for us Germans, appeared clutching a piece of paper and looking very self-important.

He asked us to be quiet, opened up his 'files', and everyone had to listen. He read us the unconditional surrender of the German Wehrmacht. Then he delivered a brief address in which he said among other things, 'The Germans are all political criminals and must be treated accordingly.' It should be said that a Russian woman spoke to us in quite different terms a few days after the surrender. Whether someone spoke to us well or badly was, given our situation, a matter of complete indifference to us, we took it all impassively.

**A soldier**              *prisoner-of-war camp, Soviet Union*

We experience 8 May 1945 in Morshansk. All prisoners had to take up position, divided according to nation. We were told about the end of the war. A march-past of Russian officers. Together we sang the 'Internationale'. The next day I was lucky and was allowed to clean the Russians' victory party room. The occasional trampled crust of bread, a few herring-heads were welcome additions to our diet.

**Wilhelm Winkelmann, b. 1917**      *prisoner-of-war camp near Kiev*

I owe the Russian-Jewish doctor a great deal. His name was Major Reifmann, he put himself out a great deal for us prisoners of war. But he came to us a little late, because most of the prisoners were already dead.

Another German doctor came to see us and put us back on our feet with massages.

After the last survivors had recovered to some extent, we were transferred to a former school which was opened up as a hospital. Now we were joined by a lot of capitulating prisoners, there were probably a few hundred of them, and the spaces were all overcrowded again. Then we were joined by a Russian doctor who was very kind to us. She kept our spirits up, had a good word for everybody. She had a good memory and soon knew everyone's name and illness.

*

**Paulheinz Wantzen, editor, 1902–74**                    *Münster*
The list of 'Nazis' at the occupation of Telgte was supposed to include
170 names, and to become longer by the day because people acted as
informers in a rather unpleasant way, particularly the women. The
American commander is said to have spoken very disparagingly about
the German population and the women because of this.

**Hans Friedrich Blunck, 1888–1961**               *Greben, Holstein*
Not easy to adjust to the ceasefire. You still look up at the sky as soon
as a plane appears and want to take cover.

Pathetic examples of self-humiliation.

As predicted, the radio, which hammers away at us from every
country, means that we risk losing our discrimination and our independent opinions. Even if we are Protestant in these matters and
things cannot be otherwise, some of the others are succumbing to
the reassuring, lulling repetitions that they hungrily hear on the radio
news.

But we critics have not yielded to external criticism over the last few
years, and we are not going to yield to it now.

But yesterday I was taught a bitter lesson. A captain, a confectioner
by trade, had detailed information about what was happening in the
concentration camps. He said more or less: 'The horrific propaganda is
being brought out now to make us forget that hundreds of thousands
of our women and children were mown down, pointlessly, to no good
military end.' But it is also wrong to close one's eyes to something
that happened here. There were a few hundred criminals who went
wild in the Gestapo (not SS) concentration camps, some of them real
released jailbirds who were sworn to complete secrecy about anything
that went on in their circles. That the widest circles of our nation knew
nothing about it is correct, that even the higher levels of the leadership
were not aware of the details is likely, otherwise they would never have
left the concentration camps to be found by the enemy.

In every nation we find examples of such criminal groups; Russian
and English history are both full of them. But it is now the case that we
have lost the war, that we have no opportunity to reply, and that the
victor as witness has power on his side.' The captain claimed to know

about people who had been hung by their feet, who had been nearly suffocated in sewers. All day I felt like vomiting over the defilement of the name of our nation.

Troops arriving from Denmark are announced. For the time being we have new groups in the courtyard, who had been eating only porridge and soup for days, and who demanded meat. In general things are proceeding in an exemplary fashion, but the pressure is mounting. It's very hard for me to explain to people that I have only stud animals, both among the cattle and among the pigs, and that breeding animals aren't meant for the slaughter.

Major Ruppert, who became my friend, and the boy Otto August Ehlers are leaving today, I'm sorry about that. I have spent beautiful hours of consolation and distraction through philosophy with both of them, and by chance I met one of the finest thinkers within the Catholic leadership of our nation in Ruppert.

## Olga Gindina, 1902–66                         *Moscow*
*To her husband*

8 o'clock in the evening

My darling!

I didn't take you firmly by the hand in time and you have let yourself go a little. On your last visit here you seemed greatly aged, you were gaunt – one can see that those other women are having a bad effect on you, and have sapped your strength. But you must know that nothing, none of your little parcels, brings me any happiness if you aren't with me. No one can replace you for me and I am completely lonely. Certainly, the children are near me, but that isn't the same thing. They have their own interests and can't pay me much attention. And you sort out, as I can see, your own household economy, and don't plan to come and see me. And I don't plan to come to you either: I don't want to 'disturb' you, as I did last summer – when I suffered, and it was a nuisance to you.

We have no shortage of food, we live in luxury in that respect. We just buy bread and potatoes. We have everything else. We ran out of butter ages ago, because as it turned out it was mixed with curd cheese and went rancid very quickly, so I got rid of it.

The preserves you sent are delicious. It is, as it turns out, buffalo meat. Ganja brought a tin like that as well, and we'd already emptied that one, while we only opened yours today. If we have no electricity, we eat that for breakfast, for dinner etc. The honey is delicious, but bear in mind that it isn't pure honey, it's mixed with flour, and you can taste that. The parcel of sweet things was very appropriate, especially on a holiday. We used the condensed milk to make pastry for the holiday, and baked milk rolls. But there was such sadness in my heart.

You promise to let us have some eggs – that's good, because we're fed up with the ones we've got. If you should send a parcel it would be good if you could send along some onions as well, because we're nearly out of them.

I have the impression that you are fulfilling your duties towards the family, but don't really feel much like talking to me, even in a letter. Fine, then! I will survive all this. I'm only worried that when my great day of joy arrives and I'm living with you as before, it'll be time to die, it'll be too late. So, Lasinka, I have fulfilled my duty towards you: I have told you in detail about everything and everyone. Forgive me if I have bored you with my long letter.

Greetings from all of us.

I kiss you. Yours Olja

**Semyon Vorogulin, Red Army soldier**                    *in the east*
*To his mother*

Hello, Mama!

Everything is going well.

Tonight we heard the news that the cave of the Fascists, Berlin, has fallen. With the fall of Berlin we glimpse the way into a glorious future!

Greetings from the front!

Your son Semyon

**Natalya Krishanovskaya, b. 1909**          *Ashgabat, Turkmenistan*
*To her husband*

Hello, dear Vitaly!

As I am not accustomed to hiding anything from you or writing anything that isn't true, I shall now tell you openly what has annoyed me.

You wrote that everything in your life has gone back to the old ways, and that there is nothing to write about, and then that you've got used to being far away from the family that it seems very natural. And then you started talking about the weather. It looks as if you really have nothing to write to your family (I'm not talking about myself personally, I never received such letters in any case).

Then to the question of the parcel. Why do you write that you're 'worried' that you haven't been able to send the parcel before? If that's really the case, why don't you just do it? We'd be delighted. I think I wrote to you a long time ago (in December) to tell you not to send me any money, but that shoes for myself and the children would be better. But if it's difficult to send a parcel then that's not the end of the world. We've lived without parcels until now, so we won't die if none arrive!

By the way, lots of women here have had several parcels from their husbands, and in this respect they're developing an unseemly appetite, and I don't want you to be like those men who (how do they do it, they must be fighting at the same time?) struggle to keep up with their wives' demands.

Of course I don't want to hide the fact that I need help. I've already written to tell you about the terrible state of my shoes. I go to work in wooden clogs (for the first time in my life). Shoe repairs cost 130 roubles and I have no right to take that away from the children, i.e. to take it out of their food.

But these are all things that pass, we'll probably sell something that isn't very necessary, and then things will sort themselves out. There's only one thing I want: I'm not interested in parcels containing silk dresses or anything.

Warm kisses from all of us – Natasha, the children and the Mamas

P.S. You asked about the children's shoe sizes, I'd already written to tell you those (Nadya: 33–34, Kolya: 24–25).

\*

**Naim Khafizov, Soviet captain**                                    *Poland*

Breslau has been taken. 40,000 Hitler people have been taken prisoner. That's the right term – not Germans, but Hitler people: there were Vlasov people there.

For three nights in a row I've been dreaming about Mariya – and always in an unsettling way: now she's wearing a black dress and doesn't talk to me, now she's wearing a black headscarf and walking away from me.

**Alexander Fedotov, Red Army soldier**                            *(Breslau)*

It might sound funny, Mama, but what I've longed for most over the last few months was silence. Silence without the thunder of the machine guns, without the roar of shells. Yesterday my superior gave me a pass. The others went trophy-hunting, looking for sub-machine guns, binoculars and medals. I went to the river and spent two hours staring at the flowing water. And in the evening, for the first time in my life, I heard nightingales singing in the bushes.

**André Drouillat**                                                 *Breslau*

I take a trip to the factory. The comrades had a visit from the Russians during the night (they just dropped in), but Senftleben, his wife, his daughter (very young) and his niece had difficulties, they escaped to us with 2 women from the quarry.

In the city everyone's telling stories about what he's seen, looting, rapes, theft of watches rings, etc. […] The shops are shut. The ones that are open have been 'totally' emptied. I was able to get hold of some supplies with M., as we went into the shops through the back entrance.

At midday a visit from 3 Russians, I try to speak, but they couldn't care less whether we're French or whatever. They seem happy enough drinking from the eau de cologne bottle and then go on. Another few visits throughout the day. The tricolour cockade that we put on display has no effect.

In the city the great show goes on: the Russians discover bicycles and want to go cycling without having learned to do it. What are you supposed to say to the soldier who throws an alarm clock at the opposite pavement because it started ringing in his pocket.

In the city, crossing the Oder bridges north–south and east–west is forbidden.

### Horst G. W. Gleiss, schoolboy                              *Breslau*

According to eyewitness reports, last night in the cellar at number 66 Rosenthalerstrasse an elderly woman was raped by a drunken Russian. To be safe from the other 22 compatriots in the cellar, the horde shot the electric light bulb out with their pistol as they came charging in, and began the crime in complete darkness. Early in the morning two of these beasts of the steppes looked through the handbags of Aunt Sidÿ, Mutti and the two other women staying with us, although without – thanks to everyone's precautions – finding anything.

At about midday a Bolshevik with the rank of an NCO dragged away my Mutti, whom he met on the stairs in my company. When I tried to go and protect her, I was struck in the ribs with a fist. A frightened Aunt Sidÿ followed the two of them in spite of incessant threats and insults. In the end the Russian disappeared into a cellar with Mutti, and when my aunt wanted to follow them the Bolshevik pulled his revolver out of his pocket and held it up to my aunt's chest, so that she had to retreat. What happened next was outside of our knowledge, but we could tell from Mutti's pale, exhausted face, when she came back after some time, that it was a crime against morality.

Often today we've watched Russian war reporters and planes filming Breslau's skyline and our beaten German soldiers.

### Wilhelm Bodenstedt, postal official, 1894–1961            *Breslau*

Today from 8–5.30 negotiations in the cellar at 28 Ohlauer Stadtgraben. Was fired because I'm *not* a party member. Unfortunately nothing to eat. Bad headache from hunger. I was at home shortly after 6 p.m. Goodnight, my Wifey.

### Sister Josepha                                             *Breslau*

I was on night watch this evening. The Russians visited us again today, but more decent than yesterday. Unfortunately there has been stealing everywhere and the girls and women have been harassed.

O dear God, enlighten these souls that know you not. Oh, help our nation, that it may bear all suffering in a spirit of atonement. We have a lot to make up for. Today everything in the whole Reich is at peace. Dear Mother of God, thanks to you.

*

**Gerhart Hauptmann, 1862–1946**                         *Agnetendorf*
01 minute (…) of absolute fame
<u>Ceasefire declaration</u> of absolute, universal nature
From night 1 minute
Bliss of peace

**Gerhart Pohl, 1902–66**                         *Krummhübel, Silesia*
On 8 May the unconditional surrender was announced. The next morning the Red Army marched into Krummhübel in single, orderly columns.

The sight of the well-fed, well-rested troops shortly after the fall of Breslau was distressing and at the same time a little bit comical. Only the light tanks of the vanguard were a reminder of the war. The other soldiers rolled in on Canadian trucks, American jeeps or the simple, stable carts of the national agricultural association. Then they squatted around the place at random, smoked cigarettes and played the balalaika or the mouth organ. Some had requisitioned old farm coaches as well as horses, and rode comfortably up and down Bergstrasse. Most of them came on foot. They all wore medals, some of them several of the things in a row. Most of them pushed bicycles. There were even some women in uniform. They were all in a relaxed mood.

In the afternoon the situation was difficult for the Germans. The Soviet soldiers had found alcohol in the cellars of the hotel. They howled and crashed around, collecting pocket watches and wristwatches, the most expensive and the cheapest, and started harassing the women and girls who had soon disappeared from the roads and fields and from the houses. The next day most of the army had moved on via the mountain pass roads to Czechoslovakia. Only a relatively weak occupying force was left in the district of Hirschberg. We sighed with relief.

Then the news reached me that Gerhard Hauptmann had left

Wiesenstein and been taken in by the Americans in the German–Czech border town of Polaun (near Schreiberhau). I immediately reported this news to Agnetendorf. That is: I wanted to report it... The electricity was switched off.

As I myself wasn't allowed to leave Krummhübel, I sent a fourteen-year-old boy to Agnetendorf. He disappeared along lonely forest paths and came back after eight hours, without having encountered a single person along the way. His report released us from a nightmare: Gerhart Hauptmann and his family were on the Wiesenstein. His condition was satisfactory. No Russian had entered his house.

*

**Helmut Richter, vicar**                                   *Wittgendorf, Silesia*

Today, because of the announcement, the church in Bittamt was full, and a procession of people, longer than ever, walked behind the cross and the flags in the new, fine morning, still swathed in the night's fog, but then made so glorious by the sun. Long rows of young people, including lots of men; and behind the Blessed Sacrament, that I carried with great joy and with such curiously cheerful love, came the long, long crowd of women. Again singing the litany of the Blessed Sacrament. And everyone had the same feeling of joy within them, as many of them assured me afterwards. The excitement of the days and hours was discharged with expressions of please and thank-you, as if the sun of God's mercy warmed us to the depths of our soul. For a long time, perhaps until the end of my life, I will remember the moment when we stood on the slope in a big semicircle, with the wonderful mountains before us, looking at the scattered village, and how we prayed to Christ to take us all under his wing. At three o'clock in the afternoon we heard the peace message from Churchill, the British Prime Minister; thank God the killing is over at last. We will have difficult times ahead, but at least the war is over. The suggestion I made in the late afternoon to ring the bells for an hour – when peace takes effect at 1 minute past midnight – to express our thanks to God for the war being over, and also our grateful respect for those who gave their lives for the nation, and also the exhortation to build the nation according to God's order;

and the plea to God not to impose excessively heavy burdens on our nation; to celebrate High Mass with the same view in mind: our parson allowed it all. Unfortunately the lack of electricity made bell-ringing impossible.

### Inge Merten, schoolgirl                                   *Gleiwitz*
*To a friend in Vienna*

My dear Gretelein!

Last night a lot of flares were fired off here. The magic lasted an hour, it was like fireworks. People said it was a peace salute because Germany had surrendered her weapons. I was so excited I couldn't get to sleep. If that isn't true, as long as it isn't true! It can't be so!

I have a lump in my throat. The Lord can't allow this to happen! How can it be possible?! I ask the Russians. The ragman says it's true. He must be fibbing! Another one knows nothing, a third says Breslau has fallen, hence the salutes. What is true, what are we supposed to believe? I creep to the bench that we like to sit on and am quite low. It can't be true! What if it is? It takes my breath away.

And then nature helped me once again. Would there be a blossoming tree, a cheerful summer bird, blue sky and sunshine, if our Germany were doomed? It's all still there, like birds, the forest and glorious sunshine, and will not fade! How can one doubt? How often did we sing: Germany, thou sacred word... The lines have been going round in my head all morning. How much strength our songs sometimes give us!

May providence look kindly upon us, and may our salvation never fail us!

### Hans Hoffmann, farmer                       *Gnadenfrei–Eulengebirge*
As considerable crowds had now gathered, the trek advanced only slowly and fitfully. The fleeing military, mainly SS formations, ruthlessly occupied the road, and some of the refugees were forced off the thoroughfare. The soldiers burned things, took off their uniforms and left more or less everything where it was. Things looked terrible on either side of the road. The trek from Gnadenfrei to the Eulengebirge, normally an hour by coach, took from 7 in the morning until early

evening. In Habendorf I threw away my Volkssturm kit and put on civilian clothes. Our covered coach, in which my wife was sitting with the children, was pulled by 1 old horse and the two 2-year-old foals Neptun and Peter; both foals had only just learned to pull, but managed very well. [...]

We were glad when after a lot of anxieties and hardship we reached the protecting ranges of the Eulengebirge near Tannenberg and it began to get dark. Through mutual assistance, leadership etc. we reached the ridge of the Volpersdorf plateau. Here, as best we could, we stopped, as the draught animals were in real need of a break, and setting off again in darkness was too dangerous. On the plateau I saw Mayor Mannsperger for the last time.

## Charlotte Rosowsky                                    *Grafschaft Glatz*

In our village there was a famous distillery. Moritz Thienelt's Kroatz-beere blackberry liqueur had a great reputation. The Russians demanded schnapps from there by the bucketload. Drunken Russians! I was in absolutely no doubt about what would happen next.

The women had to be brought to safety at all cost. On a mountain, beyond the summit, in the depths of the forest, there was a little farmyard whose owners I knew. Evening had fallen by now. In the half-darkness my sister-in-law with her 2-year-old child, our friend's wife and daughter and I went up the mountain with my two boys. We reached the farmyard and were allowed to sleep in the hay-barn. At about 2 o'clock things suddenly got noisy down below.

I went down to look for the cause. Out of the village had come weeping women who had already been raped by the Russians, some of them several times. It must have been insane. In our quiet little corner no one troubled us. Dawn came. We hadn't had much sleep. Now I needed to go into the village to feed the animals. I must say that seldom in my life have I been in a situation stranger than this one.

I stood on the top of the mountain and looked down at the village. Smoke came from only a few chimneys. Everything lay in silence. What would I find? Perhaps the corpses of my parents? Nothing was beyond drunken Russians. Perhaps the horses would have been taken away already? What awaited me personally?

In the end I had no choice, I had to go down there. I slowly climbed down the hill, staying in the cover of the forest where possible. But eventually I had to come out into the open. I reached my father's house. Everything was unchanged, and the horses were still there too. My parents had had Russian visitors all night, and had had to drink with them. Again and again they had pointed at the empty beds and said, 'Where are daughters?' How glad I was that we had all brought ourselves to safety. Otherwise things could have got really unpleasant.

**Helga Felmy, b. 1911**                                    **Bad Landeck, Silesia**
*To her husband in a prisoner-of-war camp in the USA*

The time has come, old fellow! We have surrendered. The Russians will occupy us soon. A terrible feeling, old fellow, to say that it was all in vain. You know we always expected it. You know that I never thought of victory for so much as a minute! But it's still hard to bear when defeat is suddenly there, and we have lost. The thought is so terrible! How will you think of us, with what concerns and emotions? You will wonder whether they fled. No, old fellow! After lengthy, lengthy reflections I stayed. Where was I supposed to go? Germany has been bombed, millions of people are in the streets, desperately searching for shelter. I met Dr Werners who wanted to take me through Czechoslovakia with the children. I was close to saying yes, but when I got home and met Aunt Ruth and Mutti sitting in the annexe like offertory collectors, and they didn't want to leave, I stayed too and was quite calm in my decision. Whether it was the right thing to do, time alone will tell. There were no more trains available, and the railway bridges had been blown up. We could have set off on foot and wouldn't have got far. I only pray that the Russians will invade while I'm asleep, to spare me too much excitement.

*

**Kuno Gerner, d. 2002**              *Howze prisoner-of-war camp, Texas*
When night had fallen and the guards had been running back and forth for a long time, because we would soon be 'there', the familiar string of lights went on, the kind that lights up a prisoner-of-war camp, or

its fence, at night. The train pulled into the end of a branch line, right up against the lights, and then there were shouts of 'Let's go!' Weird at night, the change in personnel is disagreeable – the escorts were easy-going – the haste with which they drive a herd, albeit a herd of people, is revolting. After counting us several times (it's going to be like this from now on), over the field we went to the fence, where we were ordered to sit down in the headlights of cars that had pulled up in a circle. A fat captain speaking broken German delivered a brief speech to the effect that everyone would be called forward, would get a tag around his neck that would entitle him to breakfast, and which would be valid as an ID for processing – working in the paper mill – that we were to obey orders, because otherwise we would be shot, and we'd get two bullets to the belly. One would be enough, he repeated, always to a ripple of laughter. It soon turned out that he was a famous fellow. Literary-minded subalterns, fit only for the home guard, bowed and scraped in front of him saying 'Yes, sir', as one normally does to superiors, but his 'okay', in English, trumped anything that might have been said between German superiors and underlings. [...]

During the following examination of the ragged clothes and belongings, bad-tempered sergeants were very rigorous, and the rest of my notebook was gone for a burton. And then we marched to the fence.

Inside the fence, after we had been counted once again, the column received a lieutenant who had very elegant manners and aristocratic Spanish features. At every subsequent stop required at new fences or anywhere else, he made everybody sit down, probably a military method of seeing everyone at once, and told us all through an interpreter that Germany had capitulated; it was about 11 o'clock at night on 8 May 1945, the ninth in European time. He stressed, curiously – as it was no longer the case – that the capitulation had only been to the western powers, and not to Russia. Which caused great satisfaction among the Nazi sympathizers. They said that then we would soon be 'deployed' by the Americans against Russia.

**Wolfgang Soergel**                    *(prisoner-of-war camp in Scotland)*
Adolf Hitler is dead. There is still fighting around Chemnitz. In the scrappy newspaper reports I read about civil-war-style situations in the area where I'm looking for you. Will I see you again?

At the end of April Nazi concentration camps were liberated by British troops, and the British intelligence officers have been giving out the most terrible reports of them. Serious criminals were arrested, the picture of Commandant Koch, the 'beast of Belsen', is pinned to the information board, a vulgar, contemptible face. The reality is much worse than the whispers and mutterings of the past few months, the portals of the underworld are opening up. No one lies honourably defeated on the ground, we are seen as gangs of murderers whose masks have been torn off. Blood, suffocating torture, skeletons and mass deaths drag their traces behind the beaten troops of the Reich. No cry for mercy helps, where ears are deaf and eyes blind. All Germans stand accused, from the youngest to the oldest, now burdened with the fate of Sisyphus, seeking in vain torment to throw off the stone of guilt, again and again, always in vain, as there can be no forgetting.

**Paul Gross, b. 1925**  *prisoner-of-war camp near Arbuckle, California*
From 8 May the Yanks made us aware that they had won the war. Until then they had stuck to the prisoner-of-war regulations. At this point a lot of relief and comfort has been taken from us. In our work deployment we had so-called quotas (fulfilment of work duties) imposed upon us. The good food got worse and free purchase of food in the canteen has been abolished. We sensed that we had lost the war. These torments lasted a little over six months, then things slowly got better.

\*

**Arthur Miller, 1915–2005**                                      *USA*
You ask what feelings I had at the end of the war. It was as if one had pressed oneself against a steel door that was suddenly pulled open from inside – end of Fascism! In a curious, almost comical way we had needed Fascism to give our minds a direction. Now all of a

sudden it was as if we were floating weightlessly in a space capsule: 'top', 'bottom', 'left', 'right' had become meaningless. Of course the old meanings would soon come back, but for a brief moment – in historical terms – we had no compass, no certainty from which to take our bearings. For that brief moment we were human, in a painful way. There was only what was just happening, and the expression in the eyes of whoever happened to be talking, which might give a clue about whether he was telling the truth or lying. It was such an exciting, such an elementary situation that we found ourselves in – like animals with their ears pricked and their noses in the wind. And suddenly one had to wonder why we had to kill so many millions to get back to where we had started before the fog of ideology rose up.

As it soon would.

## Kurt Weill, 1900–1950                                      *Los Angeles*
*To Lotte Lenya in New York*

Here is 'Happy V-E Day!' for my Linnerl darling. I am thinking of you all day because this is the day we've been waiting for twelve long years, ever since that night when we drove to Munich, March 1933. You never gave up that firm belief that we'll live to see the end of this horror – and here it is. I can imagine how exciting it must be in New York today and I am sure that you are celebrating, probably with the Hustons. Out here one doesn't feel much of a celebration. They are much nearer to the Pacific war here, and that doesn't let a real spirit of armistice come up. I have been working at the studio all day. But when I got up in the morning (I heard Truman's and Churchill's speech [*sic*] at 6 A.M.) I realized, more than ever before what this meant – and when I drove down to the studio I felt like a million dollar [*sic*] because this happened at a time when we are still young and can enjoy what is considered the best part of our lives in a world without nazis. Lets [*sic*] hope that they'll be really tough with the Germans this time. I think they will because those atrocity stories that were discovered in Germany in the last weeks made a devastating impression on the public opinion here – and even America's sweetheart [Mary Pickford] said today she wants 70 million Germans to be sterilized.

[…] So long, baby. Sei niiiedelich, spiel dich nicht zu sehr auf [Be nice, don't carry on too much], take it easy, have fun, eat well, don't drink and smoke and schlipel dich aus und sei hochachtungsvoll ergebenst gegrüsst [sleep a lot and be greeted with high devotion and deep respect]

von deinem Ehegatten [from your spouse]

Knuti

## Alfred Döblin, 1878–1957                                 (*Hollywood*)
*To Elvira and Arthur Rosin*

So what we are experiencing now, if not the end of this war, is at least the fall of Nazism. If you are anything like me, I can barely find it in me to be pleased. That the beast lies there at last, fine; but what has it done? The other criminal, in Italy, has been hunted down as well. If only a collective revival were coming into being, if only we were experiencing a storm of freedom and human emotion, pain and solidarity – but there is hardly a sign of such a thing. A new time, a new global political period is getting under way, the powers are regrouping, a long period of weakness (thank God) is in prospect; what a blow for us that Roosevelt passed away – certain voices are missing. But perhaps we will crawl our way upright; we had a gruesome time of 'great' men; perhaps humanity, undisturbed by the shameful gentlemen, will deal better with things. My personal need for historical events is now completely satisfied – yours too, probably. Still, it becomes apparent once again: too much heroism pays off badly even for the heroes; in the end they are hung up by the feet (that's what they should start with). [...]

Perhaps in a few months my exile will be over – and what comes next? Life is a series of adventures.

Warmest regards to you both yours Alfred Döblin

*

## Lieutenant Kurt S., b. 1918                         *Zeiden bei Kronstadt*
On the evening of 28.4 I march off. Everything is guarded. I have to head inland and wade through the rivers. Particularly difficult right now the rivers are in flood again. Still, I get spotted on the first night,

and the next day, when I can hardly stand or move, a big squad of Communists comes looking for me. Twice they're standing almost directly alongside me, as I cower under a little spruce tree. If they don't see me I can only call it a little miracle. For the next few days I drag myself towards Kronstadt with the greatest difficulty.

On 3 May, at 3 o'clock in the morning, I arrive in the German town of Zeiden bei Kronstadt, completely exhausted. I am given a good reception. All German men of 16–45 and all women of 16–35 were deported from here by the Russians to Russia. Here in this village alone about 700 people. The ones who are still here (the old) are completely baffled. I won't be able to stay in a German house. At the moment – today, 5 May '45 – I am in a Hungarian house. I have recovered, and my feet, which were completely shattered, are healing again. I've found out how things are in Germany. I'm very shaken. What will my dear ones do? Will we see each other again? In Covaszna I wrote three diaries and recorded my thoughts about everything. We can predict what comes next. We are now the slaves of the others. It's going to be terrible.

[6.5.] Romanian Easter: I've made myself a hiding place in the cellar under a big woodpile. I'm there by day, and I don't come up until night. I hope it stays that way. I keep thinking about home. As I sit here in peace, my dear ones are being dragged away. The future looks terrible. What's going to happen? It's unimaginable. At any rate, over the next few days the hostilities will have abated. The German army is finished.

[7.5.] Last night I listened to the radio for the first time in ages. Only enemy broadcasters. But I must say, I no longer know what I'm supposed to think. Everyone's surrendered! The German broadcasters are silent, only Graz had dance music. It's terrible.

Every night I have the most dreadful dreams. The Elbe is the demarcation line between Russia and Anglo-America. The Germans are now the slaves of the others. My thoughts are with my loved ones. Are they still alive? Under what circumstances? I can hardly think clearly now. Yes, it's over.

One war – and the new one begins. The battle for personal freedom. Perhaps I can hear again today. We will see how the prisoners of war are treated. I don't think they'll be hurrying back.

[8.5.] Breslau fell yesterday, and 40,000 Germans were taken prisoner.

The fear for my loved ones gives me no rest. But perhaps they were evacuated in advance. But I can't go back to Germany yet. If I did, I would be taken prisoner straight away as well.

The war is over today. Dönitz has ordered the cessation of all fighting. Peace is there, but what sort of peace? I don't dare to look into the future. Will I be allowed to run my cash register company ever again? That more than any other was the idea that kept me going through recent times. My lovely flat. All gone. Who knows if I will ever see my loved ones again? If they're dead, there's no point in my going on living.

[9.5.] The bells are ringing here. The factory sirens are wailing. The war is over and won for the Allies. Which includes the Romanians. My ideas won't stray from Germany. What will happen? I firmly believe that everyone from east Germany will have to go to Russia. Yesterday I heard that Stalin is demanding reparations on all sides. It will take a lifetime.

## Manfred Klein, Waffen-SS officer, b. 1926                    Slovenia

I was on night duty from the evening of 6 May onwards. After a few hours, there was total radio silence, and I was sitting alone in the car, I put the headphones on and looked for the BBC on the receiver; because of its striking interval signal, four rhythmical beats, it was easy to find. Of course it was strictly forbidden to listen to broadcasters. But I'd turned the volume down, and in any case I was listening on headphones, so I hardly needed to be afraid of being caught. And in any case, who could catch me? Instead of the expected reports about the day's military events there was a great surprise for me. At 1.50 p.m. the BBC reported: 'England is celebrating tomorrow, Tuesday, 8 May, as Victory Day.' So if England wanted to celebrate victory, it meant that the war must be over. I had mixed feelings, but I didn't feel great cause for rejoicing.

Certainly, the war was over, I had come out of it alive, but it was equally certain that we now faced a prisoner-of-war camp. We wouldn't see home for a long time, perhaps a very long time.

There was no opportunity to tell my closest colleagues what I had heard in secret. They were still asleep, I was on duty until the morning, and it turned out that my news was no longer news. Since early morning, army units had been patrolling the area, almost endlessly, and already in loose formation. At the same time, Volkssturm men kept turning up, in groups or individually, often grotesquely dishevelled. It was an image of chaos, the picture of a defeated army flooding back. Most of them trotted mutely along and some, when they saw us, said, 'The war is over.'

The ceasefire came into effect at one minute past midnight on 8 May. Our great good fortune consisted in the fact that the division had not been part of the front line for some days, but lay detached far behind the front. Otherwise the division would probably have been taken prisoner by the Soviets. Before we set off from Lichendorf the commander had the regiment fall in. Obersturmbannführer Josef Maier, an Austrian by birth, delivered an impassioned address. He said more or less: We know how terribly the Bolshevik soldiers are raging in Hungary and eastern Styria. The population was being murdered, women were being raped. He practically implored us to go with him into the mountains, to keep on fighting and protect women and children in Styria and Carinthia against further misfortune. That fell on deaf ears, not a single soldier in the regiment proved willing to engage in an underground struggle that was doomed from the outset.

### Liesbeth Flade on the flight to Karlsbad

It got going at 6 in the evening. Vati was in charge. Maria and I stayed near the company vehicle with our bicycles, and when it became too much of an effort, since at first we were always going uphill, Maria was allowed to get into the car with her bicycle. Where we had been almost alone at first, we soon became a huge caravan. Units of various sizes were joining us on all sides, with handcarts, prams, on foot. A huge number of them were trying to seek safety in escape. I certainly wouldn't have chosen to flee out of fear for our lives, but under no circumstances did I want our fate to be divided from Vati's, and if we had to go through difficult things, at least we were together.

It must have been about midnight, we were in quite a remote place, and there were big flares nearby. We didn't know what it meant, we puzzled over it – was it a ceasefire? No one knew. And now we went uphill on a narrow path, where a car could hardly drive. On a bend a car had rolled down the hill, plainly no one had been hurt, but it couldn't be brought up again. We felt very sorry for the people. When we had gone down the winding road, on a sharp bend we happened upon a very broad road. It took us about half an hour to get there: the huge crowd pushed forwards side by side in threes and fours, the pedestrians heavily laden, women with handcarts, cyclists, horse-carts. The saddest sight of all was women with little children in carts. Overtaking was out of the question, only motorized military dashed past us every now and again, all fleeing.

**Dr Wilhelm zur Linden,**             *Milowitz barracks,*
**staff physician, 1896–1972**             *Czechoslovakia*
On the night of Tuesday, 8 May, we set off on our escape westwards. We had put everything I needed as a doctor on the journey in my official car, and the passenger seats were occupied by my closest colleagues, when, in the deep darkness of a moonless night, I heard the voice of the Oberstabsrichter [Senior Judicial Officer], Ritter von Fabrizius, asking if we had room for him too. It was impossible to take him with us, but before I could find him a seat somewhere else, he had been swallowed up by the darkness. I still reproach myself for that, because later after making inquiries I discovered he had starved to death in Siberia.

Night had fallen by the time the two-thousand-strong troops from Milowitz drill ground prepared to march away on 8 May 1945. General R, the camp commandant, thought he would be able to march in a solid unit to Germany with this huge column of military vehicles, including six hundred tanks and hundreds of carts, laden with food from the so-called Wehrmacht farms. The decampment was scheduled for 11.00 p.m., when we realized the Czech coachmen had disappeared. Naively we had believed they would march with us, and drive their harvest wagons to Germany.

So soldiers were assigned to harness up the horses and drive the carts; in complete darkness, of course, and it was a raven-black night.

In the end the decampment was postponed until four o'clock in the morning, and the general went to bed; he sensed nothing of the charged atmosphere in the camp, which increased every fifteen minutes.

*

### Victor Klemperer, 1881–1960                                    *Bavaria*

Now that the threat to our lives has passed, we are truly fed up with the minor but concentrated sufferings of our condition, and find no consolation in its romanticism. But the feeling of gratitude remains present, and many hours of the day are pleasurable once again. Bucolic hours, so to speak. And 'down-to-earth' and hence instructive.

### Ernst Jünger, 1895–1998                                    *Kirchhorst*

The cuckoo called for the first time in the moorland woods. The grapes at the house are bursting voluptuously, abundantly from the vines; the Dionysian force is apparent even in the foliage, in the grapes themselves. Once, years ago, I cut it too late and in the night I heard the sap dripping like blood from the wounds.

A delectable aroma rises from the flowerbeds. That too is language, and it is wonderful when the plant, at the moment of its supreme power and opulence and, at the same time, of the deepest joy, breaks the silence on a quiet spring night and starts to spill its secret. That delicious side of things echoes the words of the ancients such as *odor*, *aroma*, *balsamon*, while in our own words *Dunst*, *Ruch* and *Duft* [*scent*, *smell* and *aroma* ] the darkness and mystery of the message predominate.

We spent the evening without the blackout for the first time in six years. Still, that is a modest improvement for us on a day when the victory celebrations in all the capital cities of the Allies, from New York to Moscow, are brightly glowing while the defeated sit deep in their cellars, their faces veiled.

I heard the address of the British king, which was dignified, moderate and appropriate to the sovereign of a great nation.

*

**Joachim Halfpap, private soldier, b. 1927**          *near Deutsch-Brod,*
                                                       *Czechoslovakia*

By 8 May the time had come. With soldiers of the infantry, artillery
and the Luftwaffe, we marched westwards. From time to time we are
allowed to sit on a truck. At my turn, I sat on the right mudguard
and held on to the bonnet. We were constantly being fired at. The
rifle bullets and machine-gun fire came from Czechs in plain clothes.
They also threw hand grenades at us. They were trying to stop us, and
to damage us. Our column had to pause more and more frequently,
vehicles stopped working, soldiers cursed.

We advanced very slowly. We often had to take cover. In the end we
could only continue on foot. At dawn the march was over once and
for all. We were stuck. We could only go onwards, there was no going
back. We were in a hollow. We were surrounded by hills with a thin
covering of trees. On the slope ahead of me, if you followed the road,
there were tanks. A lot of comrades were pushing their way through
from the same direction as me. People started panicking. A lot of us
hadn't yet noticed that there was no chance of going forwards. Not a
step. The Russian was in front of us.

Conditions became increasingly chaotic. Newly arrived German
soldiers were constantly jostling their way – what else were they
supposed to do? – into the hollow. They certainly thought there must
somehow be a way onwards. In front of us, in front of me, was the
Russian. Strictly speaking, not one single Russian, but the soldiers of
the Soviet army. The men were no longer being fired at, we didn't
constantly have to take cover. But neither was there any going back. The
pressure from the comrades coming up from behind was intensifying.
I didn't actually want to go on, because I couldn't tell exactly what
was going to happen. On all the slopes and mountains around us, in
the fields, everywhere, in fact, there were tanks, armoured and other
vehicles.

The Russian soldiers came down the slopes towards me. Some
Russians drove us up the path or the road by force of arms. As they
did so they roared and shouted loudly. They fired into the air, and into
the ground beside us. Perhaps they also hit a few of our comrades. I
wished I was very small. In a sign of surrender I raised my hands high

over my head and ran rather than walked up the hill. Up on the slope stood a row of Soviet soldiers with steel helmets, fully armed. They had sub-machine guns or rifles with bayonets at the ready.

Now the main thing for me was to be as inconspicuous as possible. Reckless and hasty movements could be interpreted as a provocation. Nervous actions were to be avoided at all costs. Our opposite numbers were also in a highly stressful situation that was hard to get under control. The Russian soldiers were constantly shouting, 'Ruky vyerch', which means more or less 'hands up'. But I only found that out later. But I could tell from the situation what was meant. Now and again one of the Russians fired as if to emphasise his words and gestures. But perhaps it was also nerves and tension; I can't tell. At any rate guns were fired. It was one of the most horrible moments of my life. A bullet could easily have hit me.

Of necessity I approached a Russian. I noticed how some soldiers were being separated from the rest. Shots rang out again and again. I got closer and closer to the Russian soldier. He was probably not much calmer than I was, and no older. He was aiming a pistol at me. We were barely a metre apart.

The Soviet soldier patted me down with his free hand and searched me for weapons. Suddenly I was being punched, kicked and beaten with the butt of a gun. The reason: in my right boot there was a knife that in my excitement I hadn't thrown away. I always used it as a breadknife. But the Russian saw it as a weapon. The knife could have been used as that too. The Russian probably doubted my peaceful intentions. Perhaps he was just frightened, as I was. Those were terrible moments. Everyone involved was in a situation that occurs extremely rarely in life, an extremely dangerous and exceptional situation.

I was driven towards an increasingly large crowd of comrades who had already been searched. My body hurt from the blows. I was very agitated, and worried that even more unfortunate things could happen to me. I immediately tried to disappear into the group. I managed it too. Luckily I had survived those moments of extreme danger. The Soviet soldiers who took me prisoner left me alive.

**Heinz Dost, radio operator**                    *Melnik, near Prague*

As radio operator with the 1st Tank Corps Signal Detachment 457 I
was detained by the Czechs on 8 May 1945. Place of detention: Melnik,
near Prague. My mechanic was detained at the same time. We were
taken prisoner by Czech partisans, who had armed themselves with
discarded German weapons, and after being briefly searched put us up
against the wall to be shot. On the order of the partisan leader, the rifles
were loaded. We were ordered to lower our heads slightly. Then the
execution was aborted. People whose language we didn't understand
approached from the road. But we could understand enough to
know that they were former Russian prisoners of war. These Russian
prisoners of war had also armed themselves with German weapons,
and were ordered by the Czechs to bring us to the nearby farm, about
100 to 150 metres away. By now other German prisoners of war had
also appeared, officers, Wehrmacht officials and civilian staff with their
wives and children. The unit leader of the Czech partisans now stirred
up the Czech population against us, shouting, 'Here come the ones
who raped your women and girls.'

Whereupon the Czechs laid into this little group of prisoners of
war with cudgels and stones. Many were injured. When we had left
the farm, we were divided by sex. We men had to strip to the waist.
They checked us to see if we had SS tattoos on our upper arms. Some
of my fellow prisoners had this tattoo and were summarily shot by the
Czechs in front of the stable.

**Dieter Wiechmann, officer, b. 1922**                    *near Karlsbad*

In Komotau I first went to a restaurant in the city centre and had lunch
on travel coupons, as if the world outside hadn't changed. I sat down
at the table of a major who told me he was driving his car (a DKW
Meisterklasse) to see the Americans, and wanted to take me along as
his companion. I quickly used up all my travel coupons in a grocer's
shop, getting not only bread but also margarine in return.

Towards evening we arrived in Karlsbad, where we heard that there
was a ceasefire on all fronts from 11.00 p.m. onwards. Major von L.
had acquaintances in Karlsbad, at whose lovely villa we were able to
spend the night. The next morning we went into town to be formally

dismissed from the Wehrmacht. A special office had been set up in a barracks. It was full of armed Czech civilians who stood around wearing red arm-bands and with red flowers in their lapels. They left us in peace, as the town was swarming with armed German soldiers anyway.

After our formal release from the Wehrmacht, we were of the opinion that if the cockade and braids on our caps had been removed, along with the swastikas from our jackets and our epaulettes, we would have the status of civilians and would be treated accordingly by the Americans. We even hoped we would be able to travel to our home destinations.

The wife of our host removed all our military markings, and we got back into the DKW as 'civilians'. Previously I had given the gentleman of the house, who was a huntsman, my 10 x 50 service binoculars and my .38 pistol.

So we headed west towards the endless stream of people. At Eger, all motor vehicles were suddenly separated off from the refugees on foot, apparently by the Americans, although we didn't see them anywhere.

So we were driving more or less alone on one such farm track, as instructed, when there was suddenly an American tank in front of us. The squad ordered us to get out and put our hands up. The car and our luggage were searched, our arms and hands 'examined', i.e. relieved of watches and rings. Then we had to fasten a white handkerchief to the window and were able to travel on.

After a few kilometres along the farm path we reached a huge 'car park', where only German vehicles were parked. We had to leave our car as well and walk to a transit camp.

### Captain Arthur Mrongovius, 1905–92                              *Krummau*

American sentries stood on either side of the thoroughfare in their olive-green uniforms, their steel helmets low over their foreheads. And behind their ranks their jeeps and tanks had driven up. And so the limousine in which I was sitting with four Russian officers passed this cordon unmolested. Our column was ordered by the Americans to stay in the car park until we were assigned the place where we were to be interned. So, standing behind the row of the American sentries, we were able to witness one German unit after another forcing its way through the cordon of American sentries, and giving up their weapons. Even today the metallic rattle with which the discarded weapons landed on a big pile on their right side still rings in my ears. These German soldiers had not yet assumed the typically dragging gait of later columns of prisoners; instead they strode with their heads held scornfully high through the ranks of victors into the darkness of the future.

Among the capitulating units there were also a lot of Waffen-SS squads, including some real Titans, which repeatedly prompted the Russian ROA officers to exclaim in admiration. 'Kakiye orly!' (What eagles!) I heard them calling out again and again. Typically, during my long imprisonment with the Soviets, I encountered this admiration very often, directed specifically at members of the Waffen-SS by simple officers and soldiers of the Red Army.

**Boris Gindin, Red Army soldier, 1926–45**           *Czechoslovakia*
*To his sister*

Hello Musya!

I am now in a little Czechoslovakian village. The Germans have run away from here. The only ones left are the 'Czech people' – 'tschechish Leud' – as they write on the doors here. Some Germans have tried in vain to present themselves as such 'Leud'.

The weather is glorious now. It's hot. There is green everywhere. I am now writing the letter on a balcony like the one on which Romeo and Juliet once declared their love. Two Czech girls live in the flat where I'm staying. One is 19, the other 20. A shame my Czech isn't very good. It's hard to talk to them. But they are wonderful girls. In my time off I dance with them to music from the portable gramophone. That's what life is like here, with all its pleasures.

Write more to me. What is your school doing? How is Ganya? I'm interested in everything.

Yours, Boris

**Alisah Shek, b. 1927**                *Theresienstadt concentration camp*
All day and all night cannon-fire, very nearby. Morning SS fired into
ghetto. Old man killed. Southern barracks – at first overcome with
disinfestations in Bodenbach [barracks]? Typhus continues. Men from
May and December transports from Black Forest. 3 weeks on the road,
arrived on foot, 250 left of 1,000. News: Red Cross, Raschka – lunatic,
hysteric, commands Sudeten [barracks]. Anti-Semite. 68) The […] Jews
(cheering in the streets; the Russians coming are chivvied and cursed
(shouting outside) and have dirt thrown at them. Application for
40,000 arrivals, all due by tomorrow evening. Wooden fence around
Bauschowitzer Kessel [Bauschowitz Hollow, used as a mass grave]
(cheers), then roof on top! Meissner – taken over. Meeting – Jews,
Sudeten [barracks]. Czechs. Zirka [Georg Vogel] has run away. Refused
to assume part of the responsibility. Absolutely impossible. Tomorrow
people (Czechoslovaks) are to leave at great speed – regardless of
whether there was firing or what. On foot – it's called going home.
The whole thing will go wrong, has to. At half past nine in the evening
the first Russians. Shouting and cheers. Yesterday they sang Czech
songs, wore tricolours, today they are singing the 'Internationale' and
carrying red flags through the town. There is a bitterness inside me, I
can no longer go with them because something within me has broken,
and I bear a burden of centuries, troubled and vivid. I only have one
path, and all this repels me. Human beings disgust me. Although I
must think of them, I am overwhelmed with the despair of one who
must carry the undigested matter of those who sing.

**Erich Kessler, b. 1912**                *Theresienstadt concentration camp*
This morning at 6.30 I'm woken to the news that my brother Hans has
arrived on a transport to Theresienstadt.

Of course I was out of bed and dressed in a shot, and ran to the
collection point. That was a joyful reunion, after so many years of
painful separation! So often I was completely dejected and didn't dare
believe we would see each other again. But then I felt hope again, and
thank God it proved to be justified. But the way we had to see one
another. Emaciated, with the typical expression of the camp inmate,
which speaks of unimaginable horror. Hans's normal weight was

72–73 kg. Today he weighs 48. The poor fellows had to go through a lot before they stepped on the soil of Theresienstadt, under the protection of the Red Cross, and their life was given back to them. They were on the road for three weeks. Almost without food and largely on foot. The last 2 nights were particularly dreadful. The rain was streaming down, and they stood crammed together in the open freight wagon, drenched to the skin. They were starving too, so that one after the other fell dead with complete exhaustion. There were 70 fatalities in the last, most terrible night. Hans sat down on his bowl and was so weak that he fell asleep. When he woke up, he was in water, and as a consequence he had terrible diarrhoea. He had to do his business no fewer than 40 times. He asked me to find some kind of remedy. Of course I went to the hospital, to a nurse I knew, but all I got was bone charcoal. Luckily I had some dried bread which I brought him so that he wasn't tempted to eat something that might harm him. In December 1943 1,500 people left here, and yesterday 280 came back. All the others were gassed, or starved to death or died of the strain. We won't see our dear, kind Mama again, either. What these people have seen and experienced is so terrible that it is almost impossible to believe. The east-bound transports prepared in Theresienstadt went to Birkenau, a satellite camp of Auschwitz, under barbed wire. The whole transport spent 6 months under quarantine there. Then the camp administrators in Berlin asked what was going to happen to the transport, and at the same time a general overview was given of the people's state of health, and their ability to work. According to this estimation, the judgement was then delivered from Berlin: 'destroy' or 'work detail'. In the first case the whole transport, men, women or children, old or young, sick or healthy, were gassed. In the second case those capable of work were selected by the SS camp doctor and the rest were gassed. Only men under 50 and women under 40 were taken into account for a work detail. Of course anyone on that dangerous border tried to make himself younger to save his life again. Hans told me that they were led past the gas chambers three times before the decision was made to examine the transport. Hans spent the night before being transported on to further slave labour in Germany with our dear mother. It must have been terrible for her, and then Hans had to go through a lot, but luckily he's here today. At about midday the whole transport was sent to be disinfested, as they call it. Of course I went there quite often to see how they were doing. In the afternoon retreating SS troops passed by the ghetto, and although the Red Cross flag was flying, they threw hand grenades in and fired sub-machine guns. The people had to stay in their houses. In the early afternoon Allied planes attacked Leitmeritz, and as I was in the attic of the Genie barracks I saw the impact very distinctly. Later, pressing against the walls of the houses, I went back to the disinfestation building, but it still wasn't Hans's turn. When it was dark, I went back. Hans was still outside, and they were sitting around a pile of burning concentration camp uniforms. All of a sudden we heard the sound of driving tanks and cheers. It was the Russians! I ran across the courtyard of the hospital, where I often sat and looked longingly at the road. Now the boarding had been torn down and the columns of the victorious Red Army was moving past us in the direction of Prague. It was pitch-dark, and only the headlights of the vehicles illuminated the road. We cheered them on, and everyone sang the 'Internationale' to the best of his ability. German, Czech, Polish, Hungarian, all at the same time but with the same enthusiasm. I ran back to Hans, who was still sitting by the fire, and they had just started their evening meal. They were preparing to spend the night in the open. It was wonderful to see the sign of German tyranny and ignominy going up in flames, while the troops of the liberating Red Army routed what was left of the 'undefeatable' German army: it was late when I said goodbye to Hans, who was spending the night with two comrades at a friend's place.

*

**Ilse Schulz, b. 1913** *Aussig*

In the morning the radio broadcast the first reports of ceasefire negotiations. The war was over. We heard it with our eyes lowered. No feeling of relief or hope ran through our hearts. Our oppressed silence was interrupted by Ulli's jubilant little voice: 'Mum, it's Dad!'

On tottering knees I hurried to the garden gate. There he stood. Pale and stubbly, in a crumpled uniform without a weapon, without a belt, without shoes and with blood-drenched bandages on both feet. But he was alive! He looked like the personification of the lost war – but he was alive. We hugged blissfully. Then the little children danced around us; the parents, housemates and neighbours came running. What a joyful moment.

**Hildegard Holzwarth, seminarian, b. 1928**   *Hermannshütte, Sudeten*

Today was our enemies' victory celebration. Yesterday we were aiming our guns at the western powers. We are still fighting against Bolshevism. But it can last a few hours at most. The battles in Prague are over too. We have succumbed to superior forces, and are now abandoned to the caprice of the enemy. Our soldiers are being led around as prisoners. Today we had to keep Sunday rest, and wave flags for the victory celebration. Of course we flew the white flag. In the afternoon an American paid us a visit, a real gangster type. I'm terrified of those men. Brrr! Over the next few days we wait for the occupying American troops. At the moment the Czechs are leading the regiment in their stead. They humiliate us at every opportunity. It has been so hard for the whole population to hold out for six years. Now everything has happened so suddenly that we don't feel at all defeated. Again and again we have to get used to the idea of the collapse of the Reich and our being handed over. I know we have a long journey of suffering ahead of us. The peace conditions are terribly severe. The Americans are violent people. German girls are fair game as far as they are concerned. But we will defend ourselves with hands and feet. The best thing to do will be simply to ignore these people. Things will get better, yes, it is as it must be. We Germans have the great will needed to do this. And those of us who are young will do it in spite of everything. If only a benign fate could send us another Führer, otherwise we are abandoned by internal feuding to external circumstances. The victory celebration was the first great humiliation.

**Ernst Hammen, private soldier, 1902–84**   *Czechoslovakia*

It must have been 8 May 1945 when the great getaway got going here as well. The start was hesitant, as it usually is. Two French civilians transporting large amounts of luggage walked past. The tricolour they carried with them marked them out as such. 'Where are you heading?' I asked them. 'West,' was the reply. 'That's where I want to go,' I said. In this way we fell into conversation. They had been sent to Germany to work as students. After the fall of Dresden, where they had worked, fate had dispatched them to Setzdorf. They were two handsome young men, who inspired trust. Over the two weeks that we went on to spend together they proved to be true comrades.

Accordingly, I told them the following: 'You won't get far with all that insane amount of luggage, chuck it in the back of the car and march with me as long as you feel like it, or take a seat back there. Afterwards you can take me along as a French civilian.' I knew the language well enough for that. An Alsatian who left school in 1917 doesn't need to speak perfect French! It all made sense to them. We sat down on the edge of the field. I took out the supplies that my kind landlady had packed for me, butter and ham – we have a whole car full of bread – and divided it cleanly into three pieces. Everyone had his share, and our comradeship was sealed.

*

**Klaus Mann, 1906–49**                                    *(Berchtesgaden)*
*To his father*

From Innsbruck we travelled on to Berchtesgaden. The seething mass of Allied troops, most of them Frenchmen and 'displaced persons' of every nationality, was even denser there, even noisier, a wild carnival of exuberance. Lots of drunks were conspicuous by their uninhibited manners; the wine with which they had lubricated themselves came from Hitler's cellar. For two days the 'Berghof' had been systematically looted by our soldiers (GIs and *poilus* [French soldiers]); it must have been an orgy of robbery and triumph of the grand, grim style. Unfortunately my friend Tewskbury and I got there too late to join in. We found the famous estate guarded by military police – albeit unnecessarily. After the bombs that made such a terribly clean sweep here, the looters did a lot of very conscientious work. Shattered walls and charred beams, deep craters full of ash and debris, furniture in pieces, broken glass and dirt, a heap of rubble. Nothing else left. In the ruins of the main building you can still make out the structure of the enormous window of which the master of the house is said to have been so proud. Here he used to delight in the sight of the Alpine panorama with his guests, his courtiers and victims. The panorama is still impressive; but the ugly remains of the 'Berghof' disturb the beautiful picture. The various constructions for guests, servants, journalists and Gestapo officers, Martin Bormann's villa, Göring's pavilion, just black caves, black heaps: just dirty stains and marks of shame in an otherwise pure landscape. Of the whole massive complex, which was once Hitler's pleasure palace and stout fortress, all that remains is a relatively modest side wing, it too burned out and plundered. A blue, white and red banner adorns the ruined roof. The tricolour!

At our arrival in Salzburg, on the evening of the same day, at every kiosk we saw the special edition of the *Stars and Stripes* with the big inscription 'IT'S ALL OVER HERE! VICTORY IN EUROPE IS OURS...'

'It's all over...' Over! Done! Finished. No one's thinking of what is yet to come, not today! Today everyone is thinking only: *Phew...*

And the Pacific front? No such sigh of relief over there, not yet. Pessimists say the war with Japan will drag on for many months, perhaps even years. I can't believe it. Admittedly I wouldn't have thought it possible that the Germans would end their suicidal, iniquitous struggle only on 8 May 1945.

*

**Martin Hauser, sergeant in the British army, b. 1913**          *Trieste*
Trieste. Things have come full circle, after twelve years. Back then I was on the way to Palestine and left a peaceful city – today, the 'day of victory', peace has not yet returned here. There has been severe friction between the Allies here too – between Britain and America on the one hand and the Yugoslavs on the other, because of their occupation of the city. The Yugoslavs see Trieste as compensation for 20 years of suffering under the Italian regime and the years of bitter, bloody fighting against Italian and German Fascism. They stress the

fact that while most of the city's inhabitants are Italian, the bulk of the rural population are Croatian. They say Yugoslavia urgently needs a big harbour for the development of the country. All well and good, but what we can't agree with is the way they want to achieve their goal. Negotiations? Yes. Conference? Fine. Referendum? Good. But don't just grab everything and appropriate the population along with its soil. We have waged this war, among other things, against the assertion that 'the end justifies the means'.

Victory celebration. In front of the city hall the big square is filled with a huge crowd of people. Flags with red stars in the middle flutter above their heads, big posters with political slogans in Italian and Yugoslavian in the hands of many participants. Hanging from the balcony of the city hall is a big red flag, on its right the Union Jack and the American flag, on its left the Yugoslavian and Croatian colours with the red star in the middle. Speech follows speech, everything translated into Italian and Yugoslavian, congratulations to the Allies for their victory – along with the demand for an annexation of Trieste! In the hall, from which a big glass door leads on to the balcony, senior officers of the British, American, Russian and Yugoslavian armies. Everyone is being 'reserved'. Now that we have won the war together, may the gods help us if we don't win the peace together as well.

First steps towards the reorganization of the Jewish community and provisional aid measures.

**Vittorio Segre, b. 1920**                                              *Italy*
There are black holes in my memory. In one of them the memories of the end of the war do battle. The news of the ceasefire in Italy reached me in Zadar, to which the British unit to which I was assigned had returned after Tito's troops had blocked the road to Trieste. I drowned the idea of ending the war in such a banal fashion in gin. My drunkenness must have thrown my memories into confusion. I can still see the ruined harbour, the pregnant Yugoslavian partisan running around in what was left of the city park with a hand grenade pressed to her belly, the absurd seaman, bayonet over his shoulder, guarding the cruiser *Columbus*, moored on the quay under the D'Annunzio slogan 'We will stay here for ever'.

I remember the patrol boat that brought me to Italy, the journey to Turin, where I tried to find news of my family. The city was celebrating, they were dancing in the streets, there were no Allied troops, and a partisan who heard me speaking Italian pressed his rifle against my chest, assuming that I was a Fascist in disguise. I can't remember what I did on 8 May. Perhaps that was the day when the bombed synagogue opened again. Or the one when I went to a cobbler who was repairing shoes with the leather from stolen Torah rolls. 'I didn't know it was sacred leather,' he said. We collected all the pieces together, and he refused the money that I tried to give him for a few ladies' shoes with Hebrew letters written in ancient ink on the soles.

## Major Erwein Karl Graf zu Eltz, 1912–75                    Croatia

Events are rushing ahead, and the situation is forcing us to take quick evasive action. We turned the corps staff into as strong a convoy as we could. I preferred to use my own car, and manoeuvred my way in front of the general's car, armed to the teeth. Our journey took us first via Trakostan to Windisch-Freistritz. All our attention was devoted to the mountain terrain. We crouched, relaxed and ready to jump, on the car seats, with fingers on the triggers of our sub-machine gun. Only when darkness began to fall did we reach Windisch-Freistritz, where we were received by Nandi Attems in his hospitable form. In his beautiful, tidy house he placed a series of comfortable guest-rooms at our disposal, and we were promptly supplied with the necessary information by our staff personnel. Count and Countess Attems were touchingly determined to make everything as comfortable for us as possible. I was extremely surprised and unsettled that our kind hosts hadn't even remotely thought of moving to the west and putting themselves in safety. I visited Nandi in his study, and saw that his habits hadn't changed at all, just as they hadn't anywhere else in the castle. Silver and other valuables were in their places, as they presumably always had been. I mentioned this to him and tried to persuade him at least to pack up the most important things and join us, as we still had enough room in our vehicles. He said he had no serious fears for his family, as one of his sons was on the best of terms with the partisans. Although those soft beds invited us to lay down our weary bodies, it was not to be, since the news reached us around midnight that Germany had also surrendered to the east, and that from 1 o'clock in the morning all movements were to be suspended. Nevertheless, our divisions received the order to fight on to the Austrian border, come what may.

**Dr Hans Uhlemann, staff physician, 1907–98**     *Croatia–Austria*
We travelled on the following day, along the Drau, constantly concerned that we might suddenly be fired at from the dense forests. But nothing happened, the ceasefire had already come into force. En route we passed a big food supply warehouse. We wanted to get hold of some cigarettes etc., but the senior paymaster wouldn't spend anything without special instructions from his superiors, even though the capitulation had already been announced. Although in the end he softened a bit.

Then at last, at last, we crossed the old Reich border and drove into Lavanttal. It was cramped, the road was narrow and ahead of us car after car, and Cossacks of the Vlasov Army fighting on our side, trying almost in a blind panic to get away on their horses into the mountain forests.

The news came in that the Red Army was already waiting for us to the north. So everybody turned round in a crazed bid to escape to the British in the west. Many Cossack officers shot themselves because they knew exactly what to expect from the Soviets. In fact those who didn't were handed over, as agreed, to the Russians, and summarily shot with machine guns, one after the other, in Judenburg.

After a few breakdowns we slowly made it to the Austrian village of Völkermarkt – 'People's Market'. At the edge of the town it looked like its name: Tito partisans, including women, some wild figures as in a tale of brigands (a scene from *Das Wirtshaus im Spessart*!) with broad belts lined with cartridges, hand grenades, sub-machine guns, daggers etc., hardly a body part without murderous-looking weapons. And these bandits stopped us and wanted to take our money. Luckily at the last moment a British armoured car turned up. We surrendered, and were taken into town under its protection because of our red cross. Now we were safe.

＊

**Isa Vermehren, b. 1918**                                  *on the way to Naples*

We left the cosy hotel on Tuesday at ten o'clock on the dot. Our departure and everything related to it had proceeded smoothly and calmly, without any shouting, without any loud commands or any trace of agitation. It is hard for a German to believe that a military apparatus can operate without those dreadful accompaniments, but it actually works, and the sense I get is more than pleasant. In a convoy of forty cars, including about ten limousines and thirty 'bucket cars' as they are called here, we snaked our way down the mountain in a southerly direction. It had been decreed that a top speed of forty kilometres an hour should not be exceeded, in order to safeguard the older people and the children. So we had ample opportunity to enjoy all the beauties of this spring journey into the north of Italy. The country seemed still to be tied up in the happy rapture of the war, over at last. Flags hung everywhere, and in the little marketplaces the people stood side by side as if they were all on holiday. Now and again we met smaller or larger groups of German soldiers who were waiting to be taken prisoner, or who were already on the way there. Many must have been in a painful state, having only ever been able to get to know this beloved country as enemies, first as hostile invading victors, and now as expelled, defeated enemies; helplessness lay on all sides like a lead weight upon everyone.

In the early afternoon we stopped in a charming garden restaurant, where long tables had been set up for our reception, with white bread, buckets of wonderful jam and inexhaustible quantities of coffee, sugar and cream. At around midnight we reached Verona, which seemed to have suffered severe damage during the war, and at the Hotel Colombo d'Oro a delicious dinner awaited us – with roast chicken, salad and asparagus, ice cream, cigarettes and, of course, coffee again.

The early breakfast the following morning was no less appetizing. Again we boarded our forty automobiles, but this time just to travel the short distance to the airport, where five planes waited, engines running, to take off for Naples. The sun was shining, the air was calm and clear and gave us a clear view of the land below. I was filled with intense longing at the sight of Florence, and I greedily craved a glimpse of Rome. Our pilot was cordial, he let us join him in his cabin, and always made sure to fly the route that gave us the best view. During the flight we were given sandwiches and a mug of coffee.

Just like the children of our party, we looked forward to continuing our Prague idyll in the warmer climate of the more southerly city of Naples. These many hours were all made wonderful by the idea of liberation. We felt liberated from fear and horror, terror and oppression, murder and war, liberated from the bitter necessity of having to protect and defend ourselves, we were really swimming in a sea of bliss, we flew through a sky of sun-drenched joy, of cloudless happiness, of perfect peace.

When we arrived in Naples, we were met first by the innumerable lenses of countless press photographers, and then by the girls of the American Red Cross. They pounced on us with overwhelming kindness, treated us to coffee and the children to lemonade and cocoa, little pancakes, they gave us bags full of useful things; a piece of soap, a toothbrush, a facecloth, a pack of cigarettes, etc. They pressed newspapers into our hands, beamed at us as if we were their dearest children, and kept coming up with new ideas for the part they played in 'Our Peace'.

Suddenly the dream was shattered: a sentry stepped in our way, with orders to separate the members of the Axis powers from those of the Allies, and to forbid any further contact between them. As swiftly as night follows day at the equator, the light made way for engulfing darkness; being German became a bad fate that cast a sudden shadow over us. With a rather forced smile we waved adieu to our new friends, and had to battle for a long time against a painful feeling of nausea. The American girls, undaunted, maintained their natural warmth, and in their unrivalled sympathy there appeared genuine maternal feelings that did not alter for national differences, but that was feeble consolation in this profound sadness over the fact that 'being a human being among other human beings' only ever happens in dreams of a perfect world.

After a wait of about three hours we were told to get into the twenty limousines that had just drawn up, which took us from

the airport to the Hotel Terminus, where our lodgings had been prepared. We Germans were staying on one floor, and the other Axis
powers on the other, and on every landing there was an American
military policeman with a sub-machine gun over his shoulder, making
sure no one left their corridor. We were given twenty-four hours to
come to terms with the new situation, which was all the more difficult
since, in our present state, our ears, suspicious by now, could no longer
ignore the quiet sense of everything starting all over again: all questions
about our future fate were answered with a familiar and stereotypical
'I don't know'. These things have etched themselves so sharply in
my memory less because of any lurking bad intention on the part of
the Americans, but chiefly because it was through these measures, as
understandable as they were objectively necessary, that I first saw the
German face reflected in a foreign mirror. If we were placed under
such a strict watch it was primarily for our own protection, because it
could not remain hidden from the Italians that so many Germans were
lodged in the building, and their reaction was deeply unpredictable. So
the armed military police didn't shine a bad light on the Americans,
but instead on us, whose quiet presence could be enough to unleash a
storm of wild and furious rage. We could almost have wished ourselves
back in the concentration camp, where one could have felt like an
innocent party in the hands of the guilty; here, on the other hand,
the weight of 'German' guilt lay so oppressively upon us that it was
difficult to guarantee peace and order in the unchained contradiction
of our own emotions.

*

**Erich Kästner, 1899–1974**                            *Mayrhofen*
Jodl has signed the unconditional surrender. In Rheims. The radio
broadcasts the victory celebrations and the jubilation that prevails
outside. Everyone is proud of what they have achieved in five years of
war. And they have good reason to boast. But they reproach us with
the fact that it took their efforts to do it. What they did was something
we should have done. We, the German minority, failed, they say. It's
an ambiguous accusation. It only contains half the truth. They hide

the other half. They ignore their own guilt. What they hide turns what they say into a slogan, and over the course of time we have become very sensitive to slogans. Even liberal slogans. Even slogans from overseas. The victors who want to see us in the dock will have to sit next to us. There's room.

So who, when the executioner was publicly consorting with us, drew up a pact with Hitler? Not us. Who concluded accords? Signed trade agreements? Sent diplomats to send congratulations and athletes to the Olympics in Berlin? Who shook hands with the criminals rather than the victims? Not us, my dear Pharisees!

You call us the 'other' Germany. It's supposed to be praise. But you only praise us the better to blame us. Do you pretend to have forgotten that this other Germany was the land first and longest-occupied and tormented by Hitler? Don't you know how power and impotence are distributed in the totalitarian state? You reproach us for not being capable of making attempts on their lives? For the fact that the very best of us were dilettante one-off murderers of outstanding mass murderers? You are right. But you don't have the right to throw the first stone at us! It has no place in your hand. You don't know what to do with it? It belongs, behind glass and catalogued, in the Museum of History. Beside the neatly painted number of Germans who were murdered by Germans.

The world awaits. Stalin has declared that Germany is not to be fragmented. But it must feed itself, British ministers have said. They will intervene only if epidemics of starvation occur. Captain Gerngross has told us that Hitler's greatest devotees lived only north of the Main. And the Vorarlberg radio station praised the angelic innocence of the Austrians. The future fate of the Old Reich does not affect them. They are not interested in it. Their friends live behind different borders. Innocence is spreading like plague. Even Hermann Göring has been affected by it. He has been condemned to death by Hitler and arrested by the SS. He was only saved by members of the Luftwaffe. We can see that the angel of innocence has visited almost everybody, and now they all want to go to hospital.

Prague and Dresden have been taken. Mayrhofen is governing itself. No one is allowed in the streets after 9.00 p.m. And an attack signifies that because of the tense food situation we, the refugees, are to be cast out.

## Göring's adjutant                                   *Zell am See*

A lot of packing in the morning, Toni is very concerned about the distribution of vehicles. We set off at 12.00, first car Sis, Christa and I, then RM with family, Robert, Gerch and others following after. The pass is jammed as usual, largely by SS, who want to retreat to join the 'partisan fighting' in the mountains, but are for the time being drunk and have brought girls with them. After four hours the first cars get through, the rest by evening. In the meantime we rest in the Untertauern sawmill, where RM is soon surrounded by soldiers and civilians who listen exasperatedly to his account of his fate, and offer him their services for whatever purpose. That's also what it was like during the last few days in Mauterndorf; those Luftwaffe soldiers who came from the south immediately appointed themselves to RM's security, and placed themselves unhesitatingly at his disposal: 'Our honour is loyalty.'

Meanwhile in Radstatt a road block has been erected on the orders of the Americans, and German officers are guarding it carefully to ensure that no soldiers escape from the Russian side to the American! After a great fuss they let us through. Just after the village two American cars come towards us. It is 8.10 p.m. A general and Major Müller get out of the limousine, RM gets out, walks up to the general, a greeting takes place involving al the formalities without which an arrest would be impossible. The general, the Deputy Division Commander of the 36th Texas Division, General Stake [in fact General Stack – translator's note], informs RM that his letter has arrived and been passed on, but there has not yet been a reply. He asks him to take lodgings in a specially prepared house in Zell am See. Driving at the head of the column, he then drives us there, to the former SS riding school. Some SS leaders are sitting in the kitchen with a few Polish girls, getting drunk. They all still have their guns, and are delivering highly unambiguous speeches like 'I hope that fellow [RM] has drawn up his will' and so on. At our request the American general lets us keep a few guns, and I share a constant guard outside RM's bedroom. First appearance of press photographers.

**Field Marshal Wilhelm Keitel, 1882–1946**        (Dobbin–Neustadt,
Holstein)

The following events reveal how little Himmler understood about the
political situation and his personal responsibility. He sent from his
lodgings, which were unknown to us, via an army officer who had
until then been part of his staff, and whom he dismissed at the same
time, a letter to General Eisenhower, with a request that it be passed
on. The officer was authorized to inform me of the contents of the
letter. In a few words it contained the offer to surrender himself of
his own accord to Genral Eisenhower, if he received an assurance that
he would under no circumstances be handed over to the Russians.
Himmler had mentioned this intention to me at my last discussion
[with him] in the presence of Jodl. Since the officer, as deliverer of
the letter, did not return to Himmler, Himmler never learned that
the letter was not passed on, but was destroyed and never reached
Eisenhower. Himmler had, incidentally, informed me via the courier
officer reporting to Dönitz that he was going to disappear from
the Northern Sector and go into hiding; he would not be found for
the next six months, he said. His arrest, some weeks later, and his
suicide by poison in prison are well known.

**Paul Schmidt**                                                      *Salzburg*

On 8 May, at 3 o'clock in the afternoon, we heard Churchill: 'Yesterday
morning, at 2.41, at General Eisenhower's headquarters, General Jodl,
the representative of the German High Command and of Grand
Admiral Dönitz, the designated head of the German state, signed the
act of unconditional surrender of all German land, sea and air forces
in Europe to the Allied Expeditionary Force, and, simultaneously, to
the Soviet High Command.' When in later years I came face to face
with the surrender document, I was able to establish that General Jodl
had surrendered only 'by authority of the German High Command'
and not as representative of the head of state Grand Admiral Dönitz.
In terms of international law, particularly if one draws comparisons
with the ending of the First World War and the Japanese surrender,
an interesting point that is not insignificant for the course of further
developments.

Of course in May 1945 these details were entirely lost upon us. We were struck only by the lack of drama with which the British prime minister communicated this world-shattering event: 'Hostilities will end officially at one minute past midnight tonight, Tuesday, 8 May.' No big words. Only the sober statement: 'The German war is therefore at an end.'

Then, in the evening, we heard reports from London about the victory celebrations that were taking place there. In London's White-hall, the crowd shouted not, 'We want to see our Churchill', but 'We want Winny', and 'Winny' appeared not in his uniform with a stiff expression and an even stiffer outstretched arm, but in his familiar siren suit with a top hat and, in the floodlights, conducted the choral singing of the crowd in the street. There could hardly be a more telling characterization, condensed into such a short and easily graspable scene, of the difference between 'Germany since 1933 and England since 1066', as we noted in our diary.

'Every ceasefire is the first step to peace and reconstruction,' I said to General Huntzinger, the leader of the French delegation, in 1940 in the Forest of Compiègne after the signing of the armistice with France in the historic dining car, in an attempt to do something to help him get over the infinite sadness expressed on his face and in his posture. At that moment I couldn't help thinking – not least because I had experienced at first hand the countless discussions and conferences on the diplomatic scene of the 1920s and '30s – about how Germany had risen again and regained its place in the family of nations after the difficult defeat of 1918.

But our diary says: 'Where others have so much reason to be pleased, and we so much reason not to complain about our misfortune, but to be deeply ashamed for others who claim, rightly or wrongly, to belong to us and even to lead us, in spite of all our intellectual resilience a deep despondency settles in. One person voices it, the others think it. In spite of everything we greet this first little step away from war in the hope that the completely negative result of the experiment of 1933, pursued according to all the rules in the recipe book, right through to the end, is now generally acknowledged. Any German equipped with a normal level of intelligence must say to himself that the search for new paths, which is inherent in the German character, must in any case reject the road taken in 1933.'

### Günter Cords, b. 1928                                              (*Linz*)

Clusters of people in grey and white prisoners' uniforms appeared by the roadside. I had never seen such terrible-looking figures, emaciated to the bone. A little group crouched around a fire by the roadside, stirring cooking pots. When they realized that we weren't from the victorious powers, they stopped our horses and also searched our vehicles. Even our protest that everything was precisely recorded and we were travelling on the instructions of the American army didn't stop them taking down two boxes from the cart. As we travelled on one of these miserable figures, a 23-year-old Pole, climbed up and crouched on our cart. His head, which sat on a thin neck, looked more like a skull or a mask than a living person, particularly as he had only one eye. Thin bones stood out under his prison uniform, and running along his head was a swathe three fingers wide cut with hair-clippers. I had to struggle to look at him.

'Where do you come from?' Ignatz asked.

'Mauthausen concentration camp.'

'Never heard of it.'

'No, it's true,' he nodded eagerly, and reported on thousands of foreigners who had been locked up there and freed by the Americans that morning, and then he reported on the incredible conditions that were supposed to have prevailed there.

*

### Konrad Adenauer, 1876–1967                                    *Cologne*
*To Colonel John K. Patterson, military government*

Given that Ascension Day is imminent, I should like to ask you whether this day should be a holiday and hence a day off for the staff of the city administration. Acension Day has always been a High Holiday, even though it had been abolished by the National Socialists over the past few years.

A[denauer]

**Walter Ulbricht, 1893–1973**                                    *Berlin*
*To Georgi Dimitrov*

Comrade Dimitrov!

We have concentrated our work primarily on the selection of anti-Fascists for the district administrations and the city administration of Berlin. In many circles the Communists who had emerged from illegality were at first isolated from the district administrations that were organizing themselves at the time. The spontaneously set up KPD offices, the people's committees, the committees of the 'Free Germany' movement and the commissions of the people of 20 July who had hitherto been working illegally, now came out into the open. We sealed the doors of the offices and made it clear to the comrades that all forces must now be concentrated on work in the city administration. Committee members must also be transferred to work in the urban district administrations, and the committees themselves liquidated. The red vehicles with hammer and sickle are also slowly disappearing from the city. In the context of the new administrative organizations we are succeeding in introducing a broad association of anti-Fascist democratic forces. The following have agreed to collaborate with us: Dr Hermes, Prof. Sauerbruch, Prof. Gorbrandt, City Councillor Otto Schulz, Headmaster Karl Schulz, the actor and director Karl Rühmann, Dr Flechtheim – a person who has contacts with many bourgeois opponents of Hitler.

In many districts the traces of illegality are still discernible. The Communists there have little contact with the people of other social strata and political tendencies. As there are neither newspapers nor political training, more time is required for the satisfactory orientation of comrades.

Suggestions: we have suggested Maron and Schwenk as deputies to the mayor, Lorenz and Erpenbeck for the department of public education and Gyptner for the personnel department. I urgently need more staff: ten qualified Communist instructors for work in the district administrations and in Brandenburg, one member of staff for personnel questions and a secretary with shorthand skills. I suggest Försterling. If he's still ill I'll have to take Köpe. The work is getting easier, as the consultants for personnel issues in the district administrations are Communists. Zaisser is needed for training work. For propaganda and Dr Hermes's further work I need Hörnle. For the selection of trade union staff I shall take Chwalek. I have distributed ten prisoners of war around the district administrations. I need Kohlmey and ten assistants for the work in the public education department of the district administrations. It would be desirable for Hans Becher to come here at the end of May to work in intelligence. I request your opinion about whether we might be able to start publishing an anti-Fascist democratic newspaper about 2 weeks after the organization of the city administration. For the preparation of the newspaper and the press I need Comrade Wendt. A series of leading comrades have come out of prison. I will send on the list.

Ulbricht.
Politicial Administration of the I. Byelorussian Front

**Wilhelm Hausenstein, 1882–1957**  *Tutzing*
For two weeks I have been reading Hermann Grimm's Goethe biography. A strong, a very strong impression. I am ashamed to have come to this book so late. I will copy out some extracts over the next few days. Today just this: 1. The analysis of the relationship between Goethe and Frau von Stein seems inadequate to me, however sophisticated. I have a sense that he has missed the real thread. The real one: I don't mean the physical, certainly not the issue of the physical alone, but the absence (relative absence) of any *intensity* in the idea of the relationship – the intensity of the *real*, in fact.

2. Grimm's Protestantism restricts his judgement. The magnificent perspective on the Roman 'world', on the history of Rome, leads noticeably and annoyingly to the inadequacy of the idea of Rome in the nineteenth century. The Protestant is incapable of feeling the *reality* of *spiritual* Rome in the nineteenth century.

But these are also my only objections to the first volume and the beginning of the second, unless it is the tangible, drastic overestimation of Luther, whom Grimm places on a level far beyond what this character deserves. But apart from that: what a biography!

A subject for a book that should *soon* be written by a skilled practitioner: 'Goethe and the Germans'. It would need to make clear how *little* an effect Goethe has had on the Germans. Today he has no public existence at all – because the fact that academic lectures are still given about him does not by any means constitute an existence!

In France: Corneille, Racine and others have defined the style of the national language and way of thinking *until the present day*. Theatre, parliament, national assembly: in France one lives on the *grand siècle*. In its public expressions, in the mental attitude of the nation Germany does *not* live on Goethe at all: *it is as if he had never existed, never written*.

*

**Martin Hauser, sergeant in the British army, b. 1913**    *near Trieste*
10.30 p.m. As I write these lines, I hear rifle fire outside, the reports of fireworks, the singing of the crowd of people surging through the narrow streets of this village very near Trieste. It is night, and red, green and white lights shine in through the windows, from fireworks that stand out against the dark sky and compete for a moment with the brilliance of the stars. The world is celebrating the end of the war in Europe.

I am sitting here in the garage of a small New Zealand unit. It was announced on the radio a few minutes ago that the Germans have surrendered, that Churchill will address the British people tonight, that tomorrow will be the 'day of victory' – Victory in Europe.

I hold a glass of beer in my hand, look into the transparent yellow liquid, and my thoughts wander. So this is the end. Is this what peace looks like? Is this what it feels like? Here we sit, a group of men who left their homes and families a long time ago, who freed themselves from the routine of daily life in the past to assure their lives in the future. Here we sit, happy to have got through these years full of danger and horror sound of limb and mind. But where is the joy, the enthusiasm that can be expected of us? Not a bit of it – a smile here, a chuckle there, a joke as we drink our beer. Time passes with an exchange of memories – memories of past times, serious struggles, friends who have fallen. The past weighs heavily on everyone. We feel their pressure. I feel it too. For five years, eight months and five days the Furies of war raged over Europe and Africa, millions died, millions suffered, cities were devastated, industries and agriculture destroyed, death was sown in the form of bombs and mines over fields and forests. People's energies and intellectual creativity are concentrated primarily on ways of destroying the civilization of the twentieth century – in so far as one could even talk about civilization. For over five years physical and intellectual servitude prevailed over the European continent, the struggle for freedom and justice was identical with the danger of an agonizing death.

And yet there are two sides to everything – even war. It encouraged collaboration between individuals and nations, it made taking care of others an absolute prerequisite and created an awareness of the necessity of engaging with the fate and needs of our neighbour nations. It put us in contact with people from a great variety of countries, with the greatest variety of political or religious views. It helped to extend the perspective and achieve a clearer understanding of things playing out on the stage of world history. On my personal balance sheet are the loss of six of the most precious years of my life and the breakdown of my marriage. By way of compensation I have the awareness of fulfilling my duty as a Jewish soldier to the Jewish people by helping people and setting communities back on their feet.

It's almost midnight. I go on sitting and writing, because I'm not in a position to lie down. I had often wondered: 'How will you react when the end is there? Enthusiasm? Emotion? Relief? Apathy?' In fact it is a mixture of the last two feelings – the anticlimax after all the tension. Rockets are still going up outside, and rifle fire going off. For the last time?

**Gerhard Hessel, b. 1912**     *Bad Kreuznach prisoner-of-war camp*
Kreuznach camp. Hardly a glorious chapter. Either for the Americans or for the German army. And certainly not for me. Point zero had been reached, now I was right at the bottom. Behind barbed wire. There is no complaining here. It's how things were. The setting was well chosen, a shallow, endless dip, the Nahetal. Not a tree, not a bush, not a roof, not a tent. Constant rain from above, moisture seeping from below. Lying down? Inadvisable, many didn't get up again. So we

slept standing, crouching. No shortage of water, it's easy to transport and runs straight out of the hose. But hunger. There were no supplies, often for days, then once a day, at random times and uncooked. I don't want to talk about the latrines, many people fell in, exhausted. There was nothing left to shit. Then came the diarrhoea. Anyone who hasn't experienced that doesn't understand anything. And as there were no medical supplies – and where would they have come from? – this was the end. Into the mass grave, with lime on top of you. Morning after morning the same. No more '...for Führer and Fatherland'. Bloody death isn't as honourable as that. Where is the respect? Just a good thing that the Second World War has given us no war memorials.

Days, days, weeks, weeks. April, May, June... What does time mean? Horror? Forget it. The Yanks were simply overtaxed, they hadn't reckoned on that. In the upper echelons a misapprehension, a wrong decision, cramming crowds like that into such a small space could only go wrong. They should have been allowed to run away. They were no longer anything to be afraid of. That's the crux, fear echoes on. And then the administration, pure madness. This mash of humanity, the last sludge of a war that has come to an end needed – 'needed?' – to be sorted, registered, given decent papers and released. In the summer of '45 Kreuznach was divided up, with a shift of population to the disimprisonment camp in Babenhausen.

But before I get there I want to remember my teacher, he did me proud. A private from Greiz, an elderly chap, first name 'Willi', in peacetime – when was that? – a bus driver in Greiz. An ascetic, the only member of that species of human being that I have ever met. A level-six mountain-climber, tough and resolved not to give up. He taught me to throw away my last bit of supplies, that handful given after a hungry day: 'Tread it into the dirt. You don't need it!' He taught me to concentrate. Far on the horizon, outside the camp, there was a box tree and we concentrated on it – that is, I learned to concentrate for the first time. It wasn't that hard because we didn't have any needs, you just have to forget them.

You also have to forget what's going on around you. That was harder in the chaos of the crowd. Perceiving nothing, even forgetting perception, reducing yourself to your animal functions. So we crouched there for hours, days, with a view of the box tree, forgetting even time. Perhaps – I wonder if that wasn't the greatest degree of freedom that I have ever enjoyed.

I look back at Kreuznach without rancour. A lesson in the history of lost wars on the loser's side. A sideways glance at humanity in the raw, not exactly encouraging for God's own image. And something from my own experience: '...a shadow falls from every life into other lives, and the heavy are bound to the light as they are to air and earth'.

### Elfie Walther, b. 1928        *(Sandbostel concentration camp)*
They are dying before our eyes. There isn't much we can do. When we get there in the morning we have to clear away the dirt. There's a pile by almost every bed, and everywhere we find pools of urine, but we aren't allowed to let on. They think we're nurses.

Once we're finished and have washed everything with Lysol, it all starts over again.

More and more patients are coming in. There are 6 barracks in our complex. They're all overcrowded. 600 new ones are supposed to be coming in today. But yesterday and today over 100 people died.

Over all – a British soldier told me – there are about 3,000 people in the camp.

The work is hard and strenuous. My legs and hands are swollen from walking and carrying pots around.

The patients don't want the porridge any more. When we appear in the doorway with the pots, they throw cups at us.

They want bread. I can understand that! But there isn't any yet. The British have a lot of difficulty getting hold of it.

Our mental state is much worse than our physical state. We will probably never rid ourselves of these impressions. What we're going through here can't be put into words.

Today the patients were washed. We didn't get round to it for the first few days. Now they're all naked in their beds, and some of them have already cheered up a little, they're even jumping around in the room.

I think they've only just worked out that they've been liberated from the Germans.

In the evening, I have a bad sore throat. The British doctor examined me. Angina, he says. There's nothing they can do about it. There's hardly any medicine. At least, we're not getting any. Some of us are wearing these funny louse-caps. A lot of us are lying on sacks of straw with fever and diarrhoea. We have to take on their work as well as our own.

This afternoon I was close to despair. Inge has fallen ill as well, and I'm faced with the work in our barracks all on my own. As everything's going a lot more slowly now, some patients are getting a bit aggressive, and it's been making me really scared. Thank God there's a room full of nice, educated people. They come from Holland and Belgium. Some of them are doctors, and there's also a lawyer who's always comforting us and giving us words of encouragement.

Just imagine: this man, to whom our people have done so much, is giving us encouragement! He says what we're doing here is quite wonderful. But it's a disgrace to make people who are basically children sort out things that grown-ups have done.

This man only made one remark against the German occupying forces in Holland. For that he was sent to the concentration camp.

Instead of the usual barley soup we've just been given a tin of lard and a bit of bread. Six girls were able to share a tin and a loaf of bread. It was really delicious. There was coffee, too. We're really full again, and the coffee is warming. It has kept our spirits up for a few days.

*

**Ray T. Matheny, American prisoner of war, b. 1925**

*Braunau am Inn*

Late in the afternoon May 7th we were marched a short distance south of Braunau to Ranshofen where a new aluminum factory was to be our billet. This facility was intended to serve as our shelter until transportation home could be arranged. Not everyone was rounded up and taken to the factory at the same time, and patrols were sent out to bring in all of the men. A few men had been busy raiding the local museum, and one man had taken a jewel-encrusted sword while another had a diamond broach [*sic*] set in silver. One of our men had gone into the house where Adolf Hitler had been born, which had been made into a national shrine housing memorabilia of Hitler and his rise to power. He had taken a gold plaque with a swastika on it that was inscribed: 'To Adolf Hitler from Admiral Karl Doenitz [*sic*].' These items were all kept secret and presumably taken to the United States when the ex-Kriegies [POWs] were sent home.

At the aluminum factory, we found a place for our blankets so we could bed down for the night. The Third Corps of Engineers' cooks brought in cases of '10-in-1' field rations for us to eat. These rations included cans of concentrated egg yolks and sausage, ham, and beef, designed to mix with other foods such as potatoes. Some men ate whole cans of these concentrated foods but in a few hours they were sick. Their digestive systems were unable to handle these rich foods after their long diet of meagre food. [...]

Trucks arrived and took us to Pocking Field, a German–Hungarian airfield 25 kilometers northeast of Braunau. [...] The barracks and facilities would accommodate hundreds of men at this airbase. The Major told us we would spend a few days here until air transportation arrived to take us to our next stop on our way home. We were turned loose at the airfield early in the afternoon [...]. I immediately headed to the flight line to have a look at the German airplanes. There were several Heinkel 111s, Junker 88s, Messerschmitt 109s, a Messerschmitt 107, Focke-Wulf 190s, and a small airplane used as a trainer. One Kriegie got a Ju-88 started and was taxiing around the field. He got careless and ran into a Heinkel 111, sending a propeller through a wing. Fortunately it did not catch on fire. I found a Me-109G that had not been spiked with an explosive charge. Many of the airplanes had been sabotaged by placing a small explosive device in the magneto rendering the ignition system inoperative.

The Me-109 was fascinating to me for many reasons. I admired its performance as a high altitude fighter and its speed. I suppose the fact that I had fought a duel with the pilot of one of these on my last combat flight, also contributed to my respect for this aircraft.

In a nearby hangar I found a hand crank for the engine, and I found the master electrical switch right where the British Intelligence reports said it would be.

A small amount of fuel in the tanks made me eager to get it started. I stood on the right wing root, inserted the crank into its receptacle, and cranked the starter flywheel up to a high whine. Then I leapt into the cockpit and pulled the T-handle to engage the starter. It took two tries to get the engine started, because the hand crank is on the right side of the fuselage, and entry to the cockpit was on the left side. I crawled over the engine cowl in front of the cockpit to get inside to work the controls.

The engine sounded great as it rumbled to life, but there wasn't much fuel. I did not know how to fly the plane, so I ran the engine for five minutes or so, and then I pulled the control stick full back which put the elevators up to keep the tail down. Next, I lashed the stick in place with the safety belt, jumped out on the left wing, and opened the throttle. The engine roared and the propeller blast was powerful – but only for a moment – then the engine quit. It had run out of fuel – what a disappointment. My plan was to run the engine at high power and let it blow up from over heating, thereby destroying another enemy fighter.

Harold Brown [German text has Jerry Smiley – translator's note] motioned me over to a hangar where he had found spare parts for the Nazi planes. Among these parts were American BG spark plugs and Leece-Neville carbon-pile voltage regulators along with many other things made in America. The presence of these American-made spare parts infuriated us. We called over other men to witness that American airplane parts were being used on German airplanes.

*

**Norman Kirby, British sergeant, b. 1913**                    *Lüneburg*
                                                               *Heath–Flensburg*

It was a sparkling spring day, but apart from the bright May sunshine this unforgettable day started as so many other days of Army life – with a host of unexciting chores. After tidying my bed space in the tent, taking two pairs of boots to the cobbler, giving the daily strength return to the Camp Sergeant Major and packing my small kit, I reported for duty soon after dawn at the given map reference on Lüneburg Heath.

Punctually at the appointed time I was met by two British officers in a jeep. One of them was Major O'Brien and the other turned out to be an observer from the BBC, Chester Wilmot. Giving them my smartest salute I climbed into the jeep. We were driven across the bumpy heath and through the outskirts of the town of Lüneburg to the airfield where an Anson was already waiting for us as we pulled up. Excitement took complete possession of me as I boarded the plane on this, my very first flight – air travel had not yet become the everyday experience it is now. We were strapped into our seats, the small iron ladder was drawn up into the plane, the door was shut, and with a roar of engines we slid along the runway towards that warm blue sky. Soon Germany lay neat and geometrical far below us. Where were the dust and the potholes, the wreckage of the marshalling yards, the endless, untidy, heartbreaking processions of displaced persons in that now over-simplified landscape? I gazed down upon the sunlit Elbe, gliding in a sinuous ribbon through a bright patchwork of green and yellow fields; in the distance rose the few remaining chimneys of Hamburg. Later the Kiel Canal cut a straight line across the view. Now and again the plane bumped up or dropped down as it hit an air pocket. I looked at Major O'Brien for some hint of information about the object of our journey. Drawing from his pocket a large envelope he said to me: 'This, my boy, is the end of the war.' [...]

This day was to signal the end of all hostilities in the west. I was elated at the prospect of final surrender, which would at least bring peace throughout Europe; I felt like singing.

But what was a mere sergeant doing on this vital mission? Major O'Brien caught my look of inquiry.

'You speak German, don't you, Sergeant?'

'Yes, Sir.'

'Well then.'

I thought, 'What is that supposed to mean?' and imagined having to play the usual boring part of standing guard or telling my two superior officers where the cloakrooms were. I could not have been more mistaken. Major O'Brien had been entrusted with the task of delivering a letter containing the final surrender terms into the hands of Field Marshal Keitel, Supreme Head of the German Armed Forces, and I was to be the interpreter. The BBC reporter was to be introduced as an army captain, assistant to the major.

A large German aerodrome hove in sight with planes bearing the swastika standing in neat rows round the edges of the field. These, we learned, were all that remained of Goering's mighty Luftwaffe. I remembered having seen other planes with those same markings littering the fields of Kent. I had memories too of the planes which kept Londoners awake during the long nights of the Blitz. The Anson veered over and twice circled the airfield before landing. Owing to some misunderstanding there was no one to meet the delegates from Field Marshal Montgomery's Tactical Headquarters, but a German general, General Blaskowitz, who happened to be on the spot, came towards us and announced:

'I know of no such mission.'

He did, however, volunteer to drive the party to the OKW (*Oberkommando der Wehrmacht*, the High Command of the German Armed Forces) in his car.

In the streets of Flensburg, crowded with German soldiers, sailors, airmen and civilians, the three British uniforms in the open-top car caused a great stir. The soldiers in that mass of people were a remnant of the retreating armies that had escaped capture on the Russian Front. They looked demoralised and abandoned, gaunt and grey-faced: many were unshaven and unshod, with bare feet poking through strips of rag. Some wore long tattered coats and dirty, frayed trousers – a scene reminiscent of the retreat from Moscow. Arms raised stiffly in Nazi salutes greeted the general all along the road, but the events of that day would bring about the end of such demonstrations. Major O'Brien whispered:

'Don't get big ideas, Sergeant – they're not saluting you. It's the swastika on the bonnet.'

From that day it would be a punishable offence to raise the arm in a '*Sieg Heil*' salute or to display the Nazi flag in public.

The German Supreme Headquarters was located in a Naval School where steel-helmeted sentries guarded the entrances and patrolled the grounds, a duty which, in a matter of minutes, was to lose its point. As we stepped out of the car there was a general clicking of heels, like hundreds of castanets, and a flutter of Nazi salutes. Chester Wilmot and I both caught a glimpse of Field Marshal Keitel standing at an upstairs bay window, before we were ushered into the building. A long passage lay before us. More helmeted sentries with rifles slung and hand-grenades wedged in their belts were giving more Nazi salutes outside office doors. Two civilian visitors were having their identity checked in the all-too-familiar way. At the end of the corridor our party was shown into a small barely furnished room crammed with German officers. As we entered we were asked to sit down and one of them rose to his feet and took up his position, legs astride, with his back to the door. We were asked to explain the purpose of our visit.

'Tell them,' said Major O'Brien to me.

In quivering German, but struggling to steady my voice, I explained that the major and the captain his assistant had come from Field Marshal Montgomery's Headquarters with a copy of the final terms of surrender. Major O'Brien carried the document and demanded to place it in the hands of Field Marshal Keitel. They appeared not to believe us. Major Buchs who was the spokesman for the Germans said in a quiet, measured voice:

'This message comes as a surprise.'

It was then that I noticed, through the high window opposite to where I was sitting, the tip of a bayonet passing at intervals backwards and forwards. They had placed a guard on the room. We were kept waiting what seemed a very long time and Major O'Brien's impatience with his treatment had to be translated into firmer German. I shall always remember that dingy room, where a solemn picture of Adolf Hitler was jostled by lighter works of art including a humorous study of some little boys fishing.

Major Buchs objected that we could not see Field Marshal Keitel as he had just gone out. The news came as a shock to us: the urgent message required the instant delivery by hand of the surrender terms and had we not just seen Field Marshal Keitel? There was something not quite straightforward about this reception. We protested: did they not realise the importance of our mission? I repeated:

'We insist that we have come from Field Marshal Montgomery's Headquarters with the requested copy of the final terms of surrender.'

At this moment the proceedings were interrupted by a sharp rap on the door. A German orderly, bowing stiffly from the waist, announced *Mittagessen*.

'It is time for lunch,' declared Major Buchs, shelving any further decision.

Major O'Brien held firm:

'My instructions from General Eisenhower are to place this letter in the hands of Field Marshal Keitel.'

'But that is impossible if he is not here,' replied the major.

There was nothing to be done about that and presumably the business of checking our credentials was proceeding somewhere in the background. All sorts of unpleasant thoughts were beginning to stir in my mind and I could sense that my companions shared my un-easiness. While we were waiting in the room we heard gangs of soldiers return from their morning's work singing staccato marching songs. Then came a ray of hope in the form of a telephone message from Tac with instructions to collect Seyss-Inquart, the infamous Gauleiter (Provincial Governor) of Holland, and bring him back in the same plane with us.

Shortly after this two staff cars (the only Mercedes Benzes left in Germany, according to Major Buchs) drew up outside the main entrance and we were invited to travel in them to lunch. Major O'Brien and Chester Wilmot took their seats in the rear car while I sat in British isolation in the leading car. Beside the driver sat the German major and, standing stiffly next to me in the back of the open Mercedes, a German guard with steel helmet concealing all of his face but his lower jaw, waved traffic to one side with a white baton. This white stick with a red disc at one end of it gave us priority. Nazi salutes and clicking heels greeted our passage through the town as, with siren screaming, we swept into the approach to the German Officers' Mess down by the water's edge. It was here that I saw Denmark for the first time. Unfortunately this last country to be liberated by the armies of the West was across the water, inaccessible yet so tantalisingly near.

On arrival at the officers' mess I waited for the other car containing my only two allies in a hostile Germany. Looking across the lake I thought, 'After they've shot us I suppose that is where they'll dump the bodies.' I was shaken out of this dispiriting reverie when, to my relief, Major O'Brien and Chester Wilmot came at last and went into the Mess. I waited outside. A few moments later Major O'Brien reappeared and said:

'Come on in, Sergeant.'

'I can't, Sir,' I answered.

'Why not?'

'I'm only a sergeant.'

'Well, they're only Nazis.'

So I went in, to be confronted by an assembly of German officers of all ranks, from the lowest to the highest.

The lunch in the Officers' Mess, where the waiters seemed petrified whenever an order was given, consisted of thick barley soup resembling dirty rice pudding, one slice of black bread and a glass of wine. The latter was excellent and proved to be the one redeeming feature of the meal. With ambiguous modesty my German neighbour at the table (a brigadier) apologised:

'You see to what Germany has been reduced when the leaders of the people have to eat such filth. But never mind. We did save this good wine with which to celebrate our victory. Ha! Ha!'

This sarcastic reference to their defeat was surprising on the lips of a high-ranking German officer before the publication of the surrender terms.

When the meal was over an orderly burst into the room and, jumping to attention with clicking heels, breathlessly delivered his message to the senior officer present.

'Field Marshal Keitel awaits the British representatives.'

We again climbed into the staff cars and drove back to Field Marshal Keitel's office in the OKW. This proved to be an unpretentious room overlooking the main entrance from where we had caught our first glimpse of Keitel. Clerks were bustling about in what appeared to be an undisciplined and undignified muddle in the small anteroom from which we were ushered into the presence of Keitel himself. We had to edge our way between an obtruding filing cabinet and a dishevelled girl typist who, with hair falling over her machine, was tapping out a training programme for the German Army for the year 1947. Training for what? The next war? And what German Army?

As the narrow door leading into Keitel's room swung open I was still wrestling mentally with the ordeal of having to translate military jargon into German. Suppose he rejected the terms! That would be awkward. All sorts of embarrassing possibilities suggested themselves, but it was too late. We were already over the threshold and the august figures of Keitel and his Chief of Staff stood silhouetted against the window. That is how I shall always remember them. There was a tense moment of deathly silence. Of course! They were waiting for the interpreter to speak first! We walked up to the field marshal's desk and, with a brisk salute, I took the plunge by introducing Major O'Brien the Liaison Officer, and the captain, his assistant, and was struck by the weighty climax to which my words built up when spoken in the German order:

'Herr Feld Marschall may I present to you Major O'Brien who, from Field Marshal Montgomery's Headquarters, on behalf of General Eisenhower, Supreme Commander of the Allied Forces in Europe, has brought the final terms of surrender of German Armed Forces on land, on sea and in the air.'

I was even more amazed to think that it was my voice which had actually made this solemn announcement of the war's end to the Supreme Head of the German Wehrmacht. Field Marshal Keitel, an imposing figure in those drab surroundings, opened the letter which the LO presented to him and with a face like granite replied:

'Thank you for this document containing the text of the surrender terms. I am already acquainted with those terms through General Jodl, who has communicated with me from General Eisenhower's Headquarters, whither I despatched him this morning, but I require and will keep this letter as security.'

When people speak English or French you know what they are saying while they are saying it. When people are speaking in German you don't know what they are saying until after they have finished. Field Marshal Keitel's reply went something like this:

'I you, for this surrendertermscontainingrequireassecuritydocument the message of which has been communicated to me from General Eisenhower's Headquarters by the thitherdespatched General Jodl this morning, thank.'

Waiting desperately for the final verb (suppose it had been 'curse' or 'defy' or 'challenge'?) which was to make sense of what seemed an endless sentence, I turned half-left in military style to the liaison officer and translated the Field Marshal's words by simply saying:

'He said "Thank you".'

Major O'Brien's raised eyebrows seemed to imply, 'Did he really?'

In conclusion Keitel said:

'And thank Field Marshal Montgomery for the promptitude with which he has sent you.'

He grasped his baton and gave a smart salute by holding it obliquely across his chest. The monocle in his eye wobbled with this sudden movement of his body. We too saluted, in less spectacular fashion, turned right-about and walked out of the room.

Our next duty was to find Seyss-Inquart. He must have been tipped off, because he had made his getaway, and our inquiries only met with negative response. He could not be found. He was, however, picked up later on the road by the Canadian Army, who in order to discourage any further absconding took away his false teeth. It was our suspicion that Admiral Doenitz had also deliberately made himself scarce, leaving Field Marshal Keitel in charge, but he did not get very far either and all were eventually brought to trial at Nürnberg.

In the course of our inquiries we learned a few facts about the last days of Hitler's Headquarters. The German colonel whom we pumped, though he had seen Adolf Hitler himself as late as 20 April, could give no facts about the Führer's death: he had only heard of it over the wireless. Shortly after this, on about 23 April, OKW moved from Berlin to Flensburg. Their convoy was not attacked during this move, which took place both in daylight and at night. The colonel had watched Allied planes attack another convoy acting as a decoy, but theirs arrived unscathed. We asked if Himmler were at Flensburg. He said, 'Perhaps.' He volunteered the already stale information that Goering had been taken prisoner by the Americans in the south, and that Goebbels as well as Hitler had died.

In the middle of our rather one-sided conversation, which had resolved itself into a political quiz, the German liaison officer returned with the dubious information that unfortunately Seyss-Inquart had left for Field Marshal Montgomery's Headquarters by car.

As our small party of three emerged from OKW, walked down the front steps and climbed into the Mercedes Benz which was to take us to the airfield, German officers lined up with their cameras and took photographs.

Only when the Anson roared up towards the blue again did I sink back in delicious relaxation.

*

**Thea Sternheim, 1883–1971**                                      *Paris*
The end of the slaughter in Europe. For how long? I feel as if I'm recovering from a long illness. My legs dangle like rubber hoses. But never has my hope on earth been smaller than it is today. [...]

People promenade, sing, sweat, most faces express a joy unseen for a long time, often with an almost animal quality. I recognize clearly all kinds of animal physiognomies: birds, cats, pigs.

**Marguerite Duras, 1914–96**                                      *Paris*
The Germans are what frightened me most in my life. Not the tigers, devils or snakes of childhood, or death, it was the Germans that frightened me most. I still dream regularly about them. And in my dreams I am always guilty. The Germans are the eternal victors. It is always the same scenario: I am part of the Resistance and am betrayed. In my dreams the Germans return to Paris after fifty years.

I can't even remember writing *La Douleur*. The book was published a decade ago – I had completely forgotten it, and found the manuscript by chance at my house in the country. It contains these words: 'If one makes a German fate from the Nazi horrors, one limits the people of Bergen-Belsen to the dimensions of a regional figure. The only response to this crime is to turn it into a crime that belongs to everyone. Likewise the idea of equality, of fraternity.' When I read these texts again after forty years I fell ill and needed treatment. I couldn't bear to be reminded of them. I must have written them immediately after the war, but probably not until 1946. In 1945 I would not have been capable of it.

## Paul Valéry, 1871–1945                                      (*Paris*)
League of Nations: 'Société des Nations'. Even the name is an absurdity. Because one would have to start with the very term *Nation* (in the political and legal sense).

*Nation* means difference, opposition, competition, jealousy etc. *of conventional* or *historical origin* (which amounts to the same thing, because that which exists *because of the past*, which *exists as a conventional value* of *the disappeared* – just as inheritance law exists – is traditional and contestable). There are also genuine values of the past, which are unconscious, *unlearned*, but *acquired*. […]

Of the errors of nations. Who will dare to illuminate them? Voltaire had a very strong sense of them – and since then they have grown unhindered – they have assumed power.

No government can try to 're-educate' the nation – certainly no democratic one. Regardless of what its name might be – every regime is in these terms 'democratic' – and thus subject to the moment.

Our great failures have their source in the incapacity to have longer-term foresight – and to act according to that foresight at the cost of the comfort of the moment. (Irreplaceability) – It is clear that it happens at the cost of momentary freedom, if one does something that nothing requires in the moment – It is clear that 'Après moi le déluge' is not just a monarchical phrase.

'To be satisfied with little' is also a justification for greed and hence for everything unkempt and dirty – a shabby virtue.

This kind of parsimony is an aberration. Behind it there lies a fear of the future, of the next day, so people hoard, but at the same time refuse real foresight. […]

No people in Europe is believed to have had the qualities necessary to assert itself and create a common and viable organization. Not since the Romans.

Europe is at the end of its career. See map. 1945–1815 = 130. Religious unity is missing – 3 conflicting Christian religions. Fateful role of the 'nations' – no advantages of his historical-political formation given clearly demonstrated dangers. Absurd personifications.

### Albert Schweitzer, 1875–1965                         (*Lambarene*)

We receive the news of the end of the war in Europe on Monday, 7 May, at around midday. As I sit at my table after dinner preparing urgent letters which are to be brought to the sea-bound river steamer at two o'clock, a white patient appears at my window. He has brought his radio with him. He calls to me that according to German reports being passed on by the Leopoldville radio station in the Belgian Congo, a ceasefire is to be concluded on water and land. But I have no choice but to go on sitting at the table to deal with the letters that have to be sent straight away. Then I have to go down to the hospital, where the cardiac patients and others are due to be treated at two o'clock. In the course of the afternoon the bell rings and the gathering residents of the hospital are informed that the war is over. Later, in spite of my great fatigue, I have to drag myself to the plantation to see what work is being done there.

It's only in the evening that I come to my senses and am able to try to imagine what the end of hostilities in Europe means, and what the many people must be feeling who are able to experience their first night in years without fear of threatened bombing. While outside in the dark the palms rustle quietly, I take the little book of the sayings of Lao Tzu, the great Chinese thinker of the sixth century BC, off the shelf and read his gripping words on war and victory.

'Weapons are tools of evil, not tools for the noble man. He uses them only in dire necessity… Calm and peace are the highest qualities for him. He is victorious, but takes no pleasure in it. Anyone who delighted in it would be delighting in the murder of human beings… At the victory celebration the leader should take his place after the custom of the funeral service. The killing of people in large numbers should be mourned with tears of compassion. Therefore he who wins in battle should weep as if at a funeral.'

**Ludwig Marcuse, 1894–1971**                                  *(Beverly Hills)*
A Leipzig doorman stands in the street amidst the rubble and shouts, 'We have been lied to and betrayed.' A Leipzig professor apologizes: 'We have nothing to do with it.' By 'with it' he means the past twelve years. Did they all have nothing to do 'with it'? [...]

But I am passionately opposed to the term that could come from the *Malleus Maleficarum* [*Hammer of the Witches* – an anti-witchcraft document from the fifteenth century – translator's note]: collective guilt. It is the product of a collective delusion. It is the expression of a method of Hitler's, the practice of sheer inhumanity; ignoring the individual and thinking only in groups. Moral judgement concerning what has happened in Germany can be captured in a single sentence. But moral judgement about 'The German people', about eighty million people, cannot consist of a single sentence. A girl who has learned credulously about Hitler at her school desk is to be judged differently from an elderly professor who has lived incredulously under Hitler. No list of horrors should make us as unresponsive to the individual as was German power, recently deceased.

**Wilhelm Hausenstein, 1882–1957**                                  *Tutzing*
It is horrific, no, shocking to see that disaster causes no kind of moral change in people. Admittedly I observe this only in the narrow sector that I am able to see (it is impossible to go beyond the village boundaries, even the forest behind the house is a kind of Wild West, where suspicious figures roam, and leaving the village is strictly forbidden). But we must sadly assume that things are very similar elsewhere: events have exerted *no transforming force* on people's emotions – apart from the few who didn't want to see a complete collapse and Jews begging from house to house. *What in God's name are people still waiting for?* They weep if you (for the first time) take their houses away to billet officers and soldiers in them; that is: they weep over the loss of their traditional comforts, but they make no connection, no connection at all, with the idea of the punishment that every German must endure (every German, and I'm really not excluding myself). If only the Church would speak out at last! If only they wanted to send out preachers like Savonarola! He has always horrified me, but now the time has truly

come for him and his kind! Meanwhile, over the past few years the Church has kept far too quiet – quiet both deep and wide, because *one* Count Galen in the end merely demonstrated the *exception*.

Today people creep their way around the three flags of the occupation, just as they crept their way around the red banner with the black spider in the white field: submissive as fellaheen – and they have already worked out how to do business with the new situation. I am just waiting for the moment when food is reserved only for buyers with foreign currency, by shopkeepers and farmers. It is understandable of course when they speculate; not understandable if it is their *only* concern.

When Margot came here (a good twenty–five years ago now), she said impulsively to me: 'I wouldn't be at all surprised if all of a sudden all women took their clothes off in the street, all men walked on their hands, and children threw stones at everyone who didn't do the same.' The vision of the state of the German 'soul' seemed absurd to me at the time; since then I've understood that an uncorrupted eye, from outside, really saw the German condition; what was once a potential has become a horrific reality. Reality not in the literal sense but far beyond that single aspect: the whole and the individual 'moral insanity' identified with the name 'Hitler' was unfortunately more, infinitely more than the gruesome Expressionist farce that haunted Margot's perception in such an immediately frightening way. That 'moral insanity' that became Hitler's actual climate, his greenhouse – that 'moral insanity' is by no means removed by the horrific evidence of the disaster; it goes on working, it remains the people's state of mind.

What else can the heavens allow, so that this terrible situation may change?

The occupation is surrounded by a German public that still wore the party insignia yesterday, or bowed and scraped before 'the party'. The occupation doesn't notice.

*

**Alexander Werth, 1901–69**                                    (*Moscow*)

The German Wehrmacht surrendered on 7 May. Marshal Zhukov signed for the Russian side; for the Soviets the surrender in Rheims was only a prelude, to which merely a younger officer had been sent. On 8 May, when Churchill announced the end of the war in a radio broadcast, Radio Moscow calmly transmitted a children's hour programme with a pretty story about two rabbits and a bird. In Russia the end of the war was not announced until the morning of 9 May. The reason why Victory Day was held in the Soviet Union a day later than it was in the West was that Prague had not yet been liberated. The western Allies thought that was a trivial detail, but the Russians didn't.

9 May became an unforgettable day for Moscow. The spontaneous joy of the 2 or 3 million people who gathered in Red Square that evening, processed down Gorky Street and streamed along the banks of the Moskva, was deeper than I have ever experienced it in that city. People were dancing and singing in the streets. Soldiers and officers were hugged and kissed. People stood in a dense crowd outside the American Embassy, chanting, 'Long live Roosevelt!', even though the President had died a month before. (Outside the British Embassy which, being on the opposite shore of the Moskva, was far from the actual scene of the demonstrations of joy, there were only a few sympathy demonstrations.) I had never seen anything like it in Moscow. The firework display set off that evening was the biggest I have ever seen.

**Ilya Krichevsky, Red Army soldier, b. 1907**                *Berlin*

My command was coming to an end. In the evening I had to make my way back to the editorial office that was now stationed in a suburb of Berlin.

The day was springlike, sunny. Light clouds that looked as if they had been dabbed there with watercolours drifted slowly across the sky. An actual encampment clamoured in front of the Reichstag. Soldiers shaved in the street, in front of mirrors that had somehow been set up on the armour of combat vehicles.

I set off on an expedition through the city and kept a lookout for telling images. A member of the military painted a study on canvas, using a car chassis as an easel. I stepped closer: was he an acquaintance? During those days I met a lot of people with whom fate had thrown me together at various times during the war. Gradually it even started to seem to me as if all the roads of the front had led to Berlin. But I didn't know this man. In my thoughts I wished him success in his artwork, then I walked on.

I had long been fascinated by the Brandenburg Gate. I walked to Unter den Linden. From this straight avenue, planted with linden trees, the gate looked more interesting. The bronze quadriga that had been under fire was now crowned with the red banner of our home, which fluttered in the wind and the sun. The horses, mutilated by a grenade, seemed to be stopping just before the abyss.

How many times before the war had I seen photographs of his construction? In the pictures it looked solemn and monumental. Perhaps a shot fired through one of the columns or something else had spoiled the picture, but the gate didn't look majestic to me as I drew it.

At its other end, Unter den Linden reached a square in which the Berlin Palace stood. In front of the building was a pompous monument to Wilhelm I. The Kaiser was surrounded by various allegorical figures; among others I remember a woman striding along beside a man who was reining in his horse. The monument had been damaged by gunfire, and bits of the bronze rider lay around at the bottom of the plinth; I was startled by the dimensions of his huge, gloved hand.

In the middle of the square, on a pedestal, a Soviet traffic conductor stood. She waved her flags with brisk deftness. Perhaps she was one of the girls who had shown us the way through the rain and snow in the district of Kalinin. I watched her trim, familiar little figure and was cheered to the depths of my heart to see her here in the centre of Berlin. I couldn't resist the temptation, and drew this image that had appeared before me of the last day of life at the front, 8 May.

At sunset I went back to the editorial office. It was getting dark. An unusual silence still prevailed, and the evening, filled with the scent of young growth, was wonderful.

All of a sudden rockets shot into the air, one after the other. Fountains of coloured light dissolved in the sky, leaving dense trails of smoke. Cheerful little sparks danced around, promising a long-awaited peaceful life. I didn't know where the fireworks were coming from. Perhaps someone was celebrating the end of the war, as we had prematurely done the day before? It was the eve of the great day of celebration, Victory Day.

### Fritz J. Raddatz, b. 1931                                    *Berlin*

I wasn't unfamiliar with corpses, in May 1945 they were lying around in parks, at the roadside, often looted to such an extent that it was impossible to tell whether a body belonged to a shot soldier or a murdered civilian. Raped women with their mouths wide open, their gold teeth torn out by robbers. Some half charred in the ruins of burnt-down houses. It wasn't lilac, it wasn't hyacinths that gave this spring its sweet scent.

### A radio broadcast                                          *(Berlin)*
BBC report about Berlin in ruins
   4'20

Reminds him of photographs of the desert in Colorado/ Situation at Tempelhof airport/ On the way to Karlshorst he has hardly seen a house that hasn't been destroyed/ The population is apathetic/ The state of Berlin can be summed up in five words: 'Berlin has ceased to exist'/ The destruction of Berlin cannot be compared with that of any other German or Allied cities/ The situation is 'terribly im– and depressing'/ The number of the population living mostly in cellars is estimated at about 2 million, most of them children or old people.

Reporter: Thomas Cadett (Engl.)

*

### Field Marshal Wilhelm Keitel, 1882–1946                    *Berlin*
On 8.5, after Jodl's return on 7.5 from the Headquarters of General Eisenhower near Rheims, I flew to Berlin on a British transport plane on behalf of the Grand Admiral – as head of state and Senior Commander of the Wehrmacht – with the preliminary agreement drawn up by Jodl and Eisenhower's chief of staff. [...]

We first flew to Stendal. There a squadron of passenger planes had been assembled, under the leadership of the British Air Marshal and the commissioned representative of General Eisenhower. After a kind of lap of honour above Berlin we landed, myself last of all on my passenger plane, at Tempelhof airport. A Russian battalion of honour with a music corps received the British and American delegation; we were able to observe the ceremony from our landing spot a long way away. I had been assigned a Russian officer as escort – I was told he was General Zhukov's general quartermaster. He drove with me in the car, and the other cars of my entourage followed.

We drove via Belle-Alliance-Platz through the suburbs to Karlshorst, and were dropped at a small, cleared villa right next to the barracks of the school of pioneers and engineers. It was about 1.00 p.m. We were entirely on our own. Occasionally a reporter appeared, photographs were taken of us, sometimes we were visited by a Russian interpreter officer. He couldn't tell me when they would hold the act of signature of the surrender negotiations of which I had been handed a German printout at the airfield.

So I couldn't compare the preliminary agreement initialled by Jodl with the wording of this one, but I did notice some unimportant changes. The only crucial one was the addition of threatened punishments for troops who refused to lay down their arms and surrender at the time decreed. So I demanded that the interpreter officer provide a representative of General Zhukov, because I would not sign this addendum without reservations. A few hours later a Russian general appeared with the interpreter officer and listened to my objections; I think he was Zhukov's chief of staff.

I told him the reason for my objection, namely that I had no responsibility over the timely reception of our order to lay down weapons, so that the commanders of troops could feel justified in not complying with such an order. I demanded the inclusion of a clause to the effect that the surrender (capitulation) should only come into effect 24 hours after the order is given to the troops, before punitive measures can become effective. After about an hour the general came back, with the answer that General Zhukov agreed to a delay of 12 hours rather than 24. He also demanded my legitimation for perusal by the representatives of the victorious powers, saying I would have it back straight away. As to the appointed time for the signature he said 'towards evening'.

At about 3.00 p.m. Russian girls served us an ample breakfast. Our patience was put sorely to the test. At around 5.00 p.m. we were led to another house and served a snack, but nothing else happened. My certificate of authority was brought back to me, with the observation that everything was in order, but the time scheduled for the signature was apparently not known. At around 10.00 p.m. I became impatient and asked in my best official voice when the act of signature would be taking place; the answer came, in about an hour. Towards evening I had had our modest luggage fetched from the plane, because the return flight, which we had been told was a certainty, was no longer possible.

Shortly before midnight, when the surrender was due to take effect, my entourage and I were taken to the barracks mess. As midnight struck we entered the big hall through a big side door, and were led to the long table immediately facing us where three seats had been left free for me and my two companions. Our entourage had to stand behind us. The room was crammed full, and brightly lit by Klieg lights. One cross-wise row and three lengthwise rows were fully occupied. At the head of the cross-wise table was General Zhukov, and on either side of him the representatives of Britain and America.

When Zhukov's chief of staff presented me with the treaty in three languages I called upon him to enlighten me about the limitation of the punitive measures which I had demanded, and which did not yet appear in the text. He went back to Zhukov, and after a brief discussion with him, which I was able to observe, he came back to me to tell me that Zhukov expressly agreed that punitive measures would not be applied until a period of 12 hours had passed.

The solemn act began with a few introductory words then Zhukov asked me if I had read the surrender treaty. I replied, 'Yes.' The second question was whether I was ready to acknowledge this by signing. Again I replied with a loud 'Yes!' The signature ceremony began immediately, followed by the administration of the oath, after I had signed... Once this was concluded, I left the hall with my entourage, through the door just behind me.

Now we were to drive back to our little villa; in the afternoon a fully laden table was set up with cold food and various wines, and clean sleeping arrangements – a bed for everyone – had been set up in the other rooms. The interpreter officer announced a Russian general, saying that food would be served immediately after his arrival. After half an hour Zhukov's senior quartermaster arrived and asked us to take our seats; he asked us to accept his apology. The food was significantly more modest than we were accustomed to; but he asked us to make do. I couldn't help replying that we were not used to such luxury, and such an ample spread. He clearly didn't feel very flattered by this remark.

We had imagined that the cold starters laid upon the table would bring our last meal to an end. Then, when we were quite full, the hot food began with roast meat etc. Last of all there were frozen fresh strawberries, which I was served for the first time in my life. Plainly a sybaritic Berlin restaurant had supplied this supper, because the wines were also of German origin. After the meal the interpreter officer, who had clearly been acting as a deputy host, took his leave. We went to bed, after I had ordered the plane for our return flight at 6.00 a.m.

### Neue Zürcher Zeitung

Karlshorst, 10 May. (Exchange) While Keitel was placing his signature under the surrender document, his adjutant, Lieutenant Brehm, burst into tears. Keitel, who showed no sign of his awareness of the weighty consequences of the act, immediately turned to Brehm with astonishing harshness, in a tone that could clearly be heard: 'Stop that. After the war you can make a fortune by writing a book: "With Keitel in the Russian Prisoner-of-war Camp".'

**Yakov Makarenko, author**          *Tempelhof airport, Berlin*
A white flag flew over the enormous airport building. It was a sunny day. At two o'clock two Douglas planes appeared in the sky over Berlin. They flew in a circle by way of greeting and then landed. In the first plane was the British Air Marshal Tedder, in the second the American General Spaatz, in the third the French General de Lattre de Tassigny. Then another plane landed with Field Marshal Keitel on board. No one shook his hand. The victors met in silence with the

defeated parties, and that is the language of history. They drove to Karlshorst to sign Germany's surrender.

**Georgy Zhukov, Soviet general, 1896–1974**        *Karlshorst, Berlin*
On the early morning of 8 May Vyshinsky arrived by plane in Berlin. He brought all the documents required for Germany's surrender and informed me of who was to represent Allied Supreme Command.

At almost the same time journalists, reporters and photo-journalists of the world's big newspapers and magazines met in Berlin to report on the historic moment, as the defeat of Fascist Germany was given a legal anchorage, and the definitive collapse of all Fascist plans, of all its far-reaching barbarous intentions, were acknowledged by its representatives.

At around midday the representatives of Allied Supreme Command landed at Tempelhof airport: the British Air Marshal W. Tedder, American Air Force commander General Spaatz and the senior commander of the French army General de Lattre de Tassigny [...].

From the airport our allies travelled to Karlshorst, where the unconditional surrender of the OKW was to be accepted.

Also at Tempelhof airport, coming from Flensburg and guarded by British officers, were Field Marshal Keitel, General Admiral von Friedeburg and Luftwaffe Generaloberst Stumpff, who were authorized by Dönitz to sign the unconditional capitulation.

In Karlhorst a room had been prepared in the one-storey officers' mess of the former pioneer school.

After a short break all the representatives of Allied Supreme Command came to me to discuss matters of procedure for this stirring event.

As soon as we had entered the room assigned for the discussion, countless American and British journalists streamed in and immediately swamped me with questions. In the name of the Allied troops they gave me a flag as a sign of friendship, with a greeting from the American troops to the Red Army embroidered in gold. After the journalists had left the meeting room, we began our discussion of the surrender of imperialist Germany.

Meanwhile Keitel and his entourage stayed in another building. As our officers reported, Keitel and the other members of the delegation were extremely nervous. Keitel said to his entourage, 'When we drove through Berlin, I was shaken to note how seriously damaged the city is.'

One of our officers replied, 'Field Marshal, were you not shaken when thousands of Soviet towns and villages were levelled on your orders, places under whose ruins millions of our compatriots, including tens of thousands of children, met their deaths?'

Keitel shrugged nervously, but didn't say a word.

As previously agreed, the representatives of Allied Supreme Command, Tedder, Spaatz and de Lattre de Tassigny, as well as Vyshinksy, Telegin, Sokolovsky and others, met at 23.45 p.m. in my study, abutting the hall where the Fascist military officers were to sign the document for unconditional surrender. We entered the hall at exactly midnight.

Everyone sat down at a table, with the national flags of the Soviet Union, the USA, Great Britain and France hanging on the wall behind it.

Sitting in the hall at long tables covered with green cloth were the generals of the Soviet army whose troops had broken through the defences of Berlin within a very short time, and had brought the arrogant Fascist Field Marshals, the Fascist ringleaders and the whole of Nazi Germany to its knees. Also present were many Soviet and foreign journalists and photo-journalists.

At the opening of the meeting I declared, 'We representatives of the Supreme Command of the Soviet forces and the Allied Supreme Command are authorized by the governments of the anti-Hitler coalition to accept the unconditional surrender of Germany from the German military leadership. Bring the representatives of the Supreme Command of the Wehrmacht into the hall.'

Everyone's eyes were directed at the door in which, in a few moments, we would shortly see the people who had boasted to the whole world that they would defeat France and Great Britain in a Blitzkrieg, destroy the Soviet Union in a month and a half or two at the most, and conquer the whole world.

First to enter the room was General Field Marshal Keitel – Hitler's closest military colleague – who came in slowly, trying to appear relaxed. He greeted the representatives of Soviet and the Allied Supreme Command by raising his hand with his marshal's baton. After him came Stumpff. His eyes were filled with impotent fury. At the same time Friedeburg entered the room. He looked prematurely aged.

The German representatives were invited to sit at the table assigned to them, which was not far from the door.

Keitel sat down carefully and looked across to the top table. Stumpff and Friedeburg sat down beside Keitel. The officers of their entourage took up position behind them.

I turned to the German delegation: 'Do you have the document of the unconditional surrender with you, have you studied it and are you authorized to sign it?'

Air Marshal Tedder repeated my question in English.

'Yes, we have studied it and are ready to sign it,' Keitel said in a muted voice, and handed us a document signed by Dönitz. It said that Keitel, von Friedeburg and Stumpff were authorized to sign the document concerning the unconditional surrender.

This was no longer the arrogant Keitel who had accepted the surrender of defeated France. He looked beaten now, even though he was trying to maintain his composure.

I rose to my feet and said, 'I invite the German delegation to come to this table. Here you will sign the document confirming Germany's unconditional surrender.'

With a hostile glance at the top table, Keitel rose quickly from his seat, then lowered his eyes, slowly took his marshal's baton from the table and walked unsteadily towards our table. His monocle fell off and dangled on its string; his face was covered with red blotches.

Next to him Stumpff, von Friedeburg and the German officers of the entourage stepped to the table. Keitel straightened his monocle, sat down on the edge of his chair and awkwardly signed all five copies of the document. After Keitel, Stumpff and Friedeburg put their signatures underneath his.

After signing, Keitel stood up, put on his right glove and tried to adopt the posture of the tough military officer. He failed to do so, however, and walked back to the table assigned to him.

On 9 May at 0.43 a.m. the document confirming the unconditional surrender had been signed by everyone. I invited the German delegation to leave the hall.

Keitel, Friedeburg and Stumpff rose to their feet, bowed and left with heads lowered, followed by their staff officers.

In the name of Soviet Supreme Command I warmly congratulated everyone present on their long-awaited victory. An unimaginable noise rose up in the hall. They all congratulated each other and shook each other's hands. Many people had tears of joy in their eyes. My comrades-at-arms Sokolovsky, Malinin, Telegin, Antipenko, Kolpakchi, Kusnetzov, Bogdanov, Bersarin, Bokov, Belov, Gorbatov and others came up to me.

'Dear friends,' I said to my brothers in arms, 'We have been paid a great honour. The people, the party and the government have trusted us with the task of leading our heroic Soviet troops in a charge on Berlin. The Soviet troops, including yourselves, who issued the orders to the troops fighting in Berlin, have justified that trust with honour. Sadly, many are no longer with us. How they would have rejoiced over the long-awaited victory for which, without hesitation, they gave their lives!'

Remembering their good friends and comrades who were not given the chance to experience this joyful day, these men, who were used to looking death fearlessly in the eye, could not hold back their tears. On 9 May 1945 at 00.50 a.m. the meeting at which the unconditional surrender of Fascist forces was accepted, came to an end.

I opened the banquet and raised a toast to the anti-Hitler coalition's victory over Nazi Germany. Then Marshal Arthur Tedder, de Lattre de Tassigny and General Spaatz delivered addresses. Soviet generals also took the floor. They all spoke of the things that had filled their hearts during those difficult years. I remember that a lot of cordial talking was done, and that the wish was vigorously and repeatedly expressed that friendly relations between the countries of the anti-Fascist coalition be maintained for ever. This wish was expressed by Soviet, American, French and British generals, and we all voiced the hope that it might be fulfilled.

The feast ended in the morning with singing and dancing. The Soviet generals were unbeatable in this. In the end I too was unable to contain myself, I felt young again and performed a Russian folk dance. When we parted, some driving straight to the airport, salutes in honour of the victors were fired by guns everywhere, both in and out of Berlin. They fired into the air, but the bullets and shell splinters that fell to earth made strolling in Berlin on the morning of 9 May a dangerous business. But how fundamentally that danger differed from the one that had almost become a habit in the long war years.

The same morning the signed unconditional surrender document was handed in to the Headquarters of Supreme Command.

Point 1 of the document reads:

'1. We the undersigned, acting by authority of the German High Command, hereby surrender unconditionally to the Supreme Commander, Allied Expeditionary Force and simultaneously to the Supreme High Command of the Red Army all forces on land, at sea, and in the air who are at this date under German control.'

**Konstantin Simonov, war reporter, 1915–79**   *Berlin*

Tempelhof. Morning. No planes have landed yet. The airfield is empty. Only in the middle a fat little colonel is practising the guard of honour before the Allies arrive. He practises long and hard: during the war the soldiers have forgotten how to do these things. We sit in the grass and get bored. In the end the representative of the Senior Commander, Sokolovsky, appears in the company of several generals. I know one of them. I met him in Italy. At the time fighting was still going on in the area around Florence. How long ago that seems!

The first plane lands! Out of it steps Vyshinsky, accompanied by some of our diplomats. They immediately get into a car and drive away. An hour and a half later another plane lands. Yesterday we expected Eisenhower to come, and only here, at the airfield, when not Zhukov but Sokolovsky appeared, we told ourselves that someone else would come instead of Eisenhower. Now the British Air Marshal and Deputy Supreme Commander of the Allied Expeditionary Forces in Europe, Arthur W. Tedder, and the Senior Commander of Strategic Air Forces in Europe, the American General Carl A. Spaatz, arrived. Spaatz is a man of middle size, well fed, square-shaped, Tedder is gaunt, youthful, of indeterminate age, nimble, agile, and he smiles often and in a slightly forced manner. They and Sokolovsky greet one another. The soldiers present arms, the band plays three national anthems, the Allies and Sokolovsky march past the guard of honour.

Meanwhile another plane lands, bringing the Germans: Wilhelm Keitel, Admiral General Hans-Georg von Friedeburg and Generaloberst Hans-Jürgen Stumpff. In their entourage there are several German officers. The guard of honour that has stepped up to welcome the Allies stands between the aeroplane in which the Germans came and the cars at the end of the airfield to which the Germans have to walk. As soon as the Germans have left the plane, some Soviet officers walk up to them, and while the Allies walk past the formation of honour, on the other side the Germans are led to the cars. At their head walks Keitel in a long coat, with a big, tall general's cap whose brim is bent. He deliberately avoids looking to the left or the right, and walks with big, striding steps.

We follow the Germans through Berlin. When I see the ruins flashing past us, the lonely figures of the inhabitants, I reflect that it would be hard to imagine a gloomier image than that of the German generals driving to sign the surrender document.

Karlshorst. First of all we visit the banqueting hall of the engineering school. This is where the signing is to be done. The hall is not very big. Two hundred square metres. At the front the wall is decorated with flags: the Soviet, the American, the British and the French. The Senior Commander of the 1st French Army, Jean de Lattre de Tassigny, is said to have arrived as well, or is about to. Below the flags is a long table that takes up almost the whole width of the wall. That is where the representatives of the Allied Command will sit. At right angles to it are three tables, two long and one short. The short one is meant for the German delegation, the one in the middle for the Soviet and the Allied generals and officers who will witness the surrender. The last table, finally, is for the correspondents.

We spend almost an hour in the engineering school. Everything is drawn out because the Soviet and Allied representatives are still negotiating certain matters of procedure. The surrender, which was originally scheduled for 2.00 p.m., is not going to start until the evening. Finally Zhukov and Telegin come into the room, and with them come Vyshinsky, Tedder, Spaatz and Lattre de Tassigny, whom I see for the first time. He is a young general of about forty-five.

The correspondents and military staff who are supposed to be present at the capitulation hurry to the seats that are still free. An officer who has been deployed as a steward walks over to them and hastily whispers something to them. Our generals at the table meant for the surrendering Germans jump to their feet as if bitten by a tarantula and switch seats.

Zhukov smiles. Tedder smiles. Lattre de Tassigny smiles. They smile at each other and at the non-smiling Spaatz and take their seats at their table. The photographers and cameramen come out of their shells. They jump on the tables, press their bellies against the shoulders of the generals and snap, snap, snap...

One of our cameramen brushes an American admiral's head. The admiral, who is clearly used to the frantic activity of the reporters, laughs benignly and waves a hand: 'Okay!' But our steward, unfamiliar with this atmosphere, would love to throw the poor fellow out of the door.

The people at the middle table behave in very different ways. Spaatz maintains a poker face. Vyshinsky is over-eager.

Zhukov beams. Tedder, who is sitting next to him, has a faint smile on his pleasant but expressionless face. Through the interpreter he says something to Zhukov, and I think that of everyone present he is the only one who has maintained a little irony about the imminent solemn procedure. Lattre de Tassigny seems worried about having arrived later than the others, and concerned that they will very shortly be moving on to the order of business. I see Zhukov, his handsome, strong face, and I remember having met him during the battles against the Japanese at Khalkhin Gol, when he was a Corps Commander and I was leading our army unit in Mongolia. […] Six years have passed since then, I have not met Zhukov in the meantime, and back then I would never have dreamed that our next meeting would take place in Berlin, before the acceptance of the surrender of the Germany army.

When the hall has fallen silent, Zhukov rises to his feet and declares the meeting open for the acceptance of the surrender of the German army. Then there is talk of authorization, and it is established who has been authorized by which government, and the documents are read out in individual languages. That takes ten minutes.

Zhukov gets back to his feet, turns to the officers by the door and says drily, 'Bring in the German delegation.'

The door is opened and Keitel, Friedeburg and Stumpff come in. They are followed by some officers, presumably adjutants. Keitel only needs to take three steps to reach his table. He walks over to it, stops behind the middle chair, holds out his hand with the short marshal's baton, and makes a nimble forward and backward motion that reminds me of an exercise with dumb-bells. He pulls the chair back, sits down and sets his baton down in front of him.

Zhukov stands up and says something, but it is impossible to make out what.

It is translated for the Germans. Keitel lowers his head in agreement. Further details of procedure follow.

I study Keitel. He has rested his gloved hands on the table, Stumpff seems absolutely calm. Friedeburg is frozen, but hidden behind his stillness is boundless dejection.

Keitel too sits motionlessly, looks straight ahead, then turns his head slightly and looks attentively at Zhukov, then looks back at the table in front of him, then back at Zhukov. This is repeated several times, and although the expression is highly inappropriate in the circumstances, I am not mistaken in thinking that he is looking curiously at Zhukov. No one but Zhukov, and really curiously, as if he is looking at someone in whom he has taken an interest for a long time and who is now sitting only ten feet away from him.

Now, at the middle table, the signing of the document begins. Zhukov, Tedder, Spaatz and, last of all, Lattre de Tassigny add their signatures.

As they are signing, Keitel's face changes terribly. Waiting for the second when his turn comes to pick up his pen, he sits there stiff and frozen. The big officer standing to attention behind his chair, hands along the seams of his trousers, weeps, although his face doesn't move a muscle. Keitel sits there for a moment, then stretches out his hands and clenches them into fists on the table. He keeps throwing back his head as if to force back the tears that are threatening to burst from his eyelids.

Zhukov gets up and says, 'It is suggested to the German delegation that they sign the document of unconditional surrender.'

The interpreter translates the invitation into German, and Keitel, who has grasped the meaning of the words even before they have been uttered, motions towards himself as an indication that the document should be presented to him for signature.

But Zhukov abruptly darts his arm towards the Germans, points to the table where the Allies are sitting and says harshly, 'You will come here to sign.' Keitel stands up first. He walks to the narrow side of the table, sits down at a chair waiting there and signs several copies of the document. Then he walks back to his table, sits down and adopts his old pose. He has taken off one of his gloves to sign. Now he puts it back on.

After him Stumpff and Friedeburg go to sign. Meanwhile I go on looking at Keitel. He has half turned towards the table of the Allies, looks at them and broods intently on something, unconsciously bringing his gloved right hand to his face and running it over his sagging cheeks.

The last of the three Germans comes back to his seat.

Zhukov stands up and says, 'The German delegation can leave the hall.'

The Germans rise. Keitel makes the same movement with his marshal's baton that he made at the beginning when he came in, turns round and walks out. The others follow him. The door is closed.

And suddenly the pent-up tension dissipates from the room. It flees as if everyone had been holding in their breath, which now flows from their chests. A general sigh of relief and exhaustion spreads through the room.

The surrender is sealed, the war is over.

### From the last German Wehrmacht report                    *Berlin*

The weapons on all fronts have been silent since midnight. On the orders of the Grand Admiral the Wehrmacht has halted what had become hopeless combat. Almost six years of heroic fighting is over. It has brought us great victories, but also serious defeats. In the end the

German Wehrmacht has honourably submitted to a mighty superior power.

The German soldier, true to his oath, has in the service of his nation achieved feats that will never be forgotten. The home front has supported him to the last with all its might, amidst the heaviest of sacrifices. The unique achievement of front and home will find its definitive appreciation in the later, just judgement of history.

And even the enemy will give his respect to the achievements and sacrifices of the German soldiers on land, on the water and in the air. So every soldier can stand upright as he proudly sets down his gun, and in the most difficult hours of our history go bravely and confidently to work for the eternal life of our people. At this hour the Wehrmacht remembers its comrades who fell before the enemy. The dead compel us to unconditional loyalty, to obedience and discipline towards the Fatherland, bleeding from countless wounds.

*

*Spring*

The sun shines, the pastures bloom,
The days come mild and blossom-filled,
The evening blooms too, and bright days fall
From the sky, where the days begin.

The year with its seasons seems
A glory that brings forth feasts,
Man's activity begins with a new goal,
Such are the signs of the world, of its many wonders.

Your obedient servant
Scardanelli
24 April 1839

Friedrich Hölderlin

# Epilogue

> Be kindly affectioned one to another
> with brotherly love; in honour
> preferring one another; Not slothful
> in business; fervent in spirit; serving
> the Lord.
>
> DAILY READING: ROMANS 12:10–11
> (21 JUNE 1941)

### *Fuldaer Nachrichtenblatt*
New street names

The changed political conditions have made a change in various street names appear necessary. Thus 'Adolf-Hitler-Platz' – formerly Friedrichsmarkt – has been given back the name that it bore from the first settlement of Fulda into the nineteenth century. From now on it will be called 'Unterm heilig Kreuz' ['Under the Holy Cross']. This sign formerly referred to Fulda parish church, which stands in the middle of the square.

### Harry S. Truman, 1884–1972            *Washington*
All Fascism did not die with Mussolini. Hitler is finished – but the seeds spread by his disordered mind have firm root in too many fanatical brains. It is easier to remove tyrants and destroy concentration camps than it is to kill the ideas which gave them birth and strength. Victory on the battlefield was essential, but it was not enough. For a good peace, a lasting peace, the decent peoples of the earth must remain determined to strike down the evil spirit which has hung over the world for the last decade.

The forces of reaction and tyranny all over the world will try to keep the United Nations from remaining united. Even while the military machine of the Axis was being destroyed in Europe – even down to its very end – they still tried to divide us.

They failed. But they will try again.

They are trying even now. To divide and conquer was – and still is – their plan. They still try to make one Ally suspect the other, hate the other, desert the other.

But I know I speak for every one of you when I say that the United Nations will remain united.

They will not be divided by propaganda either before the Japanese surrender – or after.

### Leonid Voytenko, Red Army soldier, b. 1922      *near Berlin*

The soldier Popov was a strange person. He had nothing but bees in his bonnet. Thus he kept a diary in a thick volume of soft newsprint that he had bound himself. It was his pride and joy. At every free moment he had written something in it with the stump of an indelible pencil. As he was forever putting the pencil in his mouth to moisten it, he was always walking around with blue lips. Hence his nickname – Ivan-Pencil Brigade. Just outside Berlin his diary disappeared without a trace. He tried very hard, offered a big reward for its return, even reported it to the battalion commander. He wept! 'It's all over. For two years I've written down every village, every metre of the roads we travelled, from Stalingrad to Berlin. Now my book will be used to roll cigarettes. No I can't bear such a thing. Sooner an enemy bullet…'

He complained like that for about a week, and then an enemy bullet found him. A German tank unit had broken through near Erkner, and our battalion suffered severe casualties. In this battle diary-writer Popov fell. Next morning we found his notebook behind the seat of his truck. He had probably put it there himself, and forgotten about it in the heat of battle.

# Acknowledgements

I should like to thank the archives that have helped me with my search for material, the publishing houses for granting reproduction permission, and all individuals for their kind willingness to make their texts available to us for *Swansong*.

I should also like to thank, for research and transcriptions, Carla Damiano, Andrej W. Doronin, Hans-Wilhelm Eckert, Kirsten Hering, Hildegard Kempowski, Ulrich Krüger, Anette Lienert, Simone Neteler, Mireille Onon, Anatoli Philippowitsch Platitsyn, Angela Scheffel, Peter Steege, Frank Wagner; for translation Kirsten Bühler (from Danish), Nicole Fester (from English), Andrea Gotzes (from Russian), Manfred Hempel (from English), Annette Kohler (from Italian), Mireille Onon (from French), Anatoli Philippowitsch Platitsyn (from Russian), Anne L. Schippmann (from English), Ingeborg Schröder (from Russian), Frank Wagner (from English), Regine Wagner (from English) and for collecting reproduction permissions Barbara Münch-Kienast.

W.K.

The publishers have not been able to trace all rights holders to the texts reproduced. We request that they inform Albrecht Knaus Verlag of any claims.

The translator and the publishers would also like to thank Sandra Bance, Stephen Walton of the Imperial War Museum and the staff of the Mass Observation Archive for their help in tracing English-language texts and securing permissions for their use.

S.W.

# Acknowledgements

# Sources

To find the source for a particular entry, please refer to the index, which lists sources in bold type at the end of each entry.

## 1. Published and Broadcast Sources

Copyright to works protected by copyright law belongs to the publisher of each source unless otherwise stated. The publisher has made every attempt to trace all copyright holders and to obtain permission to reproduce the material. Copyright holders of material who have not been acknowledged should contact the publisher.

Unlike in the original German, letters with umlauts are arranged here according to their nearest equivalent letters in the English alphabet, for example, 'ö' as 'o'. Where the English transliteration of the Russian names of authors included in this volume differs from the German, the English version is given in square brackets.

The source given in the German edition, most often a German-language source, is listed first, followed, where applicable, by the original, non-German, edition referred to for this English-language edition, and the relevant credit. Sources not originally given in the German edition are preceded by an asterisk*.

1   Adenauer, Konrad, *Briefe 1945–1947* [Letters: 1945–1947], edited by Hans Peter Mensing (Berlin: Wolf Jobst Siedler Verlag, 1983). Copyright © Stiftung Bundeskanzler-Adenauer-Haus. Reproduced with the kind permission of Stadt Köln Historisches Archiv.

2   Adler, H. G., *Theresienstadt 1941–1945: Das Antlitz einer Zwangsgemein-schaft* [Theresienstadt 1941–1945: The face of an enforced community] (Tübingen: Mohr Siebeck Verlag, 1960). Reproduced with the kind permission of Mohr Siebeck Verlag GmbH.

3   Alilujewa, Swetlana [Aliluyeva, Svetlana], *Zwanzig Briefe an einen Freund* [Twenty letters to a friend], translated from the Russian by Xaver Schaffgotsch (Zürich and Vienna: Verlag Fritz Molden, 1967).

4   Alper, Benedict S., *Love and Politics in Wartime: Letters to My Wife, 1943–45*, selected and edited by Joan Wallach Scott (Urbana and Chicago: University of Illinois Press, 1992), copyright © 1992 by the

Board of Trustees of the University of Illinois. Used with permission of the University of Illinois Press and Joan W. Scott.

5 Alvensleben, Udo von, *Lauter Abschiede: Tagebuch im Kriege* [Nothing but farewells: Diaries in wartime], edited by Harald von Koenigswald (Berlin: Propyläen Verlag in der Ullstein Buchverlage GmbH, 1971). Reproduced with the kind permission of Ullstein Verlag GmbH.

6 Anonymous, *Eine Frau in Berlin: Tagebuchaufzeichnungen vom 20. April bis 22. Juni 1945* copyright © 2002 Hannelore Marek and AB – Die Andere Bibliothek GmbH & Co. KG, Berlin 2011 (Frankfurt am Main: Eichborn Verlag, 2003). First published in Great Britain in English translation as *A Woman in Berlin* in June 2005 by Virago Press, London. Translation copyright © Philip Boehm 2004.

7 Axmann, Artur, *'Das kann doch nicht das Ende sein': Hitlers letzter Reichsjugendführer erinert sich* ['Surely that can't be the end': Memories of Hitler's last youth leaders] (Schnellbach: S. Bublies Verlag, 1995)

8 Bahnsen, Uwe and O'Donnell, James, *Die Katakombe: Das Ende der Reichskanzlei* (Stuttgart: Deutsche Verlags-Anstalt, 1975). Copyright © 1975, Deutsche Verlags-Anstalt, München, in der Verlagsgruppe Random House GmbH. *The Bunker* by James P. O'Donnell. Reprinted by permission of SLL/Sterling Lord Literistic, Inc. Copyright © by The Estate of James P. O'Donnell.

9 Ballhorn, Franz, *Die Kelter Gottes: Tagebuch eines jungen Christen 1940–1945* [God's wine-press: Diaries of a young Christian 1940–1945] (Recklinghausen: Regensberg Druck- und Verlags GmbH, 1980).

10 *Baltische Studien, Neue Folge Bd. 68* [Baltic studies, new series vol. 68] (1982) (Marburg: Verlag N. G. Elwert, 1982).

11 Barth, Emil, *Lemuria: Aufzeichnungen und Meditationen aus den Jahren 1942 bis 1945* [Lemuria: Notes and meditations from 1942 to 1945], edited and annotated by Bernhard Albers and Karin Dosch-Muster (Aachen: Rimbaud Verlagsgesellschaft, 1997). Reproduced with the kind permission of Rimbaud Verlasgesellschaft GmbH.

12 Bauer, Fritz, *Würzburg im Feuerofen: Tagebuchaufzeichnungen und Erinnerungen an die Zerstörung Würzburgs* [Würzburg in flames: Diaries and memories of the destruction of Würzburg] (Würzburg: Echter Verlag, 1985).

13 Bauer, Robert, *Heilbronner Tagebuchblätter* [Heilbronn diaries] (Heilbronn: self-published, 1949).

14 Baur, Hans, *Mit Mächtigen zwischen Himmel und Erde* [Between heaven and earth with those in power] (Coburg: K. W. Schütz Verlag, 1971).

15 Beckmann, Max, *Tagebücher 1940–1950* [Diaries: 1940–1950], compiled by Mathilde Q. Beckmann and edited by Erhard Göpel, with a foreword by Friedhelm W. Fischer (Munich: Piper Verlag, 1984, revised edition 1979).

16   Behrens, Erwin, *Tagebuch aus Moskau* [Moscow diaries] (Hamburg: Christian Wegner Verlag, 1964).

17   Below, Nicolaus von. *Als Hitlers Adjutant 1937–45* [I was Hitler's adjutant 1937–45] (Mainz: v. Hase & Koehler Verlag, 1980). Reproduced with the kind permission of v. Hase & Köhler Verlag GmbH.

18   Benz, Wolfgang and Distel, Barbara (eds), *Die Befreiung, Heft 1* [Liberation, volume 1] of *Dachauer Hefte: Studien und Dokumente zur Geschichte der nationalsozialistischen Konzentrationslager* [Dachau journals: studies and documents on the history of Nazi concentration camps] (Brussels: Comité International de Dachau, 1985). Copyright © Max Mannheimer.

19   Bergau, Martin, *Der Junge von der Bernsteinküste: Erlebte Zeitgeschichte 1938–1948* [A young man from the Bernsteinküste: History as lived 1938–1948], with a foreword by Michael Wieck and including documents about the Jewish death marches of 1945 (Heidelberg: Heidelberger Verlagsanstalt, 1994). Copyright © Heidelberg, Universitätsverlag C. Winter.

20   Berthold, Eva, *Kriegsgefangene im Osten: Bilder. Briefe. Berichte* [Prisoners of war in the east: pictures, letters and reports] (Königstein im Taunus: Athenäum Verlag, 1981).

21   Besymenski, Lew, *Der Tod des Adolf Hitler: Unbekannte Dokumente aus Moskauer Archiven* [The death of Adolf Hitler: Unknown documents from the Moscow archives], with an introduction by Karl-Heinz Janßen, translated from the Russian by Valerie B. Danilow (Munich: F.A. Herbig Verlagsbuchhandlung, 1982). Used with the kind permission of F.A. Herbig Verlagsbuchhandlung u. Allunionsagentur für Urheber Moscow.

22   Besymenski, Lew, *Die letzten Notizen von Martin Bormann: Ein Dokument und sein Verfasser* [The last writings of Martin Bormann: A document and its author], from Verlag der Presseagentur Nowosti, Moscow, translated from the Russian by Reinhild Holler (Stuttgart: Deutsche Verlags-Anstalt, 1974).

23   Boldt, Gerhard, *Die letzen tage der Reichskanzlei* (Reinbeck: Rowohlt Verlag, 1949). Lines from *Hitler: The Last Ten Days* reproduced with permission of Orion Books Limited, Orion House, 5 Upper St Martin's Lane, London WC2H 9EA. Copyright © Reinbek, Rowohlt Verlag 1947.

24   Bonifas, Aimé, *Häftling 20801: Ein Zeugnis über die faschistischen Konzentrationslager* [Prisoner 20801: A testimony from the fascist concentration camp] (Munich and Berlin: Buchverlag Union, 1983).

25   Borkowski, Dieter, *Wer weiß, ob wir uns wiedersehen: Erinnerungen an eine Berliner Jugend* [Who knows if we'll meet again: Memories of a youth in Berlin] (Frankfurt am Main: S. Fischer Verlag, 1980).

**26** Bourke-White, Margaret, *Deutschland April 1945*, with an introduction by Klaus Scholder, translated from the English by Ulrike von Puttkamer (Munich: Schirmer/Mosel Verlag, 1979). Excerpt from *Dear Fatherland Rest Quietly.* Text © Estate of Margaret Bourke-White/Licensed by VAGA, New York, NY.

**27** Brecht, Bertolt, *Arbeitsjournal Bd. 2: 1942–55* [Journals vol. 2: 1942–5] (Frankfurt am Main: Suhrkamp Verlag, 1973). Lines from *Arbeitsjournal Vol 2 1942–55* copyright © Bertolt Brecht, edited by Werner Hecht, Methuen Drama, an imprint of Bloomsbury Publishing Plc.

**28** Breloer, Heinrich (ed.), *Mein Tagebuch: Geschichte vom Überleben 1939–47* [My diary: A story of survival 1939–47] (Cologne: vgs Verlagsgesellschaft Schulfernsehen, 1984) Copyright © 1984, EGMONT Verlagsgesellschaften mbH.

**29** Bryant, Arthur, *Sieg im Westen 1943–1946: Aus dem Kriegestagebüchern des Feldmarschalls Lord Alanbrooke, Chef Des Empire-Generalstabs*, translated by Hans Steinsdorff (Düsseldorf: Droste Verlag, 1960). *Triumph in the West 1943–1946: Based on the Diaries and Auto-biographical Notes of Field Marshal, the Viscount Alanbrooke* (London: Harper Collins, 1959). Reprinted with kind permission from Harper Collins.

**30** *Cadett, Thomas, 'Devastation in Berlin', a despatch, copyright© British Broadcasting Corporation, 9 May 1945, radio broadcast. Reproduced with the permission of the BBC, London.

**31** Canetti, Elias, *Die Provinz des Menschen*: *Aufzeichnungen 1942–1972* [The human province: notes 1942–1972] (Munich and Vienna: Carl Hanser Verlag 1973), copyright © by Elias Canetti 1972 by the heirs of Elias Canetti 1994. Published by kind permission of Carl Hanser Verlag München.

**32** Carossa, Hans, *Ungleiche Welten* [Unequal worlds] (Frankfurt am Main: Insel Verlag, 1951). Reproduced with the kind permission of Eva Brinkmann-Carossa.

**33** Churchill, Winston S., *Der zweite Weltkrieg* (Bern and Munich: Alfred Scherz Verlag, 1989). *The Second World War* (London: Pimlico, 2002). Reproduced with the permission of Curtis Brown Group Ltd, London on behalf of the Estate of Sir Winston Churchill. Copyright © Winston S. Churchill

**34** *Churchill, Winston S. 'Victory in Europe' speech, 8 May 1945, House of Commons and Broadcast, London. Reproduced with the permission of Curtis Brown Group Ltd, London on behalf of the Estate of Sir Winston Churchill. Copyright ©Winston S. Churchill.

**35** *Churchill, Winston S., Letters of correspondence from Winston S. Churchill to Joseph Vissarionovich Stalin dated between April and

May 1945 from collection CHAR20/2014 held at the Churchill Archive Centre, Cambridge. Reproduced with the permission of Curtis Brown Group Ltd, London on behalf of the Estate of Sir Winston Churchill. Copyright ©Winston S. Churchill.

36 Colville, Sir John, *Downing-Street-Tagebücher 1939–1945*, translated by Karl H. Schneider (Berlin: Wolf Jobst Siedler Verlag, 1988). *The Fringes of Power: Downing Street Diaries, 1939–55*. Extracts from diary entries 25 April 1945, 26 April 1945, 30 April 1945, 8 May 1945. First published by Hodder and Stoughton, London, 1985. Copyright © Sir John Colville 1985. Reproduced by permission of Hodder and Stoughton Limited.

37 Cranz, Martin, *Ich, ein Deutscher: Erfahrungen mit meinem Vaterland und unserer Welt 1926–1986* [I, a German: Experiences with my Fatherland and our world 1926–1986] (Dülmen: Laumann-Verlagsgesellschaft, 1987).

38 Degrelle, Léon, *Die verlorene Legion* [The lost legion] (Preußisch-Oldendorf: K W Schütz Verlag, 1972). Copyright © Deutsche Verlagsgesellschaft

39 *Der Prozeß gegen die Hauptkriegsverbrecher vor dem Internationalen Militärgerichtshof Nürnberg. 14. November 1945–1. Oktober 1946. 42 Bde.* [The trial of the principal war criminals at the international military court of Nuremberg, 14 November 1945 to 1 October 1946, 42 volumes] (Nuremberg: 1947–49).

40 *Der Spiegel*, 3 (1966).

41 Diem, Liselott, *Fliehen oder bleiben?: Ein dramatisches Kriegsende in Berlin* [To flee or to stay?: A dramatic end to the war in Berlin] (Freiburg im Breisgau: Verlag Herder, 1982).

42 Dirks, Walter, et al., *Das Ende das ein Anfang war: die letzten Tage des dritten Reiches* [The end that was a beginning: The final days of the Third Reich] (Freiburg im Breisgau: Verlag Herder, 1981).

43 Döblin, Alfred, *Ausgewählte Werke. Bd. 13: Briefe* [Selected works vol. 13: Letters] (Olten, Freiburg im Breisgau: Walter Verlag, 1970). Letter, 'To Elvira and Arthur Rosin', dated 2 May 1945, from Alfred Döblin, *Das Lesebuch* [A reader], edited by Günter Grass (Frankfurt am Main: S. Fischer Verlag, 2012), copyright © S. Fischer Verlag GmbH, 2012.

44 Doderer, Heimito von, *Tangenten: Tagebuch eines Schriftstellers 1940–1950* [Tangents: Diaries of a writer 1940–1950] (Munich: C. H. Beck Verlag, 1964).

45 Dollinger, Hans (ed.) *Kain, wo ist dein Bruder? Was der Mensch im Zweiten Weltkrieg erleiden mußte. Dokumentiert in Tagebüchern und Briefen* [Cain, where is your brother?: The human suffering of WWII documented in diaries and letters] (Cologne: Komet Verlag, 2004).

46 Ehrenburg, Ilja [Ehrenburg, Ilya] *Menschen – Jahre – Leben:*

*Autobiographie, Bd. 2* [People, years, life: Autobiography, vol. 2] (Munich: Kindler Verlag, 1965). Copyright © Paleyeva Faina.

47  Eltz, Erwin Karl Graf zu, *Mit den Kosaken: Kriegestagebuch 1943–1945* [With the Cossacks: War diaries 1943–1945] (Donaueschingen: private publication, 1970). Reproduced with kind permission from Dr Erwin Graf zu Eltz and Ernst D Hohl.

48  Enzensberger, Hans Magnus (ed.) *Europa in Ruinen. Augenzeugenberichteaus den Jahren 1944–1948* [Europe in ruins: Eyewitness accounts from 1944–1948] (Frankfurt am Main: Eichborn Verlag, 1990). English language excerpt from 'London in Midsummer' from *Europe Without Baedeker: Sketches Among the Ruins of Italy, Greece and England* by Edmund Wilson. Copyright © 1966 by Edmund Wilson. Renewed copyright © 1994 by Helen Miranda Wilson. Reprinted by permission of Farrar, Straus and Giroux, LLC.

49  Fest, Joachim, *Das Gesicht des Dritten Reiches: Profile einer totalitären Herrschaft* (Munich: Piper Verlag, 1993). English translation by Michael Bullock published as *The Face of the Third Reich: Portraits of the Nazi Leadership* (London: I. B. Tauris, 2011). Reprinted with permission from I. B. Tauris.

50  Findahl, Theo. *Letzter Akt: Berlin 1939–1945* [Final act: Berlin 1939–1945], translated from the Norwegian by Thyra Dohrenburg (Hamburg: Hammerich & Lesser, 1946).

51  Frankfurter Allgemeine Zeitung, 6.5.1995; 19.4.1999.

52  Frankfurter Presse, 3 (1945).

53  *Fuldaer Nachrichtenblatt*, 6.5.1995; 19.4.1999.

54  Galland, Adolf, *Die Ersten und die Letzten: Jagdflieger im Zweiten Weltkrieg* [The first and the last: Fighter pilots in WWII] (Munich: Schneekluth Verlag, 1953). Reproduced with kind permission from Medien Büro München and Philosophia Verlag GmbH.

55  Gaulle, Charles de, *Memoiren 1942–1946: Die Einheit, das Heil*, translated by Wilhelm and Modeste Pferdekamp (Düsseldorf: Droste Verlag, 1961). Originally published in French as *Mémoires de guerre*. Reproduced with kind permission from Editions Plon, Paris, 1954.

56  Geouffre de la Pradelle, Raymont and de Pange, Jean (eds), *Verjagt – Beraubt – Erschlagen* [Chased out, robbed, murdered] (Wiesbaden: Verlag Karlheinz Priester, 1961)

57  Gleiss, Horst G.W. (ed.) *Breslauer Apokalypse 1945: Dokumentarchronik vom Todeskampf und Untergang einer deutschen Stadt und Festung am Ende des Zweiten Weltkrieges, Bd. 4 u. 5* [Breslau apocalypse 1945: A documentary record of the fight to the death and destruction of a German city and stronghold at the end of WWII, vols 4 and 5] (Rosenheim Obb.: Natura et Patria Verlag, 1986)

58  Goebbels, Josef, *Goebbels Reden 1932–1945* [Goebbel's speeches 1932–1945], edited by Helmut Heiber (Düsseldorf: Droste Verlag, 1971).

59  Golowko, Arseni Grigorjewitsch [Golovko, Arseniy Grigoriyevich], *Zwischen Spitzbergen und Tiksibucht* [Between Spitzbergen and Tiksibucht], translated by Horst Both (Berlin: Militärverlag der Deutschen Demokratischen Republik, 1986).

60  Görlitz, Walter (ed.), *Generalfeldmarschall Keitel. Verbrecher oder Offizier? Erinnerungen, Briefe, Dokumente des Chefs OKW* [Field Marshal Keitel: Criminal or officer? Memoirs, letters and documents by the head of the German High Command of the Armed Forces] (Göttingen and Berlin: Musterschmidt Verlag, 1961). Copyright © Schnellbach, S. Bublies Verlag.

61  Graff, Sigmund, *Von S. M. zu N. S.: Erinnerungen eines Bühnenautors (1900–1945)* [Memoirs of a playwright: 1900–1945] (Munich, Wels: Verlag Wesermühl, 1963).

62  Gross, K.A. *Fünf Minuten vor Zwölf: Des ersten Jahrtausends letzte Tage unter Herrenmenschen und Herdenmenschen. Dachauer Tagebücher des Häftlings Nr. 16921* [Five minutes to twelve: The last days of the first millennium among members of the master race and followers of the herd. Dachau diaries of prisoner no. 16921] (Munich: Neubau Verlag, n.d., c.1946)

63  Gun, Nerin E., *Eva Braun – Hitler: Leben und Schicksal* [Eva Braun and Hitler: Life and fate] (Velbert: Blick u. Bild Verlag, 1968). Copyright © Lesen & Schenken GmbH, Kiel.

64  Haltermann, Udo (ed.), *So erlebten wir das Ende: Als Deutschland den Zweiten Weltkrieg verlor. Erinnerungen* [How the end was for us: Memories of Germany losing WWII] (Nettetal: Steyler Verlag, 1988).

65  Hammen, Ernst, *Glückliche Heimkehr. Die Geschichte des Kriegsendes 1945 und einer glücklichen Heimkehr zum Hunsrück* [Happy homecoming: The end of the war in 1945 and a happy return home to Hunsrück] (Bad Kreuznach, Pandion Verlag 1985.

66  Hansen, Thorkild, *De søde piger. Dagbog 1943–1947* (Copenhagen: Gyldendalske Boghandel, Nordisk Forlag, 1974)

67  Hansen, Thorkild, *Der Hamsun Prozess* [The Hamsun Trial], translated from the Danish into the German by Ulla Leippe and Monika Wesemann (Munich: Albrecht Knaus Verlag, Random House Publishing Group, 1979).

68  Hartung, Hugo, *Schlesien 1944/45: Aufzeichnungen und Tagebücher* [Silesia 1944/45: Notes and diaries] (Freiburg im Breisgau, Bergstadtverlag Wilhelm Gottlieb Korn, 1956).

69  Hausenstein, Wilhelm, *Licht unter dem Horizont. Tagebücher von 1942–1946* [Light beneath the horizon: Diaries 1942–1946] (Munich:

F. Bruckmann Verlag, 1967). Copright © Stiebner Verlag. Lines reproduced with permission from Stiebner Verlag.

70  Hauser, Martin, *Wege jüdischer Selbstbehauptung. Tagebuchaufzeichnungen 1929–1967* [Ways of Jewish self-assertion: diaries and notes 1929–1967], fourth revised edition (Bonn: Bundeszentrale für politische Bildung, 1997). Copyright © Martin Hauser.

71  Hedinger, Annemarie, *Vertrieben: Aufzeichnungen aus den Jahren 1945/46 [Expelled: Notes from 1945/46]*, volume 133 (H. 133) of *Eckart-Schriften* (Vienna: Österreichische Landsmannschaft, 1995), copyright © Wien, Österreichische Landsmannschaft.

72  Heer, Hans (ed.), *Als ich 9 Jahre alt war, kam der Krieg: Schüleraufsätze 1946. Ein Lesebuch gegen den Krieg* [War broke out when I was nine years old: school compositions. An anti-war reader], with a forewod by Hermann Glaser (Cologne: Prometh Verlag, 1980).

73  Hessen, Heinrich Prinz von, *Der kristallene Lüster. Meine deutsch-italienische Jugend 1927–1947* [The crystal chandelier: my German-Italian youth 1927–1947] (Munich: Piper Verlag, 1994), copyright © Milano, Gruppo Longanesi.

74  Höcker, Karla, *Die letzten und die ersten Tage: Berliner Aufzeichnungen 1945* [The last and the first days: Berlin notes 1945] (Berlin: Verlag Bruno Hessling, 1966) copyright © Dr. Viola Hammetter.

75  Hölderlin, Friedrich: *Sämtliche Werke Bd. 2* [Collected works, vol. 2], edited by Friedrich Beissner (Stuttgart: Verlag W. Kohlhammer, 1951)

76  Hupka, Herbert (ed.), *Letzte Tage in Schlesien. Tagebücher, Erinnerungen und Dokumente der Vertreibung* [The last days in Silesia: Memories and documents of expulsion] (Munich: Langen Müller Verlag in der F. A. Herbig Verlagsbuchhandlung 1988) copyright © Helmut Richter (for his work).

77  Irving, David, *Die geheimen Tagebücher des Dr. Morell, Leibarzt Adolf Hitlers* [The secret diaires of Dr Morrell, Adolf Hitler's doctor] (Munich: Wilhelm Goldmann Verlag, 1983) copyright © David Irving.

78  Jahnn, Hans Henny, *Briefe II 1941–1959* [Letters II: 1941–1959], edited by Ulrich Bitz et al. (Hamburg: Hoffmann und Campe Verlag, 1994)

79  Jahnn, Hans Henny, *Fluss ohne Ufer III* [River with no banks III], edited by Uwe Schweikert and Ulrich Bitz (Hamburg: Hoffmann und Campe Verlag, 1986).

80  Junge, Traudl, with Melissa Müller, *Bis zur letzten Stunde: Hitlers Sekretärin erzählt ihr Leben* (Berlin: Claassen Verlag in der Ullstein Buchverlage GmbH, 2002). English translation published as as *Until the Final Hour* (London: Weidenfeld & Nicolson, 2003). Lines from *Until the Final Hour* reproduced with permission of Orion Books Limited, Orion House, 5 Upper St Martin's Lane, London WC2H 9EA.

Copyright © Ullstein Heyne List GmbH & Co. KG, München 2002. Translation copyright © Anthea Bell 2003.

81   Jünger, Ernst, *Sämtliche Werke in 18 Bänden, Bd. 3: Tagebücher III. Strahlungen II* [Collected works in 18 vols: vol. 3, diaries III: Rays II] (Stuttgart: Verlag Klett-Cotta, 1979) copyright © Ernst Jünger.

82   Junger, Gerhard, *Schicksale 1945: Das Ende des 2. Weltkrieges im Kreise Reutlingen* [1945 destinies: The end of WWII in the Reutlingen district] (Reutlingen: Verlagshaus Oertel & Spörer, 1971).

83   Kantorowicz, Alfred. *Deutsches Tagebuch: Erster Teil* [German diaries: part one](Berlin: Kindler Verlag, 1959).

84   Kardorff, Ursula von, *Berliner Aufzeichnungen 1942–1945* [Berlin notes: 1942–1945], revised new edition with illutrations (Munich: nymphenburger in der F. A. Herbig Verlagsbuchhandlung, 1976), copyright © Petra von Kardorff.

85   Kasack, Hermann, *Dreizehn Wochen: Tage- und Nachtblätter. Aufzeichnungen aus dem Jahre 1945 über das Kriegsende in Potsdam* [Thirteen weeks: day and night diaries. Notes from 1945 on the end of the war in Potsdam], edited by Wolfgang Kasack with an introduction by Walter Kempowski and an afterword and notes by Günter Wirth (Berlin: Edition Hentrich, 1996).

86   Kästner, Erich, 'Mayrhofen, Montag 30. April 1945' (chapter: 'Mayrhofen I, 22.März bis 3. Mai) and 'Mayrhofen, Dienstag 8. Mai / Mittwoch 9. Mai 1945 (chapter: 'Mayrhofen II, 4. Mai bis 15. Juni'), both published in *Notabene 45: Ein Tagebuch* [Nota bene 45: A diary] by Erich Kästner (Zürich: Atrium Verlag, 1961) copyright © Atrium Verlag, Zürich 1961 and Thomas Kästner.

87   Katz, Casimir, *Jeder sah es anders: Erinnerungen an meine Kindheit und Jugend im Dritten Reich* [Everyone saw things differently: memories of my childhood and youth in the Third Reich] (Gernsbach: Casimir Katz Verlag, 2000).

88   Keim, Heinrich, *Gefangener der Wälder: Erlebnisbericht* [Prisoners of the woods: An experience] (Stuttgart: Buchdienst Hans Jürgen von Elterlein, 1983). Extract from *Gefangener der Wälder* by Heinrich Keim copyright © Wolfram von Elterlein. Reproduced with permission from Verlag von Elterlein.

89   Kempka, Erich, *Die letzten Tage mit Adolf Hitler* [The final days with Adolf Hitler], third edition, revised and annotated (Preußisch Oldendorf: Deutsche Verlagsgesellschaft, 1991). English translation extracts from *I was Hitler's Chauffeur* (London: Frontline Books, an imprint of Pen and Sword Books, 2010).

90   Kempka, Erich, *Ich habe Adolf Hitler verbrannt* [I cremated Adolf Hitler] (Munich: Kyrburg Verlag, n.d., *c.*1950). English translation

442  *Swansong 1945*

extracts from *I was Hitler's Chauffeur* (London: Frontline Books, an imprint of Pen and Sword Books, 2010).

91  Kennan, George F., *Memoiren eines Diplomaten: Memoirs 1925–1950*, with a foreword by Klaus Mehnert (Stuttgart: Henry Goverts Verlag, 1968). English language extracts from *Memoirs: 1925–1950* by George F. Kennan. Copyright © 1976 by George F. Kennan. By permission of Little, Brown and Company. All rights reserved.

92  Kersten, Felix, *Totenkopf und Treue. Heinrich Himmler ohne Uniform. Aus den Tagebuchblättern des finnischen Medizinalrats Felix Kersten* [Skulls and loyalty: Heinrich Himmler without his uniform. From the diaries of the Finnish doctor Felix Kersten] (Hamburg: Robert Mulich Verlag, 1952).

93  Kessler, Erich, '*Ein Theresienstädter Tagebuch: Der Theresienstädter 20. April 1945 und die Tage danach*' [A Theresienstadt diary: the people of Theresienstadt on 20 April 1945 and in the days after'] in *Theresienstädter Studien und Dokumente 1995* [Theresienstadt studies and documents 1995] (Prague: Institut Terezínské Iniciativy, 1995).

94  Kirby, Norman, *1100 Miles with Monty: Security and Intelligence at Tac HQ* (Stroud, Gloucestershire: Allan Sutton Publishing, 1989) copyright © Norman Kirby 1989, 2003.

95  Klein, Manfred *Eine deutsche Jugend, 1926–1945* [A German youth: 1926–1945] (Würzburg: self-published, 2001), copyright © Dorothea Klein.

96  Klemperer, Victor, *Ich will Zeugnis ablegen bis zum letzten: Bd. 2, Tagebücher 1942–1945*) Edited by Walter Nowojski with Hadwig Klemperer (Berlin: Aufbau-Verlag, 1995). Extract from *To the Bitter End*. Translation copyright © Martin Chalmers 1999. Published in 2000 by Phoenix, an imprint of Orion Books Ltd, Orion House, 5 Upper St Martin Lane, London WC2H 9EA. Originally published as *Ich will Zeugnis ablegen bis zum letzten*, copyright © Aufbau-Verlag GmHB, Berlin 1995.

97  Klüger, Ruth, *Weiter leben: Eine Jugend* [Keep on living: A youth] (Göttingen: Wallstein Verlag, 1992).

98  Kokoschka, Oskar, *Briefe III: 1934–1953* [Lettters III: 1934–1953], edited by Olda Kokoschka and Heinz Spielmann (Düsseldorf: Claassen Verlag, 1986).

99  Koller, Karl, *Der letzte Monat. 14. April bis 27. Mai 1945: Tagebuch-aufzeichnungen des ehemaligen Chefs des Generalstabs der Deutschen Luftwaffe* [The final month: 14 April to 27 May 1945: notes from the diaries of the head of staff of the German Luftwaffe], with a foreword by Walter Görlitz. (Esslingen, Munich: Bechtle Verlag, 1985)

100  Kraushaar-Baldauf, Elisabeth, *Nimm das Brot und lauf: Biographie*

[Take the bread and run: A biography] (Baden-Baden: Schwarz Verlag, 1983), copyright © Dr. E. A. Kraushaar.

101 Kronika, Jakob, *Der Untergang Berlins* [The fall of Berlin] (Flensburg: Verlagshaus Christian Wolff, 1946).

102 Kuby, Erich, *Das Ende des Schreckens: Dokumente des Untergangs Januar bis Mai 1945* [The end of the horror: Documents on the fall from January to May 1945] (Munich: Paul List Verlag, 1961), copyright © Susanne Kuby.

103 Kuby, Erich, *Mein Krieg. Aufzeichnungen aus 2129 Tagen* [My war: Notes from 2129 days] (Munich: nymphenburger in der F. A. Herbig Verlagsbuchhandlung, 1975), copyright © Susanne Kuby.

104 Kunze, Karl (ed.). *'Kriegsende in Franken und der Kampf um Nürnberg im April 1945'* [The end of the war in Franconia and the battle for Nuremberg in April 1945] in *Nürnberger Forschungen Bd. 28 [Nuremberg studies vol. 28]* (1995), copyright © Nürnberg, Verein für Geschichte (Stadtarchiv Nürnberg, C 36/I Nr. 322).

105 Kupfer-Koberwitz, Edgar, *Dachauer Tagebücher. Die Aufzeichnungen des Häftlings 24814* [Dachau diaries: Notes by prisoner 24814], with a foreword by Barbara Distel (Munich: Kindler Verlag, 1997), copyright Kindler Verlag, 1997. Published by permission of Rowohlt Verlag GmbH.

106 Lammers, Marie (ed.), *'Jutta'*, from *Lebenswege in Ost- und Westdeutschland: Frauen aus einer Stettiner Schulklasse erzählen* [Lives in east and west Germany: The stories of women who were in the same class at a school in Stettin] (Frankfurt am Main: S. Fischer Verlag, 1996), copyright © Fischer Taschenbuch Verlag GmbH, Frankfurt am Main, 1996.

107 Lange, Eitel, *Mit dem Reichsmarschall im Kriege: Ein Bericht in Wort und Bild* [With the Reich Marshal in the war: A report in words and pictures] (Stuttgart: Curt E. Schwab Verlag, 1950).

108 Lange, Wilhelm (ed.), *Cap Arcona: Dokumentation* [Cap Arcona: Documents] (Eutin: Struves Buchdruckerei u. Verlag, 1988)

109 Laqueur, Renata, *Bergen-Belsen Tagebuch 1944/45* [Bergen-Belsen Diaries 1944/45], translated from the Dutch into the German by Peter Wiebke (Hanover: Fackelträger-Verlag, 1989), copyright © Renata Laqueur.

110 Lehfeldt, Walburg, *Gut Lehfelde: Eine deutsche Geschichte 1932–1950 (Wie konnte das geschehen?)* [Lehfelde manor: A German history, 1932–1950 (How could it have happened?)] (Munich: Limes Verlag in der F. A. Herbig Verlagsbuchhandlung, 1986) copyright © Walburg Lehfeldt.

111 Lehndorff, Hans Graf von, *Ostpreußisches Tagebuch: Aufzeichnungen eines Arztes aus den Jahren 1945–1947* [East Prussian diaries: A doctor's

notes, 1945–1947] (Munich: C. H. Beck Verlag, 1961)

112 Leonhard, Wolfgang, *Die Revolution Entlässt Ihre Kinder* [The revolution dismisses its children] (Cologne: Kiepenheuer & Witsch, 1955).

113 Liddell Hart, Basil Henry, *Lebenserinnerungen*, translated from the English into the German by General Leo Freiherr Geyr von Schweppenburg (Düsseldorf and Vienna: Econ Verlag, 1966). *Memoirs* (London: Cassell Publishers, 1965).

114 Lilje, Hanns, *Im finsteren Tal: Rechenschaftsbericht einer Haft* [In the dark valley: Report from an imprisonment] (Hanover: Lutherisches Verlagshaus, 1999), copyright © Eggo Hafermann and Augsburg Fortress Publishers.

115 Linden, Wilhelm zur. *Blick durchs Prisma: Lebensbericht eines Arztes* [Looking through a prism: Memoirs of a doctor] (Frankfurt am Main: Vittorio Klostermann), copyright © Vittorio Klostermann GmbH.

116 Linge, Heinz, *Bis zum Untergang: Als Chef des Persönlichen Dienstes bei Hitler*, edited by Werner Maser (Munich: F. A. Herbig Verlagsbuchhandlung, 1980). *With Hitler to the End: The Memoirs of Hitler's Valet*. Copyright © F.A Herbig Verlagsbuchhandlung GmbH, 1980. English translation copyright © Pen and Sword Books Ltd, 2009. Reproduced with permission from Frontline Books, an imprint of Pen and Sword Books Ltd.

117 Mack, Joanna, and Humphries, Steve (eds), *The Making of Modern London 1939–1945: London at War* (London: Sidgwick and Jackson, 1985). Copyright © ITV.

118 Mann, Heinrich, *Briefwechsel mit Barthold Fles 1942–1949* [Letters to Barthold Fles 1942–1949], edited by Madeleine Rietra (Berlin and Weimar: Aufbau-Verlag, 1993). Copyright © Madeleine Rietra

119 Mann, Klaus, *Der Wendepunkt: Ein Lebensbericht* [The turning point: A memoir] (Frankfurt am Main: S. Fischer Verlag, 1952), copyright © Reinbek, Rowohlt Taschenbuch Verlag 1984.

120 Mann, Klaus, *Tagebücher 1931 bis 1949* [Diaries: 1931 to 1949], edited by Joachim Heimannsberg, Peter Laemmle et al. (Reinbek: Rowohlt Verlag, 1995).

121 Mann, Thomas, *Tagebücher 1944–1.4.1946* [Diaries: 1944 to 1 April 1946], edited by Inge Jens (Frankfurt am Main: S. Fischer Verlag, 1986). Copyright S. Fischer Verlag GmbH, 1986.

122 Marcuse, Ludwig, *Mein zwanzigstes Jahrhundert: Auf dem Weg zu einer Autobiographie* [My twentieth century: Notes for an autobiography] (Berlin: Paul List Verlag (Ullstein Buchverlage GmbH), 1960).

123 *Marineforum 70*, Jg 5 1995 (Hamburg: Verlag E. S. Mittler & Sohn, 1995)

124 Matheny, Ray, T., *Die Feuerreiter: Gefangen in Fliegenden Festungen*

(Munich: Albrecht Knaus Verlag, Random House Publishing Group, 1988). *Rite of Passage: A Teenager's Chronicle of Captivity in Nazi Germany*. Copyright © American Legacy Media, Clearfield, Utah.

125 Matt, Alphons. *Zwischen allen Fronten: Der Zweite Weltkrieg aus der Sicht des Büros Ha*. [Between all fronts: WWII for the Ha. Office] (Frauenfeld, Stuttgart: Verlag Huber, 1969).

126 Mende, Erich. *Das verdammte Gewissen: Zeuge der Zeit* [The cursed conscience: Witness to the times] (Munich: F.A. Herbig Verlagsbuchhandlung, 1982) copyright © 1982 by F.A. Herbig Verlagsbuchhandlung GmbH, München.

127 Meneghello, Luigi, *Die kleinen Meister* [The Little Master] (Berlin: Verlag Klaus Wagenbach, 1990) Lines from *I Piccoli Maestri* Rizzoli, Milano 1976 Copyright © 1976–2013 RCS Libri S.p.A, Milano.

128 Menzel, Matthias, *Die Stadt ohne Tod. Berliner Tagebuch 1943/45* [The city without death: Berlin diaries 1943/45] (Berlin: Carl Habel Verlagsbuchhandlung, 1946).

129 Michelet, Edmond. *Die Freiheitsstraße: Dachau 1943–1945*, translated from the French into the German by Georg Graf Henckel von Donnersmarck (Stuttgart: Europa-Contact-Gesellschaft, n.d., *c.* 1955). *Rue de la liberté: Dachau (1943–1945)*. Copyright © Editions du Seuil, 1955.

130 Montgomery, Bernhard Law, Viscount Montgomery of Alamein. *Memoiren*. Translated from the English by Dietrich Niebuhr (Munich: Paul List Verlag, 1958). Lines from *Memoirs of Field-Marshal Viscount Montgomery* reprinted with permission from A. P. Watt at United Agents, on behalf of Viscount Montgomery of Alamein.

131 Moran, Lord, *Churchill: Der Kampf ums Überleben 1940–1965. Aus dem Tagebuch seines Leibarztes Lord Moran*. Translated from the English by Karl Berisch, edited by Sir Charles MacMoran Wilson (Munich: Droemer Knaur Verlag, 1967). *Winston Churchill: The Struggle for Survival 1940–1965*. Copyright © Constable & Robinson Publishing Ltd, London 1966.

132 Mussolini, Benito, *Colloquio con il Giornalista Cabella*. In: *Opera Omnia Vol. XXXII*. A cura di Edoardo e Duilio Susmel. (Florence: La Fenice, 1960).

133 Mussolini, Rachele, *Mein Leben mit Benito* [My life with Benito](Zürich: Thomas Verlag, 1948).

134 Mussolini, Vittorio, *Vita con mio padre* (Milan: Arnoldo Mondadori Editore, 1957).

135 Nansen, Odd, *Von Tag zu Tag: Ein Tagebuch* [From day to day: A diary], translated from the Norwegian by Ingeborg Goebel (Hamburg: Hans Dulk Verlag, 1949)

136 *Neue Zürcher Zeitung*, 20. 4. 1945; 10. 5. 1945.

137 Neumann, Flora, *74559: Erinnern, um zu leben. Vor Auschwitz, in Auschwitz, nach Auschwitz* [74559: Remember in order to live. Before Auschwitz, in Auschwitz, after Auschwitz] (Hamburg: Klaus Reichelt und Selbstverlag des Alternativen Wohlfahrtsverbandes (SOAL), 1991). Copyright © Flora Neumann

138 Nicolson, Harold, *Diaries and Letters 1930–1964*, edited and condensed by Stanley Olson, with an introduction by Nigel Nocolson (London: Wm Collins, 1968). Reproduced with permission of the Curtis Brown Group Ltd, London on behalf of the The Estate of Harold Nicolson. Copyright © Harold Nicolson 2014.

139 Niekisch, Ernst, *Gewagtes Leben: Begegnungen und Begebnisse* [A bold life: Encounters and events] (Cologne: Kiepenheuer & Witsch, 1958).

140 Nin, Anaïs, *Die Tagebücher der Anais Nin 1944–1947*, edited by Gunther Stuhlmann. Translated from the English by Manfred Ohl and Hans Sartorius (Munich: nymphenburger in der F. A. Herbig Verlagsbuchhandlung, 1977). *Diary of Anais Nin 1944–1947*. Copyright © Houghton Mifflin Harcourt Publishers, New York 1971 and The Anaïs Nin Trust.

141 Panofsky, Walter. *Richard Strauss: Partitur eines Lebens* [Richard Strauss: The score of a life] (Munich: Piper Verlag, 1965).

142 Paquin, Grete, *Wie hinter einem Vorhang: Ein Göttinger Tagebuch von 1938 bis 1947 für meine Kinder geschrieben* [Behind a curtain: A Göttingen diary from 1938 to 1947] (Neukirchen-Vluyn: Friedrich Bahn Verlag, 1968).

143 Pavese, Cesare, *Das Handwerk des Lebens. Tagebücher 1935–1950* [The work of a life: Diaries 1935–1950], translated from the Italian by Maja Pflug (Berlin: Claassen Verlag in der Ullstein Buchverlage GmbH, 1988). *Il mestiere di vivere: Diario 1935–1950*. Copyright © 1952, 1990, 2000, 2006 Giulio Einaudi Editore SpA Torino.

144 Pechtold, Friedrich, *Der Pimpf. Eine Familie erlebt den Krieg im Kölner Land und in Coburg* [The little rascal: A family experience of the war in the Cologne countryside and in Coburg] (Sulzbach: self-published, 1987) copyright © Karin Pechtold.

145 Peikert, Paul, *«Festung Breslau» in den Berichten eines Pfarrers. 22. Januar bis 6. Mai 1945* ['The fortress of Breslau' in a clergyman's report, 22 January to 6 May 1945], edited by Karol Jonca and Alfred Konieczny (Munich and Berlin: Buchverlag Union, 1974).

146 Pentzien, Arno, *Kriegstagebuch: 2. (mot.) A. R. 18 vom 7. Juni 1941 bis Kriegsende 1945* [War diaries 2: 7 June 1941 to the end of WWII, 1945] (Hamburg: self-published, 1974).

147 Pohl, Gerhart. *Bin ich noch in meinem Haus? Die letzten Tage Gerhart*

*Hauptmanns* [Am I still in my house? The final days of Gerhart Hauptmann], edited by and with an afterword by Günter Gerstmann (Herne: Stiftung Martin-Opitz-Bibliothek, 2003) copyright © Peter Pohl, Kiel.

148  Rad, Gerhard von, *Erinnerungen aus der Kriegsgefangenschaft Frühjahr 1945* [Memories from war imprisonment in spring 1945], edited by Luise von Rad (Neukirchen-Vluyn: Neukirchener Verlag, 1976) copyright © Ursula von Rad.

149  Raddatz, Fritz J. *Unruhestifter: Erinnerungen* [Troublemaker: Memoirs] (Berlin: Propyläen Verlag in der Ullstein Buchverlage GmbH, 2003).

150  Riedel, Hermann, *Halt! Schweizer Grenze! Das Ende des Zweiten Weltkrieges im Südschwarzwald und am Hochrhein in dokumentarischen Berichten deutscher, französischer und Schweizer Beteiligter und Betroffener* [Stop! Swiss border! The end of WWII in the southern Black Forest and the Hochrhein area in documentary reports from German, French and Swiss nationals] (Konstanz: Südkurier Verlag, 1984).

151  Roosevelt, Eleanor, *Eleanor Roosevelt's My Day. Her Acclaimed Columns. Vol.1: 1936–1945*, edited by Rochelle Chadakoff with an introduction by Martha Gellhorn (New York: Pharos Books, 1989), copyright © Nancy Roosevelt Ireland.

152  Rürup, Reinhard (ed.), *Der Krieg gegen die Sowjetunion 1941–1945. Eine Dokumentation [Topographie des Terrors]* [The war against the Soviet Union 1941–1945. A documentation (Topography of Terror)] (Berlin: Argon-Verlag, 1991).

153  Ruhl, Klaus-Jörg (ed.), *Deutschland 1945: Alltag zwischen Krieg und Frieden in Berichten, Dokumenten und Bildern* [Germany 1945: Everyday life between war and peace in reports, documents and images] (Darmstadt, Neuwied: Hermann Luchterhand Verlag 1985), copyright © Klaus-Jörg Ruhl.

154  Sägebrecht, Willy, *Nicht Amboß, sondern Hammer sein: Erinnerungen* [Be the hammer, not the anvil], edited by Fanny Rosner and Heinz Vosske (Berlin: Karl Dietz Verlag, 1968).

155  Saenger, Erna, *Geöffnete Türen: Ich erlebte hundert Jahre* [Opened doors: I lived through a hundred years] (Berlin: self-published, 1975).

156  Schellenberg, Walter. *Aufzeichnungen des letzten Geheimdienstchefs unter Hitler* [Notes by the last head of the secret service under Hitler], edited by Gita Petersen with a foreword by Klaus Harpprecht and notes by Gerald Fleming (Munich: Limes Verlag in der F. A. Herbig Verlagsbuchhandlung, 1979).

157  Schenck, Ernst Günther, *Patient Hitler: Eine medizinische Biographie* [Hitler the patient: A medical biography] (Düsseldorf: Droste Verlag, 1989), copyright © Michael Schenck.

**158** Schmidt, Paul, *Der Statist auf der Galerie 1945–50: Erlebnisse, Kommentare, Vergleiche* [The extra in the gallery 1945–50: Experiences, commentary, comparisons] (Bonn: Athenäum Verlag, 1951).

**159** Schmidt, *Das Tagebuch des Herrn Schmidt. Ein Zeitdokument aus Berlin vom 20. April bis 27. Juli 1945* [The diary of Herr Schmidt: a documentary record from Berlin, 20 July to 27 July 1945], edited by Michael Schütz (Hamburg: AVH Verlag, 1999).

**160** Schön, Helmut, *Die letzten Kriegstage: Ostseehäfen 1945* [The final days of the war from the ports on the Baltic Sea, 1945] (Stuttgart: Motorbuch Verlag, 1995).

**161** Schramm, Percy E. (ed.) *Kriegstagebuch des Oberkommandos der Wehrmacht (Wehrmachtführungsstab) 1940–1945. Bd. IV/8* [War diary of the high command of the Wehrmacht (Wehrmachtführungsstab) 1940–1945. Vol. IV/8], edited by Helmuth Greiner and Percy E. Schramm (Bonn: Bernhard & Graefe Verlag, n.d.)

**162** Schroeder, Christa, *Er war mein Chef. Aus dem Nachlaß der Sekretärin von Adolf Hitler*, edited by Anton Joachimsthaler (Munich: Langen Müller Verlag in der F. A. Herbig Verlagsbuchhandlung, 1985). *He Was My Chief: The Memoirs of Adolf Hitler's Secretary*. Copyright © Langen Müller in der F.A Herbig Verlagsbuchhandlung GmbH, 1985. English translation copyright © Pen and Sword Books Ltd, 2009. Reproduced with permission from Frontline Books, an imprint of Pen and Sword Books Ltd.

**163** Schultz-Naumann, Joachim, *Mecklenburg 1945* copyright © 1989 by Universitas in der F.A. Herbig Verlagsbuchhandlung GmbH, München.

**164** Schultz-Naumann, Joachim, *Die letzten dreißig Tage: Das Kriegstagebuch des OKW April bis Mai 1945* [The last thirty days: The war diary of the German High Command of the Armed Forces], April to May 1945 (Augsburg: Weltbild Verlag, n.d.) Copyright © Bonn, Bernhard & Graefe Verlag 1961–1979. Reproduced with kind permission from Mönch Publishing Group, Bonn (MPG).

**165** Schweitzer, Albert, *Albert Schweitzer Lesebuch* [Albert Schweitzer reader], edited by Harald Steffahn (Munich: C. H. Beck Verlag, 1984).

**166** Shek, Alisah, '*Ein Theresienstädter Tagebuch: 18. Oktober 1944–19. Mai 1945*' [A Theresienstadt diary: 18 October 1944 to 19 May 1945] in *Theresienstädter Studien und Dokumente 1994* [Theresienstadt Studies and Documents] (Prague: Institut Terezínské Iniciativy, 1994)

**167** Shindel, Aleksandr Danilovich (ed.) *Auf beiden Seiten der Front. Briefe sowjetischer und deutscher Soldaten 1941–1945 (Po obl storony fronta. Pis ma sovetskich i nemeckich soldat 1941–1945)* [From both sides of the front: letters by Soviet and German soldiers, 1941–1945] (Moscow: Sol, 1995)

168 Shirer, William L., *Berliner Tagebuch. Das Ende. 1944–1945*, edited and translated by Jürgen Schebera (Leipzig: Gustav Kiepenheuer Verlag, 1994). April 25, 1945 and April 30, 1945 entries from *Berlin Diary*. Reprinted by permission of Don Congdon Associates Inc. copyright © 1941, renewed 1968 by William L. Shirer.

169 Shukow, Georgi Konstantinowitsch [Zhukov, Georgy Konstantinovich], *Erinnerungen und Gedanken. Bd. 2. 5.* [Memoirs vol. 2. 5], revised and updated edition (Berlin: Militärverlag der Deutschen Demokratischen Republik, 1976).

170 Simonow, Konstantin [Simonov, Konstantin], *Kriegstagebücher. Bd. 2: 1942–1945* [War diaries vol. 2: 1942–1945]. Translated from the Russian into the German by Corinna and Gottfried Wojtek and Günter Löffler (Berlin: Verlag Volk und Welt 1979), copyright © Ekaterina Simonowa-Gudzenko, Mariya Simonowa, Alexander and Alexej Simonow [Ekaterina Simonova-Gudzenko, Mariya Simonova, Alexander and Alexei Simonov]

171 Spitta, Theodor, *Neuanfang auf Trümmern. Die Tagebücher des Bremer Bürgermeisters Theodor Spitta 1945–1947* [Starting anew from rubble: the diaries of the mayor of Bremen, Theodor Spitta, 1945–1947], edited by Ursula Büttner and Angelika Voss-Louis, a publication of the Institut für Zeitgeschichte (Munich: R. Oldenbourg Verlag, 1992), copyright © 1992 Oldenbourg Wissenschaftsverlag, München.

172 Stalin, Josef and Churchill, Winston S., *Die unheilige Allianz: Stalins Briefwechsel mit Churchill 1941–1945* [The unholy alliance: Stalin's correspondence with Churchill, 1941–1945], edited by Gerhard Schoenberner with an introduction and notes by Manfred Rexin (Reinbek: Rowohlt Verlag, 1964 and Zürich: Orell Füssli Verlag) copyright © Gerhard Schoenberner, Mira Schoenberner. Reproduced with the kind permission of Mira Schoenberner.

173 *Stars and Stripes*, 12. 2. 1945; 20. 4. 1945; 24. 4. 1945; 26. 4. 1945.

174 Steinbock, Johann, *Das Ende von Dachau* [The End of Dachau] (Salzburg: Österreichischer Kulturverlag, 1948).

175 Steiner, Herbert, *Zum Tode verurteilt: Österreicher gegen Hitler. Eine Dokumentation* [Sentenced to death: documentation of Austrians against Hitler], with a foreword by F. Heer (Vienna: Europa Verlag, 1964).

176 Sternheim, Thea, *Tagebücher III 1936–1951* edited and selected by Thomas Ehrsam and Regula Wyss on behalf of the Heinrich Enrique Beck-Stiftung (Göttingen: Wallstein Verlag, 2002), since republished in the compilation *Tagebücher 1903–1971* [Diaries 1903–1971] (Göttingen: Wallstein Verlag, 2011).

177 Sternheim, Thea, *Tagebücher V* annotated, edited and selected by Thomas Ehrsam and Regula Wyss on behalf of the Heinrich Enrique Beck-Stiftung (Göttingen: Wallstein Verlag, 2002) since republished in

the compilation *Tagebücher 1903–1971*[Diaries 1903–1971] (Göttingen: Wallstein Verlag, 2011).

178 Storm, Ruth, *Ich schrieb es auf: Das letzte Schreiberhauer Jahr* [I wrote it down: The final year in Schreiberhau] (Freiburg im Breisgau: Bergstadtverlag Wilhelm Gottlieb Korn, 1961).

179 Sullivan, Matthew Barry, *Auf der Schwelle zum Frieden. Deutsche Kriegsgefangene in Großbritannien 1944–1948*, translated from the English by Margarete Venjakob (Vienna: Paul Zsolnay Verlag, 1981). *Thresholds of Peace: Four hundred thousand German prisoners and the people of Britain, 1944–1948* (London: Hamish Hamilton, 1979).

180 Susdalew P. K. and Jumatow, W. A. (eds), *Mit Eigenen Augen moskauer Künstler im Grossen Vaterländischen Krieg* [With their own eyes: Moscow artists in the great war in the fatherland], translated from the Russian by Joachim Wilke (Berlin: Militärverlag der Deutschen Demokratischen Republik, 1988).

181 Sweers, Weert, *Die Turteltaube: Heimweh nach Ostfriesland. Ein Zeitzeuge berichtet* [The turtle dove: Homesick for East Frisia. A witness of the times.] (Neermoor: self-published, 1993), copyright © Weert Sweers. Lines reproduced with the kind permission of Weert Sweers.

182 Thape, Ernst, *Ernst Thapes Buchenwalder Tagebuch von 1945* [Buchenwald diaries 1945 by Ernst Thape], edited by Manfred Overesch, in Vierteljahrshefte für Zeitgeschichte 29, H. 4 [Quarterly journal for contemporary history 29, vol. 4] (1981) copyright ©Manfred Overesch. Lines reproduced with permission from Vandenhoek & Ruprehct GmbH & Co.

183 Tissier, Tony le, *Der Kampf um Berlin 1945. Von den Seelower Höhen zur Reichskanzlei* translated from the English by Wolfgang Bergt and Hans-Ulrich Seebohm (Berlin: Ullstein Buchverlage GmbH, 1991). *The Battle of Berlin* (London: Jonathan Cape, 1988). Copyright © Tony le Tisser.

184 Trampe, Gustav (ed.), *Die Stunde Null: Erinnerungen an Kriegsende und Neuanfang* [The zero-hour: Memories of the end of the war and a new beginning] (Stuttgart: Deutsche Verlags-Anstalt 1995).

185 Tremayne, Julia. *War on Sark: The Secret Letters of Julia Tremayne*, with an introduction by Michael Beaumont (Exeter, Devon: Webb & Bower, 1981) copyright © Xan Franks.

186 Truman, Harry S., *Memoiren. Bd.1: Das Jahr der Entscheidungen (1945)* [Memoirs, vol. 1: The year of decisions] (1945 translated from English to German by Eduard Thorsch (Stuttgart: Scherz & Goverts Verlag, 1955). Truman, Harry S., United States President, radio broadcast to the American people 8 May 1945, and address to the United Nations Conference, San Francisco, 26 June 1945.

187 Uhland, Ludwig, *Uhlands Gedichte und Dramen in zwei Bänden. Bd. 1: Gedichte*.[Poems and plays in two volumes. Vol. 1: poems] (Stuttgart: J. G. Cotta'sche Buchhandlung Nachfolger n.d., c. 1890).

188 Valéry, Paul, *Cahiers / Hefte 1*, edited by Hartmut Köhler and Jürgen Schmidt Radefeldt. Translated from French to German by Reinhard Huschke, Hartmut Köhler, et al. (Frankfurt am Main: S. Fischer Verlag, 1987), copyright © Paris, Éditions Gallimard 1973 and 1974. *Cahiers, Tome 1*, copyright © Gallimard 1973.

189 Vaupel, Helmut, '*Kriegsende 1945 – Letzte Tage in der Prignitz*' [The end of the war, 1945: Final days in Prignitz] in Blätter zur Stadtgeschichte H. 4 [Notes on town history vol. 4] (1998), copyright © Jorg Lüneberg.

190 Vermehren, Isa, *Reise durch den letzten Akt: Ravensbrück, Buchenwald, Dachau: eine Frau berichtet* [Travelling through the final act: Buchenwald, Dachau. A woman reports] (Reinbek: Rowohlt Taschenbuch Verlag, 1979) copyright © Isa Vermehren.

191 '*Vor 50 Jahren: Hamburg in den letzten Wochen des Zweiten Weltkrieges*' [Fifty years ago: Hamburg in the final weeks of WWII] in Hamburgische Geschichts- und Heimatblätter 13, H. 6–7 [Hamburg history and home journals 13, vol. 6–7] (1995) copyright © Hamburg, Verein für Hamburgische Geschichte.

192 Wantzen, Paulheinz, *Das Leben im Krieg 1939–1946. Ein Tagebuch. Aufgezeichnet in der damaligen Gegenwart* [Life during the war 1939–1946: A diary written at the time] (Bad Homburg: Verlag Das Dokument, 2000).

193 Warlimont, Walter, *Im Hauptquartier der deutschen Wehrmacht 1939–1945: Grundlagen, Formen, Gestalten* [In the headquarters of the German Wehrmacht 1939–1945: Principles, forms, people] (Bonn: Bernard & Graefe Verlag, 1962), with permission from Mönch Publishing Group, Bonn.

194 Warren, Hans, *Geheim Dagboek 1945–1948* (Amsterdam: Prometheus / Bert Bakker, 1982).

195 Wassiltschikow, Marie [Vassiltchikov, Marie 'Missie'], *Die Berliner Tagebücher der «Missie» Wassiltschikow 1940–1945*, translated from English to German by Elke Jessett (Berlin: Wolf Jobst Siedler Verlag, 1987). *The Berlin Diaries 1940–1945* (London: Pimlico Press, Random House Publishing Group, 1985), copyright © The Estate of Marie Harnden 1985.

196 Weichmann, Elisabeth, *Zuflucht: Jahre des Exils* [Refuge: Years of exile], with a foreword by Siegfried Lenz (Munich: Albrecht Knaus Verlag, part of Verlagsgruppe Random House GmbH, 1983).

197 Weidling, Helmuth, '*Der Endkampf in Berlin (23.4.–2.5.1945)*' [The final battle in Berlin, 23 April to 2 May 1945] in *Wehrwissenschaftliche*

*Rundschau 12. Jg.* [Military history journal 12th edition] (1962).

198  Weill, Kurt and Lenya, Lotte, *Sprich leise wenn Du Liebe sagst. Der Briefwechsel Kurt Weill–Lotte Lenya.* Edited and translated by Lys Symonette und Kim H. Kowalke (Cologne: Kiepenheuer & Witsch, 1998) copyright © New York, The Kurt Weill Foundation for Music. Lines from *Speak Low (When You Speak of Love): The Letters of Kurt Weill and Lotte Lenya, reprinted with the permission of the Kurt Weill Foundation for Music, New York. All rights reserved.*

199  Weiss, Franz-Rudolph von, *Kriegsende und Neuanfang am Rhein. Konrad Adenauer in den Berichten des Schweizer Generalkonsuls Franz-Rudolph von Weiss 1944–1945* [The end of the war and a new beginning on the Rhine: Konrad Adenauer in the writings of the Swiss Genral Consul Franz-Rudolph von Weiss 1944–1945], edited by Hanns Jürgen Küsters and Hans Peter Mensing, a publication of the Institut für Zeitgeschichte (Munich: R. Oldenbourg Verlag, 1986).

200  Wellershoff, Dieter, *Die Arbeit Des Lebens: Autobiographische Texte* [The work of a lifetime: Autobiographical texts] (Cologne: Kiepenheuer & Witsch, 1985)

201  *Welt am Sonntag* 19.4.1985

202  Werth, Alexander, *Rußland im Krieg 1941–1945. Bd. 2.* Translated from English to German by Dieter Kiehl (Munich: Droemer Knaur Verlag, 1964). *Russia at War 1941–1945* (London: Barrie and Rockliff, 1964) copyright © Cyrus Gabrysch and Kolya Werth.

203  Westphal, Siegfried, *Erinnerungen* [Memoirs] (Mainz: v. Hase & Koehler Verlag, 1975).

204  Wieck, Michael, *Zeugnis vom Untergang Königsbergs. Ein «Geltungsjude» berichtet* [Witness to the fall of Königsberg: A 'Geltungsjude' (person considered a Jew) reports], with a foreword by Siegfried Lenz (Heidelberg: Lambert Schneider Verlag, 1988) copyright © Heidelberg, Universitätsverlag C. Winter.

205  Willis, Donald J, *The Incredible Year* (Ames, Iowa: Iowa State University Press, 1988).

206  Wischnewski, Alexander [Vishnevsky, Alexander], *Tagebuch eines Feldchirurgen* [Diary of a field surgeon] (Berlin: Militärverlag der Deutschen Demokratischen Republik, 1978).

207  Wolff-Mönckeberg, Mathilde. *Briefe, die sie nicht erreichten: Briefe einer Mutter an ihre fernen Kinder in den Jahren 1940–1946* [Letters that they never received: Letters from a mother to her children far away in the years 1940–1946], edited by Ruth Evans (Hamburg: Hoffmann und Campe Verlag 1980), copyright © Rhys Evans.

208  Wyndham, Joan, *Love Lessons & Love is Blue: Diaries of the War Years* (London, Mandarin, 1995) with the permission of United Agents.

**209** *Yanks treffen Rote: Begegnung an der Elbe. Erinnerungen amerikanischer und sowjetischer Soldaten des Zweiten Weltkrieges*, translated from English to German by Karl Heinz Berger and from Russian to German by Heinz Kübart (Berlin Militärverlag der Deutschen Demokratischen Republik, 1990) Yanks meet Reds: An Encounter on the Elbe, edited by Mark Scott (Santa Barbara: Capra Press and Moscow: Novosti Agency, 1988) Copyright © the authors.

## 2. Archives and Institutions

A1    Archives Nationales à Paris, Centre Historique. M. Chereau (AJ/72/321. All.23)

A2    Bayerisches Hauptstaatsarchiv, Munich. Kriegsarchiv. Franz Ritter von Epp (Nachlass Epp 94)

A3    Bundesarchiv-Lastenausgleichsarchiv, Bayreuth

A4    Bundesarchiv-Militärarchiv, Freiburg. Wehrmachtsbericht (RW4)

A5    Das Kempowski Archiv, Nartum [now transferred to A23]

A6    Deutsches Rotes Kreuz Suchdienst, Munich

A7    Deutsches Rundfunkarchiv, Frankfurt am Main

A8    Evangelische Kirchengemeinde Marien, Berlin

A9    Hans Fallada Archiv, Feldberger Seenlandschaft. Elisabeth Ditzen. © Dr. Ulrich Ditzen

A10   Imperial War Museum, London. Department of Documents. © with the kind permission of the copyright holders

A11   Institut d'Histoire du Temps Présent – Centre National de la Recherche Scientifique, Cachan. Archivar Chobaut (cote ARCo 83); Ferdinand Picard (Picard D.24)

A12   Kreisgemeinschaft Angerburg Archiv, Rotenburg (Wümme). Walter Wendel. © Maria Wendel

A13   Marinemuseum Dänholm Archiv, Stralsund

A14   Marineschule Mürwik. Wehrgeschichtliches Ausbildungszentrum. Gert Kochskämper (Archiv Nr. 16460)

A15   Nordost-Institut, Lüneburg. (Names have been changed) Wilhelm Bodenstedt (P O/144); Irma von Blanck-Heise (P O/50)

A16   Schleswig-Holsteinische Landesbibliothek, Kiel. Nachlaß Hans Friedrich Blunck (Cb 91). © Dr. Jürgen Blunck

A17   Senatsverwaltung für Stadtentwicklung, Berlin

A18   Siebenbürgische Bibliothek mit Archiv, Gundelsheim

A19   Staats- und Universitätsbibliothek Hamburg. Handschriftenabteilung. NL Walter Teich (46:1157: Bl. 80)

A20   Staatsarchiv der Freien und Hansestadt Hamburg. Luise Solmitz (622–I: Familie Solmitz I Bd. 34)

**A21**    Staatsbibliothek Berlin, Preußischer Kulturbesitz. Handschriften-abteilung. NL Hauptmann

**A22**    Stadtarchiv München. Anni Antonie Schmöger (NL Schmöger)

**A23**    Stiftung Archiv der Akademie der Künste, Berlin. Fritz Hochwälder (Georg-Kaiser-Archiv) © Ullstein Buchverlage GmbH, Berlin; Eva Richter-Fritzsche (Eva-Schmidt-Fritzsche-Archiv) © Gisela Harich-Hamburger; Walther von Seydlitz-Kurzbach (Erich-Weinert-Archiv); Mary Wigman (Mary-Wigman-Archiv) © Marlies Heinemann;Dr Hedwig Müller and Dr Patricia Stöckemann.

**A24**    Stiftung Archiv der Parteien und Massenorganisationen der DDRim Bundesarchiv Berlin. 8. Sitzung des Lagerkomitees (Dy 55/V 278/2/23); Bertram 490 archive und institutionen Bietz, unbekannter KZ-Häftling, August Richard Protz (Dy 55/V 278/2/29); Wilhelm Pieck (Ny 4036/544); Walter Ulbricht (Ny 4182/851); Erich Weinert (Ny 4065/1)

**A25**    The Mass-Observation Archive, Brighton. © reproduced with the permission of the Trustees of the Mass-Observation Archive, University of Sussex

**A26**    Traditionsarchiv Unterseeboote, Cuxhaven-Altenbruch

**A27**    University of Oregon Library System, Eugene, Oregon. Division of Special Collections and University Archives. Edward Morton (Ax 783)

**A28**    Zentrum der Dokumentationen «Volksarchiv», Moscow

**A29**    Zentrum zur Aufbewahrung der Dokumente der Jugendorganisationen, Moscow

# Index

The index lists in alphabetical order all texts included in the work under the names of the people in question, pseudonyms or the names of institutions, followed by the page number(s) they appear on. The arrow → at the end of each entry refers to the sources: numbers in bold refer to published and broadcast sources (see p. 433), and the letter 'A' followed by a number in bold refers to archives and institutions (see p. 453).

Unlike in the original German, letters with umlauts are arranged here according to their nearest equivalent letters in the English alphabet, for example, 'ö' as 'o'.

the 2nd White Russian Front. She became an accountant after the war. 240 → **A5**

Axmann, Artur (1913–96; German). From 1940 Reich Youth Führer of the NSDAP. After the war he worked as a sales representative. In 1949 he was sentenced to three years' imprisonment by a denazification tribunal and was fined in 1958. 67, 147, 295 Doctor (d. 1945; German). 67, 147, 296 → **A5**

B., Dmitry (b. 1918; Russian). Soviet major, commander of a bomber squadron. After the war he became an engineer and head of department in an electronics firm. 276 → **A5**

Bagh, Peter (German). 201 → **A5**

Baker, H. M. (Canadian). Lieutenant colonel in a Canadian tank regiment. 87 → **A10**

Ballhorn, Franz (1908–79; German). Imprisoned in a concentration camp from 1940 [until the end of the war]. From 1964 to 1974 he was a president of the Deutsche Jugendkraft youth sports organization. 153 → **9**

Bartelt, Günter (German). Chief engineer on a U-boat. 326, 341 → **A26**

Barth, Emil (1900–1958; German). Writer. 160, 271 → **11**

Bauer, Fritz (b. 1913; German). Cathedral chaplain in Würzburg. 255 → **12**

Bauer, Robert (German). 258 → **13**

Baur, Hans (1897–1993; German). SS brigade leader and chief

of police. After 1933, Hitler's pilot, chief pilot and leader of the 'Reichsregierung' flying squadron. Returned from captivity in the Soviet Union in 1955. 1, 106, 133 → **14**

Bayanov, Boris Pavlovich (Russian). Red Army soldier. 131 → **A29**

Bayer, Gertrud (name changed; b. 1909; German). 155 → **A5**

Beckmann, Max (1884–1950; German). Painter and graphic artist who fled to Amsterdam in 1937. 238, 316 → **15**

Beerbohm, Hans-Heinrich (German). Company Commander of the 5th Company of the 1st Schiffsstammabteilung on Dänholm in Stralsund. From April 1945, port commander. 274 → **A13**

Below, Nicolaus von (1907–83; German). Colonel. From 1937 until 1945 he was Hitler's Luftwaffe adjutant. 83 → **17**

Bergau, Martin (b. 1928; German). Flakhelfer from Palmnicken. Held in Soviet prisoner-of-war camp until 1948. 112 → **19**

Bietz, Bertram (German). 142 → **A24**

Bittkowski, Franz (b. 1915; German). 24, 140 → **A5**

Blanck-Heise, Irma von (name changed; b. 1916; German). Daughter of a landowner near Hanover, trained in estate management and agriculture, married in 1943. She managed an estate near Deutschkrone, Pomerania. 272 → **A15**

Blunck, Hans Friedrich (1888–1961; German). Author; from 1933

Colville, John (1915–87; British).
From 1939 private secretary to
Winston Churchill. 97, 128, 213,
309 → **36**

Concentration camp inmate
(German). 266 → **A24**

Cords, Günter (b. 1928; German).
Member of an SA marching band;
driving instructor after the war. 5,
390 → **A5**

Cowles, B. R. (British). Artillery
captain. 226 → **A10**

Cranz, Martin (b. 1926; German).
Soldier; mortar crew leader.
139 → **37**

D., Walter (b. 1921; German).
230 → **28**

Dalgas, Hans Erich (1896–1987;
German). Worked as an engineer
on the Siegfried Line in senior
construction management with
a Bremen construction company
from 1941 until 1966. 59 → **A5**

Damaschke, Willi (1892–1957;
German). Teacher. 282 → **A5**

Degrelle, Léon (1906–94; Belgian).
Fascist politician; Waffen-SS
officer, commander of the SS
tank division 'Wallonie', he was
sentenced to death in absentia in
1945. Lived out his days in Spain
as a businessman. 65, 110, 250,
344 → **38**

Dengler, Gerhard (1914–2007;
German). Captain, leader of a
gun emplacement, he went over
to the Soviets late January 1943
near Stalingrad and worked in
the NKFD. After the war he was
the first Bonn correspondent
of GDR newspaper *Neues*

*Deutschland* and from 1959
to 1968 vice-president of the
National Front of the GDR.
323 → **51**

Diem, Carl (1882–1962; German).
Sports scientist and official,
organized the 1936 Olympic
Games, first rector of the German
Sports College in Cologne.
278 → **41**

Diem, Lieselott (German). Wife of
Carl Diem. After the war she was
the head of the sports college in
Cologne. 167 → **41**

Dirks, Walter (1901–91; German).
Catholic journalist; imprisoned
in 1933. From 1935 to 1943 he
worked for the arts section of
the *Frankfurter Zeitung*; in 1943
he was banned from writing. In
1946 he founded the *Frankfurter
Hefte* with Eugen Kogon. From
1956 to 1967 he was the director
of the cultural department of
Westdeutscher Rundfunk. 45 → **42**

Ditzen, Elisabeth (1868–1951;
German). Mother of Rudolf
Ditzen (Hans Fallada). 279 → **A9**

Doctor (d. 1945; German). 141 → **A5**

Doctor (German). 167 → **A5**

Doctor (German). 182 → **183**

Documentation *Cap Arcona*.
76 → **108**

Döblin, Alfred (1878–1957;
German). Writer and doctor, he
emigrated to France in 1933 and
to the USA in 1940. 363 → **43**

Doderer, Heimito von (1896–1966;
Austrian). Writer; captain in the
war. 9, 342 → **44**

Dölker-Rehder, Grete (1892–1946;
German). Author. 96, 112,

Morell, Dr Theodor (1886–1948; German). Adolf Hitler's personal physician. 1 → **77**

Morton, Edward Perry (1894–1954; American). Chief of Staff of the US Military Government of the Province of Littoria (Italy). 214 → **A27**

Mrongovius, Arthur (1905–92; German). Captain; grew up in Russia but expelled at the start of the First World War; studied law, then became a journalist, working with propaganda units in the war, among others for the Eastern Volunteer Divisions (Turkish Propaganda Squad); autumn 1943 Eastern Department of the Propaganda Ministry, September 1944 liaison officer with the staff of the general of volunteer units, early 1945 on the liaison staff of Vlasov's Russian Liberation Army; taken prisoner by the Americans on the Moldau and handed over to Soviet troops at the end of May; returned to the Soviet Union at the end of 1955. 7, 263, 372 → **A5**

Munzinger, Ludwig (1921–2012; German). Journalist, commentator and publisher; in the war, latterly leader of an intelligence unit; prisoner of war in France, 1945–6, then until 1949 in the Soviet Union; director of the Munzinger Biographical Archive. 56 → **A5**

Mursina, Nina (b. 1925; Russian). Forced labourer from Voronezh in Silesia from 1942; after the liberation in February 1945 paramedic in a Soviet field hospital in Częstochowa, then a waitress in a Soviet sanatorium in Austria. 28 → **A5**

Mussolini, Benito (1883–1945; Italian). Dictator until July 1943, then head of government of a Fascist 'Social Republic of Italy'; end of April 1945 taken prisoner by partisans and shot. 2, 53, 62, 74, 88, 97 → **132**

Mussolini, Rachele (1892–1979; Italian). Wife of Benito Mussolini. 103, 216 → **132**

Mussolini, Vittorio (1916–97; Italian). Italian film producer, son of Benito Mussolini. 103 → **134**

N., B. (b. 1921; German). 171 → **A5**

Nansen, Odd (1901–73; Norwegian). Son of Fritjof Nansen, architect and philanthropist, founder of Nansen Aid for Refugees and Stateless People, 1937; from January 1942 imprisoned in Norway, then later in concentration camps in Germany. 75 → **135**

Naval news service. 326 → **A26**

Nemeskei, Paula (1904–89; German). 42 → **104**

*Neue Zürcher Zeitung.* 36, 417 → **136**

Neumann, Flora (b. 1911; German). → **137**

Neumann, Peter (German). 247 → **10**

Nicolson, Harold (1886–1968; British). Diplomat and writer; Member of Parliament, married to Vita Sackville-West. 213, 314 → **138**

Niekisch, Ernst (1889–1967; German). Writer, politician;

Protz, August Richard (German).
Patissier and master baker
77→**A24**

Rad, Gerhard von (1901–71;
German). From 1934 Professor of
Old Testament Theology in Jena;
conscripted in late summer 1944;
professor in Heidelberg, 1949. 23,
139, 235→**148**

Raddatz, Dr Fritz J. (b. 1931;
German). Literary critic and
writer; son of the director of the
UFA film company, he became
an editor after the war in East
Berlin; from 1960 to 1969 deputy
director of Rowohlt Verlag; from
1977 to1985 features editor of
*Die Zeit.* 414→**149**

Radloff, Fritz (1916–89; German).
Senior lieutenant. 35, 177,
291→**A5**

Radio broadcast 303, 414.→**A7, 30**

Reidt, Hella (name changed; 1901–
78; German). 256→**A5**

Reinhardt, Klaus (German).
Agricultural apprentice. 26→**A5**

Reuschel, Horst-Harry (German).
338→**A5**

Richter, Helmut (German). Catholic
priest. 356→**76**

Richter-Fritzsche, Eva (1908–86;
German). After secondary school
attended art college in Berlin;
in 1927 joined the KPD and
married an art student who had
been called up to the Wehrmacht;
after 1945 in the office of popular
education in Pankow, Berlin,
made documentary films for
DEFA, the East German film
studio, director of the DEFA

dubbing studio; after 1957
artistic director of the theatres in
Stralsund and Güstrow. 71, 191,
290→**A23**

Riemann (German). 240→**A3**

Röhrich, Margit (German) 191→**A5**

Romanova, Antonina (b. 1927;
Russian). Forced labourer,
librarian after the war; wife
of Andrei Filin, sister of Soya
Romanova. 274→**A5**

Romanova, Soya (b. 1934; Russian).
Daughter of a forced labourer
in Mecklenburg; after secondary
school studied at a technical
college in Riga; sister of Antonina
Romanova. 275→**A5**

Roosevelt, Anna Eleanor (1884–
1962; American). Wife of the
US president Franklin Delano
Roosevelt and human rights
campaigner. 107→**151**

Rosowsky, Charlotte (German).
358→**A5**

Rummelsburgerstrasse Cemetery,
Berlin. 292→**A17**

S., Kurt (b. 1918; German). Senior
lieutenant, born in Silesia. Clerk
with a cash register company;
in the war head of a telephone
company in Romania; escaped
from Soviet prisoner-of-war
camp and lived in various hiding
places in Romania until 1947;
after the war director of a sale
and rental cash register company.
363→**28**

S., Paul (German). Businessman
from Berlin. 116, 277→**28**

S., Ulli (b. 1928; German). Born in
Hamburg. Stayed hidden from

Writer and diplomat; lives in
Israel and Italy. 380→**51**

Seib, Agnes (1901–83; German).
Teacher from Hamburg, in the
KLV. 99→**A5**

Seifert, Thea (b. 1903; German). A
woman from Breslau. 244→**A5**

Seiler, Erna (1906–90; German).
From the district of Oels, Silesia.
12→**A5**

Seydlitz-Kurzbach, Walther von
(1888–1976; German). General;
late January 1943 imprisoned
near Stalingrad; president of
the League of German Officers,
vice-president of the NKFD;
after refusing to work in the SBZ,
sentenced to death, then twenty-
five years' imprisonment; released
1955. 102→**A23**

Shek, Alisah (b. 1927; Czech).
Daughter of a Prague civil
engineer who was deported
to Auschwitz; she worked
in Theresienstadt, first in
agriculture, then in the poultry
yard, and secretly collected
documents. 82, 115, 222,
374→**166**

Shirer, William (1904–93; American).
Journalist and commentator;
from 1934 to the end of 1940
correspondent in Berlin, then in
Great Britain and Switzerland;
reporter at the 1946 Nuremberg
Trials. 205, 298→**168**

Simon, Claude (b. 1913; French).
Writer, born in Madagascar;
received the Nobel Prize for
Literature in 1985. 306→**51**

Simon, Harald (b. 1927; German).
Luftwaffe assistant in Neuss,

Rhine, 1943; with RAD, 1944;
from January 1945 soldier, losing
the sight of both eyes at the end
of April; after the war attended
an institution for the blind, then
studied law and became a judge.
224→**A5**

Simonov, Konstantin (1915–79;
Russian). Soviet war reporter
with the army newspaper
*Kraznaya zvezda.* 149, 422→**209**

Smend, Helmut (1894–1984;
German). 233→**A5**

Soergel, Wolfgang (German).
Medical senior ensign. 229,
361→**A5**

Soldier (German). 95→**A5**

Soldier (German). 329, 348→**64**

Soldier (Russian) 286→**153**

Solmitz, Luise (1889–1973;
German). Housewife. 59→**A20**

Speer, Frau (d. 1968; German).
Sister-in-law of Albert Speer,
(1905–81; German), architect and
Reich Minister for Armaments
and War Production, 1942–5,
who was imprisoned as war
criminal, 1946–66. 199→**A5**

Spitta, Dr Theodor (1873–1969;
German). Lawyer, barrister;
from 1911 to 1933 member of the
Bremen Legislative Assembly,
senator and deputy mayor, but
dismissed in 1933; after 1945
deputy mayor and senator
for law and the constitution.
245→**171**

SS man (French). Member of the
SS 'Charlemagne' battalion.
182→**183**

St., H. (b. 1925; German). Soldier
with the 12th Panzer Division;

prisoner-of-war camp. 34 → **A5**

Tittmann, Senta (b. 1919; German). 11 → **A5**

Tremayne, Julia (b. 1903; British). Boarding-house keeper on Sark, in the Channel Islands, which was occupied by German troops from 1940; her letters to her daughter in England only reached her after the war. 148 → **185**

Truman, Harry S. (1884–1972; American). President, 1945–53. 300, 429 → **186**

Uhland, Ludwig (1787–1862; German). Writer. xxiii → **187**

Uhlemann, Hans (1907–98; German). Staff doctor; before the war medical activity with the regional insurance institution of Saxony; after war captivity consultant doctor with social insurance for the state of Thuringia; from 1958 fiduciary doctor with the national insurance institution of Upper Bavaria. 382 → **A5**

Ulbricht, Walter (1893–1973; German). Politician; from 1933 in Paris and from 1938 in exile in Moscow; from July 1950 secretary general of the central committee of the SED. 391 → **A24**

Ullrich, Rita (b. 1922; German). Student teacher in French internment until 1946; later teacher. 54 → **A5**

Unknown man (b. 1924; German). 114 → **A5**

Unknown man (German). 117 → **A5**

Unknown man (German). 247 → **164**

Unknown man (British). Probably a teacher in Reigate. 308 → **A25**

Valéry, Paul (1871–1945; French). Writer. 137, 215, 408 → **188**

Vassiltchikov, Marie 'Missie' (1917–78; Russian) Born in St Petersburg, daughter of a prince; at the outbreak of war she was in Germany and worked in the Cultural Policy Department of the Foreign Office in Berlin; spent the last few months of the war in Vienna as a nurse. 8, 118 → **189**

Vasilenko (Russian). Soviet lieutenant; commander of a tank unit. 247 → **164**

Vasilyev, Vasily I. (Russian) Red Army soldier. 228 → **A28**

Vaupel, Helmut (b. 1928; German). Early March 1945 conscripted as reserve officer recruiter with the Luftwaffe; after secondary school in 1947 studied Protestant theology in Heidelberg, then a teacher of religion. 65 → **189**

Vermehren, Isa (b. 1918; German). Cabaret artiste and film actress in Berlin; in 1938 converted to Catholicism; during the war employed to entertain the troops; because of her contacts with the political resistance imprisoned in 1944 in Ravensbrück, Buchenwald and Dachau concentration camps; studied from 1946 to 1951, when joined the Order of the Society of the Sisters of the Sacred Heart of Jesus; ran girls' secondary schools in Hamburg and Bonn. 255, 383 → **190**

Spanish Civil War; became vice-president of the Central Administrative Board of popular education in the Soviet Occupied Zone. 204 → **A24**

Weiss, Franz-Rudolph von (1885–1960; Swiss). Swiss Consul General. 258 → **199**

Weitzsch, Erich (b. 1920; German). Senior lieutenant. 134 → **A5**

Wellershoff, Dieter (b. 1925; German). Writer. 36, 112, 246 → **200**

Wendel, Walter (1928–98; German). 251 → **A12**

Werth, Alexander (1901–69; British). Born in St Petersburg, studied in England, worked from 1929 as a correspondent with leading British newspapers; from 1941 until 1948 he reported for the *Sunday Times* and the BBC from Moscow. 412 → **202**

'Werwolf Oberbayern'. A flyer. 157 → **102**

Westphal, Siegfried (1902–82; German). Cavalry general; from 1944 Chief of the General Staff of Commander in Chief West; after being held as a prisoner of war under the Americans and the British various posts in business. 59 → **203**

Westphalen, Otto (b. 1920; German). Senior naval lieutenant; U-boat commander. 99 → **A26**

Wick, Hans-Georg von (1907–64; German). Senior lieutenant. 230 → **A5**

Wiechmann, Dieter (b. 1922; German). From April 1943 infantry lieutenant on the eastern front; seriously injured October 1944. 371 → **A5**

Wieck, Michael (b. 1928; German). From a well-known Jewish family of musicians; survived in Königsberg and was able to emigrate to Berlin in 1948; violinist in symphony orchestras. 122, 241, 337 → **204**

Wigman, Mary (1886–1973; German). Dancer, choreographer. 37 → **A23**

Wilking, Horst (b. 1926; German). From 1941 with the Kriegsmarine; after the invasion in 1944 deployed on patrol boats in British waters. 316 → **A5**

Willis, Donald J. (b. 1919; American). US Army soldier; was called up in 1941 and served with the 3rd Armored Division until October 1945. 47 → **205**

Wilson, Edmund (1895–1972; American). Writer and literary critic. 137 → **48**

Winkelmann, Wilhelm (b. 1917; German). 348 → **A5**

Winkler, Paul (German). 315 → **A3**

Wolf, Markus (1923–2006; German). In 1933 emigrated with his family and from 1934 in Moscow; from 1943 to 1945 editor with the *Deutsche Volkssender* in Moscow; from 1953 to 1986 head of the GDR Foreign Intelligence Service. 322 → **184**

Wolf, Richard (German). Colonel. 41 → **104**

Wolff-Mönckeberg, Mathilde (1879–1958; German). Married to a professor of English; her letters, which were never sent, were addressed to her children living abroad. 60 → **207**

Woman (German). 174, 284 → **6**

Wyndham, Joan (1922–2007; British). In the WAAF; after the war ran a restaurant and wrote articles for magazines 153, 312 → **208**

Youth group leader (German). 77 → **164**

Z., Emmi (b. 1893; German). Housewife. 202 → **A5**

Zaporozhets, Alexei Abramovich (Russian). Red Army soldier. 184 → **A29**

Zevelyov, Pyotr Mitrofanovich (Russian). 184, 261 → **167**

Zhukov, Georgy Konstantinovich (1896–1974; Russian). From February 1941 Chief of the General Staff of the Red Army and marshal from 1943; after the war senior commander of Soviet ground forces; from 1955 to 1957 defence minister. 3, 131, 418 → **169**

Zimmermann, Erich (1900–1987; German). Musician; at the age of nine he had polio and was in a wheelchair after that. He worked first with a band in the silent cinema, then, at the start of the war, he was first cellist in the Danzig Symphony Orchestra and played with the City Orchestra, Graudenz, from 1943; after the war he worked in Göttingen as a music teacher and with dance bands. 18, 272 → **A5**

This book has been selected to receive financial assistance from English PEN's Writers in Translation programme supported by Bloomberg and Arts Council England. English PEN exists to promote literature and its understanding, uphold writers' freedoms around the world, campaign against the persecution and imprisonment of writers for stating their views, and promote the friendly co-operation of writers and free exchange of ideas.

Each year, a dedicated committee of professionals selects books that are translated into English from a wide variety of foreign languages. We award grants to UK publishers to help translate, promote, market and champion these titles. Our aim is to celebrate books of outstanding literary quality, which have a clear link to the PEN charter and promote free speech and intercultural understanding.

In 2011, Writers in Translation's outstanding work and contribution to diversity in the UK literary scene was recognised by Arts Council England. English PEN was awarded a threefold increase in funding to develop its support for world writing in translation.

www.englishpen.org

*Also by Walter Kempowski and forthcoming from Granta Books*
www.grantabooks.com

# ALL FOR NOTHING

Translated from the German by Anthea Bell

'I love this book . . . *All for Nothing* is Kempowski's crowning
achievement: his last, and lasting, work of fiction'
Rachel Seiffert

Winter, January 1945. It is cold and dark, and the German army
is retreating from the Russian advance. Germans are fleeing the
occupied territories in their thousands, in cars and carts and on
foot. But in a rural East Prussian manor house, the wealthy von
Globig family tries to seal itself off from the world. Protected
by their privileged lifestyle and caught in the grip of indecision,
they make no preparations to leave.

Brilliantly evocative and atmospheric, sympathetic yet painfully
honest, *All for Nothing* is a devastating portrait of the self-
delusions, complicities and denials of the German people as the
Third Reich comes to an end.